CULT WATCH

John Ankerberg & John Weldon

HARVEST HOUSE PUBLISHERS
Eugene, Oregon 97402

This book is a compilation of eight Harvest House Pocket Books written by John Ankerberg and John Weldon, published by Harvest House Publishers, with material added on Mormonism, the occult, and positive confession.

CULT WATCH

Copyright © 1991 by John Ankerberg and John Weldon
Published by Harvest House Publishers
Eugene, Oregon 97402

Library of Congress Cataloging-in-Publication Data

Ankerberg, John, 1945–
    Cult watch / John Ankerberg, John Weldon.
    ISBN 0-89081-851-7
    1. Cults—Controversial   literature.   2. Sects—Controversial   literature.
    3. Occultism—Controversial   literature.   4. New   Age   movement—Contro-
    versial   literature.   5. Spiritualism—Controversial   literature.   I. Weldon,
    John   II. Title.
    BP603.A65   1991
    291—dc20   90-23715
                                                           CIP

Printed in the United States of America.

96 97 98 99 00 01 02 / BC / 12 11 10 9 8 7 6 5

In memory of our good friend,
Walter R. Martin, 1928–1989

CONTENTS

Part Five: *Spirit Guides*

Part Six: *Astrology*

Part Seven: *The Occult*

Part Eight: *False Teaching in the Church*

Foreword

This text discusses eight religious beliefs/sects that command the attention of masses of modern Americans: Mormonism, Jehovah's Witnesses, the Masonic Lodge, the New Age Movement, spiritism, astrology, occultism, and Christian Positive Thinking/Positive Confession.

Those who accept these religious philosophies are often committed individuals genuinely seeking after God and spiritual truth and growth. This is, after all, an American heritage. We pride ourselves on being a nation of religious freedom and pluralism. But such freedoms carry responsibilities. Wouldn't you agree that religious freedom, like political freedom, is first of all a personal responsibility to be accurately informed on the issues, and that it presumes we make our choices based on discernment, and hopefully wisdom?

One of the blessings of religious freedom is the freedom to believe what we are convinced of. But are all religious beliefs equal? Can all religious beliefs be true at the same time? If not, isn't it important for each one of us to critically evaluate what we believe is true—to be sure it really is true?

With at least 40-50 million people collectively interested in the topics discussed in this book, few people can doubt either their influence or the importance of carefully evaluating their claims.[1]

The title of this book, *Cult Watch*, underscores the need for each of us, including members of the Christian church, not only to be accurately informed on the religious practices and beliefs we see around us, but on our own religious beliefs as well. (See Note 6.)

Why is this task of being accurately informed on religious issues necessary? Because whether ideas are religious or political, they have consequences—either for good or ill. Just as is true in politics, in religion there are beliefs that are good and those that are not so good. Let us ask another question. What happens when millions of people adopt wrong ideas, even if these people are sincere and have good motives? Will there not still be consequences to wrong ideas?

Unfortunately, a book this size would not permit sketching the personal problems and even tragedies wrought through wrong ideas in religion in the last several decades alone: spiritual deception and depression, atheism, family breakups, occult bondage—even mental illness, suicides, and death. Religious beliefs that started out so promisingly have unfortunately often ended in heartbreak and even disaster. Jonestown is perhaps the most visible example, but many other religions in America carry the seeds of disappointment and potential tragedy. For example, how many hundreds or thousands have needlessly been injured or died from the Christian Science faith's rejection of medical care, or the Jehovah's Witnesses' refusal to permit blood transfusions?[2] Nor is the

Christian church immune from wrong ideas. Consider the belief of some charismatic churches that faith is all that is needed to cure even life-threatening illness—and that to seek medical care constitutes a "lack" of faith. Scores of well-meaning people have also died from such teachings.[3] Doesn't all this prove that we need to be informed about what our neighbors believe, especially if, as the Scripture admonishes us, we are to love our neighbors as ourselves?

What about the New Age Movement, astrology, channeling, and other aspects of the paranormal and the occult? National polling consistently reveals high interest in these topics. For example, a Gallup poll of 1,236 adults over 18 years of age conducted June 14–17, 1990, reveals some unexpected information:

- Belief in the paranormal is widespread in society and is categorized as "surprising."

- Such beliefs are almost as common among people who are "deeply religious in a traditional sense" as among those who are not, even though "such beliefs contradict [the beliefs of] more traditional religions."

- The majority of Americans are unaware of the New Age Movement, at least by that name (almost all the topics included in the poll were New Age subjects).

- One in four Americans believes in ghosts (for example, poltergeists); one in four believes in astrology; one in five believes in reincarnation—including 22 percent of those who classify themselves as born-again Christians. More than one in ten Americans believes in channeling, although if similar and related terms had been included, such as mediumism and spirit healing, the figure would undoubtedly have been higher.

- Incredibly, only 7 percent of Americans deny "believing in any of a list of 18 paranormal experiences [UFOs, astrology, ESP (telepathy, clairvoyance, telekinesis), reincarnation, psychic healing, contact with the dead, witchcraft, channeling, etc.]. . . ." Almost 50 percent say they believe in five or more of these items and fully 75 percent have had a personal experience in at least one of the categories.[4]

These beliefs are apparently widespread in society—but what if they are really false beliefs having harmful consequences? For example, the national organization headed by Billy Graham receives letters every day, in the words of Graham, "from individuals who have become enslaved by the occult."[5] But how many people realize that most people who become involved in the occult do so under another name? If most occult practices are not called occultic and are thought of as something else, it is not surprising that many people become involved in dangerous spiritual pursuits.

What some people may not understand is that the dramatic increase in unorthodox religions, plus the increase of modern social problems (drugs, crime, abortion, corruption in politics and business, the economy, AIDS, etc.), are really symptoms reflecting a deeper and more serious social condition: defection from the God of the Bible. Consider that the entire process of emerging social disintegration occurring around us would probably never have existed if the majority of our culture had not abandoned God but rather had turned to Christ for salvation, been regenerated, and consequently adopted the basic principles of biblical morality and a biblical worldview. But in their personal search for meaning, people instead turned to humanism, materialism, skeptical philosophies, and rationalistic (liberal) religion—worldviews that are unlikely to satisfy man's genuine spiritual needs. In essence, a spiritual vacuum was created which thrust open the door to the world of the cults, the New Age Movement, and the occult.

Still, the Bible teaches that most neglect of God is deliberate (Romans 1:18-25) and, because of that, the consequences of such actions are unavoidable (Galatians 6:7). So what does all this have to do with the content of this book?

Unfortunately, the specific religious and moral views of the philosophies in this book undercut personal knowledge of God and work powerfully to insulate tens of millions of people against biblical teaching. And to the degree we are morally and spiritually floundering, perhaps it is largely because we are theologically naive and uninformed. Doesn't it seem that, as a nation, we prefer to accept almost any belief or practice other than what God says is true and necessary in the Bible? As a nation, how well do we know the teachings of the Bible? Are not tens of millions of us biblically illiterate? We want to believe in God, or at least think we believe in God, but who really is God to us? More importantly, who are we to God? What does God really think of us? What does He expect of us?

But given our biblical illiteracy, at a moment of vulnerability might not such illiteracy make us susceptible to the attractive claims of many of the new cults and religions, even before we really have time to understand their true beliefs and implications?

Why have we written this book? We have written this book, in part, to inform people on some of the more popular and influential modern religious beliefs. In this text we have included three leading religious sects (Mormonism, Jehovah's Witnesses, and Masonry), four new religious practices having ancient roots (the New Age Movement, spiritism, astrology, and the occult) plus one more recent Christian practice called "Positive Confession."

Why were these specific topics selected? These groups were selected to show the wide range of belief, influence, and even consequences that nonbiblical religious teaching and practice can have in our culture and, specifically, why they are consequential.

In what context do we define these philosophies as cultic? The term "cult" is often misused. It has various meanings.[7]

By use of the term "cult," we mean nothing necessarily derogatory or pejorative. But from the viewpoint of biblical revelation, most cults and most cultic religion have serious errors of belief and often incorporate dubious ethical values. For our purposes a "cult" may be loosely defined as a religious group having biblically unorthodox and/or heretical teachings and which may fail to meet basic ethical standards of Christian doctrine or practice. (See Note 7.) Thus, in light of this definition there are many unbiblical "cults" today—Jehovah's Witnesses, Mormons, and Masons among them. There are New Age cults, spiritistic cults, and astrological cults. But for us, the word "cultic" may describe more than religious groups: It may also describe philosophies and practices having cult-like elements. Looking at the lowest common denominator in much religious cultism today, we discover at least some cultic elements in all the topics discussed herein. The common characteristics of such cultism often include 1) spiritual deception; 2) unbiblical theology (often justified by new, supernatural [occultic] revelations); 3) spiritistic and other occultic influence; and 4) authoritarianism or spiritual intimidation. Below we briefly discuss these four points in turn, supplying a brief illustration from each of our selected topics.

Spiritual Deception

Cultic religion is often less than frank concerning its real beliefs, whether by design or ignorance. It also often makes claims that are simply not true. For example, if we look specifically at the topics discussed in this volume, we may note the following:

Mormonism claims it believes in the Trinity and salvation by grace and that it alone represents genuine Christianity.

Jehovah's Witnesses claim a perfect record in prophetic accuracy and that their translation and interpretation of the Bible is superior to all others.

Masonry claims it is only a universal brotherhood of men seeking to better the world and that its teachings are not in conflict with those of any other religion, including Christianity.

The New Age Movement claims harmony with the teachings of Jesus and that its primary concern is the welfare of men and the knowledge of God.

Spiritism claims biblical support and that the spirits it endorses are benevolent entities sent from God to help men evolve spiritually.

Astrology claims it is a unified science capable of "reading" the heavens' "influence" on our lives and can therefore accurately predict the future.

The occult claims to offer a progressive form of spiritual security, knowledge, and enlightenment; that its methods are trustworthy; and that it advances human values and true spiritual wisdom.

Positive Confession claims its practices are biblical and, therefore, that it will result in true spiritual growth, and that it will command God's blessing and make people healthy and rich.

But as we document in this book, none of the above claims are true. The willingness to be less than frank or to actually deceive may also lead to duplicity in other areas as well, such as the suppression or alteration of historical material. For example, Mormons and Jehovah's Witnesses have censored historical documents which damage their claims to be the only church of God on earth. In a different manner, Masonry has also engaged in purposeful deception as we have documented in *The Secret Teachings of the Masonic Lodge* (Moody, 1990) pp. 254-64.

Unbiblical Theology and New Revelations

Another element of cultic religion is 1) the rejection of biblical teaching often resulting from 2) the acceptance of new, supernatural (occultic) revelations. For example, with the exception of our last topic, all the groups we discuss deny the major doctrines of historic Christianity, and all of them have accepted new revelations in one form or another. If we again examine the groups in this text and supply examples, we can see how each of them fits this description.

Mormonism rejects biblical teaching. It is polytheistic (believing in many gods), and thus rejects the monotheism (belief in one God) of the Bible. It also accepts new allegedly divine revelations in the Book of Mormon, *Doctrine and Covenants*, and *The Pearl of Great Price*.

Jehovah's Witnesses reject biblical teaching. They believe that Christ is not God, but a creation of God, and thus reject what the New Testament teaches about Christ. They too claim "angelic" guidance in their Bible translation and doctrinal views.

Masonry rejects what the Bible teaches. The Masonic Lodge is syncretistic, attempting to merge all religious beliefs under Masonic doctrine and thus cannot be considered biblical. As we have documented in *The Secret Teachings of the Masonic Lodge* (Moody Press, 1990), Masonry is also historically dependent on various occultic beliefs and revelations for many of its teachings.

The New Age Movement rejects what the Bible teaches. It is eclectic in its worldview, drawing from many diverse sources for its beliefs and practices, thereby opposing biblical exclusivism (John 14:6; Acts 4:12; 1 Timothy 2:5,6). It also often incorporates "channeled" and other allegedly "divine" revelations as part of its program of spiritual education and development.

Spiritism rejects what the Bible teaches. It is gnostic in its worldview, holding that salvation comes by knowledge (*gnosis*), not faith. Like the New Age Movement, it too is largely dependent upon contact with supernatural spirits for its beliefs and practices.

Astrology rejects what the Bible teaches. Astrology is prescientific, pantheistic (God is all; all is God), and pagan. Like almost every other teaching discussed in this volume, it also rejects all major biblical doctrines. Further, it depends entirely upon the alleged "divine" revelations from the planetary alignments for its beliefs, predictions, and supposed "insights" into human nature and behavior.

The occult rejects what the Bible teaches. It is monistic in its worldview (see Part 7, Question 5), and openly opposes Christian belief. It too prefers supernatural revelations and practices that it claims will lead to spiritual advancement.

Positive Confession rejects what the Bible teaches in particular areas, such as the doctrine of faith and the intent of Christ's death on the cross. It claims that a person's "faith" has almost magical powers that will bring health, wealth, and prosperity. Positive Confession advocates think that God or "divine laws" can be influenced or manipulated by our "faith," and that Christ died on the cross for our prosperity and healing in this life. It too claims its messages are based on direct revelation and counsel from God.

Spiritistic and Occultic Influences

Perhaps the lowest common denominator of all modern religious cultism and phenomena is direct or indirect contact with the spirit world.[8] This is taken for granted in spiritism and the occult in general, but is also true for the other topics in this book.

Mormonism's founder, Joseph Smith, was dependent upon spiritistic revelations for the founding of his religion; even today, Mormons look to the spirits of the dead for ministry and assistance.

Jehovah's Witnesses claim the guidance of spirits ("angels") in the formulation of their doctrine and organizational activities.

Masonry has significant occultic influences historically and today, as we have documented in *The Secret Teachings of the Masonic Lodge: A Christian Appraisal* (Moody Press, 1990), pp. 215-53.

The New Age Movement, spiritism, and the occult accept spiritism and occultism as a matter of course.

Astrology is a potent occult art largely dependent upon the spirit world, as we have documented in our *Astrology: Do the Heavens Rule Our Destiny?* (Harvest House, 1989), pp. 157-74, 201-56.

Positive Confession has also been influenced historically and in the present by spiritism and occultism.[9]

Authoritarianism and Spiritual Intimidation

Another characteristic of cultic religion is an authoritarian element leading to spiritual intimidation and often the suppression of independent, critical thinking. People are taught to fear alleged religious leaders and organizations rather than to first reverence and respect God and His Word.

Mormonism—Mormons are warned to listen only to the general authorities of the Church and are told that disobeying Church leadership and Mormon doctrine can have eternal consequences.

Jehovah's Witnesses—The Watchtower Society rules its membership with an authoritarian hand. Individual members are warned against reading

any literature critical of their beliefs and threatened with disfellowshipping and complete abandonment for disagreeing with official teaching
and practice.

Masonry—As we document in *The Secret Teachings of the Masonic Lodge: A
Christian Appraisal* (Moody Press, 1990) pp. 178-91, Masons are spiritually
intimidated with terrifying oaths and warned of severe consequences of
breaking their vows.

The New Age Movement—Because the New Age Movement constitutes a
combination of spiritism and occultism, followers of New Age practices
and philosophy are subject to the characteristic hazards of these practices:

Spiritism—The spirits who first appear so friendly and kind can easily
turn into cruel taskmasters who punish the slightest disobedience with
swift retribution and who warn of greater torments on "the other side"
(i.e., after death) for disobedience to them now.

Astrology—Few greater fears exist than the fatalistic pronouncements of
zealous astrologers claiming "cosmic law" as the source of their dire
predictions of personal disaster or calamity such as illness, divorce, tragic
accident, or death (see our *Astrology*, pp. 257-84).

Occultism—No greater fear is found than among those who may
encounter the living hell which can result from Satanism, witchcraft,
voodoo, death magic, and very real demons who openly display their true
natures to those foolish enough to taunt, manipulate, ignore, or flaunt
them (e.g., see Part 5, note 88).

Positive Confession—People who are promised great things from Positive
Confession teachings are often disappointed instead. After exercising
what they think is great faith in God, and often proving their faith by large
financial sacrifices to those who have promised them wonderful rewards,
they become subject to spiritual discouragement and depression when
what is promised fails and "God" seems to abandon them. Such persons
often feel they are a spiritual failure and that they lack true faith (as Positive
Confession defines it). Finally, they may question both their salvation and
God's love and care for them. This can lead to fear of the consequences of
not being saved, or doubt as to the nature and reality of God. Some people
lose valuable years of fellowship with God and ministry, having been
sidetracked into a false Christianity that left deep wounds requiring years
to recover from.

Other cultic elements could be listed for the groups discussed herein,
but the point is made. Denials aside, the religions and philosophies discussed in this volume evidence degrees of cultic belief and practice.

Why have false teachings in the church been included in this volume?
Simply to emphasize that the church, like society in general, is not
immune from false ideas having harmful consequences. For example, with
literally millions of charismatic Christians accepting a teaching so potentially destructive as Positive Confession, with its ties to cultic religion,
spiritism, and the occult,[9] such a topic could hardly be ignored. Even the
"father" of modern positive thinking, Norman Vincent Peale, confesses
his indebtedness to *Science of Mind* founder Ernest Holmes: "Only those

who knew me as a boy can fully appreciate what Ernest Homes did for me. Why, he made me a positive thinker."[11]

Few can deny that the church today does have cultic and occultic influences within its ranks. Dr. Harold Bussell points out in *Unholy Devotion: Why Cults Lure Christians* (Zondervan, 1983, that the reason some Christians join cults is because they are unable to distinguish cultic belief and practice from what they learned as Christians. This simple, tragic fact should make every Christian grieve in his heart and increase his resolve to know God and His Word, both doctrinally and practically.[12] Unfortunately, as Dr. Van Baalen once observed, "The cults are the unpaid bills of the church"—debts past due (but now being paid) for failing to educate Christians in sound doctrine and apologetics. In essence, whether false teachings occur in the culture itself or within the church, both result from the same failing: neglect of God.

The Pentecostal, charismatic, and Positive Confession movements in this country might be in more serious spiritual condition than they realize. Those Christians who are part of these movements need to carefully evaluate what their leaders are really teaching (or failing to teach). For example, at least one-fourth of all Pentecostals, representing over 5000 churches and millions of professed Christians, are members of the United Pentecostal Church, an organization which adamantly denies the Trinity and teaches other serious errors.[13]

Despite many positive aspects, the charismatic movement as a whole has yet to integrate the great doctrinal truths of Scripture into the lives of its people. In its great emphasis upon experience with the Holy Spirit, the value of diligent study of theology is often neglected. But perhaps the truest and greatest fellowship with the Holy Spirit occurs when we thoroughly know and obey what He has written (2 Peter 1:21; 2 Timothy 3:16; 1 John 1:5-7; 2:3-6,29; 3:24; 4:13).

The Positive Confession movement alone is neutralizing, distorting, or destroying the spiritual life of thousands (and perhaps tens of thousands) of Christians. Leaders in this teaching and those related to it, such as Kenneth Hagin, Kenneth Copeland, Robert Schuller, Paul Yonggi Cho, Oral Roberts, Robert Tilton, Charles Capps, John Osteen, Agnes Sanford, Benny Hinn, and all the rest are *not* always teaching sound biblical doctrine, but incorporating with it false teaching that can harm people spiritually.

Anyone who wants to help Christians caught in false teaching needs to know how to recognize it and how to defend against it. Thus, the need for this material also is clear: The Positive Confession movement encompasses one of the cutting edges of error in the church, and to ignore it is folly.

Our analysis of all these beliefs has been based upon our personal conviction that the Bible alone constitutes God's revealed word to mankind and that a Christianity based upon it alone is fully true.

What can we say to those who think that we are being "narrow" in holding to biblical exclusivism? We can say three things. First, this was the attitude of Jesus Christ Himself (John 14:6; John 10:108; Acts 4:12; 1 Timothy 2:5,6), and Jesus proved Himself an infallible authority by resurrecting from the dead.[14] Therefore, what He believed and what He said was true should matter to everyone.

Second, what we accept as true in a religious sense is really a matter of the historical and logical evidence. If the objective evidence that is available for any man to investigate[15] strongly favors the truth of Christianity—and no other religion—than we may be free to accept or reject the evidence, but we cannot logically ignore it.

We agree with the assessment of one of the leading intellectual giants of our day, the esteemed philosopher Mortimer Adler. In a recent interview he noted, "I believe Christianity is the only logical, consistent faith in the world."[16] If anyone knows what he is talking about in the areas of philosophy, logic, and evidence, it is Adler. He is the director of the Institute for Philosophical Research in Chicago, chairman of the board of editors of *Encyclopeida Britannica*, the architect behind the monumental *Great Book of the Western World*, and developer of its phenomenal *Syntopicon*. He is author of *Aristotle for Everybody, Six Great Ideas, Ten Philosophical Mistakes, Reforming Education* and more than 20 other works. Men like Adler do not lightly embrace Christianity. But one reason Christianity has such a long history of intellectual conversions to it[17] is precisely because there is so much evidence for it. If the evidence compels us to conclude Christianity is true, and if we sincerely care about what is true, then we also should embrace it.

Third, it is neither being "narrow" to reject other religions and beliefs, nor necessarily being "broad" and "open-minded" to accept them. Ideas are not primarily narrow or broad; they are either true or false. And it is not necessarily "broad" and "open-minded" to accept ideas that may be false and wrong.

Nevertheless, without an absolute standard by which to judge other beliefs, practices, and actions, all of us are uncertain, floundering in a sea of relativism. We are logically unable to have a true basis for making final judgments on anything. If there is no absolute truth, no one can say with absolute authority that anything is either right or wrong, or good or evil.

This is one of the greatest tragedies of our modern era—the assumption that absolutes are unknowable, truth is relative, and that therefore almost anything goes and almost anything may be believed.

If we need an absolute standard, what then is that absolute standard and how may we know it? That standard is God Himself, and it may be known through His revealed word, the Bible. The Bible alone provides the infallible standard by which ideas and practices can be judged. Because Christianity alone is based on God's Word, it stands unique among all the world's religions and philosophies. And if Christianity is true to Scripture, it can speak authoritatively to any situation because it offers God's mind on the subject. Indeed, the only reason the Bible has absolute authority is because the Bible really *is* God's revelation to man.

Our prayer for the church echoes the words of Jesus, who prayed for His people: "Sanctify them by the truth; your word is truth" (John 17:17 NIV) and who also said, "If you abide in My word, then you are truly disciples of Mine; and you shall know the truth, and the truth shall make you free" (John 8:31,32 NASB).

P A R T   O N E

CULT WATCH

MORMONISM

*A handy guide
to understanding
the claims
of Mormonism*

1

Introduction to Mormonism

The Church of Jesus Christ of Latter-day Saints (the Mormon Church) is a multibillion-dollar institution, perhaps the wealthiest per member in the world. It has vast holdings in real estate, insurance, financial services, broadcasting, and publishing, making it an 8-billion-dollar-a-year conglomerate. In state and national politics, Mormons have a substantial influence. Mormons have headed the following posts and departments: Secretary of Agriculture, Treasurer of the United States, the Department of Interior, the Department of Urban Housing and Development, the Federal Reserve Board, and the Securities and Exchange Commission. Mormons also head or have headed Walt Disney Productions, the Marriott Hotel Chain, Max Factor, Save-on Drugs, Standard Oil, and other corporate giants. Further, the Mormon church is the single largest sponsor of Boy Scout units in the United States, supporting some 17,000 troops.[1]

Mormonism claims to be authentic Christianity. Because it alleges that it is the only true Christian religion, it aggressively seeks to lead members of other churches into its fold. Indeed, it has achieved a measure of success. The late Harry Ropp was director of Mission to Mormons, one of several organizations founded to, in the words of Ropp, "stem the flow of converts from Christian Churches to Mormonism."[2]

Because of the claim that Mormonism makes, millions of people, including many Christians, think that Mormonism is a Christian religion. One example of how Mormonism has been accepted as a Christian denomination is in the fact that the Navy Chief of Chaplains, Rear Admiral Alvin B. Koeneman, has officially designated Mormon Navy chaplains as "Protestant."[3] The idea that Mormonism is Christian illustrates one of the basic problems that the Christian church faces concerning Mormonism.

One purpose of this unit is to show why it is incorrect for anyone to believe that the Church of Jesus Christ of Latter-day Saints is associated with historic, biblical Christianity.

In recent years the Mormon Church has waged an extensive media campaign to introduce itself to the American public as a church that believes in the biblical Jesus Christ. Advertisements have been taken out in major magazines (e.g., *Reader's Digest*) and, more recently, nationwide television ads, claiming that Jesus Christ visited the Americas after His resurrection. This teaching comes from the purported history taught in the Book of Mormon.

Both the Book of Mormon and its alleged translator, Joseph Smith, the founder of Mormonism, are central characters in the story of the Church of Jesus Christ of Latter-day Saints.

What is the Book of Mormon and what does it teach?

The Book of Mormon is the "Bible" of the Mormon Church along with two other Mormon scriptures, *Doctrine and Covenants* and *The Pearl of Great Price*.

The Book of Mormon claims to represent the history of three different groups of people, all of whom allegedly migrated from the Near East to Central and South America. Two of the groups supposedly traveled as far north as Mexico and North America (the Book of Mormon, Ether, and First Nephi).[4]

These two groups, the Nephites and Mulekites were semitic, with the most important group being led by Lehi of Jerusalem. His descendents became the Nephites. The main history of the Book of Mormon concerns the Nephites.

How did the alleged Nephites originate?

Around 600 B.C. the family of Lehi left Jerusalem. By the time of Christ, his descendents had migrated to North America. Earlier, two of Lehi's sons, Nephi and Laman, disputed and the people took sides. This began two quarreling camps named after Lehi's sons: the Nephites and Lamanites. Nephi was a righteous leader, but Laman was not, which had unfortunate consequences for his descendents. Native American Indians are held by Mormons to be descendents of Laman and, along with Blacks, their dark skins are considered the sign of a curse by God (1 Nephi 12:23; 2 Nephi 5:21).

When Jesus resurrected, He allegedly came and preached to both these peoples and they were converted. Unfortunately, a few centuries later, the Lamanites apostatized and were at war with the Nephites.

The Book of Mormon teaches that in A.D. 385, during the final battles that wiped out the Nephites (around A.D. 380 to 420), some 230,000 Nephites died near the hill Cumorah in New York (Mormon 6:10-15; 8:2). By A.D. 421 all the Nephites had been killed, with only the apostate

Lamanites left in the land. (These were the supposed "Jewish Indians" whom Columbus discovered in 1492.)

Before this time, one Nephite historian-prophet named Mormon (the commander of the Nephites) had gathered all the records of his predecessors. From them he penned an abridged history of his people— allegedly written on gold plates in "reformed Egyptian." This synopsis by Mormon was largely derived from plates written by Nephi (2 Nephi 5:28-31).

Thus Mormon wrote the "history" of his people from about 600 B.C., when they left Jerusalem, to A.D. 385. He entrusted the plates to his son Moroni, who supposedly finished the history and then hid the accounts in the hill Cumorah around A.D. 421. Fourteen hundred years later Joseph Smith was allegedly led to the same hill by the "angel" Moroni (the same Moroni, now a resurrected being) to discover the gold plates which Mormon had written.

By use of a magical seer stone, the young Smith translated the "Egyptian heiroglyphics" (so they claim) of the Jew called Mormon into English—the result being a perfect translation "by the power of God." Named after its author, this became known as the Book of Mormon.

But, in spite of the Book of Mormon's claimed "history," no evidence— archaeological or other—exists to support it.

Joseph Smith

As we have noted, the "translator" of the Book of Mormon was Joseph Smith, the founder of the Mormon Church. Joseph Smith was an occultist whom the Mormon Church views as a true prophet of God in the biblical meaning of that term. This alleged prophet, who had been the recipient of numerous visions and supernatural revelations, felt his divine calling in life was unsurpassed. He believed the entirety of Christendom was in deep ignorance. But because he had the Holy Ghost he felt, "I am learned, and know more than all the world put together."[5]

Smith boasted that he comprehended "heaven, earth and hell," and that God was his "right-hand man."[6] In his own words, he confessed, "*I have more to boast of than ever any man had. I am the only man who has ever been able to keep a whole church together since the days of Adam. . . . Neither Paul, John, Peter nor Jesus ever did it. I boast that no man ever did such a work as I.*"[7] In *Doctrines and Covenants* 135:3 it asserts that, "Joseph Smith, the Prophet and Seer of the Lord, has done more, save Jesus only, for the salvation of man in this world than any other man that lived in it."

The tenth president of the Church, Joseph Fielding Smith, said bluntly that there was "no salvation without accepting Joseph Smith" and that a man "cannot enter the kingdom of God" if he rejects the truth of Joseph Smith's prophethood.[8] Brigham Young even claimed that for any man to enter heaven, Joseph Smith's *permission* was required, and that Smith reigns in the spirit world today as supremely as God Himself does in heaven.[9]

Mormonism

The sixth president of the Mormon Church, Joseph F. Smith, stated that *"Joseph Smith's name will never perish"* and that his name will be held in reverence and honor among men as universally as the name of Jesus Christ.[10]

Nevertheless, the prophetic status of Joseph Smith is not borne out by an objective perusal of the evidence. Anyone who wishes to may compare Smith's teachings, prophecies, and moral character with the Bible and prove for themselves that they are inconsistent with that of a genuine biblical prophet.[11]

Mormonism is a powerful and influential religion today—one that the Christian church ignores at its peril. Christians and non-Christians need to be informed about what this group really teaches and believes. Let's examine the specific claims of the Mormon Church and assess their credibility.

2

The Origin
and Claims
of Mormonism

Question 1

What is Mormonism and why is it important?

Mormonism is a religion founded upon the teachings of Joseph Smith (1805-1844). Although some 100 Mormon sects have existed historically (many of which are polygamous), the two largest divisions are the Church of Jesus Christ of Latter-day Saints (headquartered in Salt Lake City, Utah) and the Reorganized Church of Latter-day Saints (headquartered in Independence, Missouri; see Appendix A).

The subject of Mormonism is important because of the Church's influence, power, and evangelistic operations. For example, it maintains over 30,000 missionaries who actively engage in proselytizing activities throughout the world.[12] Further, Mormonism is one of the largest of the leading U.S. non-Christian religions originating in the last 200 years. It boasts a membership of 6 to 7 million worldwide, which it hopes to double by the year 2000.[13]

No one can doubt the power and influence of Mormonism,[14] and this is why a discussion of this subject is important.

Question 2

How did Mormonism originate and how important are supernatural revelations to the founding and sustaining of the Mormon Church?

Like most other religions, Mormonism claims divine inspiration as its source. Mormons argue that their religion was divinely instituted in 1820 when God the Father and Jesus Christ allegedly appeared to Joseph Smith in a dramatic vision. "Jesus" told Smith that Christianity was in complete apostasy and that he (Smith) would be guided into the truth, presumably the reestablishment of true Christian faith.

This crucial "first vision" of Joseph Smith in 1820 is the official account of Mormon beginnings. Although it allegedly establishes the Church's divine origin, there are at least six contradictory versions of this key event.[15] (See Question 15.) We cite the Church's official version below.

Joseph Smith claimed that in his fifteenth year, while living in Manchester, New York, a religious revival of significant proportions took place "and great multitudes united themselves to the different religious parties."[16] Smith claimed that the strife among these parties was so great as to confuse a person as to which one was correct in its teachings—Presbyterian, Baptist, Methodist, or some other denomination. Because of this alleged strife, Smith determined to privately seek God's counsel as to which of the various denominations he should join.

One day while reading James 1:5 (which refers to asking God for wisdom), Smith was greatly moved. In Smith's own words:

> Never did any passage of scripture come home with more power to the heart of man than this did at this time to mine. . . . [Smith then retired to a secluded place in the woods to seek God's counsel]. . . . I kneeled down and began to offer up the desire of my heart to God. I had scarcely done so, when immediately I was seized upon by some power which entirely overcame me, and had such an astonishing influence over me as to bind my tongue so that I could not speak. Thick darkness gathered around me, and it seemed to me for a time as if I were doomed to sudden destruction.
>
> But, exerting all my powers to call upon God to deliver me out of the power of this enemy which had seized upon me . . . just at this moment of great alarm, I saw a pillar of light exactly over my head, above the brightness of the sun, which descended gradually until it fell upon me.
>
> It no sooner appeared than I found myself delivered from the enemy which held me bound. When the light rested upon me, I saw two Personages, whose brightness and glory defy all description, standing above me in the air. One of them spake unto me, calling me by name, and said, pointing to the other— "THIS IS MY BELOVED SON. HEAR HIM!"
>
> My object in going to inquire of the Lord was to know which of all the [religious] sects was right, that I might know which to join. No sooner, therefore, did I get possession of myself, so as to be able to speak, than I asked the Personages who stood above me in the light, which of all the sects was right—and which I should join.

> I was answered that I must join none of them, for they were all wrong, and the Personage who addressed me [presumably Jesus Christ] said that all their creeds were an abomination in his sight: that those professors were all corrupt; that: "they draw near to me with their lips, but their hearts are far from me, they teach for doctrines the commandments of men, having a form of godliness, but they deny the power thereof." He again forbade me to join with any of them; and many other things did he say....[17]

Although Smith's claims were considered impossible by the Christian community, Joseph remained true to his vision. His "mind [was satisfied] so far as the sectarian [Christian] world was concerned.... It was not my duty to join with any of them, but to continue as I was until further directed."[18]

Unfortunately, if Joseph Smith had truly believed in the authority of the Bible and had really studied it, he could have determined for himself that the various Christian denominations were *not* "all corrupt" and that the vision was, therefore, a false one.[19] Nor, apparently, was he aware of the characteristic methods of spiritistic imposture.[20]

But Smith was convinced that he had been called of God and, although in the next three years he confesses he "frequently fell into many foolish errors" (cf. James 1:20-22,26), he waited patiently for the next revelation.[21]

On September 21, 1823, an "angel" appeared to Smith telling him of the location of certain "gold plates." It was from the writings on these gold plates that eventually the Mormon scripture known as the Book of Mormon was "translated." These plates allegedly contained the historical records of a tribe of Jewish people known as the "Nephites" concerning their supposed early migration to the Americas.[22]

Smith had many more supposedly angelic revelations. Just as the Church ostensibly began through supernatural revelation, it was also sustained by this process. For example, from 1831 to 1844, Smith allegedly "received 135 direct revelations from God," helping the new movement to grow and solidify itself.[23] Smith believed that he received revelations from God, Jesus, and many spirits of the dead, such as Peter, James, John the Baptist, and others.[24] (Many of these revelations are printed in *Doctrine and Covenants*, the second and doctrinally most important volume of Mormon scripture.[25] (See Questions 17, 21-23.)

Question 3

How can we know if these revelations were from God or whether they originated from some other source?

We can know whether or not these revelations were from God by comparing them with what God has already said in His Word, the Bible. If these revelations deny what God has clearly said is true, then they cannot logically originate in God. As Abraham Lincoln noted during the Civil War when both sides were claiming God's support, "God cannot be for and against the same thing at the same time."

That Joseph Smith or anyone else claims to have divine visions does not automatically prove the visions are from God; people may invent stories of divine visions for unknown reasons or they may even be the recipient of mental delusions. Even if Joseph Smith was the recipient of *real* supernatural manifestations, how does anyone know they were not clever counterfeits by deceiving spirits who were lying when they claimed to be angels and saints?[26]

Literally thousands of people claim to have seen divine visions or to have received revelations from angels and spirits of the dead, and yet subsequent events have usually proved them wrong, so no one should automatically assume Joseph Smith's revelations were really divine. Before such things can be accepted, they must be carefully tested, as the Bible itself commands (1 Thessalonians 5:21). The Bible further teaches, "Dear friends, do not believe every spirit, but test the spirits to see whether they are from God, because many false prophets have gone out into the world" (1 John 4:1 NIV).

The issue of Mormon revelations is finally reduced to one simple test. If Joseph Smith's revelations deny, contradict, and oppose the Bible, then whatever their source, they cannot possibly have originated in God. And if they did not originate in God, they have no divine authority and should not be heeded.

We think that Mormons would agree with Orson Pratt, an early apostle of the Mormon Church, who confessed, "Cursed be that man or angel who preaches another gospel, or perverts the true gospel of Christ."[27] This agrees with what the apostle Paul himself taught, "But even though we, or an angel from heaven, should preach to you a gospel contrary to that which we have preached to you, let him be accursed" (Galatians 1:8).

Most of this unit will be devoted to supplying documentation that Mormon revelations and the doctrines derived from them cannot be considered divine. If you are a Mormon, we ask you to carefully weigh the arguments presented. Every conscientious religious person has a responsibility to be certain that what he or she claims to be from God really is from Him.

Question 4

Does Mormonism claim to be the only true church on earth?

Mormonism does not claim to be merely one part of the Christian religion, such as a Christian denomination. Rather, it claims to alone comprise the only true Christian religion on earth. This claim is in harmony with the "first vision" of Joseph Smith where Jesus supposedly condemned all Christian religions as corrupt abominations. *Doctrine and Covenants* emphasizes that Mormonism is "the only true and living church upon the face of the whole earth."[28]

Indeed, from their earliest days, Mormons have claimed they were the only people of God on earth. In 1854, Orson Pratt argued, "All other churches are entirely destitute of all authority from God."[29] A leading doctrinal theologian of the modern Mormon Church, the late Bruce McConkie, asserted that "Mormons...have the only pure and perfect Christianity now on earth."[30] He also taught, "All other systems of religion are false."[31] The Mormon Sunday school text, *The Master's Church, Course A,* informs children, "We cannot accept that any other church can lead its members to salvation. . . ."[32]

Question 5

Is Mormonism a Christian religion?

As we have now seen, there is no doubt that Mormonism *claims* to represent authentic Christianity. Indeed, because it alleges it is the only truly Christian religion on earth, it aggressively seeks to lead members of other churches into its fold. And it has achieved a measure of success.[33,34,35]

Many Christians accept the Mormon faith as genuinely Christian. But when Christians view Mormons as fellow Christians, they fail to understand Mormonism correctly. They have accepted Mormon claims without determining whether those claims are true.

Virtually all knowledgeable Christian authorities recognize that not only is Mormonism not Christian, it is really anti-Christian. Dr. Anthony Hoekema declares in his book *The Four Major Cults*: "We must at this point assert, in the strongest possible terms, that Mormonism does not deserve to be called a Christian religion. It is basically anti-Christian and anti-biblical."[36] Gordon Fraser, the author of four books on Mormonism, explains, "We object to Mormon missionaries posing as Christians, and our objections are based on the differences between what they are taught by the [Mormon] General Authorities and what the Bible teaches."[37] One of the leading modern authorities on the cults, the late Dr. Walter Martin, correctly asserted, "In no uncertain terms, the Bible condemns the teachings of the Mormon Church."[38] Former Mormons and leading experts on Mormonism, Jerald and Sandra Tanner, also correctly affirm, "The Mormon Church is certainly not built on the teachings of the Bible."[39]

If the teachings of Mormonism are biblical, then they deserve to be called Christian. But if Mormon teachings deny and oppose biblical teaching, then it is wrong for anyone to consider Mormonism a Christian religion. In our next question, we will briefly illustrate how Mormon teachings oppose biblical teachings. We will do this by showing that when the Mormon Church uses a Christian term, it typically rejects the biblical definition of that term and substitutes a false, non-Christian definition in its place.

Question 6

Does the Mormon Church give biblical words an entirely false meaning?

In order to illustrate that Mormon teachings are not biblical, we have

provided a selected list of key biblical/Christian words and the false definitions that the Mormon Church gives to them. This redefinition of words
underscores the problem that Christians face when discussing religious
issues with Mormons. Mormons may use the same words that Christians
use, but they use them with different, or even opposite, meanings. Unless
Christians pursue the meaning of such words, and unless Mormons are
frank in giving them their true Mormon definition, Christians and the
public in general will continue to be confused over the religious status of
Mormonism.

In any discussion with a Mormon, the following redefinition of biblical/
Christian terms must be kept in mind. Although Mormons themselves
may be ignorant of some of the definitions cited below, they represent true
Mormon teaching as proven by an evaluation of standard Mormon theological works.[40] (Chapter 3 provides illustrations.)

Christianity: sectarianism; a false and damnable apostate religion.

God: "Elohim"; one of innumerable self-progressing bodily deities; formerly a man, a finite creature. In early Mormon theology, Adam (of the
Garden of Eden) was considered by many Mormons as the true earth
deity.[41]

Jesus Christ: a self-progressing deity ("Jehovah" of the Old Testament) and
the first spirit child of "Elohim" and his wife.

Holy Ghost: a man with a spiritual body of matter.

Trinity: tritheistic; coordinated under general Mormon polytheism; thus
the Father, Son, and Holy Ghost are separate deities.

The Gospel: Mormon theology.

Born-again: water baptism into Mormonism.

Immortality: Mormon salvation by grace (limited to the universal resurrection of all men).

Atonement: the provision God has supplied for an individual to earn their
true salvation "by obedience to the laws and ordinances of the Gospel"
(*Articles of Faith,* 3).

True salvation/eternal life/redemption: Exaltation to Godhood in the highest
part of the celestial kingdom based upon individual good works and
personal merit; exaltation incorporates ruling a new world and sexual
procreation in order to produce spirit children who will eventually be
embodied and inhabit that world, each then having the opportunity to
be exalted.

The Fall: a spiritual step upward; a blessing permitting the production of
physical bodies for preexistent spirits to inhabit and thus have the
possibility of attaining their own "exaltation" or Godhood.

Death: generally a step upward; death represents the possibility of a form of salvation (if not exaltation) for those who have never heard of Mormonism.

Heaven: three "kingdoms of glory" comprising various spiritual gradations.

Hell: generally purgatorial; possibly eternal for a very few (primarily apostate Mormons).

Virgin birth: the birth of Christ through a physical sex act between God the Father (the Mormon earth god "Elohim") and Mary (hence, not a *virgin* birth).

Man: a preexistent spirit with the potential to earn Godhood by obedience to Mormon dictates.

Creation: the reorganization of eternal matter.

The Scriptures: the Book of Mormon; *Doctrine and Covenants*; *The Pearl of Great Price*; and the Bible "as far as it is translated correctly" (*Articles of Faith*, 8).

The Bible: an erring and often unreliable inspired record, properly interpreted only by Mormons and only in light of Mormon theology.

Consider this list of words. For 2,000 years the Christian church has expressed general agreement on the meaning of these terms. Yet the Mormon definitions and descriptions of the words cited above are anything but Christian. Why has the Mormon Church supplied false definitions to common Christian terms? Simply because it has not relied upon the Bible alone to formulate its views. Rather, it has depended upon revelations from the spirit world (see Chapter 4) and these revelations have forced a redefinition of the above terms. Once these revelations had become the Church's standard scriptures, the doctrinal teachings of the Mormon Church were predetermined.

This is why Mormonism cannot be considered Christian—its new revelations deny the true meaning of biblical terms and offer non-Christian teachings in their place.

In Chapter 3, we will contrast specific Mormon and Christian doctrines so the reader can easily see the fundamental irreconcilability of Mormonism with Christianity.

3

Is Mormon Teaching the Same as Biblical and Christian Teaching?

Question 7

How do Mormon teachings differ from Christian teachings?

Because Mormon theology is Mormon and not Christian, it is easy to compare the beliefs of Mormonism with the beliefs of Christianity. As an introduction to this section, we offer the following chart contrasting basic Mormon and Christian teaching.

Mormonism	*Christianity*
BIBLE	BIBLE
Unreliable	Reliable
Incomplete as it is	Complete as it is
Adds new revelations to God's Word	Rejects new revelations
Unbiblical theological presuppositions utilized in interpretation	Accepted historical, grammatical principles utilized in interpretation
GOD	GOD
Tritheism/polytheistic	Trinity/monotheistic
Physical (evolved man)	Spirit
Finite	Infinite
Morally questionable	Holy
Organizer of eternal matter	Creator of matter from nothing
Sexual polygamist	Nonsexual

Mormonism	*Christianity*
JESUS	JESUS
A god	God
Created	Eternal
Earned salvation (exaltation to Godhood)	As eternal God neither salvation nor exaltation was required
Not virgin born	Virgin born
Polygamist*	Unmarried
SALVATION	SALVATION
By works	By grace
Denies biblical atonement	Affirms atonement
Possible after death	Impossible after death
DEATH	DEATH
"Purgatorial"; three celestial kingdoms; almost universalistic	Eternal heaven or hell; no purgatory; not universalistic

For anyone to maintain that Mormonism and Christianity teach the same thing is logically, historically, and doctrinally an indefensible position. We will now document some of the key doctrines of Mormonism and show why they are not biblical teachings.

Question 8

How does Mormonism view the Christian religion?

The Mormon Church teaches that shortly after the time of the disciples, the Christian church apostatized and was not restored until Joseph Smith's "first vision" in 1820. (See Question 14.)

Mormonism considers Christianity its enemy because it believes Christianity is an apostate religion, teaching false doctrines. For example, one allegedly false doctrine Mormonism strongly opposes is the Christian teaching of salvation by grace through faith alone (Ephesians 2:8,9; Romans 4:6; 11:6). Because Mormonism holds that Christian doctrines lead men astray spiritually, the Mormon Church views Christianity as a damnable religion and Christians as deceived people. Below we present selected citations in documentation.

Brigham Young taught that Christians were unbelievers; they may falsely claim to believe in Christ, but the truth is "not one of them really believes in Him."[42] Further, Joseph Smith himself emphasized that Christian pastors "are of their father, the devil" and they and all who follow them "without one exception [will] receive their portion with the devil and

---

* primarily but not exclusively an early Mormon teaching

his angels."[43] Smith avowed they will "all be damned together."[44]

In his introduction to Joseph Smith's alleged[45] *History of the Church*, noted Mormon Church historian Brigham Henry Roberts declares that those who profess belief in the great creeds of Christendom, such as the Nicene and Athanasian Creeds "are wandering in the darkness...of old pagan philosophies."[46] Citing 2 Peter 2:1, he sees this as evidence that Christians have denied the Lord that bought them, and that they have literally turned "to fables."[47]

In *Journal of Discourses*, a 27-volume set of speeches by early Mormon presidents and leaders, we find sentiments such as the following. Second president Brigham Young taught that concerning true theology, "a more ignorant people never lived than the present so-called Christian world."[48] Further, he believed that Christians were "heathens as to their knowledge of the salvation of God."[49] John Taylor, the third president of the Church, believed that Christianity was a "perfect pack of nonsense...as corrupt as hell" and an invention of the devil.[50] He taught that Mormons were "the saviors of the world" but that the entire Christian world knew nothing about God, and that as far as "the things of God are concerned, they are the veriest fools...."[51]

The apostle Orson Pratt, another leader in the early Church, declared, "The whole of Christendom is as destitute of Bible Christianity as the idolatrous pagans."[52] In his 1854 article, "Repentance," he asked, "How long will the heavens suffer such wickedness to go unpunished?"[53] According to Pratt, Christianity teaches:

> ...doctrines which are calculated to ruin the soul....these soul destroying doctrines...are taught in Christendom...which millions have had the wickedness to believe....What will become of all these false teachers....What will become of the people who suffer themselves to be led by such hypocrites? They will, every soul of them, unless they repent of these false doctrines, be cast down to hell....every one of you will, most assuredly, be damned.[54]

The tenth president of the Mormon Church, Joseph Fielding Smith, claimed that the supposed apostasy of Christianity had caused it to become a pagan "abomination" and that even the Reformation "perpetuated these evils, and therefore, the same corrupted doctrines and practices were perpetuated in these Protestant organizations."[55]

Nor has modern Mormonism changed its mind. Leading Mormon theologian, Bruce McConkie, condemns all non-Mormon churches. He teaches that "a perverted Christianity holds sway among the so-called Christians of apostate Christendom."[56] He even refers to Christian churches as "churches of the devil"[57] because "there is no salvation outside this one true church, the Church of Jesus Christ [the Mormon Church]."[58]

In another book, McConkie alleges that Christians are enemies of God, because God's plan of salvation "has been changed and perverted by an apostate Christendom."[59] Modern Christians are not only ignorant of God's true purposes,[60] their doctrines are "the doctrines of devils,"[61] and the Christian church is part of the "great and abominable church" of the devil preparing men "to be damned."[62]

All this is proof that the Mormon Church views the Christian faith as its enemy and individual Christians as spiritually deceived people. Mormonism alone is true Christianity. But we emphasize again, the real issue is not any specific claim to Christianity, but whether one's teachings are biblical or not. Scores of modern religions and cults all *claim* to be Christian, but their teachings conclusively prove that such a claim is false.[63] The only issue is: Do Mormon teachings clearly reject what God has revealed in His Word? If they do, they are not Christian.

In the following questions, we will examine the religious beliefs of Mormonism and compare and contrast them with what the Bible teaches.

Question 9

What does Mormonism teach about God?

Mormons emphasize that they believe in the biblical God and they "believe in the Holy Trinity."[64] But this claim is demonstrably false. We can compare and contrast the Mormon concept of deity with the Christian concept in the following chart.

Mormon God	*Christian God*
Many (polytheistic)	One (monotheistic)
Evolving (changing)	Immutable (unchanging)
Material (physical)	Immaterial (spirit)
Sexual	Nonsexual
Polygamist	Celibate
Morally imperfect (requiring salvation)	Eternally holy

Let us briefly examine these Mormon views of deity in turn. First, the Mormon Church accepts and teaches what is known as *polytheism*, a belief in many gods.* This is in contrast to historic orthodox Christian teaching which asserts there is only one God. Mormons will often claim they believe in only one God and that they are not polytheists, but such claims are false.

In his own words, Joseph Smith, the founder of Mormonism, emphasized, "I wish to declare I have always and in all congregations where I

---

* Technically, Mormon belief is henotheistic—a polytheistic system stressing one central deity ("Elohim," the primary god of this earth).

have preached on the subject of deity, it has [been on] the plurality of Gods."[65] In *Mormon Doctrine*, McConkie declares, "There are three Gods— the Father, Son and Holy Ghost."[66] McConkie further confesses,

> . . . to us speaking in the proper finite sense, these three are the only Gods we worship. But, in addition, there is an infinite number of holy personages, drawn from worlds without number, who have passed on to exaltation and are thus Gods. . . . This doctrine of plurality of Gods is so comprehensive and glorious that it reaches out and embraces every exalted personage. Those who attain exaltation are Gods.[67]

In other words, not only are there three principal Gods for this earth, and not only are there an infinite number of Gods throughout infinite worlds, but every Mormon who is "exalted" will himself become a God— in the fullest sense of that term.[68]

But this is clearly not the teaching of the Bible. God Himself says, "Before Me there was no God formed, and there will be none after Me" (Isaiah 43:10). He also says, "I am the first and I am the last, and there is no God besides Me. . . . Is there any God besides Me. . . . I know of none" (Isaiah 44:6,8). Finally, God declares, "I am the Lord, and there is no other; besides Me there is no God. . . . there is none except Me" (Isaiah 45:5,21). What could be clearer?

When Mormonism teaches there are many gods—indeed an infinite number of them—it denies what God Himself teaches in His Word.

Further, Mormonism teaches that each god is evolving. Even though God Himself has said, "I, the Lord, do not change" (Malachi 3:6; cf. James 1:17; Numbers 23:19), Mormonism teaches that God was once a man, having been created by another god. But by self-perfection, this man finally evolved into absolute Godhood. McConkie confesses Mormon belief when he teaches, "God is a Holy Man."[69] Joseph Smith likewise taught that "God Himself, the Father of us all . . . was once a man like us."[70] In his own words, Joseph Smith made his beliefs plain:

> God Himself was once as we are now, and is an exalted man and sits enthroned in yonder heavens! That is the great secret. . . . If you were to see him today, you would see him like a man in form. . . . I am going to tell you how God came to be God. We have imagined and supposed that God was God from all eternity. I will refute that idea, and take away the veil, so that you may see. . . . He was once a man like us. . . . Here, then, is eternal life—to know the only wise and true God; and you have got to learn how to be Gods yourselves.[71]

Because Joseph Smith is the author of the above statement, it is not surprising that he once mistranslated Genesis 1:1 as "In the beginning the head of the Gods brought forth the Gods."[72]

Nevertheless, the Bible is clear that God is an unchanging, infinite being existing from all eternity, not a finite man who somehow evolved into Godhood (Job 9:32; Numbers 23:19). "For I am God and not man—the Holy One among you" (Hosea 11:9 NIV).

Although the Bible affirms that "God is spirit" (John 4:24), the Mormon Church denies what the Bible teaches and tells its members that God is not spirit, but rather a physical being. Joseph Smith declared, "There is no other God in Heaven but that God that has flesh and bones."[73] *Doctrine and Covenants* 130:22 teaches, "The Father has a body of flesh and bones as tangible as man's...." McConkie calls God, "a glorified resurrected Personage having a tangible body of flesh and bones."[74] But Jesus Himself taught that a true "spirit does not have flesh and bones" (Luke 24:39) and therefore, if "God is spirit," He cannot, as Mormons claim, have a tangible physical body as men do.

Nevertheless, because Mormonism teaches that its Gods are localized and physical, it is not unexpected they can have sexual intercourse. Mormonism teaches that the Gods are sexually active. For all eternity men have been evolving into Gods. Once they reach the state of Godhood, they sexually beget spirit children with their celestial wives. These spirit children then have an opportunity to inhabit a physical body on a physical earth in order to attain their own Godhood and continue the process. McConkie teaches:

> We are the offspring of God. He is our eternal father; we have also an eternal mother. There is no such thing as a father without a mother, nor can there be children without parents. We were born as the spirit children of celestial parents long before the foundations of this world were laid.[75]

In 1870, Brigham Young stated, "The scripture says He, the Lord, came walking in the Temple with His train; I do not know who they were, unless his wives and children."[76] In November, 1853, Mormon apostle Orson Pratt concluded that God honors polygamy because He is Himself a polygamist. Therefore, His Son (Jesus) and His people are also polygamists.[77] One reason for early Mormon teaching favoring polygamy is seen in the fact that Mormons were only imitating their Gods.

But again, these Gods produce spirit children who require physical bodies. Thus, earths are "created" (materially organized) and populated with physical bodies so that the spirit children might have the opportunity to progress to Godhood just as their parents did:

> Just as men were first born as spirit children to their Eternal Father and His companion, the children born to resurrected beings are spirit beings and must be sent in their turn to another earth to pass through the trials of mortality and obtain a physical body.[78]

Here we see one of Mormonism's apparent theological rationalizations for the early doctrine of polygamy. If one wife could produce ten bodies for the spirit children to inhabit and thereby have the opportunity to become gods, then 20 wives could produce 200 bodies for these spirits; the more bodies the better; hence, the more wives the better. Brigham Young stated, "The Lord created you and me for the purpose of becoming Gods like Himself.... We are created... to become Gods like unto our Father in Heaven" so that we can then create "worlds on worlds."[79] Milton R. Hunter, a member of the First Council of Seventy, taught that "God the Eternal Father was once a mortal man.... He became God.... He grew in experience and continued to grow until he attained the status of Godhood."[80]

But Mormonism also teaches that its Gods were once imperfect, including God the Father and God the Son. That is why even God the Father and Jesus Christ (two of the Gods of this earth) required salvation. If every God was once an imperfect man who was saved through his good works, which exalted him to Godhood, then God Himself once required salvation. As Marion G. Romney, a member of the First Presidency observed, in *Gospel Doctrine*, "God is a perfected saved soul enjoying eternal life."[81]

All of this is why the Mormon concept of God cannot possibly be considered Christian. The Mormon Church may claim that Christians are in a state of apostasy and have lost the true knowledge of God, but a careful examination of Mormon teaching on God reveals otherwise. In essence, Mormonism is a religion of pagan polytheism. The concept of physical, sexual, procreating gods defended by the Mormon Church coincides with pagan and occultic belief, not Christian belief.

Question 10

What does Mormonism teach about Jesus Christ?

Mormonism claims that it believes in the true, biblical Jesus Christ. One publicity booklet teaches, "Christ is our Redeemer and our Savior. Except for him, there would be no salvation and no redemption...."[82] Statements like this have confused some Christians. For example, Frank Morley of Grace Presbyterian Church in Alberta, Canada, actually permits the Mormon Church to publish and promote a lecture by him in support of Mormonism. In this booklet he says, "It has been said to me that Mormons don't believe in Jesus Christ! [It is] such superstitions and misunderstandings we have regarding them, you see, that need clearing up."[83]

But consider the following chart contrasting the Mormon Christ (whom it confuses with Jehovah of the Old Testament) with the biblical Christ.

The Mormon Jesus Christ	The Biblical Jesus Christ
A created being; the brother of Lucifer	Uncreated God
Earned his own salvation (exaltation)	As God, Christ required no salvation

Common (one of many gods) and of minor importance in the *larger* Mormon cosmology	Unique (the Second Person of the one Godhead) and of supreme importance throughout eternity and in all creation
Conceived by the physical sex act of the Father (Adam or Elohim) and Mary	Conceived by the Holy Spirit who overshadowed Mary, a true virgin
A married polygamist?	An unmarried monogamist

The following brief statements by Mormon leaders reveal the true beliefs of the Mormon Church concerning Christ. In essence, the Mormon doctrine of Christ (as with many other of its doctrines) parallels those found in the world of the occult.

First, Mormonism teaches that Jesus Christ was a created being, not eternal God as the Bible clearly instructs (John 1:1,3; Titus 2:13), and that He was the first and foremost of subsequent billions of spirit children created through sexual intercourse between the male and female earth gods. *Doctrine and Covenants* 93:21-23 teaches that "Christ, the Firstborn, was the mightiest of all the spirit children of the Father." James Talmage affirms in a standard Mormon church work, *The Articles of Faith*, "Among the spirit children of Elohim, the firstborn was and is Jehovah, or Jesus Christ to whom all others are juniors."[84]

In Mormonism, Jesus is also seen as the brother of Satan. Since Satan was also a preexistent spirit creation of the male and female earth gods, Christ must therefore be considered his relation. In other words, Christ and the devil are "blood" brothers. If the devil and his demons were all spirit children of the Mormon earth god "Elohim," it must follow that they too are Jesus' brothers, just as they are the brothers of all men. As one Mormon writer states, "As for the devil and his fellow spirits, they are brothers to man and also to Jesus and sons and daughters to God in the same sense that we are."[85] In essence then, the difference between Christ and the devil in Mormonism is not one of kind, but only one of degree.

Second, Mormonism teaches that Jesus is a saved being. Because Jesus was only one more spirit offspring of the male and female earth gods (like all men and women), He too had to earn His salvation: "Jesus Christ is the Son of God. . . . He came to earth to work out His own salvation. . . . After His resurrection, He gained all power in Heaven."[86] And, "by obedience and devotion to the truth, He [Jesus] attained that pinnacle of intelligence which ranked Him as a God."[87] This is why McConkie emphasizes, "Christ . . . is a saved being."[88]

Third, in Mormon teaching, Jesus Christ is not unique, at least in nature. His divinity is not unique, for every exalted man will attain the same Godhood that Christ now experiences. Neither is His incarnation unique, for Christ, like all men, is only an incarnated spirit man, who in a preexistent state was the offspring of sexual union between the male and female earth gods who made Him.

Mormons do refer to Christ as a "greater" being than other spirit children of the male and female earth gods, but only on this earth. Further, Christ is their senior only by priority and position, not nature or essence. In fact, as a spirit child of the earth gods, He *is* of the same exact nature as all men and all demons; this is one reason Mormons refer to Him as their "elder brother." And so, "Jesus is man's spiritual brother. We dwelt with Him in the spirit world as members of that large society of eternal intelligences, which included our Heavenly Parents."[89]

Christ is also not unique as Creator of this earth. Mormonism teaches that the preexistent spirits Adam and Joseph Smith, plus others, helped Him to create it![90]

In fact, Christ was unique in nature in only one way—by His physical birth. Rather than having a merely human father as the rest of us on this earth, His mother had physical sex with God (Elohim).[91]

Fourth, as noted above, Mormons accept the birth of Jesus Christ through sexual intercourse between God (Elohim) and Mary. Because "sexuality . . . is actually an attribute of God . . . God is a procreating personage of flesh and bone" and "the Holy Ghost was not the father of Jesus."[92] In *Doctrines of Salvation*, Joseph Fielding Smith asserts, "Christ was begotten of God. He was not born without the aid of Man and *that Man was God*"![93] McConkie declares, "Christ was begotten by an Immortal Father the same way that mortal men are begotten by mortal fathers."[94]

In other words, Mary was apparently a bigamist—married to both her earthly husband, Joseph, and God Himself. Brigham Young confessed, "The man Joseph, the husband of Mary, did not, that we know of, have more than one wife, but Mary, the wife of Joseph, had another husband [that is, God]."[95]

Fifth, some Mormons have also taught that Jesus Christ was a polygamist having several wives, another unbiblical doctrine. The early Mormon apostle Orson Pratt claimed that Jesus Christ was married at Cana of Galilee, that Mary and Martha (and others) were His wives, and that He had children. Thus, Jesus "was a Polygamist" who proved it by "marrying many honorable wives."[96]

This, then, is the Mormon Jesus Christ—a sexually created spirit-brother of Lucifer, a possible polygamist, and one of many gods who earned His salvation, immortality, and godhood.

But biblically, all of this is false. Jesus Christ is God. He is eternal, and was therefore never created (John 1:1-3; Colossians 1:16,17; Isaiah 9:6; Micah 5:2). Further, Jesus Christ is not the brother of the devil; He came to destroy the works of the devil (1 John 3:8). He was not a man who earned his salvation; He was God who (through the incarnation) died on the cross for other men's salvation (1 Peter 2:24). He never married, nor was he born by sexual intercourse between a pagan god and the virgin Mary (John 1).

In fact, not a single biblical Scripture can logically be advanced by Mormons in defense of their teachings on Jesus Christ. Yet Mormon missionaries come to the door and say in full sincerity that they are Christians who believe in the biblical Jesus Christ.

Question 11

What do Mormons teach about salvation and life after death?

Mormon teaching on salvation presents different kinds of salvation leading to different kinds of heaven.

First, there is a *general salvation* which Mormons call "salvation by grace." Mormonism affirms this occurs to all men. But this general salvation is restricted to resurrection from the dead and immortality; it does not decide a person's specific residence or degree of glory in the next life. This is decided by the second category of Mormon salvation, *individual salvation*. Individual salvation determines which one of three "heavens" one goes to, and whether or not one earns true "eternal life" (godhood).

General salvation is said to be based on grace while individual salvation is confessedly by good works. Therefore, Mormons may *claim* that they believe salvation is by grace; however, by this they mean only that every person will be resurrected from the dead. The actual destiny of that person is determined by personal righteousness (see Questions 12,13).

Talmage states in his book *Jesus the Christ* that "general salvation, in the sense of redemption from the effects of the fall [resurrection], comes to all without their seeking it; but that individual salvation, or rescue from the effects of personal sins, is to be acquired by each for himself by faith and good works. . . ."[97]

Therefore, a person's good works and personal merit determine which "kingdom of glory" he or she inherits after death. The lowest kingdom of glory is called the *telestial* kingdom. It is the place of the wicked, where most of humanity will reside. Such persons will be excluded from the presence of God and Christ. The kingdom above this is called the *terrestrial* kingdom of glory. This is where lukewarm Mormons, good nonMormons, and those who accept Mormonism after death go.

The highest kingdom of glory is the *celestial* kingdom and this is gained by "complete obedience" to gospel law.[98] This kingdom has three parts. But it is only in the highest part of the celestial kingdom that salvation in its fullest sense is found. Salvation in its truest sense is attaining absolute Godhood and eternal sexual increase.[99]

In conclusion, worthy Mormons attain exaltation or deification in the highest heaven of the celestial kingdom. All other people are said to be "damned," which is, in effect, to inherit a restricted and servant status in lesser kingdoms—but kingdoms nonetheless.

Question 12

Do Mormons teach that true salvation occurs only by good works and personal righteousness?

From its inception, the Mormon Church has consistently and adamantly opposed the clear biblical teaching of justification by grace through faith alone (Ephesians 2:8,9; Philippians 3:9). In fact, few religions are more hostile to the biblical teaching of salvation by grace than Mormonism.

Talmage refers to "a most pernicious doctrine—that of justification by belief alone."[100] Joseph Fielding Smith taught that "mankind [is] damned by [the] "faith alone" doctrine."[101] McConkie complains, "Many Protestants . . . erroneously conclude that men are saved by grace alone without doing the works of righteousness."[102]

Because salvation by grace is thoroughly rejected, Mormonism forcefully teaches a system of salvation by works of righteousness and personal merit. Both the Book of Mormon and *Doctrine and Covenants* teach "works salvation."[103] Further, virtually every Mormon authority of past and present has emphasized the absolute necessity of salvation by works and personal righteousness.

Heber C. Kimball taught, "I have power to save myself, and if I do not save myself, who will save me? All have that privilege, and naught can save us but obedience to the commandments of God."[104] Talmage refers to "the absolute requirement of individual compliance with the laws and ordinances of his [Jesus'] gospel by which salvation may be attained."[105] Joseph Fielding Smith emphasized that "the new birth is also a matter of obedience to law."[106] Bruce McConkie thinks that the great defender of justification by faith alone, the apostle Paul, is "the apostle of good works, of personal righteousness, of keeping the commandments, of pressing forward with a steadfastness in Christ, of earning the right to eternal life by the obedience to the laws and ordinances of the gospel."[107]

But none of this is biblical teaching. From the Old Testament to the Gospels and the book of Acts, from the apostle Paul's writings to the apostle John's, the Bible teaches only one way of salvation—by grace through faith alone. "Of Him [Jesus], all the prophets bear witness that through His name everyone who believes in Him receives forgiveness of sins" (Acts 10:43).

Jesus Himself taught that salvation was secured by faith alone. For example, "Truly, Truly, I say to you, he who hears My word, and believes Him who sent Me, has eternal life, and does not come into judgment, but has passed out of death into life" (John 5:24). "Truly, truly, I say to you, he who believes has eternal life" (John 6:47). "Jesus answered and said to them, 'This is the work of God, that you believe in Him whom He has sent'" (John 6:29).

Notice the testimony of the following additional Scriptures: As early as Genesis we read, "Abram believed the Lord, and he credited it to him as righteousness" (Genesis 15:6 NIV). The apostle Paul comments on this verse when he asserts, "What does the Scripture say? 'Abraham believed God and it was credited to him as righteousness'" (Romans 4:3 NIV). Paul never once taught that salvation was earned by good works and personal righteousness, as Mormons claim. To maintain this is to seriously misinterpret and distort Paul's teaching. In his own words Paul confessed that even though he was a righteous man according to the law, he counted it

but rubbish in order that I may gain Christ, and may be found in Him, not having a righteousness of my own derived from the Law, but that which is through faith in Christ, the righteousness which comes from God on the basis of faith (Philippians 3:8,9).

Does this sound as though Paul was a great defender of salvation by good works and of "earning the right to salvation" by obedience to gospel law? To the contrary, Paul repeatedly emphasized salvation was secured by grace through faith in Christ alone as the following Scriptures prove:

For we maintain that a man is justified by faith apart from works of the Law (Romans 3:28).

But to the one who does not work [for salvation], but believes in Him who justifies the ungodly, his faith is reckoned as righteousness, just as David also speaks of the blessing upon the man to whom God reckons righteousness apart from works (Romans 4:5,6).

For Christ is the end of the law for righteousness to everyone who believes (Romans 10:4).

By grace you have been saved through faith; and that not of yourselves, it is the gift of God; not as a result of works, that no one should boast (Ephesians 2:8,9).

But if it is by grace, it is no longer on the basis of works, otherwise grace is no longer grace (Romans 11:6).

I do not nullify the grace of God; for if righteousness comes through the Law, then Christ died needlessly (Galatians 2:21).

Now that no one is justified by the Law before God is evident; for "the righteous man shall live by faith" (Galatians 3:11).

He saved us, not on the basis of deeds which we have done in righteousness, but according to His mercy, by the washing of regeneration and renewing by the Holy Spirit (Titus 3:5).

In conclusion, because Mormonism teaches a religious system of salvation by good works and personal righteousness, it comes under the condemnation so clearly expressed by the apostle Paul himself in Galatians 1:6-8 (NIV):

I am astonished that you are so quickly deserting the one who called you by the grace of Christ and are turning to a different gospel—which is really no gospel at all. Evidently some people are throwing you into confusion and are trying to pervert the gospel of Christ. But even if we or an angel from heaven should preach a gospel other than the one we preached to you, let him be eternally condemned!

If Mormonism teaches personal salvation by good works and individual merit, then of what value was the atonement of Jesus Christ for our sins?

Question 13

What does Mormonism teach about the atoning death of Jesus Christ on the cross?

Mormonism claims that "salvation comes because of the atonement."[108] However, in spite of such claims, the Mormon Church does not believe in the biblical atonement, but rather in an atonement of its own devising. The value of the atonement in Mormon thinking is that it gives men the *opportunity* to earn their own salvation through personal merit.

For the individual Mormon, righteousness by works would avail nothing if the atonement had not canceled the penalty of Adam's sin which brought physical death to every man.[109] Mormons are grateful for the atonement because it raises them from the dead—but this is all it does. Mormons believe that "...the Lord died in order to bring about the resurrection of the dead."[110]

In other words, in no way has Christ's death actually purchased full salvation for anyone. The death of Christ itself did not forgive even a single sin; it only made possible the forgiveness of sins by law-keeping. This is why Mormon discussions of Christ's death on the cross do not mention actual forgiveness of sins solely through the atonement.[111]* For example, one Mormon promotional brochure teaches that "the atonement of Christ ransoms men from the effects of spiritual death [Adam's sin] in that by the obedience to the laws and ordinances of the gospel, they can be born again and have spiritual life." It further teaches:

> All men are saved by grace alone without any act on their part, meaning that they are resurrected and become immortal because of the atoning sacrifice of Christ.
> In addition to this redemption from death, all men, by the grace of God, have the power to gain eternal life. This is called *salvation by grace coupled with obedience* to the laws and ordinances of the gospel.[112]

Just as a college degree does not secure a salary, but only makes earning one possible, so Christ's death does not secure salvation, but only makes earning it possible by good works. In Mormonism, the actual *saving value* of the atonement is virtually nonexistent. In fact, Mormonism has such a low view of the atonement that during its early history, the Church taught that men must have their own blood shed (be killed) in order to atone for certain sins.[113] Unfortunately, there is little doubt that many individuals

---

* At best, Mormons teach that Christ *conditionally* died for sins predicated on good works and individual merit.

were actually murdered in the mistaken belief that this would allegedly atone for their sins and send them to heaven.[114] Mormon leaders such as C. W. Penrose have taught that the idea that Christ's death is sufficient for salvation is "the great error" and most pernicious delusion of Christianity.[115]

But Mormonism is wrong. The teaching of the Bible is clear: The death of Christ on the cross actually paid the penalty for *all* sin. In order to appropriate that forgiveness, all any person need do is believe on the Lord Jesus Christ as these Scriptures show (emphases added):

> Believe in the Lord Jesus Christ and you *shall* be saved..." (Acts 16:31).

> For I delivered to you as of first importance what I also received, that Christ *died for our sins* according to the Scriptures (1 Corinthians 15:3).

> The next day he saw Jesus coming to him, and said, "Behold the Lamb of God *who takes away the sin of the world!*" (John 1:29).

> In Him we have redemption *through His blood, the forgiveness of our trespasses*, according to the riches of His grace (Ephesians 1:7).

> And He *Himself is the propitiation for our sins*; and not for ours only, but also for those of the whole world (1 John 2:2).

> He Himself *bore our sins in His body on the cross* that we might die to sin and live to righteousness; for by His wounds you were healed (1 Peter 2:24).

In essence, Mormonism completely opposes the saving value of Christ's death on the cross. It tells men and women that their good works will save them, forgive their sins, and bring them to heaven. But in doing this, it rejects the most fundamental teaching of the Bible and all Christian faith. When Mormonism teaches men to trust in a false gospel, this teaching comes under the judgment of God Himself (Galatians 1:6-8).

One thing should be obvious from the above discussion of Mormon beliefs—Mormon faith and Christian faith are not the same. Mormonism rejects and opposes the clear biblical teaching concerning God, Jesus Christ, salvation, the death of Christ, and we could go down the list. It denies the biblical teaching on man, faith, the fall, death and the afterlife, the Bible, the Holy Spirit, and many other doctrines.[116]

In conclusion, those people who claim that Mormons are brothers or sisters in Christ or that Mormonism is a Christian religion are simply wrong. Mormonism opposes almost every biblical doctrine and, therefore, cannot possibly be considered Christian.

4

Mormonism—
A Critical
Evaluation

If a faith will not bear to be investigated; if its preachers and professors are afraid to have it examined, their foundation must be very weak.[117]

—Mormon apostle and historian George A. Smith

Smith was correct. But, in fact, few religions have such a wealth of historical, archaeological, and other data arrayed against them as the Mormon religion. In this section, we will briefly examine some of this data which prove that Mormon claims are false. We will show why it is impossible to examine this evidence fairly and conclude that the Mormon Church is a divine revelation and represents the one true church of God on earth.

Question 14

Was there a universal apostasy by the early Christian church?

The Mormon Church claims that the original teachings of Christ and the apostles reflected a Mormon worldview. However, the early church soon apostatized and was only restored through Joseph Smith 1800 years later.[118]

But the Mormon Church never has (and never will) establish 1) that a universal apostasy occurred or 2) that the original gospel was Mormon.

Jesus Himself told us that even "the gates of hell shall not prevail against" His church (Matthew 16:18 KJV). He further emphasized, "Heaven and earth will pass away, but my words will never pass away" (Matthew 24:35 NIV). Mormonism denies Jesus' teaching and claims that His church and words were overpowered, completely and totally. According to McConkie,

"Every basic doctrine of the gospel . . . has been changed and perverted by an apostate Christendom."[119] Further, Joseph Smith himself argued, "There was a complete and universal apostasy . . . the church then established was destroyed."[120]

In making such an assertion, Mormons ignore what the Bible itself teaches, that God has received glory "throughout all generations" (Ephesians 3:21 NIV), that His kingdom cannot be shaken (Hebrews 12:28), and that He always retains a remnant of believers for Himself (Romans 9:29; 11:4,5).

In conclusion, because it is historically demonstrated there was no universal apostasy and because it can be proven to anyone's satisfaction that the beliefs of Jesus and the apostles as recorded in the New Testament have not been corrupted[121] and, therefore, are Christian and not Mormon, the Mormon claim to being a restored church is demonstrably false. Without an apostasy, nothing existed to be restored.

Question 15

Is the "first vision" account forming the foundation of the Mormon Church really credible?

Joseph Smith's alleged "first vision" forms the essence of Mormonism's claim to uniqueness: that God Himself had rejected all other churches as false and was now restoring the "true" church through Joseph Smith. This is why even Mormons have confessed that the "first vision" account is absolutely crucial to the credibility and authority of both Smith and the Church. Second in importance only to Christ's "deity," the "first vision" is the "foundation of the church"; the Mormon Church stands or falls on the authenticity of this event, and the "truth and validity" of all of Joseph Smith's subsequent work rests upon its genuineness.[122] The following facts prove then, by Mormonism's own assertions, that their church is false.

The official account of the event was written by Smith about 1838 and published in *Times and Seasons* in 1842, two decades after the event supposedly took place.[123] What most Mormons have never been told is that at least five *earlier* drafts of the "first vision" exist. These conflicting accounts have been repressed by Mormon leaders because they disagree with what has come to be the preferred or official version. Of all versions, this official composition, Smith's final draft, is the least credible.[124]

The earliest known account was written by Smith in 1832. It varies in important details with the official version. There are discrepancies in Smith's age, the presence of an evil power, Smith's reason for seeking the Lord, the existence of a revival, and the number of divine personages in the vision.

For example, the revival Smith claimed happened in 1820 (he clearly gives his age as 15) actually took place in 1824–1825.[125] In other words, there was no revival in 1820, and therefore Smith had no reason to seek God's counsel over his own religious confusion.

Another account by Smith was written between 1835–1836.[126] In this different and contradictory version, there is no mention of God or Christ, but only of many spirits and "angels" who testified of Jesus.

Leading authorities on Mormonism Jerald and Sandra Tanner conclude:

> We have now examined three different handwritten manuscripts of the first vision. They were all written by Joseph Smith or his scribes and yet every one of them is different. The first account says there was only one personage. The second account says there were many, and the third says there were two. The church, of course, accepts the version which accepts two personages. . . . At any rate . . . it becomes very difficult to believe that Joseph Smith ever had a vision in the grove. On top of all of this, there is irrefutable evidence that an important reference to the first vision in the *History of the Church* has been falsified by Mormon historians after Joseph Smith's death.[127]

In other words, the crucial "first vision" account is simply not credible. Mormons who accept it must ignore and deny strong evidence to the contrary.*

Question 16

What intractable problems face the Book of Mormon?

Dr. Hugh Nibley of Brigham Young University (who some Mormons feel is one of the greatest scholars in the Church) declares: "The Book of Mormon can and should be tested. It invites criticism."[129] Tenth president Joseph Fielding Smith thinks that the evidence for it "internally and externally is overwhelming."[130]

But the only evidence is overwhelmingly negative.

First, although the Church denies it, there is little doubt that, given Smith's claims, the Book of Mormon was translated by occult means.[131] Smith put a magical "seer" stone into a hat, and then buried his face in the hat to exclude the light. Next, words in "reformed Egyptian" (no such language is known to exist) magically appeared with their translation, and Smith spoke the translation to a scribe who wrote it down. One of Smith's many wives, Emma Smith, confesses: "In writing for your father, I frequently wrote day after day. . . . He sitting with his face buried in his hat, with a stone in it, and dictating hour after hour. . . ."[132]

---

* The reader may pursue the issue of various vision accounts in *Dialogue: A Journal of Mormon Thought*, Autumn 1966 and Spring 1971 issues; *Brigham Young University Studies*, Spring 1969 and elsewhere.[128] We may also note that as a whole, Smith's vision/visions were not as unique as claimed by Mormon authorities. In fact, they fit a characteristic pattern of spiritistic contacts that have occurred throughout history. There is no doubt that Smith was subject to spiritistic visions and inspiration; what must be doubted is the authenticity and relevance of the official version of the Mormon Church.

In addition, the very content of the Book of Mormon makes it impossible to accept it as a divine revelation. The Book of Mormon claims to be a *translation* of ancient writings on gold plates. These plates were supposedly written at least 1400 years ago and detailed the history of the Jewish "Nephites" from 600 B.C. through A.D. 421. But it is virtually impossible that records written 1400 years *prior* to the time of Joseph Smith should detail specific social, political, and religious concerns unique to nineteenth-century America.

In a scholarly work for which she was excommunicated from the Mormon Church (*No Man Knows My History: The Life of Joseph Smith*), Fawn Brodie discusses the reasons supporting a nineteenth-century origin for the Book of Mormon. She observes, "In the speeches of the Nephite prophets one may find the religious conflicts that were splitting the churches in the 1820s."[133] In a similar fashion, Alexander Campbell, founder of the Disciples of Christ, wrote in one of the first able reviews of the Book of Mormon:

> This prophet Smith, through his stone spectacles, wrote on the plates of Nephi in his Book of Mormon every error and almost every truth discussed in New York for the last ten years. He decided all the great controversies: infant baptism, ordination, the Trinity, regeneration, repentance, justification, the fall of man, the atonement, transubstantiation, fasting, penance, church government, religious experience, the call to the ministry, the general resurrection, the eternal punishment, who may baptize, and even the question of Freemasonry, republican government and the rights of man.[134]

Why would 1400- to 2400-year-old records deal with distinctly nineteenth-century theological and political disputes? This is certainly puzzling, unless, of course, they were not 1400 to 2400 years old. Even noted Mormon historian B. H. Roberts confessed that Joseph Smith alone could have fabricated the Book of Mormon.[135]

But the content of the Book of Mormon presents further difficulties. For example, there are many clearly demonstrated plagiarisms. Material has been taken from Ethan Smith's *View of the Hebrews* (1823), a book that was available to Joseph Smith,[136] as well as from the King James Bible. Some 27,000 words from the King James Bible are found in the Book of Mormon.[137]

But if the Book of Mormon was first written between 600 B.C. and A.D. 421, how could it possibly contain such extensive quotations from the King James Bible, not to be written for another 1200 to 2000 years? The Tanners have listed, one by one, 400 verses and portions of verses quoted from the New Testament in the Book of Mormon in their book *The Case Against Mormonism*.[138]

The Book of Mormon even contains King James Bible *translation errors*. For example, in 2 Nephi 14:5 (Isaiah 4:5) the correct translation to the

Hebrew *Chuppah* is "canopy," not "defense." In 2 Nephi 15:25 (Isaiah 5:25) the correct translation of the Hebrew *Suchah* is "refuse," not "torn."

Another problem for the Book of Mormon is archaeology, a major embarrassment to the Mormon Church. Mormon missionaries continue to claim that the science of archaeology substantiates the Book of Mormon, but whether we consider the alleged cities, persons, animals, fabrics, metals, wars and war implements, kings, palaces, or crops, all the evidence points to their nonexistence. Ethnologist Gordon Fraser comments:

> Mormon archaeologists have been trying for years to establish some evidence that will confirm the presence of the [Mormon] church in America. There is still not a scintilla of evidence, either in the religious philosophy of the ancient writings or in the presence of artifacts, that lead to such a belief.[139]

To show how embarrassing this situation is, consider that Mormon missionaries often claim that the Smithsonian Institution or other professional organizations have utilized the Book of Mormon as an archaeological guide. In fact, the Smithsonian Institution has received so many inquiries concerning this that they actually return a standard form-letter denying it. The first of many points they make in their rebuttal of Mormon claims is "The Smithsonian Institution has never used the Book of Mormon in any way as a scientific guide. Smithsonian archaeologists see no direct connection between the archaeology of the New World and the subject matter of the book."[140] Further, its Bureau of American Ethnology asserts, "There is no evidence whatever of any migration from Israel to America, and likewise no evidence that pre-Columbian Indians had any knowledge of Christianity or the Bible."[141]

Even the prestigious National Geographic Society has flatly denied Mormon missionary claims:

> With regard to the cities mentioned in *The Book of Mormon*, neither representatives of the National Geographic Society nor archaeologists connected with any other institution of equal prestige have ever used *The Book of Mormon* in locating historic ruins in Middle America or elsewhere.[142]

In other words, no Book of Mormon cities have ever been located, no Book of Mormon person, place, nation, or name has been found, no Book of Mormon artifacts, no Book of Mormon scriptures, no Book of Mormon inscriptions, no Book of Mormon gold plates—nothing which demonstrates the Book of Mormon is anything other than myth or invention has *ever* been found.

By contrast, the archaeological evidence for the Bible is so convincing that even a former skeptic such as the great archaeologist Sir William Ramsey became converted to Christian belief. But the archaeological evidence against Mormon claims is so devastating that prominent Mormon archaeologist Thomas Stewart Ferguson quit the Mormon Church and repudiated its prophet.[143]*

In conclusion, anyone who wishes can prove to their own satisfaction that the Book of Mormon cannot possibly be divinely inspired. Its occult method of translation, plagiarisms, internal inconsistences, archaeological disproof, and many other problems reveal that the Mormon Church is in serious error when it claims otherwise.

Walter Martin, an acknowledged authority in comparative religion and author of several books on Mormonism, points out:

> The world is now in a position to judge *The Book of Mormon* on three different levels. First, the book does not correspond to what we know that God has already said in His Word. Second, its internal inconsistencies, thousands of changes, and persistent plagarization of the King James Bible decidedly remove it from serious consideration as a revelation from God. Finally, its external inconsistencies not only expose its misuse of archaeology, science, history and language, but actually allow us to investigate its true origin.[144]

Question 17

Are the Mormon scriptures really the Word of God? If so, why has the Church made significant changes in them; why do they contain demonstrable errors and undeniable contradictions?

The Mormon Church claims that the Book of Mormon, *The Pearl of Great Price*, and *Doctrine and Covenants* are genuine scriptures inspired by God. But this cannot possibly be true.

The Tanners have reprinted the original 1830 edition of the Book of Mormon noting in the text significant major changes and over 3,000 minor changes. But even a *single* minor change is incompatible with its claimed method of translation which was "by the power of God."[145] In translating the Book of Mormon, God's power was apparently limited. For example, the 1830 edition of Mosiah 21:28 refers to King Benjamin, while modern editions read "King Mosiah." According to the Book of Mormon chronology, Benjamin was no longer king at the time (he was dead, Mosiah 6:3-7; 7:1), so the inspired name was changed to read King Mosiah to cover an obvious error.

Similarly, serious doctrinal errors have been corrected. For example, in 1 Nephi 11:18 the 1830 edition teaches, "The virgin which thou seest, is the mother of God, after the manner of the flesh." However, since Mary could not literally be the mother of the earth deity "Elohim," modern editions read "the mother of the Son of God" rather than "the mother of God."

---

* Bibles often contain detailed maps describing the history and geography of its people. If the Book of Mormon is history why are there no maps?

We have two choices: either Smith copied errors that were originally on the supposed gold plates, or the Book of Mormon is not "a perfect translation by the power of God" as Mormonism claims. Either way the Book of Mormon cannot be trusted.

The Mormon scripture *Doctrine and Covenants* presents more serious problems. The original edition of *Doctrine and Covenants* was called the *Book of Commandments* and was published in 1833. This book contained allegedly direct, word-for-word revelations from God to Joseph Smith. But in 1835 the *Book of Commandments* was reissued under the title *Doctrine and Covenants* and appeared with literally *thousands* of changes made from God's earlier revelations. There are at least 65,000 changes between the *Book of Commandments* and *Doctrine and Covenants*. Joseph Smith had apparently changed his mind about what was and wasn't God's Word.[146]

Nevertheless, the Mormon Church frequently claims that the Book of Mormon and *Doctrine and Covenants* have never been changed. Supposedly, there has been no tampering with "God's Word."[147] But the evidence is there for any Mormon to see. All interested readers may examine the issue for themselves by comparing modern versions with the first editions of the Book of Mormon and *Doctrine and Covenants* as found in *Joseph Smith Begins His Work, Volumes 1 and 2* (notarized photostat copies).[148]

The third inspired scripture of the Mormon Church is *The Pearl of Great Price*. The Church also maintains this book has not undergone changes. And yet there are literally thousands of words deleted and hundreds of words added. The Tanner's text *Changes in The Pearl of Great Price: A Photo Reprint of the Original 1851 Edition of The Pearl of Great Price With All the Changes Marked* proves this beyond doubt.[149]

Further, a portion of *The Pearl of Great Price*, "The Book of Abraham," has recently been proven a forgery. It is simply a copy of a pagan text—the Egyptian *Book of Breathings*, an extension of the occultic Egyptian *Book of the Dead* relating to the alleged journeys of the soul after death.[150]

The Mormon Church refuses to acknowledge its fabrication because to do so is to confess that Joseph Smith cannot be trusted in the most vital area of all, his alleged ability to reveal the Word of God. Smith claimed that he translated both "The Book of Abraham" and the Book of Mormon under the power of God. But if "The Book of Abraham" is now a proven forgery, merely a pagan text with an entirely false translation, how then can any Mormon know that the Book of Mormon is not a similar fabrication?[151]

The Book of Mormon, *Doctrine and Covenants*, and *The Pearl of Great Price* are the "Word of God" to Mormons. Yet they have been changed in hundreds or even thousands of places—corrections, additions, deletions—all done without any indication or acknowledgment of such action. Why has this been done if these books are truly the Word of God? Why have Church leaders kept such actions hidden from their own members?[152]

There *are* many other significant errors in the Mormon scriptures. For example, the Book of Mormon teaches that Jesus was born in Jerusalem

(Alma 7:9-10), not in Bethlehem as the Bible teaches (Micah 5:2; Matthew 2:1). In Helaman 14:20, during Jesus' crucifixion, the darkness over the face of the land is said to have lasted for three *days* instead of the biblical three *hours* (Matthew 27:45; Mark 15:33).

The above information, and much more,[153] proves that the Mormon claim to receiving divine inspiration in their standard scriptures is simply not true:

> God does not lie.
> He cannot contradict Himself.
> He cannot inspire errors.

But Mormon leaders continue to present Mormonism and its scriptures as God's revealed truth to mankind, even engaging in deliberate deception and suppression of information when it contradicts their faith in the divine origin of the Church. (See note 152.)

In fact, the authors have read scores of volumes on Mormon theology and doctrine, but in 20 years of cult research have rarely found such blatant deception on religious issues in general. This was also the conclusion of the late Walter Martin, who noted:

> ...the author can quite candidly state that never in over a decade of research in the field of cults has he ever seen such misappropriation of terminology, disregard of context and utter abandon of scholastic principles demonstrated on the part of non-Christian cultists as is evidenced in the attempts of Mormon theologians to appear orthodox and at the same time undermine the foundations of historic Christianity. The intricacies of their complex system of polytheism have caused the careful researcher to ponder again and again the ethical standard which these Mormon writers practice and the blatant attempts to rewrite history, biblical theology, and the laws of scriptural interpretation that they might support the theologies of Joseph Smith and Brigham Young.[154]

Question 18

What is the irreconcilable dilemma for the individual Mormon?

The irreconcilable dilemma for the individual Mormon is that represented by all spiritistic inspiration (see Questions 21-23): contradictory revelation. On some very vital issues, the early Mormon prophets deny and contradict modern Mormon prophets and vice versa.[155]

Where does this leave the average Mormon? Should he or she accept the Church's claim that the early prophets *were* prophets and hence absolutely authoritative? If so, then he or she must charge modern Mormonism (and *not* Christianity) with apostasy for the modern Church absolutely denies many of its early divine revelations.

Or should the average Mormon discard the early Mormon prophets as men who received erroneous revelations and were therefore false prophets, since many of their teachings are rejected today by Church leadership? If so, then the entire Mormon Church collapses, for it is based squarely on divine *authority* of such men.

In the end, the individual Mormon is faced with two equally unpleasant options. Either 1) the modern Mormon Church is in apostasy and cannot be trusted or 2) the early prophets were deceivers or deceived men and cannot be trusted.

Question 19

If the Mormon prophets were divinely inspired, how does the Mormon Church explain their false prophecies?

In his own words Joseph Smith himself emphasized:

> The only way of ascertaining a true prophet is to compare his prophecies with the ancient Word of God, and see if they agree. . . . When, therefore, any man, no matter who, or how high his standing may be, utters, or publishes, anything that afterwards proves to be untrue, he is a false prophet.[156]

Bruce McConkie agrees and claims, "By their works it shall be known whether professing ministers of religion are true or false prophets. Joseph Smith was a true prophet."[157]

But the Mormon Church also admits that "if his claims to divine appointment be false, forming as they do the foundation of the Church in this last dispensation, the superstructure [of the Church] cannot be stable."[158]

If Smith did give false prophecies, then the superstructure of the Mormon Church is more than unstable; it simply collapses. According to Deuteronomy 18:20-22, if an alleged prophet's prophecy did not come true, he spoke in the name of the Lord presumptuously. But if this prophet spoke in the names of *false gods* to lead the people astray, that prophet was to die.

Joseph Smith claimed to be a true biblical prophet. Yet he spoke in the name of *false gods* and taught false doctrines, thereby leading people astray from biblical truth. The fact that his prophecies did not come true proves he was a false prophet. Consider the following:

In *Doctrine and Covenants* 1:37,38, "God" promises that all the prophecies and promises within the book's pages "shall all be fulfilled." Yet, *Doctrine and Covenants* 84:1-5,31, declares under the authority of "the Word of the Lord" that both a city and a temple are to be built "in the Western boundaries of the State of Missouri" and dedicated by the hand of Joseph Smith. This was a revelation given to Smith on September 22-23, 1832. It stated clearly that the temple would be erected during the lifetime of those then living. The prophecy promised the temple would be erected "in this generation" (*Doctrine and Covenants* 84:4,5), and that "this generation shall not all pass away" until it was built.

In 1864, 30 years after the prophecy was given, the apostle George Cannon continued to teach that the temple would be built before "this generation" passed away.[159] In 1870, almost 40 years later, Orson Pratt confirmed that the Church could expect a literal fulfillment of the prophecy because "God promised it" and "God cannot lie."[160] In 1900, 70 years later, Lorenzo Snow emphasized that the Mormons now living in Utah would still go back to Missouri and build their temple.[161] Even in 1931, 99 years after the prophecy, Joseph Fielding Smith was stating his "firm belief" that the temple would be built.[162]

But it is now *160 years* after the original prophecy and the temple has still not been built. "This generation" all passed away long ago. Joseph Smith is also long since dead and unable to dedicate the temple as "God" promised. No one can deny the prophecy was false.

Another false prediction can be seen in the so-called "Civil War" prophecy recorded in *Doctrine and Covenants* 87:1-8, given December 25, 1832. Although Mormons claim the prediction is "remarkable" and proof of Smith's prophethood, this is not the case. First, the prediction of a civil war to begin in South Carolina was not unusual. In 1832 Congress passed a tariff act refused by South Carolina, and Andrew Jackson alerted the troops. Even in 1832 "the nation was fully expecting a war to begin promptly in South Carolina."[163]

Also, the prophecy itself is wrong on a number of counts. For one thing, when the Civil War did occur, it was not poured out upon "all nations." There were no earthquakes, "thunder of heaven," or lightning. Neither did all the earth's population feel the "wrath of the Almighty" nor was there "a full end of all nations." In addition, there is some doubt the prophecy was a genuine prediction to begin with.[164]

Mormon rationalizations for these and numerous other false prophecies[165] have proved futile. Instead of admitting the fact that Smith was a false prophet, Mormons continue to deceive other people by wrongly portraying him as a genuine prophet of God.

Question 20

Why has the Mormon Church ignored the compelling historical research of Jerald and Sandra Tanner and why is this important?

In the last two decades, former committed Mormons Jerald and Sandra Tanner have produced a small library of careful historical research which casts grave doubt upon almost all the major claims of the Mormon Church.*

The question is, Why has the Mormon Church ignored this compelling historical research? Why has the Church acted almost as if it does not even exist? This issue is important, indeed vital, because the Church claims to be concerned about the truth—yet continues to reject a wealth of factual

---

* Dozens of their well-documented books were condensed into *Mormonism: Shadow or Reality?* (1966), a further condensation of which is found in *The Changing World of Mormonism* (Moody Press, 1981).

data having critical bearing on Mormon origins, history, doctrine, scripture, and Church censorship.

Even *Mormonia: A Quarterly Bibliography of Works on Mormonism* calls the Tanners' book *Shadow or Reality?* "perhaps the most exhaustive exposé of Mormonism between two covers."[166] Dr. Jennings G. Olson, professor of philosophy at Webber College, observed it was "the most comprehensive and thorough analysis and evaluation of Mormonism ever produced in the history of the Church."[167] Dr. Gordon Fraser accurately describes it as "an encyclopedia of Mormonism's lack of credibility."[168]

If indisputable historical documents have been found discrediting Mormon beliefs, it deeply concerns all Mormon people. Mormons, especially Mormon leaders, should want to look into this, if they are as concerned with the truth as they say.

But even after a quarter century, the Church has never responded to the Tanners' research. One can only ask, Why? We vigorously encourage interested readers to secure a list of materials (offered at cost) from Utah Lighthouse Ministry, Box 1884, Salt Lake City, Utah 84110. Mormons have a right to this information.

What may we conclude to this point? Even with so brief a treatment as found in this unit, there is little doubt that Mormonism is not what proponents claim. Mormonism cannot possibly be a revelation from the biblical God since it denies the nature of God Himself as revealed in the Bible and also distorts nearly every major biblical teaching. It cannot possibly be the one true church of Christ on earth because it rejects and distorts the true person of Christ as found in the historical Gospel records. Further, its "first vision" account is not credible; its scriptures, the Book of Mormon, *Doctrine and Covenants*, and *The Pearl of Great Price* also lack credibility on numerous accounts. Joseph Smith himself could not have been a prophet of God because no one can logically deny that he engaged in false prophecy.

If neither Joseph Smith nor the Mormon scriptures are credible, what remains of Mormonism? In essence, no one familiar with the canons of evidence can logically deny that Mormonism must be considered a false religion.

5

Mormonism and the Occult: Should Mormonism Be Considered an Occultic Religion?

Question 21

How important is the concept of inspiration and revelation within the Mormon Church?

In Question 2 we saw that Mormonism was founded upon alleged supernatural revelations given to Joseph Smith. Throughout its history the Mormon Church has stressed the importance of accepting supernatural revelations. For example, the 13 *Articles of Faith* represent a condensed version of Mormonism's current doctrinal beliefs. Article 9 declares: "We believe all that God has revealed, all that He does now reveal, and we believe that He will yet reveal many great and important things pertaining to the Kingdom of God."[169]

Mormonism accepts revelation on two levels: 1) canonical (the acceptance of new scripture) and 2) individual (personal, supernatural guidance).

As far as the Church is concerned, "The canon of scripture is still open; many lines, many precepts, are yet to be added; revelation, surpassing in importance and glorious fullness any that has been recorded, is yet to be given to the Church and declared to the world."[170] This is the basis upon which the Church accepted three volumes in addition to the Bible as scripture—the Book of Mormon, *Doctrine and Covenants*, and *The Pearl of Great Price*. In fact, to deny continuous revelation, as Protestantism generally does, is according to Mormonism a "heresy and blasphemous denial" of God Himself.[171]

In addition to the importance of revealed scripture, the Church teaches the urgency of personal revelation from God for both Mormon leadership and laity. Without this, one cannot, allegedly, discern God's work from

Satan's, or truth from error. Hence, the necessity of individual "divine" guidance is also actively stressed.[172] Such revelation may involve an audible voice from God, supernatural dreams, the use of angelic messengers, or communication from the dead, etc.[173]

Mormons assert that direct revelation from God is guiding Church leadership on a daily basis: "The Spirit is giving direct and daily revelation to the presiding Brethren in the administration of the affairs of the church."[174]

Bruce McConkie further emphasizes that every good Mormon also receives revelation from God and that it is the duty of Mormons to "gain personal revelation and guidance for their personal affairs."[175]

This concept of individual and corporate revelation is crucial for understanding how Mormonism was led into occult practices and unbiblical doctrines historically. Once the safeguards of biblical authority were rejected, once an uncritical openness to supernatural revelation was accepted, the fate of the Church was sealed. Mormonism could only become an occultic religion.

The Mormon doctrine of revelation promotes spiritism to both the Church and its members, who logically become predisposed to supernatural, occultic revelations from the spirit world. It cannot be expected that the faithful will necessarily deny *any* supernatural manifestation they receive, particularly when the "test" of its truthfulness is fundamentally subjective.[176]

From its inception to the present, the Church has exercised tremendous receptivity to and dependence upon supernatural manifestations in both leadership and laity categories. That these revelations are spiritistic is clear from their content. Although they are interpreted as revelations from God, their theological teaching is absolute proof to the contrary.

Indeed, the occult philosophy of many spiritistic mediums resembles the revelations given to Smith and other Mormon prophets (including the importance of revelations from the alleged dead, personal ministry to the dead [proxy-baptism], the doctrine of preexistence, polytheism, different levels of postmortem existence and schooling on the spirit plane, man as God, eternal progression, etc.).

All this is why no less an authority than Walter Martin observes, "Occultism in Mormon theology is undeniable."[177] Jerald and Sandra Tanner also document occultism in Mormonism in *Mormonism Magic and Masonry; Joseph Smith and Money Digging*, and other works.[178]

Unfortunately Mormonism is fundamentally an occultic religion promulgating occultic and pagan practices in America. No amount of false claims, outward righteousness, financial power, or misinformed public opinion can change this fact.

Question 22

Was Joseph Smith an occultist?

No one can logically deny that Joseph Smith was an occultist. Martin observes that "What most Mormons do not recognize is the fact that

Joseph Smith was an occultist, and that Mormonism had occultic origins."[179] As is true for many occultists, both Smith's parents were involved in the occult[180] and this may have brought Joseph a hereditary transference and/or predisposition to psychic ability.[181] Smith claims he received his first supernatural visitation of "angels" at the age of 14.[182]

Smith also had occult powers, and along with a number of other early Mormon leaders[183] was involved in various occult practices. (In 1826, he was arrested, tried, and found guilty of fortune-telling in Bainbridge, New York.)[184] Smith employed what he called a "Jupiter Talisman"—an amulet supposedly possessing supernatural powers intended to bring wealth, influence, and power to its possessor.[185] He would also place "peepstones" or "seer" stones into a hat, place his face into the hat, and see visions of buried treasure, lost property, etc.[186] As we have seen, this was the method by which the Book of Mormon was allegedly translated.[187]

But such activities are simply a variation upon the occult practice of crystal gazing. Further, they are similar to other occultic practices such as psychometry and radionics. Nor was Smith alone in his use of seer stones and amulets. The early Mormon people were also prone to use them as means to contact and commune with the spirit world,[188] and even today, many Mormons continue to contact the spirit world to receive its guidance and instruction (see Question 23).

That Smith had occult powers and may also have had a number of spirit guides is not surprising.[189] Like mediums and spiritists in general, he had personal experience that the so-called dead "are not far from us, and know and understand our thoughts, feelings and emotions . . . ," and that they could play an important role in spiritual encouragement and growth.[190] Both he and Brigham Young believed that "we have more friends behind the veil than on this side," and that knowledge of the spirit world was crucial to personal salvation.[191]

Smith taught, "The greatest responsibility in this world that God has laid upon us is to seek after our dead," and "those Saints who neglect it [baptism for the dead], in behalf of their deceased relatives, do so at the peril of their own salvation."[192] Thus, "work for the dead is an important determining factor in the Latter-day Saints' attempt to attain their ultimate salvation and exaltation in the Kingdom of God."[193]

Question 23

How frequently do spiritistic revelations occur within Mormonism and how often are the dead contacted?

Given its theology, Mormon interest in seeking the spirits of the so-called dead is logical, and spiritistic revelations and contacts occur somewhat frequently within Mormonism. One major Church teaching is that the spirits of the dead can be assisted and even saved in the next life by work done on their behalf under the auspices of the Mormon Church. How did the Mormon Church adopt such beliefs? Such beliefs originated from the spirits themselves.

1) From its inception Mormonism accepted spiritistic revelations from the so-called dead and other spirits.

2) Part of these revelations from the spirits concerned the importance of contacting the dead in order to allegedly assist them spiritually.

3) As a result, contacting the dead became a theological necessity within the Mormon Church.

But in Deuteronomy 18:10-12 (NIV), God commands His people to avoid all forms of contact with the dead: "Let no one be found among you ... who practices divination or sorcery ... engages in witchcraft, or casts spells, or who is a medium or spiritist or who consults the dead. Anyone who does these things is detestable to the Lord. ..."

In spite of this warning, the dead have always played a major role in the practice of Mormonism. Both Smith and many subsequent leaders in the Mormon Church were in regular contact with the spirit world.[194] When dead family members or biblical personalities appeared to Joseph Smith, he welcomed them.[195] A sermon delivered by Mormon Elder Parley Pratt in 1853 (five years after the celebrated spiritist movement began in America, which Pratt extolled) indicates early Mormon acceptance of Joseph Smith as a "divine" medium. Jesus Christ was given the role of a spiritistic mediator, and spiritism was to be practiced in the Mormon temple. Pratt gloried in Joseph Smith's role as a spirit medium:

> Who communicated with our great modern Prophet, and revealed through him as a medium, the ancient history of a hemisphere, and the records of the ancient dead? [i.e., who revealed the Book of Mormon? The spirit] Moroni, who had lived on the earth 1400 years before. ...
>
> Who ordained our first founders to the Apostleship, to hold the keys of the Kingdom of God, and these the times of restoration? Peter, James, and John from the eternal [spirit] world. Who instructed him in the mysteries of the kingdom? ... Angels and spirits from the eternal worlds. The Lord has ordained that ... conversations and correspondence with God, angels, and spirits, shall be had only in the sanctuary of His holy temple on the earth. ... One of the leading or fundamental truths of Mormon philosophy [is] that the living may hear from the dead.[196]

Temple spiritism is also noted by Walter Martin who cites a leading Mormon theologian, Charles Penrose, in *Mormon Doctrine*: "The temple where the ordinances can be administered for the dead, is a place to hear from the dead. The Priesthood in the flesh, when it is necessary, will receive communications from the priesthood behind the veil [the dead]."[197]

The sixth president of the Church, Joseph F. Smith, continued to support spiritistic/mediumistic contacts within the Church:

> Our fathers and mothers, brothers, sisters and friends who have passed away from this earth, having been faithful ... may

have a mission given them to visit their relatives and friends upon the earth again, bringing from the divine Presence messages of love, of warning, or of reproof and instruction. . . .[198]

In harmony with the tradition of occultism in general, many Mormon leaders have claimed they have received spiritistic contacts from their dead "masters"—Joseph Smith, Brigham Young, other Church presidents, etc.[199] Brigham Young himself taught:

> Is there communication from God? Yes. From holy angels? Yes; and we have been proclaiming these facts during nearly 30 years. Are there any communications from evil spirits? Yes; and the devil is making the people believe very strongly in revelations from the spirit world. This is called spiritualism, and it is said that thousands of the spirits declare that "Mormonism" is true.[200]

Young also taught the mediumistic philosophy that many of the dead are schooled in the afterlife.[201]

But if Mormon visitations from the spirit world bring unbiblical teachings (as we have documented), how are they different from any other spiritistic circles which claim visitation by the dead, such as Sun Myung Moon's Unification Church or various "Christian" spiritualist churches? These also bring unbiblical revelations which expose them as demonic deceptions (1 Timothy 4:1), as many former mediums have openly confessed.

How then does Mormonism justify its practice of contacting the dead? In harmony with much "Christian" parapsychology and religious spiritualism, the Mormon Church erects a false division between "godly" and "satanic" spirit contact. Allegedly, all Mormon contact with the dead is "godly" practice. (See Part 7, Question 13.)

But biblically there is no such division nor can Mormonism justify one. There is no biblically endorsed practice involving "godly" contact with the dead, or "godly" mediumism, "godly" channeling or spiritism; it is *all* classified as an abomination to God (Deuteronomy 18:9-13). The Mormon practice of contacting the alleged dead is little different—in nature or consequence—than similar practices found in the world of the occult. Nor is there any doubt that the spirits who claim to be the dead are really lying spirits the Bible identifies as demons.[202]

Nevertheless, there are many books by Mormons which recount temple manifestations of dead family members as truly faith-promoting experiences. Joseph Heinerman's books, *Spirit World Manifestations, Eternal Testimonies,* and *Temple Manifestations* detail scores of stories of dead family relatives and other spirits instructing Mormon leaders, missionaries, and laymen in genealogical and other Mormon work. In fact, these and other books reveal that for many Mormons, "true" religion involves not only ministering to the spirits of the dead by proxy baptism, but also receiving guidance and instruction from spirits of the dead for spiritual growth.[203] Heinerman states:

> The inhabitants of the spirit world have received special permission to visit their mortal descendants and assist them and impress upon their minds the primary importance of assimilating genealogical information and performing vicarious ordinance work in the temples.
>
> Spirit world manifestations and angelic appearances have played and continue to play a major role in the upbuilding of God's Kingdom [i.e., Mormonism] in these latter days.
>
> Among a multiplicity of Christian creeds, sects and denominations the Church of Jesus Christ of Latter-day Saints is the sole claimant to spirit world visitations and angelic communications which are inseparably connected with genealogical research and temple work.
>
> It should be gratifying to Latter-day Saints that those in the spirit world have expressed an intense interest and are increasingly concerned with the activities of God's people upon the earth.[204]

Mormon theologian Duane S. Crowther teaches standard Mormon belief when he says that allegedly good spirits return to the earth and converse with Mormons to:

1) give counsel
2) give comfort
3) obtain or give information
4) serve as guardian angels
5) prepare others for death
6) summon mortals into the spirit world
7) escort the dying through the veil of death.[205]

Such teaching is in complete harmony with the teachings of mediums and spiritists everywhere. Indeed, at this point, it is impossible to distinguish Mormon practice from spiritism in general.

In conclusion, there is absolutely no doubt that Mormonism is a spiritistic, occultic religion. It has an occult origin, promotes occultic theology and philosophy, and to this day continues to promote occult practices such as contact with the dead and other spirits.

Question 24

What is the true basis of eternal life and how is it found?

Biblically, eternal life with God and Christ is a reality that begins the moment a person receives the true Jesus Christ as his or her personal Savior from sin. "Yet to all who received him, to those who believed in his name, he gave the right to become children of God" (John 1:12 NIV).

It is absolutely impossible for anyone to inherit eternal life based on his or her own good works and personal righteousness because no one can ever be good enough to satisfy God's perfect standards. Because Mormonism is based on good works and personal righteousness, Mormons can never have an assurance of salvation. This point must be stressed and contrasted with biblical teaching:

> I have talked with scores of Mormons, high and low in the Church, and almost none of them could claim they knew for sure that they would go to that "highest" (really, the only) heaven to be with Jesus Christ forever. . . . Really—Mormons do not know where they are going when they die.[206]

Biblically, anyone can know beyond a shadow of doubt that when they die they will be with Christ forever. If salvation *is* a gift from God, then it cannot be earned. If it is by grace through faith, then faith *is* all that is needed. In 1 John 5:13, we are told, "These things I have written to you who believe in the name of the Son of God that you may *know* that you have eternal life."

If anyone believes on the true Jesus Christ and trusts in Him alone for salvation, and not in their personal works of righteousness, Jesus promises them eternal life: "Truly, truly, I say to you, he who believes has eternal life" (John 6:47). In John 17:3 Jesus also taught, "This is eternal life, that they may know Thee, the only true God, and Jesus Christ whom Thou has sent."

Jesus said that no man can serve two masters (Matthew 6:24). The practicing Mormon must choose between coming to know and serve the true Jesus Christ or continuing to serve Joseph Smith and the Mormon Church. One simply cannot serve both.

Conclusion

What words of wisdom do Mormon leaders have for practicing Mormons?

In light of our discussion to this point, we think it relevant to quote some leaders in the Mormon Church and ask that practicing Mormons consider their words very carefully.

Bruce McConkie: "An antichrist is an opponent of Christ; he is one who is in opposition to the true gospel, the true church, and the true plan of salvation."[207]

Joseph Smith: "The Savior has the words of eternal life. Nothing else can profit us."[208]

Joseph Fielding Smith: "The theories of men change from day to day. Much that is taught now will tomorrow be in the discard, but the word of the Lord will endure forever."[209]

Brigham Young: "Can you destroy the decrees of the Almighty? You cannot."[210]

If objective historical data from within the Mormon Church itself proves Mormonism a false religion, then it is tragic to remain a Mormon. Mormons who truly desire to love God have the right to know who the true God is. They have a right to know whether their own church has consistently lied to them and deceived them on vital matters.[211]

Any Mormon who wishes may examine his own heart before God and then pray the following prayer:

> Dear God,
>
> You know that I am not only uncertain of my beliefs concerning You, but also of my spiritual condition before You. I have honestly searched my heart and it is my desire to trust in You. By searching my heart, I have recognized I cannot earn my own salvation, because as You have said, even my best righteousness falls far short of Your holy standards [Romans 6:23; Isaiah 64:6].
>
> I recognize that I am a sinner worthy of Your judgment. I renounce my pride in thinking I could perfect myself and become a God. I renounce every false view of Jesus Christ and receive the true Jesus Christ as presented in the Bible. I believe that this Jesus Christ is truly God, that He died for my sins on the cross and rose from the dead three days later. I believe that by receiving Him into my life I can now inherit eternal life. Right now, I turn from my sins and from the false teachings of the Mormon Church and I receive the true Christ as my personal Savior. Help me to grow in the grace and knowledge of my true Savior Jesus Christ [2 Peter 3:18].

If you are a Mormon who prayed this prayer, we suggest you read the New Testament daily and attend a Christian church that honors Christ. You should tell the pastor that you are a former Mormon who has just become a Christian and ask his counsel. There are many organizations of former Mormons who are now Christians, and we also suggest you contact one of them for information, counsel, and encouragement.[212] Also, please feel free to write us at "The John Ankerberg Show" with any questions you have. Our desire is to help.

P A R T   T W O

CULT WATCH

JEHOVAH'S WITNESSES

*Answers to the 20
most frequently asked
questions about the
Watchtower Society*

6

Introduction to
Jehovah's Witnesses

The following material briefly examines the history, beliefs, and practices of the religious sect known as the Jehovah's Witnesses. Why is this particular religious group important? First, it is important because of the Witnesses' particular style of door-to-door proselytizing. Each year, millions of households are visited, thousands of Bible studies are initiated, and millions of pieces of literature are distributed.

Second, the Jehovah's Witnesses sect is important because it claims to be a Christian group and to teach the Bible accurately. Their claim to accuracy is why the Jehovah's Witnesses find a ready audience among many people who desire to know the Bible better. Therefore, it is important to determine whether the teachings of the Jehovah's Witnesses are biblical or not.

The third reason this religious group is important is because the Watchtower Society, the official organization of the Jehovah's Witnesses, claims that it *alone* brings the voice of God to men. The Watchtower Society gives the reasons why it makes this astounding claim, but how can we know these reasons are valid unless we examine them carefully and impartially?

Unfortunately, Jehovah's Witnesses are often warned by the Watchtower Society against reading material critical of their faith. Why? All men and women have the right to decide important spiritual issues on their own.

Most Jehovah's Witnesses have never read the Bible apart from the interpretation given to them by the Watchtower Society. Nor have they considered that the Society might be wrong in its translation and interpretation of the Bible.

Thousands of formerly committed Jehovah's Witnesses leave the Watchtower Society each year, convinced that the Society deliberately misled them by misinterpreting the Bible. This should encourage all Jehovah's Witnesses to impartially examine the reasons for their personal religious convictions.

Consider the following illustration. Recently, we took our car to the brake shop. We noticed a friend and his family with the exact make, model, and year of the car we owned. In talking to him, we discovered he had recently purchased the car, but knew little about it. On the other hand, this car was our passion. We knew the car from front to rear, had thoroughly studied the owner's manual, and did all our own repair work.

To our horror, we noticed that the mechanic was installing the wrong brake system—a mistake that could cost our friend his life. We informed him of the mistake, but he assured us that the mechanic was well-qualified and fully conversant with the owner's manual. We responded that we had read it carefully ourselves and that the repairman must *not* have understood the owner's manual. We told him, "This is the wrong brake system! You place your life and the lives of others at risk if you drive your car!"

"Who are you to question the mechanic?" he asked.

We reemphasized that the mechanic must not be properly qualified, because no responsible serviceman could make such an obvious error.

Yet the car owner did not listen. He didn't take the time to examine the background and qualifications of the mechanic, but uncritically accepted the mechanic's claim to be the only qualified machinist. Nor did he carefully read the owner's manual for himself. He simply trusted the mechanic's claimed explanation and expertise. The mechanic had assured our friend that he alone knew the truth and warned him that to seek the advice of any other repairman was dangerous.

This man, who would not even consider examining the credentials of his mechanic, placed himself, his family, and other motorists at risk.

Spiritually speaking, many people today are like this car owner. Spiritually, they are trusting their lives and the welfare of their families to a religious repairman simply because he claims to be an authority. The Watchtower Society asserts that it is the only true spiritual "mechanic" on earth and that no other mechanics need be consulted. Shouldn't these claims be tested?

7

The History of
the Jehovah's Witnesses

Question 1

Who are the Jehovah's Witnesses?

The Jehovah's Witnesses are a religious sect begun by Charles Taze
Russell in the 1870s. In formulating their beliefs, Russell drew on the
teachings of such sects as Seventh-Day Adventism and Christadelphian-
ism, plus his own interpretation of the Bible.[1] Through aggressive, door-
to-door proselytizing and authoritarian leadership, the group has grown
from a small number of Bible students to about 2.5 million members in
over 200 countries and territories.*

Question 2

Who are the leaders of the Jehovah's Witnesses?

The leaders of the Jehovah's Witnesses are a group of men who head an
organization called the Watchtower Bible and Tract Society, or simply the
Watchtower Society, in Brooklyn, New York. This small group wields
absolute spiritual authority over the 2.5 million members. The Society is
headed by a president who rules for life. To date, it has had four presidents,
each of whom has left his unique mark on the Society's religion.

---

* The Jehovah's Witnesses claim 3.2 million members in over 200 countries and territories (see the 1987 Yearbook of The Jehovah's Witnesses, pp. 2, 254) although this figure may
not take into account a large number of defections and disfellowshippings.

Question 3

How have the Watchtower Society's presidents shaped the organization?

Each president has governed with absolute power. As a result, his period of rule has been marked by his unique personality and Bible interpretation. Thus there have been four distinct "periods" of the Society: 1) the period of Charles Taze Russell (1872-1916); 2) the period of "Judge" Joseph F. Rutherford (1917-1942); 3) the period of Nathan H. Knorr (1942-1977); 4) the period of Frederick W. Franz (1977-present).

Because the Witnesses claim that God Himself was and is the source or author of their Bible interpretations and doctrines, it is important to examine these four periods. Doing so reveals the surprising fact that each president has interpreted the Bible *differently* from or even in *contradiction* of the others. Examining the writings of these men plainly shows that the claim of the Jehovah's Witnesses that God is the author of all of the Society's doctrines is absurd. The Bible teaches that God is not the author of confusion (1 Corinthians 14:33). The Society, then, is guided not by God, but by fallible men.

Charles Taze Russell, the Society's founder, wrote a new "Bible" for the faithful of his day, which he claimed "came from God through the enlightenment of the Holy Spirit."[2] This was the seven-volume *Studies in the Scriptures.** He taught that this material was necessary for properly understanding the Bible. In their principal publication, *The Watchtower* magazine, Sept. 15, 1910, p. 298, Russell wrote that without *Studies in the Scriptures* one could never "see the divine plan in studying the Bible by itself." Further, he said, even after reading *Studies in the Scriptures* for ten years, if one stopped reading it and went to "the Bible alone," "within two years he [would revert back] into darkness." Conversely, one who never read the Bible but did read Russell's volumes "would be in the light at the end of two years because he would have had the light of the Scriptures."[3] In other words, Russell claimed that a new divine interpreter was needed to understand the Bible properly. And he claimed to be that interpreter.

Yet today the Watchtower Society contradicts many of Russell's doctrines and "divine interpretations" of Scripture. The true "divine interpreter" has changed. It is now no longer Russell but the Society itself. It claims the same authority Russell did: that only its interpretations of the Bible are authoritative, and that studying the Bible alone will lead to darkness and heresy.

For example, *The Watchtower*, Aug. 15, 1981, condemns those who:

> say that it is sufficient to read the Bible exclusively, either alone or in small groups at home. . . . Through such "Bible reading,"

---

* Technically, Vol. 7, *The Finished Mystery,* was posthumously compiled and edited by George H. Fisher and Clayton J. Woodworth.

they have reverted right back to the apostate doctrines that commentaries by Christendom's clergy were teaching 100 years ago. . . .[4]

It is interesting that the Watchtower Society itself admits that anyone who reads the Bible alone will come to the same beliefs that orthodox Christianity has always held. Nevertheless, the writings Russell once called indispensable for understanding the Bible (his own) are today largely ignored.

Under the direction of the second president, "Judge" Rutherford, the organization became even more authoritarian. Rutherford instituted an "era of changes" and ignored, altered, or denied hundreds or thousands of Russell's teachings. He justified these changes by claiming a "progressive revelation" that permitted him to shed "new light" on Russell's ideas.[5]

This is why thousands of faithful followers of Russell, realizing Rutherford had abandoned Russell, left the organization. They believed Russell's claim that he was inspired by God and felt that to change his teachings drastically was to deny God. The broad majority of Witnesses, however, accepted the changes without question.

During the third major era, under the organizational leadership of Nathan H. Knorr, the number of Witnesses grew from 105,000 to about 2.2 million. New stress was placed on training in the Jehovah's Witnesses' interpretations of the Bible. A new Bible translation was produced to support these interpretations—and additional changes in Bible interpretation and doctrine occurred.[6]

The current era, under President Frederick W. Franz, could be labeled an "era of crisis" because thousands of Witnesses have begun to examine the history of the Society independently. They have become convinced that it is not God's organization and have left it or been disfellowshipped.

Even President Fredrick W. Franz's nephew, Raymond, is an example of one who has left the Watchtower. His book *Crisis of Conscience* shows why the Watchtower Society cannot be "God's sole channel" on earth. His text is an authoritative exposé by a key leader familiar with the inner workings of the Society. It portrays an authoritarian group of men who go to great lengths to retain a false image of divine guidance. Raymond Franz concludes that the Society is not of God. He cites evidence that it 1) is antibiblical, 2) has given extensive false prophecies, 3) has changed its teachings and policies, 4) has engaged in lying and cover-ups, and 5) has brought destruction into the lives of some of its members.[7] "Most of the [Governing] Body were actually not that well versed in the Scriptures," he writes (p. 97). They practiced "manipulation of Scripture and fact" to uphold their interpretations of the Bible (p. 245). The emphasis was "not loyalty to God and His Word, but loyalty to the organization and its teachings" (p. 257). The Society has reacted to those who question its authority with the threat of disfellowshipping. For most Jehovah's Witnesses, disfellowshipping means not only losing friends but also being separated or cut off from family.

Question 4

What attracts people to the Jehovah's Witnesses?

Many people are attracted to the Jehovah's Witnesses because they claim to have authoritative answers to many of life's problems. In a society torn by relative values and personal insecurities, any group is attractive that 1) claims to offer divine guidance; 2) claims to provide genuine solutions to life's problems; and 3) stresses moral and family values. The Watchtower Society is appealing to people who are looking for answers, who are frightened about the future, or who are tired of the lack of moral values in America. They are drawn to the dedication and commitment that the Witnesses show.

In addition, many people in mainline churches who have never been taught the Bible by their pastors desire to know it better. They are grateful to Witnesses who devote a lot of time and effort to allegedly helping them understand the Bible better.

8

The Worldview
of the
Jehovah's Witnesses:
Practices and
Teachings

Question 5

What is the religious worldview of the Jehovah's Witnesses, and what logical results flow from it?

Three basic beliefs, or assumptions, form the religious worldview of the Jehovah's Witnesses:

a) *Divine guidance comes only through the Watchtower Society.* This assumption leads Witnesses to live under an authoritarian organization that suppresses independent thinking in the name of God. Once a member accepts the organization's policies and decisions as being God's will, disagreement with the Watchtower Society is disagreement with God. It follows then that any criticism of the Society is defined as satanic. The Society teaches that "Jehovah's organization is in no wise [way] democratic. . . . His government or organization is strictly theocratic" (which means ruled by God alone).[8]

b) *Jehovah's Witnesses alone have the truth of God. They alone are the people of God.* This follows logically from their first assumption that divine guidance comes only from the Watchtower. This belief causes an attitude of exclusivism that stresses their uniqueness and superiority. This, in turn, leads them to accept an alleged divine command to be separate from the entire world system—social, political, military, and religious. Witnesses view the whole world system as satanic.

The Watchtower tells them with divine authority that Jehovah's Witnesses are to be separate and renounce such things as military service, patriotism, and celebrating religious holidays (see Question 7). Children of Jehovah's Witnesses are not permitted to engage in school activities prohibited by the Society—like Christmas plays, saluting the flag, and the Pledge of Allegiance—which results in their having considerably more difficulty growing up than do most other children.

c) *Jehovah's Witnesses are told that Orthodox, Protestant, and Catholic Christianity are false and controlled by Satan.* Because of this belief, Witnesses avoid all other Christians and completely reject their idea of the Christian faith (see Question 8).

Question 6

Does the Watchtower Society really claim to be the only organization on earth through which God works?

The Watchtower Society does claim that of all religious organizations, God works only through it. It alone has authority to speak for God.[9] For example, *The Watchtower* states:

> We belong to *no* earthly organization. . . . We adhere only to that heavenly organization. . . . All the saints now living or that ever lived during this age, belong to *our church organization*: such are all *one church*, and there is *no other* recognized by the Lord.[10]

Thus, Jehovah's Witnesses believe that no one on earth can discover the complete will of God apart from the Watchtower Society. Only the Watchtower Society and its publications can reveal the true meaning of the Bible. The Society is seen as "God's sole collective channel for the flow of biblical truth to men on earth."[11]

One Jehovah's Witness said to a Christian, "Your Bible was finished 2000 years ago, but our Bible has 32 pages added to it every week." He was referring to *The Watchtower*, a magazine that Witnesses are taught is the Word of God.[12]

A former member wrote,

> We were taught that we must adhere absolutely to the decisions and scriptural understandings of the Society, because God had given it this authority over His people (*The Watchtower*, May 10, 1972, p. 272). . . . To gain . . . eternal life, I was told certain things were necessary: (1) I should study the Bible diligently, and only through Watchtower publications. . . .[13]

The Watchtower of Feb. 15, 1983, p. 12, stated as a requirement of salvation ". . . that we be associated with God's channel, His organization. . . . To receive everlasting life in the earthly paradise we must identify that organization and serve God as part of it."

Thus, from the above statements, it is clear that the Watchtower Society claims to be the only organization on earth through which God works.

Question 7

Why do Jehovah's Witnesses prohibit practices like military service, saluting the flag, celebrating holidays, and blood transfusions?

These and many other practices are prohibited because the entire world system, apart from activity in the Watchtower Organization, is believed to be connected with the devil. Military service, patriotism, and celebrating holidays are all part of the devil's scheme to trick men away from God. Thus the Society asks, "Do you want to be part of Satan's world or are you for God's new system?... Getting out of Babylon the Great, the world empire of false religion... also means having nothing to do with the religious celebrations of the world."[14]

Other practices are prohibited because they are wrongly thought to be prohibited by Scripture. Although the Bible only forbids *eating* blood (something associated with pagan rituals), the Society has wrongly interpreted this as a ban on blood *transfusions*, something entirely different. The Witnesses teach that accepting a blood transfusion may "cost... [one his] eternal life...."[15] Tragically, hundreds, perhaps even thousands, of Witnesses and their children, have died because they believed the Watchtower's unbiblical view.[16]

Question 8

What do Jehovah's Witnesses believe about Christianity?

Like Mormonism, the Jehovah's Witnesses believe that Christianity is an apostate religion that has taught false doctrines and deceived people for over 1800 years. Until Jehovah's Witnesses appeared in the late nineteenth century and began teaching the Bible correctly, God's truth was largely absent from the world. Thus, the Witnesses believe that the Christian church is a satanic deception and that they alone are the true church.

Consider the following statements that have been made by some of the Watchtower presidents and official leaders:

- "Jehovah's Christian Witnesses are the ones that have identified who Babylon the Great is... the world empire of false religion. The chief component member and mouthpiece in that religious world empire is Christendom! She is the most reprehensible member thereof because she claims to be 'Christian.' Her blasphemies exceed those of 'pagandom.'... Her blood guilt exceeds that of all the non-Christian religious realm."[17]

- "Christendom's course is 'the way of death.'..."[18]

- "The Anglo-American empire system, which chiefly is 'Christendom,' Satan makes his chief spokesman on earth. . . ."[19]

- "Christendom's religion is demonism. . . ."[20]

- "As the most reprehensible ones among the people of Christendom, the clergy and religious leaders will drink the potion of death. . . ."[21]

It is clear from this that Jehovah's Witnesses view Christians and the Christian faith as one of their most powerful and hated enemies. Does this mean they have compassion on Christians and hope to rescue them from their collision course with God's judgment? Do they take Jesus seriously and love their enemies (Matthew 5:44)? Far from it! They are taught:

> Haters of God and His people . . . are to be hated. . . . We must hate in the truest sense, which is to regard with extreme and active aversion, to consider as loathsome, odious, filthy, to detest. Surely any haters of God are not fit to live on this beautiful earth. . . . We must have a proper perspective of these enemies. . . . We cannot love those hateful enemies, for they are fit only for destruction. . . . We pray with intensity . . . and plead that [Jehovah's] anger be made manifest. . . . Oh, Jehovah God of Hosts . . . be not merciful to any wicked transgressors . . . consume them in wrath, consume them that they shall be no more.[22]

Jehovah's Witnesses believe what the Watchtower has taught them even though Jesus plainly says in their own Bible they are to "continue to love your enemies . . . that you may prove yourselves sons of your father who is in the heavens" (Matthew 5:44,45 NWT).

9

The Theology
of the
Jehovah's Witnesses

Question 9

What do Jehovah's Witnesses believe about God and the doctrine of the Trinity?

Jehovah's Witnesses believe that the God of Christianity is a false and satanic counterfeit of the one true God, Jehovah. Charles Taze Russell even wrote that the Christian God was "the devil himself."[23] Jehovah's Witnesses see God as a single person, not as a single Being in whom are united three Persons, as Christians view God. They also deny that God is present everywhere and limit His omniscience.[24]

Because the Watchtower Society teaches that God is only one person, Witnesses reject the doctrine of the Trinity as an invention of "pagan imagination."[25] They call it "a false doctrine ... promulgated [promoted] by Satan for the purposes of defaming Jehovah's name."[26]

The Watchtower Society often misrepresents the doctrine of the Trinity. But Christians do not teach the view of God that the Witnesses say they do. Christians do not teach there are "three Gods" or "a complicated, freakish-looking, three-headed God."[27] We cite the Jehovah's Witnesses *New World Translation* (NWT) below:

Instead, Christians believe the Bible teaches that the one true God exists eternally as three Persons. The doctrine of the Trinity can be seen from five simple statements supported by the Bible.[28]

1) *There is only one true God*: "For there is one God, and one mediator between God and men ..." (1 Timothy 2:5 NWT; cf. Deuteronomy 4:35; 6:4; Isaiah 43:10).

2) *The Father is God*: "There is actually to us one God the Father . . . (1 Co-rinthians 8:6, NWT; cf. John 17:1-3; 2 Corinthians 1:3; Philippians 2:11; Colossians 1:3; 1 Peter 1:2).

3) *Jesus Christ, the Son, is God*: ". . . but he [Jesus] was also calling God his own Father, making himself equal to God" (John 5:18 NWT); "In answer Thomas said to him [Jesus]: 'My Lord and my God!' " (John 20:28 NWT, cf. Isaiah 9:6; John 1:1; Romans 9:5; Titus 2:13; 2 Peter 1:1—see notes 28,29).

4) *The Holy Spirit is a Person, is eternal, and is therefore God*. The Holy Spirit is a *Person*: "However, when that one arrives, the spirit of the truth, *he* will guide you into all the truth, for *he* will not speak of *his* own impulse, but what things *he* hears *he* will speak, and *he* will declare to you the things coming" (John 14:13 NWT, emphasis added). The Holy Spirit is *eternal*: "How much more will the blood of the Christ, who through an everlasting spirit offered himself without blemish to God . . ." (Hebrews 9:14 NWT). The Holy Spirit is *therefore God*: "But Peter said: 'Ananias, why has Satan emboldened you to play false to the holy spirit. . . . You have played false, not to men, but to God' " (Acts 5:3,4 NWT).

5) *The Father, Son, and Holy Spirit are distinct Persons*: ". . . Baptizing them in the name of the Father and of the Son and of the Holy Spirit"; "The undeserved kindness of the Lord Jesus Christ and the love of God and the sharing in the holy spirit be with all of you" (Matthew 28:19; 2 Corinthians 13:14 NWT).

It is clear from these verses read either from the biased New World Translation (NWT) or a modern version like the New International Version (NIV) that the Bible teaches the one true God exists eternally as Father, Son, and Holy Spirit. For 1900 years the historic Christian church has found in the Bible the doctrine of the Trinity as defined above. This can be seen by anyone who reads the Church Fathers and studies the historic Creeds.[29]

Man's incomplete comprehension of this truth is no reason to reject what Scripture teaches, as the Watchtower Society itself agrees:

> Sincere seekers for the truth want to know what is right. They realize they would only be fooling themselves if they rejected portions of God's Word while claiming to base their beliefs on other parts.[30]

Nevertheless, Jehovah's Witnesses allow human reason to judge God's Word. They reject the Bible's teaching about the one true God existing as three Persons and replace it in favor of their own view that God is only one Person. Because the idea of a triune God is to them "unreasonable," they think that it cannot be true.[31]

To see how unreasonable the Witnesses are in thinking this way, let's consider a scientific illustration.

Scientists long believed that all energy existed as either "waves" or "particles": two contradictory things. They felt it could not possibly be both because their natures were different. But modern scientific tests surprised scientists and indicated to them that light existed as both waves *and* particles. For a while some couldn't accept this conclusion because it wasn't reasonable. So some scientists insisted that light was only waves, while others insisted that it was only particles. Finally, though, scientists were forced by the *evidence* to conclude that light really was both waves and particles. Rather than clinging doggedly to their preconceived notions of reality, the evidence forced them to accept a different conclusion.

There is no scientist who understands this fact or who can explain it reasonably. But they are honest enough to accept this is what light is.

In the same way, God has told us who He is. The evidence of Scripture forces us to accept that the one true God exists as Father, Son, and Holy Spirit. We may not be able to understand it or explain it reasonably, but we accept it because this is what the facts have led us to.

Another illustration is love. Hardly anyone really *understands* what love is, how it works, how it begins, how it grows, or anything else connected with it. Yet we don't question its reality merely because we can't fully understand it.

Jehovah's Witnesses don't deny the reality of light or love merely because they don't fully understand them. Why then, do they insist that they must understand God before they accept His existence as He has revealed it?

Indeed, the Father, Son, and Holy Spirit are so effortlessly and consistently linked in Scripture that assuming that God is not three Persons makes it impossible to understand some passages (e.g., Matthew 28:19; 2 Corinthians 1:21,22; 13:14; Ephesians 2:18; 3:11-16; 5:18-20; 1 Thessalonians 1:1-5).

Try answering the following questions without concluding that the Bible teaches the doctrine of the Trinity:

1) Who raised Jesus from the dead? The Father (Romans 6:4; Acts 3:26; 1 Thessalonians 1:10)? The Son (John 2:19-21; 10:17,18)? The Holy Spirit (Romans 8:11)? Or God (Hebrews 13:20; Acts 13:30; 17:31)?

2) Who does the Bible say is God? The Father (Ephesians 4:6)? The Son (Titus 2:13; John 1:1; 20:28)? The Holy Spirit (Acts 5:3,4)? The one and only true God (Deuteronomy 4:35)?

3) Who created the world? The Father (John 14:2)? The Son (Colossians 1:16,17; John 1:1-3)? The Holy Spirit (Genesis 1:2; Psalm 104:30)? Or God (Genesis 1:1; Hebrews 11:3)?

4) Who saves man? Who *regenerates* man? The Father (1 Peter 1:3)? The Son (John 5:21; 4:14)? The Holy Spirit (John 3:6; Titus 3:5)? Or God (1 John 3:9)? Who *justifies* man? The Father (Jeremiah 23:6, cf. 2 Corinthians 5:19)? The Son (Romans 5:9; 10:4; 2 Corinthians 5:19,21)? The Holy Spirit (1 Corinthians 6:11; Galatians 5:5)? Or God (Romans 4:6; 9:33)? Who *sanctifies* man? The Father (Jude 1)? The Son (Titus 2:14)? The Holy Spirit (1 Peter 1:2)? Or God (Exodus 31:13)? Who *propitiated* God's just anger against man

for his sins? The Father (1 John 4:14; John 3:16; 17:5; 18:11)? The Son (Matthew 26:28; John 1:29; 1 John 2:2)? The Holy Spirit (Hebrews 9:14)? Or God (2 Corinthians 5:1; Acts 20:28)?

Though Jehovah's Witnesses exalt human reason against the doctrine of the Trinity, saying that it is "unreasonable," people who submit their minds to God's Word must conclude that it is unreasonable *not* to believe in it.

Question 10

What do Jehovah's Witnesses believe about Jesus?

The Jehovah's Witnesses teach that Jesus Christ was the first creation of God, the Archangel Michael.[32] They believe that He "had a beginning" and "was actually a creature of God."[33] By so believing, the Witnesses reject the Bible's teaching about Jesus.

But the Bible teaches that although Christ is fully man, He is also fully God (John 1:1; 5:18; 10:30; 20:28; Titus 2:13; Colossians 2:9; Philippians 2:1-8). It teaches that, as God, Christ is eternal, not created (Micah 5:2; John 1:1-3). The New World Translation dishonestly mistranslates all these verses which teach Christ's deity (for examples see Question 14).

The Witnesses wrongly teach that "Christ Jesus received immortality as a reward for his faithful course of action [on earth]. . . ."[34] This is because "any failure on his part would have meant eternal death [extinction] for him."[35]

However, the Bible teaches something completely different. It teaches that, as God, Jesus was already immortal and could never have ceased to exist; He is the same yesterday, today, and forever (Hebrews 13:8). Neither did He have to earn His own salvation, since He was always sinless (Hebrews 4:15) and immortal (Isaiah 9:6) and needed no salvation.

According to the Witnesses, the fundamental identity of Jesus has been altered. They believe that the angel Michael was changed into the mortal man Jesus, thus ceasing to be an angel. Later the man Jesus was changed into an improved and immortal version of the angel Michael. This happened when God recreated the man Jesus after His death. The Jehovah's Witnesses deny the physical resurrection of Christ (John 2:19-21; 1 Corinthians 15:3,4,17,35-49), teaching instead that when God "recreated" Jesus He made Him an immortal angel. Jesus no longer existed and Michael had no access to Jesus' earthly body. As Russell wrote, "The man Jesus is dead, forever dead."[36]

But the apostle Paul disagrees. Writing long after Jesus' death and resurrection, Paul taught that there "*is* one God and one mediator between God and men, the *man* Christ Jesus" (1 Timothy 2:5).

Thus, Jehovah's Witnesses deny the biblical teaching that Jesus is "the same yesterday and today and forever" (Hebrews 13:8).[37]

Finally, since the Witnesses teach that after Jesus' death, He was recreated a spirit creature (an angel), it is impossible that He could ever return to earth visibly and physically. Therefore, they teach that Michael returned invisibly in 1914.[38] But the Bible does not teach that Michael has or will return to earth. Rather, the Bible reveals that someday Jesus will return in a cataclysmic event and the entire world will recognize Him (Matthew 24:1-35). The Bible says Jesus will appear visibly, not invisibly, and physically, not spiritually, to all the world. The Bible says Jesus will appear in the same body He had while on earth, although now glorified (John 20:24-28; Acts 1:9-11; Zechariah 12:10).

The Christ of the Jehovah's Witnesses is not the Christ of the Bible.

Question 11

What do Jehovah's Witnesses believe about salvation?

The Jehovah's Witnesses believe that there are three classes of people that will be saved by good works. But each class is working to gain a different salvation.

The *first* class is an extremely small group of people the Jehovah's Witnesses call "the 144,000." Only these are elected by God for special spiritual privileges. For example, many of the blessings that the Bible teaches are given to *every* believer by faith alone are, according to the Watchtower Society, reserved exclusively for the 144,000. For example, this class is said to enjoy the spiritual privileges and blessings of justification and being born again. However, justification and being born again are redefined. Justification is not a once-for-all legal declaration God makes about a believer, giving him a perfect and righteous standing before God on account of the atonement of Christ, as is taught in Scripture (Romans 3:28; Philippians 3:9). Rather, they say justification is a "present justification" that may be forfeited at any time by disobedience.[39]

They also redefine the words "born again." The Jehovah's Witnesses say that being born again is being water baptized and anointed by God so they may be recreated by God as a spirit creature after death, just as God supposedly recreated Jesus into the angel Michael after His death. (The Witnesses teach that Jesus was "born again" at His baptism.) According to the Witnesses, the 144,000 are spiritually privileged to eventually be recreated like Jesus, and also privileged to rule with Jesus in heaven.[40] They do not understand that the Bible really teaches that all men, not just the 144,000, can be born again. They do not realize that being born again is a spiritual rebirth in the inner man that God grants, which can occur during life and brings with it eternal life (John 3:3-8; 5:24; 6:47; 1 John 1:11-13 NWT).

The *second* class includes all other Jehovah's Witnesses (called "the other sheep"). They cannot be justified in this life or born again. Indeed, the average Jehovah's Witness has no hope of ever being born again. At death God does not recreate these people as spirit beings, as Jesus was changed into Michael, but recreates their physical bodies to live only on the earth. These people are told they will be ruled over by Jesus (Michael) and the 144,000 in heaven.

The *third* class includes non-Jehovah's Witnesses who have lived good enough lives to be given the opportunity to earn salvation after death (a teaching that the Bible denies—Hebrews 9:27). All who are worthy of the second chance will be recreated by Jehovah to live in the new millennium. But they will only gain life beyond the millennium if they attain perfection during it.[41]

Not one of the above teachings is biblical. The Bible says there is only one basis upon which God grants salvation, and it is offered freely to all men (Galatians 1:6-8; John 3:16; Acts 4:12). Again, the new birth and heavenly salvation are not limited to 144,000 people, but are given freely to every believer: "Believe on the Lord Jesus Christ and you will get saved . . . (Acts 16:31 NWT). Salvation is by grace through faith alone, not by any of our works of righteousness (Ephesians 2:8,9; Titus 3:5; Romans 3:28 NWT). In fact, because salvation is "by grace [God's unmerited favor], then it is no longer by works [by our works]; if it were, grace would no longer be grace" (Romans 11:6).

Jesus declares to *all* people, "You must be born again." He warned that no one could be acceptable to God without a spiritual rebirth in this life that comes through faith in Him (John 3:3-18). He warns, ". . . unless you believe that I am He, you shall die in your sins" (John 8:24). [Here "He" applies to Himself—the divine name that God called Himself in the Old Testament; cf. Exodus 3:14; Isaiah 43:10; See Q.14, Ill. 2.]

Salvation is by personal merit and good works, not by grace through faith.

For a Jehovah's Witness, "grace" is merely the opportunity for men to earn their own salvation. It is not the free gift of God to men. Because Jehovah's Witnesses think they must earn their own salvation, they have no concept of true biblical grace.[42] Thus, the Society teaches that obeying "God's commandments . . . can [might] mean an eternal future,"[43] but this cannot give any *assurance* of salvation:

> . . . in all areas of life, we should be prepared to give our very best. We should not be half-hearted about such vital matters. What is at stake is Jehovah's approval and our being granted life.[44]

The Bible, in stark contrast, teaches that no one by his own good works can ever gain salvation (Romans 3:10-20 NWT). The Bible says that salvation cannot be earned or maintained by personal works of righteousness (Galatians 2:16,21, NWT). It is available only to those who recognize that they are unworthy and that they cannot earn it, who in repentance turn from sin and place their faith in Christ's work at the Cross for them (Romans 3:22; Luke 18:9-14 NWT).

But the Witnesses believe that God only justifies people "on the basis of their own merit."[45] The Watchtower has lied to them in teaching that salvation rests wholly on their good works, obedience to God, and personal merit. If they backslide, their salvation is forfeited and they risk being annihilated forever.[46]

This means that the only "salvation" the Witness has is the desperate hope that somehow as a fallen and sinful human being he can, through his own efforts, finally win God's approval. But only constant, diligent battling against sin and total obedience to serving God through the Watchtower gives him any hope of being recreated after death for millennial life. Even then, he is told that during the millennium if he fails he will be annihilated. If he serves faithfully all through this 1000-year period of time, he may finally win eternal life. But it will only be because he has earned it by personal effort and merit.

But the good news for every Jehovah's Witness is that God's Word opposes the Watchtower's plan of salvation. In the Bible, God guarantees eternal life. The eternal life that God promises to give does not begin in a distant future but the very moment a person believes in Christ for forgiveness of sins. In proof of this, below we quote the Jehovah's Witnesses' New World Translation (emphasis added).

> Most truly I say to you, He that hears my word and believes him that sent me *has* everlasting life, and he does not come into judgment but *has* passed over from death to life (John 5:24 NWT).

> Most truly I say to you, He that believes *has* everlasting life (John 6:47 NWT).

At the very moment a person accepts the work of Christ on his behalf and asks Jesus to save him, he is born again and made a new creation (John 3:1-16; 2 Corinthians 5:17). "For this is the will of my Father, that *everyone* [notice: this is not just the 144,000, but everyone] that beholds the Son and exercises faith in him should have everlasting life, and I will resurrect him at the last day" (John 6:40 NWT).

Even the New World Translation states salvation "is not owing to you, it is God's gift" (Ephesians 2:8,9 NWT). For a moment, let's think about what a gift is. If a boy brings a girl a box of candy or flowers and says, "This is a gift for you. All you have to do to get it is to go clean my house and wash my car." The girl would say, "If I clean your house and wash your car, then I would have earned it—it would no longer be a gift." A gift is something you get for nothing—when somebody pays for it and freely gives it. Girls know the difference between a loving gift and something you must earn. God says He is giving eternal life as a free gift. He can offer this gift because He sent Jesus to purchase it. The New World Translation says, ". . . but the *gift* God gives is everlasting life by Christ Jesus our Lord" (Romans 6:23 NWT, emphasis added). Further, the NWT emphatically states, "By this undeserved kindness, indeed, you *have been saved through faith*; and this *not* owing to you, it is God's *gift*. No, *it is not owing to works*, in order that no man should have grounds for boasting" (Ephesians 2:8,9 NWT, emphasis added).

10

Analysis and Critique: Does God Speak Only Through the Watchtower Society?

No question is more vital to the Jehovah's Witness than whether the Watchtower Society really is God's sole channel for communicating His will to mankind today. When we listen to the Society, are we listening to God? If we are, then we should listen carefully. But if we're not, then we should reject what it says.

There are four key tests by which we may discover whether or not the Watchtower Society is God's *only* channel for communicating His will to mankind today. If God does communicate to all of mankind through the Watchtower Society, then every test question below should be answered in a manner consistent with its claims.

TEST ONE: If God speaks only through the Watchtower Society, then the New World Translation must be accurate. But is it? (The next three questions examine their translation.)

Question 12

Do the Jehovah's Witnesses claim that their Bible (the New World Translation) is accurate?

The Watchtower claims that its translation of the Bible is highly accurate. It claims the New World Translation is the most accurate or one of the most accurate translations yet produced, and it states: "The translation must be appraised on its own merits."[47] (From these words the Jehovah's

Witnesses clearly challenge outsiders to examine the accuracy of their translation.) In *All Scripture Is Inspired By God and Beneficial* (WBTS, 1963) it claims precise grammatical accuracy in translation and adds, "... the New World Translation... *is accurate and reliable... a faithful translation of God's word.*"[48]

In the New World Translation itself, the Watchtower claims it has translated the Scriptures "as accurately as possible," with both a fear of and love for God—indeed with a great "sense of solemn responsibility."[49]

In *The Kingdom Interlinear Translation of the Greek Scriptures* it claims that its New Testament translation accurately renders "what the original language says and means" and that it does so unbiasedly, "without any sectarian religious coloration."[50]

The Watchtower Society has even gone so far as to say that God Himself has supervised its translation of the Bible by "angels of various ranks who controlled" the translators.

Current Society President F. W. Franz, along with then-president Nathan Knorr, headed the secret committee of seven translators. Franz testified in a court case in Edinborough, Scotland, Nov. 23, 1954. The *Scottish Daily Express* on Nov. 24, 1954, recorded his testimony word for word. In Franz' testimony he stated under oath: 1) that he and Knorr had the final word in translation; 2) that he (Franz) was head of the Society's publicity department; 3) that translations and interpretations came from God, invisibly communicated to the publicity department by "angels of various ranks who control[led]" the translators.[51] These statements by the leaders and translators concerning the accuracy of their New World Translation is evidence that they are in agreement with the Watchtower's claim to be God's sole channel on earth.

Question 13

What do recognized Greek scholars believe about the accuracy of the NWT?

Greek scholars, Christian and non-Christian, universally reject the NWT, calling it biased and inaccurate.

Until his recent death, Dr. Julius Mantey was one of the leading Greek scholars in the world. He was author of the *Hellenistic Greek Reader* and coauthor, with H. E. Dana, of *A Manual Grammar of the Greek New Testament*. Not only did he reject the NWT, he publicly demanded that the Society stop misquoting his *Grammar* to support it (see Appendix B). Of the NWT translation he wrote:

> I have never read any New Testament so badly translated as *The Kingdom Interlinear Translation of the Greek Scriptures*. In fact, it is not their translation at all. Rather, it is a distortion of the New Testament. The translators used what J. B. Rotherham had translated in 1893, in modern speech, and changed the

readings in scores of passages to state what Jehovah's Witnesses believe and teach. That is *distortion*, not translation.[52]

Dr. Bruce Metzger, professor of New Testament language and literature at Princeton Theological Seminary and author of *The Text of the New Testament* (Oxford, 1968), observes, "The Jehovah's Witnesses have incorporated in their translations of the New Testament several quite erroneous renderings of the Greek."[53]

Dr. Robert Countess wrote his dissertation for his Ph.D. in Greek on the NWT. He concluded that the Jehovah's Witnesses' translation:

... has been sharply unsuccessful in keeping doctrinal considerations from influencing the actual translation. ... It must be viewed as a radically biased piece of work. At some points it is actually dishonest. At others it is neither modern nor scholarly. And interwoven throughout its fabric is inconsistent application of its own principles enunciated in the Foreword and Appendix.[54]

British scholar H. H. Rowley asserts, "From beginning to end this volume is a shining example of how the Bible should not be translated...." He calls it "an insult to the Word of God."[55]

The scholarly community has rendered its verdict on the NWT. The Society cannot blame the verdict on alleged Christian or "Trinitarian bias," for even non-Christian scholars of New Testament Greek agree that the NWT is inaccurate. They have arrived at this conclusion by means of rules of grammar, word meanings, and principles of translation that the Watchtower Society has blatantly violated.

Question 14

What are some examples of NWT mistranslation?

The Watchtower Society has warned, "God does not deal with persons who ignore His Word and go according to their own independent ideas."[56] The Watchtower further asserts that Jehovah is against those who "steal" or change words from His Bible to make wrong applications.[57]

Yet the Watchtower has perpetrated just such error by incorporating hundreds of mistranslations in the NWT. Though space permits us to examine only a few examples of its mistranslations, even these make a mockery of the Society's claims to have tried to publish an honest, unbiased, accurate translation of the Bible.

In each of the examples below we will: a) list both the New World Translation (NWT) and the New International Version (NIV) translations for comparison, b) give the Society's reason for mistranslating, and c) explain why the Jehovah's Witnesses' New World Translation is biased, dishonest, and wrong.

Illustration 1—Titus 2:13

a) *Comparison of translations of Titus 2:13* (the same mistranslation occurs in 2 Peter 1:1). The Jehovah's Witnesses in their New World Translation have translated Titus 2:13 in this way:

> NWT: "While we wait for the happy hope and glorious manifestation of the great God and of (the) Savior of us, Christ Jesus." (Jehovah's Witnesses have added the word "the" and put it in parentheses in front of the word "Savior.")

On the other hand, the NIV translates this:

> NIV: "While we wait for the blessed hope—the glorious appearing of our great God and Savior, Jesus Christ...."

b) *The reason the Jehovah's Witnesses have mistranslated this verse is to deny the deity of Jesus Christ, a doctrine they do not accept.*

c) *Proof and documentation from scholars that the* New World *translators dishonestly translated this verse*:

By adding the word "the" in parentheses, the New World translators obscured the fact that in this verse Paul clearly called Jesus "our God and Savior." They have made it read as if Paul were speaking of two persons here, God and Jesus, rather than one, namely Jesus. Paul expressly stated that it is *Jesus* who is our great *God* and *Savior.* The Jehovah's Witnesses completely violate what Greek grammarians call Granville Sharp's rule for the use of the article with personal nouns in a series. In essence, Sharp's rule states that when two singular personal nouns ("God" and "Savior") of the same case ("God" and "Savior" are both in the same case) are connected by "and" (the Greek word is *kai*), and the modifying article "the" (the Greek word is *ho*) appears only before the first noun, not before the second, both nouns must refer to the *same* person. In Titus 2:13, "God" and "Savior" are connected by "and." Also, "the" appears only before "God." Therefore, "God" and "Savior" must refer to the same Person— Jesus. (The same rule also applies to the words in 2 Peter 1:1 which the Jehovah's Witnesses have also mistranslated in the NWT.)

In fact, scholars have conclusively shown that in ancient times the phraseology "god and savior" was used of a ruling king, clearly showing that only one person was meant.[58] In an exhaustive study, C. Kuehne found Sharp's rule to be without demonstrable exception in the entire New Testament.[59] Thus, honest and unbiased scholarship requires that the words in these verses must be translated "our God and Savior, Jesus Christ." Dr. Bruce Metzger, an authority on the Greek language and professor at Princeton University, has stated:

In support of this translation ["our God and Savior" must refer only to Jesus Christ] there may be quoted such eminent grammarians of the Greek New Testament as P. W. Schmiedel, J. H. Moulton, A. T. Robertson, and Blass-Debrunner. All of these
scholars concur in the judgment that only one person is referred to in Titus 2:13 and that therefore, it must be rendered, "our great God and Savior, Jesus Christ." ... [60]

Greek scholars Dana and Mantey, in their *A Manual Grammar of the Greek New Testament*, confirm the truth of Sharp's rule, and then explain: "Second Peter 1:1 ... means that Jesus is our God and Savior. After the same manner Titus 2:13 ... asserts that Jesus is the great God and Savior." [61] The greatest English-speaking Greek scholar, A. T. Robertson, insisted that "one person, *not* two, is in mind in 2 Peter 1:1." [62]

Even the context of Titus 2:13 shows that one Person, not two, was in Paul's mind, for Paul wrote of the "glorious appearing" of that Person. The Bible knows of only one such appearing: when "the Son of Man [Jesus] comes in his glory" (Luke 9:26). Indeed, an appearing of "the invisible God," other than as the visible Christ, who is His image and exact representation (Colossians 1:15; Hebrews 1:3), would be impossible.

From all of this, scholars conclude that the Jehovah's Witnesses' New World Translation is a biased and inaccurate translation.

Illustration 2—Colossians 1:17

a) *Comparison of translations of Colossians 1:17.* The Jehovah's Witnesses in their NWT have translated Colossians 1:17 in this way (everyone agrees this verse speaks of Jesus):

> NWT: "Also, he is before all (other) things and by means of him all (other) things were made to exist." (The Jehovah's Witnesses have dishonestly inserted the word "other" twice and placed it in parentheses when this word does not appear at all in the Greek text.)

On the other hand, the NIV translates this:

> NIV: "He is before all things, and in him all things hold together."

b) *The reason why the Jehovah's Witnesses have mistranslated this verse is to change the fact that Christ is eternal and therefore God—a doctrine they deny.* To do so, they dishonestly insert a word not found in the original Greek language which gives the false impression that Christ Himself was a created being and not eternal.

c) *Proof and documentation that the* New World *translators dishonestly translated this verse*:

Here in Colossians 1:17 the Watchtower Society's translators have inserted the word "other" twice and put it in parentheses (they also did this three more times in verses 16 and 20). They did this to imply that Christ Himself is not the Creator. But as their own Greek interlinear shows (page 896), the Greek word *panta* means "all things," *not* "all other things."

The Watchtower claims that inserting "other" is justified five times because the context implies it. But the only thing that implies it is their own bias against Christ's deity.

The Watchtower Society's own Greek interlinear version (page 896) embarrasses them, for it proves that there is no "other" in the Greek text. Yet this didn't prevent earlier editions of the NWT from inserting "other" *without* parentheses or brackets, implying that it *was* part of the original Greek text (see the 1950 and 1953 editions). Even the 1965 edition of *Make Sure of All Things* quotes Colossians 1:15-20 in this manner, implying that "other" is actually in the Greek five different times.[63]

This is not the only place the Jehovah's Witnesses have added words to the text. Recent versions of the NWT have inserted the word "other" in Philippians 2:9 without parentheses or brackets, to change the meaning of that verse. The meaning is changed from "the name above every name" to "the name above every other name."

The Society's objectivity cannot be more questionable than in examples of this type. They add to the divine text what simply is not present in order to deny what clearly is taught.

One more example of how the NWT mistranslates the Bible is John 8:58. This verse is absolute proof that Jesus claimed to be God. Obviously, the Jehovah's Witnesses do not believe that, so they have deliberately and dishonestly changed the words. Instead of translating Jesus to say ". . . before Abraham was born, I am" (NIV), the Jehovah's Witnesses translated these words, ". . . before Abraham came into existence, I have been."

Christ's actual statement that He was the "I am" was clearly understood by the Jews to mean that Jesus had applied the divine name of God used in the Old Testament to Himself (Exodus 3:14; Isaiah 43:10). That is why the next verse states that the Jews immediately tried to stone Him to death for blasphemy (John 8:59).

The Jehovah's Witnesses have dishonestly translated Jesus' words "I am" to "I have been" to obscure the fact Jesus was making a direct claim to being God. In mistranslating these words, they try to teach that Jesus was saying He merely existed before as Michael the angel.

The Watchtower Society has explained its reason for translating the Greek *ego eimi* ("I am") as "I have been" in John 8:58. It's because the verb *eimi* is in the "perfect indefinite tense." But when scholars pointed out to them that there has never been a "perfect indefinite tense" in Greek and that *eimi*, as any beginner's Greek grammar shows, is the first person singular, present, active, indicative form of *einai*, "to be,"[64] and therefore it *must* be translated "I am," not "I have been," they changed their mind and gave a new reason for mistranslating this verse. This too was incorrect—nevertheless, the Society has even admitted once that it was the present indicative tense.[65] But it hasn't followed through and translated it as such in its English Bible. Only its theological bias can explain its blatant mistranslation. Interestingly, their *Kingdom Interlinear* which shows the Greek words actually condemns the Watchtower's translation, giving correctly "I am" directly beneath *ego eimi*. But unfortunately, no Jehovah's Witness is likely to accept the truth of these words because the Watchtower translators place "I have been" in the column to the right.[66]

Illustration 3—Matthew 25:46

a) *Comparison of translations of Matthew 25:46.* The Jehovah's Witnesses in their NWT have translated Matthew 25:46 in this way:

> NWT: "And these will depart into everlasting cutting-off, but the righteous ones into everlasting life."

On the other hand, the NIV translates this verse:

> NIV: "Then they will go away to eternal punishment, but the righteous to eternal life."

b) *The reason Jehovah's Witnesses have mistranslated this verse is to deny the biblical teaching on eternal punishment and replace it with their doctrine of the annihilation of the wicked.*

c) *Proof and documentation that the New World translators have mistranslated this verse:*

All standard Greek dictionaries define the Greek word in question (*kolasin*) in Matthew 25:46 as "punishment," not "cutting-off," as the Jehovah's Witnesses have claimed it means. The Watchtower is in conflict with standard Greek authorities, including: Moulton and Milligan's *The Vocabulary of the Greek New Testament* (Grand Rapids, MI: Eerdmans, 1980, p. 352), Thayer's *Greek-English Lexicon of the New Testament* (Grand Rapids, MI: Baker, 1983, p. 353), Walter Bauer's *Greek-English Lexicon of the New Testament and Other Early Christian Literature* (second edition, William F. Arndt and F. Wilbur Gingrich, trans., F. W. Gingrich and Frederick W. Danker, eds. [Chicago: University of Chicago Press, 1979], p. 441), and Gerhard Kittel's *Theological Dictionary of the New Testament*, Vol. 3, Geoffrey W. Bromiley, trans. (Grand Rapids, MI: Eerdmans, 1978, p. 816).

These authorities all say that the word *kolasin* must be translated as "punishment." This definition is clearly substantiated by the word's use around New Testament times. For example, one early Christian writing says that "evil-doers among men receive their reward not among the living only, but also await punishment (*kolasin*) and much torment (*basanon*)."[67] They could hardly suffer "torment" if they were annihilated, as the Watchtower Society believes.

Greek scholar Julius Mantey wrote that he had "found this word in first-century Greek writings in 107 different contexts, and in every one of them, it has the meaning of punishment, and never 'cutting-off.'"[68]

Another verse the Society mistranslates to support its rejection of the biblical doctrine of eternal punishment is Hebrews 9:27. The standard way this is understood can be seen from the NIV's translation which reads: "Just as man is destined to die once, and after that to face judgment...." Next, please notice how the NWT adds words not in the original to justify the Watchtower's own biased doctrine: "And as it is reserved for men to die *once for all time* [i.e., be annihilated], but after this a judgment." The words "for all time" are not in the Greek text, as their own interlinear shows (p. 988). Dr. Mantey observes, "No honest scholar would attempt to so pervert the word of God."[69] In the Bible, God Himself warns all translators, "Do not add to His words, or He will rebuke you and prove you a liar" (Proverbs 30:6).

Space doesn't permit discussing all of the following verses, but consulting any of the standard authorities on New Testament Greek text will show in each instance that the NWT has dishonestly changed the true meaning of the words.

1) In Acts 20:28, the actual words "His own blood" have been mistranslated by the Watchtower Society as "the blood of His own (Son)" to circumvent Christ's deity.

2) In Hebrews 1:8, the proper translation, "Your throne, O God," has been mistranslated by the Watchtower Society to read, "God is your throne," in order to deny Christ's deity.

3) In Colossians 2:9, the word "deity" is mistranslated by the Watchtower Society as "divine quality," again in order to deny Christ's deity.

4) In John 1:1 the phrase, "the Word was God" is mistranslated by the Watchtower Society as "the Word was a god" to deny Christ's deity.

All of this clearly shows that the Watchtower Society miserably fails to pass the test of accurately translating the Bible. Since the Watchtower's New World Translation has universally been condemned as a biased and inaccurate translation, then it cannot claim it is faithfully presenting the Word of God. And if it is not faithfully presenting the Word of God, the Watchtower Society cannot possibly be the sole channel on earth through which God has chosen to lead all men.

Distorting God's Word is serious enough. But making God a liar by speaking false prophecy in His name so that men will worship a false god is an offense so serious that in the Old Testament it brought the death penalty (Deuteronomy 13:1-5).

TEST TWO: If the Watchtower Society is the sole channel for God on earth, then according to the Bible its prophecy must come true. How reliable have its prophecies been?

Question 15

What does the Watchtower Society teach and claim about prophecy?

In *The Watchtower*, Mar. 1, 1975, Jehovah's Witness leaders declared, "The Bible itself establishes the rules for testing a prophecy in Deuteronomy 18:20-23 and 13:1-8 . . ." (p. 151). Its own rules, with which we agree, are biblical and are our standard; they demand 100 percent accuracy for any prophecy that is made. The Society's publication *Aid to Bible Understanding* teaches all Jehovah's Witnesses that prophecy includes "a declaration of something to come" and that "the source of all true prophecy is Jehovah God."[70] This publication further states that "correct understanding of prophecy would still be made available by God . . . particularly in the foretold 'time of the end' . . . " (p. 1346). (In context, "time of the end" here includes the emergence of the Watchtower Society.)

Aid to Bible Understanding further defines a "prophet" as "one through whom the divine will and purpose are made known" (p. 1347). (What's more, the Watchtower Society makes the astonishing claim that it is the true prophetic mouthpiece for God on earth at this time.)[71] Furthermore, the Watchtower tells all Jehovah's Witnesses that "the three essentials for establishing the credentials of the true prophet" are 1) speaking in Jehovah's name, 2) "the things foretold would come to pass," and 3) these prophecies would promote true worship by being in harmony with God's already-revealed Word. The Watchtower claims that the true prophet would "express . . . God's mind on matters . . . [and] every prediction [will be] related to God's will, purpose, standards or judgment."[72]

In light of these lofty claims, the Society has succinctly declared its position and authority. It claims to speak in the name of Jehovah, to be His prophet predicting future events, and to be in harmony with His Word. It confidently predicts that what it says must "come to pass." *The Watchtower*, Sept. 1, 1979, declared, "For nearly 60 years now the Jeremiah class [the Jehovah's Witnesses] have faithfully spoken forth Jehovah's word" (p. 29).

It is clear from this that the Watchtower Society confidently claims to prophetically speak for God. We will now examine some of the implications of its own claims to be speaking for God.

Question 16

Has the Watchtower Society ever given false prophecies?

How have the predictions of the Watchtower Society stood the test of history? Let's look at a few. Frequently the Watchtower has attempted to predict the start of the Battle of Armageddon (the end of the world). (Unless otherwise noted, all quotations are from *The Watchtower*; dates appear at left.)[73] Let's look at a few predictions they have made in the name of God concerning the end of the world—what they often call Armageddon. (Because they believe Jesus has already returned invisibly, they look forward to the Battle of Armageddon, which they believe will usher in "paradise earth," not the Second Coming of Christ.) As you examine these prophecies, see if you really think that God spoke through them and gave the world the truth. Here are just a few of the predictions they have made through the years:

> In 1877 they said, *"The end of this world . . . is nearer than most men suppose. . . ."*[74]
>
> In 1886 they said, "The *time* is come for Messiah to take the dominion of the earth. . . ."[75]
>
> In 1889 they said, ". . . we present proofs that the setting up of the kingdom of God has already begun . . . and that 'the battle of the great day of God almighty' (Revelation 16:14), which will end in A.D. 1914 with the complete overthrow of the earth's present rulership, is already commenced."[76] (In their 1915 edition of this same book they changed "A.D. 1914" to "A.D. 1915.")
>
> On July 15, 1894 they said, "We see no reason for changing the figures—nor could we change them if we would. *They are, we believe, God's dates not ours* (emphasis added). But bear in mind that the end of 1914 is not the date for the *beginning*, but for the *end* of the time of trouble" (p. 1677 of *Reprints*, see note 73).
>
> In 1904 they said, "The stress of the great time of trouble will be on us soon, somewhere between 1910 and 1912 culminating with the end of the 'times of the Gentiles,' October 1914."[77]
>
> On May 1, 1914 they said, "There is absolutely no ground for Bible students to question that the consummation of this gospel age is now even at the door. . . . The great crisis . . . that will consume the ecclesiastical heavens and the social earth, is very near."[78]

But the year 1914 ended without a single one of these predictions coming true.[79]

In *Pastor Russell's Sermons* (1917, p. 676), Charles Taze Russell, founder and first president of the Jehovah's Witnesses, said of World War I, "The present great war in Europe is the beginning of the Armageddon of the Scriptures."

After Russell's death, "Judge" Rutherford continued the tradition of false prophecies given in the name and authority of God. He believed and stated that 1925 would mark the year of Christ's kingdom. He was wrong.[80] In *The Watchtower* magazine, Sept. 1, 1922, we find stated, "The date 1925 is even more distinctly indicated by the Scriptures because it is fixed by the law of God to Israel. . . . [One can see how] even before 1925 the great crisis will be reached and probably passed" (p. 262).

In *The Watchtower* magazine, Apr. 1, 1923, it stated, "Our thought is that 1925 is definitely settled by the Scriptures" (p. 106). But these and all other predictions proved false.

After utterly failing in the 1914 and 1925 predictions, finding many people leaving the Society, the leaders of the Watchtower became more cautious in setting dates. Nevertheless, they continued to hold out the promise of the imminency of Armageddon and the subsequent millennial kingdom. From 1930 to 1939 there were numerous declarations made about the future. For example:

> In 1930 they said, "The great climax is at hand."[81]
> In 1931 they said, "Armageddon is at hand. . . ."[82]
> In 1933 they said, "The incontrovertible proof that the time of deliverance is at hand."[83]
> In 1933 they said, "That [Jehovah] has now opened these prophecies to the understanding of His anointed is evidence that the time of the battle is near; hence the prophecy is of profound interest to the anointed."[84]
> In 1939 they said, "The battle of the great day of God Almighty is very near."[85]

In fact, from May, 1940, to April 15, 1943, just three short years, the Society made at least 44 predictions of the imminence of Armageddon.[86] Here are a few examples from this period and later:

> In September, 1940, they said, "The kingdom is here, the king is enthroned. Armageddon is just ahead. . . . The great climax has been reached" (*The Messenger*, Sept. 1940, p. 6).
> In *The Watchtower*, Sept. 15, 1941 they said, "The *Final End Is Very Near*" (p. 276). "The remaining months before Armageddon . . ." (p. 288).
> On January 15, 1942 they said, "The time is at hand for Jesus Christ to take possession of all things" (p. 28).
> On May 1, 1942 they said, "Now, with Armageddon immediately before us . . ." (p. 139).
> On May 1, 1943 they said, "The final end of all things . . . is at hand" (p. 139).
> On September 1, 1944 they said, "Armageddon is near at hand" (p. 264).
> In 1946, "The disaster of Armageddon . . . is at the door."[87]
> In 1950 they said, "The March is on! Where? To the field of Armageddon for the 'war of the great day of God the Almighty.'"[88]
> In 1953 they said, "Armageddon is so near at hand it will strike the generation now living."[89]
> In 1955 they said, "It is becoming clear that the war of Armageddon is near its breaking out point."[90]
> In 1958 they said, "When will Armageddon be fought? . . . It will be very soon."[91]

These are just a few of the many false prophecies *The Watchtower* has made over the years. Is there any wonder the Jehovah's Witness leaders in their *Awake!* magazine, Oct. 8, 1968, p. 23, were forced to admit that "certain persons" had previously falsely predicted the end of the world? In this article Jehovah's Witness leaders asked why these false prophecies were given. Every Jehovah's Witness should take note of what they said. They said it was because they lacked God's guidance.

In this article in *Awake!* magazine (Oct. 8, 1968, p. 23) the Watchtower leadership admitted:

> True, there have been those in times past who predicted an "end to the world," even announcing a specific date. The "end" did not come. They were guilty of false prophesying. Why? What was missing? . . . Missing from such people were God's truths and the evidence that He was guiding and using them. But what about today? Today we have the evidence required, all of it, and it is overwhelming!

Notice that the Watchtower leaders have condemned themselves as false prophets. They admit that all through the years they were speaking in the name and authority of God, they were really lying and giving false prophecies.

If we accept that they gave false prophecies, God in Deuteronomy 18:20-22 says in the New World Translation:

> However, the prophet who presumes to speak in my name a word that I have not commanded him to speak or who speaks in the name of other gods, that prophet must die. And in case you should say in your heart: "How shall we know the word that Jehovah has not spoken?" When the prophet speaks in the name of Jehovah and the word does not occur or come true, that is the word that Jehovah did not speak. With presumptuousness the prophet spoke it. You must not get frightened at him.

But in spite of their tragic record of predictions that did not come to pass, they disregarded the Word of God in Deuteronomy 18 and as the above quote from *Awake!* magazine shows, they confidently asked the people to believe that now they would speak accurately for God in predicting the future. They now began to strongly imply it would be the year 1975 in which Armageddon would occur.[92]

> In 1973 they said, "The 'Great Tribulation' is very near."[93]
> In 1973 they said, "According to the Bible's time-table, the beginning of the seventh millennium of mankind's existence on earth is near at hand, within this generation."[94]

In *Kingdom Ministry*, May, 1974, the world's end was said to be "so very near" that Jehovah's Witnesses were commended who sold "their homes and property" to devote themselves to full-time service in "the short time remaining before the wicked world's end" (p. 3).

> In 1975 they said, "The fulfillment... is immediately ahead of us."[95]
> In 1975 they said, "Very short must be the time that remains. . . ."[96]

Many Jehovah's Witnesses living today can remember when the year 1975 came and went, bringing great discouragement to the faithful and providing further embarrassment to the Watchtower Society.

But the charade still continued. From 1976 to 1981 the Society repeatedly said that Armageddon was "very near," "at hand," etc. And from 1981 to the present the Society still claims that the world is near its end.

It is said that Jehovah's Witnesses believe that the Watchtower's authoritative statements are true and genuinely reflect God's guidance. But if the Society has been indisputably wrong in every period, how can modern Witnesses trust it? Would any employer rehire a thief for the tenth time after nine offenses? The answer is no. Thousands of Jehovah's Witnesses have left the Watchtower after having lived through the high expectations and heartbreaking disappointments of these false prophecies. Thousands more have left who investigated these false prophecies in the Watchtower literature.

Still, the Watchtower Society claims that Jehovah's Witnesses' "unswerving attention to such inspired prophecy has held them true to the right course till now."[97] After reading its false prophecies through the years and its own admission that it lied, what do you think?

The Society still claims of Armageddon, "Jehovah has His own fixed date for its arrival."[98] But the Watchtower has missed that date every time it has predicted it.

Question 17

Does the Watchtower Society admit to false prophecy?

Jehovah's Witnesses have admitted serious errors. In their official Watchtower publication, *Man's Salvation* (1975), they now admit that Charles Taze Russell was wrong in his 1874 prediction of Christ's second coming.[99] They admit that they were wrong in their 1914 prediction.[100] They admit that they were wrong in their prediction of 1925.[101] They admit that they were wrong about their prediction in 1975.[102]

Yet in that same year in their *1975 Yearbook* they claim that for over a century "Jehovah's servants" have "enjoyed spiritual enlightenment and direction."[103] What do you think? Does the evidence show they have passed the second test they themselves laid down, namely that any prophecy given in the name of God must come true? Have their prophecies come true 100 percent of the time?[104] If not, can the Watchtower Society claim it is God's sole channel of communication to men on earth today?

TEST THREE: If the Watchtower Society is God's sole channel for communication on earth, then its scholarship should be trustworthy—but is it?

Question 18

Has the Watchtower Society ever lied, covered up and changed important doctrines, dates, and Bible interpretations?

If God actually speaks to all men through the Watchtower Society—giving prophecy, Bible interpretations, and other instruction—in looking at the Watchtower materials, it appears He must change His mind a great deal. These words and our question sound blunt, but we are only doing what Judge Rutherford told us to do for the Jehovah's Witnesses. He said in *The Golden Age*, Jan. 18, 1933, p. 252:

> If the message Jehovah's Witnesses are bringing to the people is true, then it is of greatest importance to mankind. If it is false then it is the duty of the clergymen and others who support them to come boldly forward and plainly tell the people wherein the message is false.

The fact is, the Watchtower Society leaders have lied and covered up important material. Even *The Watchtower*, June 1, 1960, p. 352, encourages "hiding the truth from God's enemies." They say it is proper to deceive people (God's enemies) but they claim this is not lying. This is because they have a different definition of lying as stated in their text *Aid to Bible Understanding*, p. 1060, where they say that lying "generally involves saying something false to a person who is *entitled* to know the truth. . . ." The fact is, however, it is not just "God's enemies" they have lied to, but their own people.

Here are a few of the changes in dates, prophecies, and its doctrines that the Watchtower Society has made through the years. What is so condemning is that all of this can be found in its own authoritative writings. (See note 104.)

For example, 1) The Watchtower Society changed the beginning of the "time of the end" from the date 1799 to 1914; 2) it changed the second coming of Christ from the date 1874 to 1914; 3) it changed the entire nature of the second coming of Christ from an earthly and visible return to a heavenly and invisible return; 4) it changed the time of the "first resurrection" from the date 1878 to 1914; 5) it changed the date of the termination of the 6000 years of creation from the year 1872 to 1972 and the 1975.[105] Why so many changes? Simple: The predicted happen. The changes were made to cover up its false pro the fact that God really hadn't spoken through it.

Next, here are a few changes the Watchtower Society has ing important doctrines. 1) The Watchtower Society chan concerning lifesaving vaccination from commands rejecting it to permission to accept it; 2) the Watchtower changed the identity of the "Faithful and Wise Servant" from Charles Taze Russell, its first president, to the Watchtower Society itself; 3) the Watchtower Society once said the book of Ruth should be interpreted as history, but later changed and said it should be read as prophecy; 4) the Watchtower changed the identity of "Abaddon" in Revelation 11, first saying this angel was Satan, and later saying this was Jesus Christ; 5) the Watchtower in its early years accepted blood transfusions, but then made rejection of blood transfusions a key doctrine; 6) the Watchtower first accepted the worship of Jesus, but now rejects the worship of Jesus; 7) the Watchtower changed the doctrine concerning the resurrection of the dead—first *all* were to be raised, now only some were to be raised; 8) it changed its view of Israel—from literal (a physical nation) to spiritual (all believers); 9) the Watchtower changed the definition of the "superior authorities" found in Romans 13 from political rulers on earth to God and Jesus in heaven, and then back again to political rulers on earth.[106]

With all these changes one wonders, "Can the average Witness know that what he is told is true today won't be declared false tomorrow?" Former Jehovah's Witness Edmond Gruss in his standard text *Apostles of Denial* reveals that "thousands of reinterpretations of Scripture" and many new doctrinal points developed after Russell's death and cites many illustrations.[107] Former Witness William J. Schnell notes, "I had observed *The Watchtower* magazine change our doctrines between 1917 and 1928 no less than 148 times...."[108] One example is Luke 16:19-31 which has been interpreted in five different ways.[109] How, then, can the average Jehovah's Witness know God's true mind on any passage of Scripture?[110]

These are only a sample of the changes the Watchtower Society has made in the name of God concerning its Bible interpretation, its doctrine, and its prophetic dates. Do its statements support the claim that the Watchtower Society "from the time of its organization until now" has been God's sole "collective channel for the flow of biblical truth to men on earth?" Do its false prophecies support the claim that for over a century Jehovah's servants have "enjoyed spiritual enlightenment and direction?"[111] One wonders how the Watchtower Society could say "Jehovah never makes any mistakes,"[112] since it also claims Jehovah is speaking through it. In the Bible, God Himself clearly states He is the "God of truth" who "cannot lie" (Psalm 31:5; Titus 1:2). Indeed, "it is impossible for God to lie" for "no lie is of the truth" (Hebrews 6:18; 1 John 2:21). God does not make mistakes concerning dates nor change His mind on doctrinal matters. Is there any other conclusion we can come to except that the Watchtower Society has misled millions of people in claiming it alone is God's sole channel of communication on earth today?

TEST FOUR: If the Watchtower Society admits it receives much of its teachings from angels or spirits and those teachings have proven to be false—is such a source trustworthy?

Question 19

Has the Watchtower Society ever claimed to receive information from angels or spirits?

It can be documented that the Watchtower Society in its early years dabbled in the occult,[113] although the Society's official position toward occult activity is supposedly in agreement with the prohibition found in Deuteronomy 18:9-12. Nevertheless, today the Watchtower Society appears to be unsuspectingly involved in the occult in at least one manner: It seems to accept demonic guidance and revelations which come to it in the disguise of angelic or spiritistic contacts.

The Watchtower in the past has claimed "angelic guidance" for its Bible translators in their writing of Jehovah's Witnesses' doctrine and practice. If real supernatural activity has occurred, and the Watchtower's translation, doctrines, and practices have failed to meet biblical, moral,[114] and scholarly standards, it seems hardly likely that the supernatural assistance was from God. Godly angels would never lend help to an organization that denies the true nature of who God is, deliberately distorts His word, and completely rejects His Son. But the Bible says fallen angels—demons—would. The Bible further declares that demons masquerade as "angels of light" while doing so (2 Corinthians 11:14).

Besides the Watchtower Society's express claim (Question 12) that "angels" guided its translators in translating the New World Translation of the Bible, former service department member Bill Cetnar in the Jehovah's Witnesses headquarters at Brooklyn, New York, found many Watchtower beliefs were also professed by a spirit-possessed medium the Society was quoting.[115]

"Judge" Rutherford openly stated that angels helped write *The Watchtower* magazine when he said, "The Lord through His angel sees to it that the information is given to His people in due time. . . ."[116] The current worldwide president of Jehovah's Witnesses is F. W. Franz who also speaks of angels guiding the Watchtower. He has said, "We believe that the angels of God are used in directing Jehovah's Witnesses."[117]

Among other things *The Watchtower* claims that angels enlighten and comfort, bring refreshing truths, and transmit information to "God's anointed people."[118] In another clear statement of its belief that angels guide the leaders of Jehovah's Witnesses, we read in *The Watchtower* magazine, "Jehovah's Witnesses today make their declaration of the good news of the kingdom under angelic direction and support."[119]

In *The Watchtower*, Dec. 1, 1981 (p. 27), and July 15, 1960 (p. 439), the leaders of the Jehovah's Witnesses claim to be God's "channel of communication," actively "channeling" (the use of this common New Age term is theirs) since the days of Rutherford. In the issue of Apr. 1, 1972 (p. 200), they claim that all spiritual direction is supplied by invisible angels. In the issues of Nov. 15, 1933 (p. 344), Nov. 1, 1935 (p. 331), and Dec. 15, 1987 (p. 7), they claim that the name "Jehovah's Witnesses" and their key doctrine of "Christ's" invisible return in 1914 were channeled by invisible angels.

Under the second president of the Jehovah's Witnesses, "Judge" Ruther-ford, the Witnesses received most of their basic doctrines. Yet Rutherford believed that God's "holy spirit" had ceased to function as his teacher and had been replaced by angels who taught him in his mind (*The Watchtower*, Sept. 1, 1930, p. 263, and Feb. 1, 1935, p. 41; Rutherford, *Riches* [1936], p. 316).

Today the Society's leaders claim that both "holy spirit" and "angels" communicate information to them (*The Watchtower*, Mar. 1, 1972, p. 155; Aug. 1, 1987, p. 19).[120]

In conclusion, these rather startling admissions from the Watchtower documenting that it receives information and guidance from "angels" coupled with the fact of all its false prophecies, biased Bible translation, and unbiblical teachings lead us to believe it is receiving its information from demons rather than from God. (Cf. Part 5).

Question 20

What can you do if you are a Jehovah's Witness who desires to live for God and Christ and yet are unsure about what you have been taught?

First, if you are a Jehovah's Witness, don't be discouraged. Don't give up on God because someone lied to you. Perhaps you accepted the Watch-tower's claims without first testing them carefully. Possibly your own doubts and discouragement will become the means by which God leads you into the truth and into a personal relationship with Him.

Second, realize that you aren't alone. Former worldwide Governing Body board member Raymond Franz estimates that between 1970 and 1979 over 750,000 Jehovah's Witnesses were disfellowshipped or left the Watchtower organization.[121]

Third, take the initiative: Get at the truth for yourself. The Watchtower has told you before that "sincere seekers for the truth want to know what is right."[122] If you study the Bible on your own, in humility before God, God says He Himself will show you the truth:

> But if any of you lacks wisdom, let him ask of God, who gives to all men generously and without reproach, and it will be given to Him. . . . Draw near to God and He will draw near to you (James 1:5; 4:8).

Ask Him, and He'll help you. Believe and obey His Word, don't alter it, and you will know the truth and, as Jesus promised, "the truth will make you free" (John 8:31,32).

Fourth, accept God's loving and free gift of salvation in Christ Jesus (no works to earn it!). God never intended for you to spend your life in a hopeless, never-ending attempt to earn your own salvation by measuring up to His standard of perfection. He has already told us it's impossible for any person to do so. Because of your fallen nature, you'll never be able to do it (Romans 8:3). "But because of His great love for us, God, who is rich in mercy, made us alive with Christ even when we were dead in transgressions—it is by grace you have been saved" (Ephesians 2:4,5; cf. Romans 8:3). The really good news that God gives to all of us is:

"Therefore, there is now no condemnation for those who are in Christ Jesus" (Romans 8:1).

"You see, at just the right time, when we were still powerless, Christ died for the ungodly" (Romans 5:6).

"But the gift of God is eternal life in Christ Jesus our Lord" (Romans 6:23).

"However, to the man who does not work [for salvation] but trusts God who justifies the wicked, his faith is credited as righteousness" (Romans 4:5).

"So we, too, have put our faith in Christ Jesus that we may be justified by faith in Christ and not by observing the law, because by observing the law no one will be justified. . . . I do not set aside the grace of God, for if righteousness could be gained through the law, Christ died for nothing!" (Galatians 2:16,21).

Thus, God wants you to confess your sins and accept the forgiveness He provided through Christ's shed blood. Read Isaiah 55:1-3 and see how eagerly God longs for you to come to Him to rest. Do you long for eternal life? God's Word says you can *know* that you have it:

> The one who believes in the Son of God has the witness in himself; the one who does not believe God has made Him a liar, because he has not believed in the witness that God has borne concerning His Son. And the witness is this, that God has *given* us eternal life, and this life is in His Son. *He who has the Son has the life*; he who does not have the Son of God *does not* have the life. These things I have written to you who believe in the name of the Son of God, in order that *you may know that you have eternal life* (1 John 5:10-13, emphasis added).

You can receive the gift of salvation, and know that you have eternal life, right now, by praying sincerely:

> Dear God, I'm confused. But I long to know You and serve You as You really are. Please reveal Yourself to me. I confess that I'm a sinner and incapable of earning merit in Your eyes. I believe Jesus' words, "You must be born again." I now receive Jesus Christ as my personal Lord and Savior. I receive Him as my God. I commit myself to Him and to Your Word. Please help me to understand it correctly. Amen.

PART THREE

CULT WATCH

THE MASONIC LODGE

Does Masonry conflict with the Christian faith?

11

Introduction to Masonry

Is the Masonic Lodge compatible with Christianity? In 1985 the Lodge challenged "The John Ankerberg Show's" teachings on Masonry. They claimed that Masonry was not a religion and did not in any way conflict with Christianity. But is this true?

Our Masonic guest on the television program told us that the Ritual was the authoritative source for all Masons—and he was correct. In this unit, we have cited Masonic Ritual and shown how it conflicts with Christian teaching.

We also wrote to all 50 of the Grand Lodges in the United States and asked them which Masonic authors and books they would recommend as the most authoritative commentaries concerning the teachings of Masonry. We will report to you what they said. Then we will compare the commentary of their recommended authors with some of the teachings of biblical Christianity to answer the question, "Is Christianity compatible with the teachings of the Masonic Lodge?"

The information we present is fully documented from authoritative Masonic sources and is confirmed as accurate by Masons and former Masons.

In this unit, we have stressed the Ritual of the Blue Lodge—the first three degrees of Masonry (Entered Apprentice, Fellow Craft, and Master Mason)—since these are the degrees through which *every* Mason must pass.[1]

We have examined the standard interpretations of the Blue Lodge rituals given by Masons. Most Masons believe that Blue Lodge Masonry makes one as full or complete a Mason as one can (or needs) to be. But an important fact must be noted. While the Blue Lodge is Masonry, and while it is the Masonry of most Masons, it is not all that Masonry constitutes.

Some Masons would view Blue Lodge Masonry as it is usually interpreted as an initial or beginning form of Masonry, and maintain that the real substance of Masonry—its lifeblood—lies in the higher degrees and in the initiate's search for their true meaning. Some Masons would even consider Blue Lodge Masonry as only the *cover* of the book, but not the book itself. These Masons would say that to truly understand Masonry one must open the book and read what lies *within* the cover. What one finds there will shock even many Masons.[2]

As Sovereign Grand Commander Henry C. Claussen admits, "It must be apparent that the Blue Lodge . . . degrees cannot explain the whole of Masonry. They are the foundation. . . . An initiate may imagine he understands the ethics, symbols and enigmas, whereas a true explanation of these is reserved for the more adept."[3]

It is our sincere hope that this unit will encourage Christian Masons to look seriously and frankly at Masonry and ask themselves: Can a Christian who follows Jesus Christ and accepts biblical authority really be a Mason? In good conscience, can he justify his involvement in Masonry?

As one Anglican vicar, also a Mason, observed, "I for one can never understand how anyone who takes an exclusive view of Christ as the only complete revelation of God's truth can become a Freemason without suffering from spiritual schizophrenia."[4]

(For readers who desire further documentation and a more detailed critique of Masonry than can be presented in this unit, we urge them to read our book, *The Secret Teachings of the Masonic Lodge* (Moody Press, 1990) which discusses Masonry's connection to the ancient mystery religions, occultism and spiritism, among many other topics).

12

What Is Masonry and How Does One Determine Authoritative Masonic Teaching?

As a fraternity, we are always ready to be judged—severely and critically.[5]

—Francis G. Paul, 33rd Degree
Sovereign Grand Commander
(*The Northern Light*, May 1988)

Question 1

What is Masonry?

Masonry (also known as Freemasonry or "the Lodge") is a powerful, centuries-old fraternal order that, according to Masonic authorities, began in the early eighteenth century. According to most Masonic authorities, modern Masonry (also called "speculative" Masonry) can be traced to the founding of the first Grand Lodge in London in A.D. 1717.[6]

The Lodge is also a secret society. To maintain its secrets, Masonry uses symbolism, secret oaths, and secret rituals to instruct new members, called "initiates." Each new member swears during these secret ceremonies to remain loyal to the Lodge and its teachings. The teachings instruct each new candidate on how he is to serve and the rewards he can expect.

Let us examine the definition of Masonry as given by Masons themselves. In Albert G. Mackey's *Revised Encyclopedia of Freemasonry* he states, "All [Masons] unite in declaring it to be a system of morality, by the practice of which its members may advance their spiritual interest, and mount by the theological ladder from the Lodge on earth to the Lodge in heaven."[7]

Other respected Masonic authorities define Masonry in the following words:

95

It is a science which is engaged in the search after Divine Truth, and which employs symbolism as its method of instruction."[8]

"[Masonry is] that religious and mystical society whose aim is moral perfection on the basis of general equality and fraternity."[9]

"Freemasonry, in its broadest and most comprehensive sense, is a system of morality and social ethics, a primitive religion, and a philosophy of life... incorporating a broad humanitarianism.... It is a religion without a creed, being of no sect but finding truth in all.... It seeks truth but does not define truth....[10]

A man who becomes a Mason is defined by Masonic authorities as being "one who has been initiated into the mysteries of the fraternity of Freemasonry."[11]

The next 18 questions present an analysis of *Masonry itself*, as stated by Masonic authorities recommended to us by at least half of the Grand Lodges in the United States (see Question 2). The Grand Lodge of each state sets the Ritual and the interpretation of that Ritual which is to be followed by the members of that state.

Question 2

What is the final authority for the teachings presented in each Masonic Lodge?

If anyone is going to investigate the teachings of the Masonic Lodge, who or what is the authority they should listen to?

When we asked Mr. Bill Mankin, a thirty-second degree Mason, this question on our television program he said, "The authoritative source for Masonry is the Ritual. The Ritual—what happens in the Lodge, what goes on."[12]

When one examines Masonry *today* and compares the different manuals containing the Ritual for each state, it is apparent that *today* the Ritual and the interpretations given are almost identical. Therefore, the Ritual in the Masonic manuals can be considered the authoritative teachings of the Lodge. As former Worshipful Master Jack Harris reveals: "In [all] other states... the principle and the doctrines [of the Ritual] are exactly the same. The wording only varies slightly."[13]

But we also wanted to know which authors and books Masons themselves recommend to outsiders as authoritative. In order to answer this question, a letter was sent to each of the 50 Grand Lodges in America. We addressed the letter to the Grand Master of each of the Grand Lodges and asked him to respond to the following question: "As an official Masonic leader, which books and authors do you recommend as being authoritative on the subject of Freemasonry?"

Half of all the Grand Lodges in the United States responded, that is, 25 of the 50 (AZ, CO, CT, DC, DE, IA, ID, IL, IN, KS, LA, MA, ME, MI, MO, NJ, NM, NY, OH, PA, SC, TX, UT, VA, WI).

Remember: For each state there is no higher authority than its Grand Lodge.

Question 3

Which books and authors have been recommended by the Grand Lodges as being authoritative for Masons?

When we received a reply from a Grand Lodge, we compared which authors and books they recommended as being authoritative for them with the replies from the other Grand Lodges. These are the authors that the Grand Lodges recommended:

> 44%—of the Grand Lodges recommended *Coil's Masonic Encyclopedia* by Henry Wilson Coil.
> 36%—*The Builders* by Joseph Fort Newton
> 32%—*Mackey's Revised Encyclopedia of Freemasonry* by Albert G. Mackey
> 24%—*Introduction to Freemasonry* by Carl H. Claudy
> 24%—*The Newly-Made Mason* by H. L. Haywood
> 20%—*A Masonic Reader's Guide* by Alphonse Cerza
> 20%—*History of Freemasonry* by Robert F. Gould
> 20%—*The Craft and Its Symbols* by Allen E. Roberts
> 16%—*Morals and Dogma* by Albert Pike

Notice that the Grand Lodges, by their responses, reveal that Coil, Newton, and Mackey are the three leading Masonic authorities.[14] Because of the high esteem in which these authors are held by the Grand Lodges, we will often document our analysis of Masonry from their texts. At the same time, we have not neglected the other Masonic authors recommended by the Grand Lodges. We have tried to quote fairly from as many as possible. We have done all of this so that Masons cannot say that we have based our arguments on material that no Mason would consider authoritative and reliable. Masons must acknowledge that these authors and books do represent their most authoritative interpreters of Freemasonry. Thus, by citing both their ritual and leading authorities an accurate portrayal of Masonry is safeguarded.

Question 4

What is the Blue Lodge, the Scottish Rite, and the York Rite?

All men who become Masons normally go through the first three degrees of the Blue Lodge. The Blue Lodge is the parent or mother Lodge of Freemasonry. In the Blue Lodge are conferred the first three degrees: 1) the Entered Apprentice, where a man is initiated into the beginning mysteries of the fraternity of Freemasonry; 2) the degree of Fellow Craft; and 3) the Master Mason degree.

After passing these three degrees in the Blue Lodge, the candidate may choose not to proceed further at all, or he may choose to proceed higher along one or both of two branches in Masonry.

One branch is known as the Scottish Rite, which advances by numerical degrees, beginning with the fourth and ending with the thirty-second, the thirty-third degree being either active or honorary. The other major branch is the York Rite, which goes through what is called the "Chapter," "Council," and "Commandery" degrees, ending with the degree of Knights Templar.

If a Mason is suspended or expelled from his Blue Lodge, it automatically severs his connection from all other Masonic bodies. Anyone who passes the first three degrees and becomes a Master Mason may visit Blue Lodges other than his own.

On the next page we present a diagram of the three Blue Lodge degrees that every Mason must take,* plus the optional degrees of the York and Scottish Rites.[15] (Note: Only the Scottish Rite cites its degrees by number— the York Rite designates its degrees by name. For example, the fourth degree of the York Rite is termed "Mark Master" whereas in the Scottish Rite the degree is simply called the fourth degree.)

---

* A Mason is not permitted entry into the York or Scottish rites unless he has completed the Blue Lodge degrees; occasionally a Mason may complete only the first or second degree.

Blue Lodge Degrees and Optional
York and Scottish Rites

Blue Lodge

1. Entered Apprentice
2. Fellow Craft
3. Master Mason

York Rite	Scottish Rite
Chapter (capitular degrees)	*Lodge of Perfection*
Mark Master	4. Secret Master
	5. Perfect Master
	6. Intimate Secretary
Past Master (Virtual)	7. Provost & Judge
	8. Intendant of the Building
	9. Elu of the Nine
	10. Elu of the Fifteen
Most Excellent Master	11. Elu of the Twelve
	12. Master Architect
	13. Royal Arch of Solomon
Royal Arch Mason	14. Perfect Elu
	Chapter Rose Croix
	15. Knight of the East or Sword
Council (cryptic degrees)	16. Prince of Jerusalem
Royal Master	17. Knight of the East & West
	18. Knight Rose Croix
	Council of Kadosh
	19. Grand Pontiff
Select Master	20. Master of the Symbolic Lodge
	21. Noachite or Prussian Knight
	22. Knight of the Royal Axe
	23. Chief of the Tabernacle
Super Excellent Master	24. Prince of the Tabernacle
Commandery (chivalric degrees)	25. Knight of the Brazen Serpent
Order of the Red Cross	26. Prince of Mercy
	27. Knight Commander of the Temple
	28. Knight of the Sun
Order of the Knights of Malta	29. Knight of St. Andrew
	30. Knight Kadosh
	Consistory
	31. Inspector Inquisitor
Order of Knights Templar Commandery	32. Master of the Royal Secret
	33. (Active or Honorary)

13

Is Freemasonry
a Religion?

Question 5

Is Freemasonry another religion?

There are approximately four million Masons in the United States. Many Masons are Christians and many are from other religious faiths. The question is, "Are those members of the Masonic Lodge willingly or unwillingly participating in another religion—the religion of Freemasonry?"

Most Masons are adamant in stating that Freemasonry is not a religion. Alphonse Cerza, Grand Historian of the Grand Lodge of Illinois, and many of the Masons who have written to us have argued that Freemasonry is not a religion because of the following: 1) It does not meet the definition of a religion; 2) it offers no system or teaching of salvation; 3) it has no creed, no confession of faith, no theology, and no ritual of worship; and 4) it has no symbols that are religious, like the symbols that are found in a church.[16]

To quote Bill Mankin: "All we are saying is that if you as an individual adopt the principles represented [in Freemasonry]...that you will be a better person. Not that you are going to go to heaven."[17]

Is Freemasonry a religion? Masonic author Alphonse Cerza in his book *Let There Be Light—A Study in Anti-Masonry* quoted Dr. M. W. Thomas S. Roy, Grand Master of the Grand Lodge in Massachusetts, in his address to that Lodge. Dr. Roy stated: "By any definition of religion accepted by our critics, we cannot qualify as a religion...."[18]

To see if Cerza and Roy are correct, let us begin with the definition of religion from *Webster's New World Dictionary* which defines religion as:

1) "[a] belief in a divine or superhuman power . . . to be obeyed and worshipped as the Creator and ruler of the universe; 2) expression of . . . [this] belief in conduct and ritual."[19]

Now, would any Mason deny that Freemasonry fits this definition of religion as given by Webster? Is it not true that Masonry demands belief in a Supreme Being? Would any Mason deny that their authoritative Ritual describes exactly how they are to express this belief in conduct and ceremony? In brief, can any Freemason say Masonry is not a religion? The answer is obviously "No."

But Masons do not need to take our word for it. They only need to listen to their respected Masonic authorities. The number-one author recommended by the Grand Lodges was Henry Wilson Coil and his *Masonic Encyclopedia*. Coil quotes the definition of religion given by *Funk and Wagnalls' New Standard Dictionary* (1941), and then asserts that Freemasonry fits not only this definition, but also fits the dictionary definition of what constitutes a "church." Coil states:

> Freemasonry certainly requires a belief in the existence of, and man's dependence upon, a Supreme Being to whom he is responsible. What can a church add to that, except to bring into one fellowship those who have like feelings? . . . That is exactly what the Lodge does.[20]

In other words, Coil is saying that not only is Freemasonry a religion, but Freemasonry also functions as a religion as much as a church does.

Albert Mackey in *Mackey's Revised Encyclopedia of Freemasonry*, the third most recommended author by the Grand Lodges, quotes Webster's definition of religion and then comments, "Freemasonry may rightfully claim to be called a religious institution."[21]

So is Freemasonry a religion? According to *Webster's Dictionary*, according to *Funk and Wagnalls'*, and according to leading Masonic authorities Coil and Mackey as recommended by the Grand Lodges in this country, Freemasonry *is* a religion.

Question 6
Does the Masonic Lodge teach its own plan of salvation?

Another reason Masons give as to why Freemasonry cannot be considered a religion is because "It offers no system of salvation."[22] In other words, they say Freemasonry has no teachings about how a man can go to heaven. But is this true?

Every candidate who enters the Blue Lodge is told again and again during the first three degrees of Masonry that God will reward those who do good deeds.

This can be documented by examining any Masonic manual that contains the Ritual of the first three degrees. In the manual under the explanation of the symbol of the "All-Seeing Eye"—one of the symbols for God—

you will find these words: The "All-Seeing Eye [God] . . . beholds [or "pervades"[23]] the inmost recesses of the human heart, and *will reward us according to our works.*"[24]

What is the reward Masonry teaches man will get because of his good works? Masonry teaches that God will reward man with eternal life in the "Celestial Lodge Above." This can be documented in the *Masonic Ritual and Monitor* under the explanation concerning the lambskin, or white linen apron. There it says, "He who wears the lambskin as a badge of a Mason is thereby continually reminded of *purity of life and conduct* which is *essentially necessary to his gaining admission* into that celestial Lodge above, where the Supreme Architect of the universe presides."[25]

Now does this sound to you like Freemasonry is teaching a way of salvation? If you were to hear this taught in the Lodge, wouldn't you think that Freemasonry is saying that *you* can go to the "Celestial Lodge Above" if you live a pure and honest life? Isn't that religion?

If you're a Christian, when the Lodge teaches a man that by *his* good life and by *his* good deeds God will admit him into heaven, isn't that contrary to biblical teaching? Doesn't the Bible clearly teach that salvation is *not* by a man's work—salvation is only by God's gracious provision through Jesus Christ? Ephesians 2:8,9 (NIV) very plainly says, "For it is by grace you have been saved, through faith—and this not from yourselves, it is the gift of God—not by works, so that no one can boast."

But if you are still not persuaded that Masonry is presenting a way to heaven, you should listen to Masonic authority Henry Wilson Coil, who writes the following about one of Freemasonry's religious services. In his encyclopedia he argues:

> Freemasonry has a *religious* service to commit the body of a deceased brother to the dust whence it came, and *to speed* the *liberated spirit back* to the Great Source of Light. Many Freemasons make this flight with *no other guarantee* of a safe landing than their belief in the religion of Freemasonry.[26]

Notice he says "*religion* of Freemasonry." From this evidence, all must conclude that Freemasonry *is* a religion because it does offer religious instruction and promises of how a man may get to heaven. In brief, Freemasonry *is* a religion because it presents its own plan of salvation.

So we have now seen that Freemasonry fits the definition of religion as given by Webster, and we've seen that it does offer its own plan of salvation—how a man can go to heaven.

Question 7

Does the creed of the Masonic Lodge prove that it is a religion?

Some Masons say, along with Masonic apologist Alphonse Cerza, "Freemasonry cannot be a religion because it has no creed; it has no confession of faith; it has no theology, no ritual of worship."[27] Let us now examine the claim that Freemasonry cannot be a religion because it has no creed.

Webster defines "creed" as: "a statement of belief, principles, or opinions on any subject."[28] Now, according to Webster, how can any Mason really say that he has no creed? No man can become a Mason without confessing his faith in a Supreme Being. Every Mason must believe in the immortality of the soul, give honorable service to God by practicing the secret arts of Masonry, say prayers to deity, and swear oaths of secrecy in God's name. These practices prove Masons have a definite creed.

In *Coil's Masonic Encyclopedia* we find:

> Does Freemasonry have a creed . . . or tenet . . . or dogma . . . to which all members must adhere? Does Freemasonry continually teach and insist upon a *creed, tenet and dogma*? Does it have meetings characterized by the practice of rites and ceremonies in, and by which, its creed, tenet and dogma are illustrated, by myth, symbols and allegories? If Freemasonry were not religion, what would have to be done to make it such? *Nothing would be necessary, or at least nothing but to add more of the same.*[29]

Coil goes on to point out that not only does Freemasonry *have* a creed, but that the Masonic Lodge actually functions in practice as a church. For example, he writes:

> That brings us to the real crux of the matter. The difference between a Lodge and a church is one of degree and not of kind. Some think because it [the Lodge] is not a strong or highly formalized or highly dogmatized religion, such as the Roman Catholic Church . . . it can be no religion at all. But a church of friends (Quakers) exhibits even less formality and ritual than does a Masonic Lodge.[30]

In conclusion, Coil writes, "The fact that Freemasonry is a mild religion does not mean that it is no religion."[31] Every Mason should listen to Henry Wilson Coil and stop asserting that they have no creed in the Lodge. If they do have their own creed, they should also admit as Coil does that they are practicing religion.

Question 8

Does the Masonic Lodge have its own distinct doctrinal statement like a church does?

Another reason Masons give for claiming Freemasonry is not a religion is because "we have no confession of faith in a doctrinal statement such as a church does." But is this true?

How can any Mason honestly say he has no confession of faith when he *must* believe in the teachings of the Landmarks concerning the universal

Fatherhood of God and brotherhood of man, when he *must* believe in immortality of the soul, when he *must* believe in a Supreme Being, and when he *must* believe that as a good Mason he will reside in the "Celestial Lodge Above" for all eternity? (See note 1.)

Not only do Masons have a confession of faith in their own doctrinal beliefs, but their Masonic beliefs are distinctive. It can be seen that Masonry teaches *specific* religious doctrines which are not accepted by many other religions. This means Masonry's claim of not having distinctive religious doctrines is false.

This can easily be seen from Masonry's religious teaching concerning the immortality of the soul. Just ask yourself, "Do all religions believe in the doctrine of the immortality of the soul like Masons do?" The answer is "No." Seventh-Day Adventists, Jehovah's Witnesses, Armstrongites, and Buddhists, to name just a few, do not believe in the immortality of the soul as Masons do.

Do all religious people believe in a single Supreme Being as the Masons do? No. Hindus believe in millions of gods; so do Mormons. Many Buddhists do not believe in God at all.

At death, do all religious people believe as Masons do that they will reside in the "Celestial Lodge in the Sky" for all eternity? A quick examination of other people's beliefs reveals that Hindus and Buddhists believe in the extinction of the person. Mormons believe that they can become gods themselves. Jehovah's Witnesses believe that only 144,000 will get to reside in heaven and all the rest who aren't annihilated will stay on planet earth.

In conclusion, it is absolutely clear that the Masonic Lodge does have its own distinct religious doctrinal statement just like any other religion does. That's why Masonry must be considered to be teaching religion.

Question 9

Can any Mason honestly claim that the Lodge has no theology of its own?

Another reason Masons give for believing Freemasonry is not a religion is their claim that Freemasonry has no theology. But is this true? A definition of theology ("theos" = God + "legein" = to speak) is "to speak of God." Masonry speaks of God, demands belief in God, instructs each candidate how to worship God, informs each candidate that the true name of God has been lost, and then in a later degree reveals that lost name.

For example, Masonry clearly teaches theology during the Royal Arch degree (York Rite) when it tells each candidate that the lost name for God will now be revealed to them. The name that is given is Jahbulon. This is a composite term joining Jehovah with two pagan gods—the evil Canaanite deity Baal (Jeremiah 19:5; Judges 3:7; 10:6), and the Egyptian god "On" or Osiris.[32] This equating of God with false gods is something the God of the Bible strictly forbids (see Question 16, point 2). "You shall have no other gods before me.... You shall not worship them or serve them; for I, the Lord your God, am a jealous God..." (Exodus 20:3,5); "You shall not learn to imitate the detestable things of those nations" (Deuteronomy 18:9); "Who among the gods is like you, O Lord? Who is like you—majestic in holiness, awesome in glory, working wonders?" (Exodus 15:11 NIV).

The *Oxford American Dictionary* defines theology as "a system of religion."[33] Webster defines theology as "the study of God and the relations between God and the universe.... A specific *form* or system... as expounded by a particular religion or denomination."[34] Masonry fulfills these definitions of theology. As we have seen, it has its own specific system and form of belief which clearly spells out exactly how the Masonic candidate is to perform his ceremonies before God. In the Lodge, this theological instruction is known as the Masonic Ritual.

As Joseph Fort Newton said, "Everything in Masonry has reference to God, implies God, speaks of God, points and leads to God. Not a degree, not a symbol, not an obligation, not a lecture, not a charge but finds its meaning and derives its beauty from God, the Great Architect, in whose temple all Masons are workmen."[35] Anyone who says the Masonic Lodge does not teach theology is uninformed or just plain lying.

Question 10

Is the Ritual that is practiced in every Masonic Lodge really worship?

Another reason why Masons think Freemasonry should not be considered a religion is because Masonry "has no ritual of worship" as a church does, they say. But is this true?

Webster's Dictionary defines "worship" as "a prayer... or other rite showing reverence or devotion for a deity..."—for God.[36] Do Masons have rites that instruct them how to show reverence and give devotion to God? The answer is "Yes." Masonry has 32 degrees of ritual instructing them how to live a good life before God and how to please Him. According to Webster, in actuality Masons are worshiping every time they practice the ceremonies of a Lodge. For example, Roberts admits:

> Masons walk in His [God's] presence constantly.... [In ritual the "lights"—candles] formed a triangle about the altar at which you knelt in reverence. They symbolized the presence of Deity.... The Masonic altar can be said to be one of sacrifice.... You have taken obligations [to God] that have sacrificed your self-interest forevermore.[37]

The *Standard Masonic Monitor* commands, "Let no man enter upon any great or important undertaking without first invoking the aid of Deity.... The trust of a Mason is in God...[38]

Finally, Claudy frankly confesses that "Freemasonry worships God":

> Freemasonry's Lodges are erected to God.... Symbolically, to "erect to God" means to construct something in honor, in

worship, in reverence to and for Him. Hardly is the initiate within the West Gate before he is impressed that *Freemasonry worships God....*[39]

Here again the evidence clearly shows that Masons are practicing religion when they worship God in their Lodges. As Albert Pike admitted in *Morals and Dogma*, "Masonry *is* a [system of] worship...."[40]

Question 11

Does the Masonic Lodge have religious symbols just like those found in a church or synagogue?

Another reason Masons give in claiming Freemasonry is not a religion is because it has no symbols that are religious like those symbols found in a church or a synagogue. But is this true? How can Masons say this when the building they meet in is called a "temple"? In the temple, which they believe is "sacred,"[41] they offer "prayers" to a "deity." No man can join the Masonic Lodge unless he swears belief in Masonry's "Supreme Being." The deity they pray to is called "the Great Architect of the Universe." Masons must kneel at their "sacred altar" to make their "sacred vows." Masons swear to be obedient and do the bidding of their "Worshipful Master." In the Lodge the "Worshipful Master" has hanging over his head a symbol—a big letter "G," which they are specifically instructed signifies "deity."

On the Masonic "sacred altar" is placed a "Bible," a "Koran," or another holy book called the "Volume of Sacred Law." In the third degree, every Masonic candidate is taught to accept the Masonic doctrine of the immortality of his soul, and further taught that if he is found worthy enough while on earth, his good works will earn him a place in the "Celestial Lodge Above."

How can any Mason say their symbols are not religious? What else would anyone call the big "G," hanging over the head of the "Worshipful Master," other than a religious symbol? After all, Masonry instructs each candidate that the big "G" represents the sacred name of "deity." If Masons do not want to have religious symbols, why don't they change the name of their meeting place from a "temple" to a "building"? Why do Masons swear their secret oaths at the "sacred altar" rather than at a desk? After all, *Webster's Dictionary* defines "altar" as "a raised platform where sacrifices or offerings are made *to a god* ... a table, stand, etc., used for sacred purposes in a place of worship...."[42]

If Masons do not practice religion and are not surrounded by religious symbols, what are they doing saying prayers in the Lodge? What about the funeral services the Lodge performs committing the departed Mason to the "Grand Lodge in the Sky"? Why are the secret oaths called "sacred vows"? Why call the leader of the Lodge "Worshipful Master"? Why is the Bible kissed? What is meant when the Bible, the Koran, or the Vedas are called the "Volume of Sacred Law" and placed on the altar in different

Lodges in the world? Why talk about the immortality of the soul? The reason they do all of this is because Masonry is a religion and uses many religious symbols.

We have now seen that Masonry 1) does meet the definition of religion, 2) offers its own plan of salvation, 3) has its own religious creed, 4) has its own distinct confession of faith, 5) has its own specific theology, 6) has its own unique ritual of worship, and 7) uses symbols just like those found in a church or synagogue.

All of this clearly proves *Masonry is a religion*. The only thing Masonry doesn't do is allow its members to consider it a religion.

Question 12

Should the Masonic Lodge be identified as a religion if it does not choose to identify itself as a religion?

Masonry claims it is not a religion. But because Masonry claims it is not a religion, does that change the fact that it *is* a religion? One example should be enough to show that claiming something is true when it is not is ridiculous.

Christian Science, via Mary Baker Eddy, teaches that when a man's heart stops beating and he dies, it is not really death, but only an illusion. Christian Science boldly claims there is no such thing as pain, evil, sickness, or death; there is only good. But calling pain and death an illusion (changing the labels) does not alter the feelings involved in these experiences. And if I experience the same feelings, what good does it do me to call these experiences something different?

The same is true of Freemasonry. The Lodge does not call itself a religion. But because certain people call Masonry a "fraternal organization" instead of a religion, this does not change what it is in experience. That's why two of Masonry's leading scholars, Henry Wilson Coil and Albert G. Mackey, have both concluded that Masonry is a religion.

Here is what is at stake. All Christians believe that there is only one true religion—biblical Christianity. Therefore, all other religions must be false. After all, the Bible declares, "Salvation is found in no one else [other than Jesus Christ], for there is no other name under heaven given to men by which we must be saved" (Acts 4:12 NIV). "For there is one God and one mediator between God and men, the man Christ Jesus, who gave himself as a ransom for all men—the testimony given in its proper time" (1 Timothy 2:5,6 NIV).

If the words in these verses are true, and if Masonry is another religion—and according to Mackey and Coil it meets the requirements of Webster's primary definitions of religion—then Christianity is the true religion and Freemasonry must be considered another religion and therefore a *false* religion.

Some people attempt to avoid this conclusion by saying that Freemasonry is not a religion—it is just "religious." But it would be just as sensible to say that a man has no power but is powerful; or he has no courage, but is courageous; or he has no wealth, but is wealthy; or he has no patience, but is patient; or he has no intellect, but is intellectual; or that he has no honor, but is honorable.

Others say, "But the Lodge is not a church so it is not really a religion." As we saw earlier, Coil responds to this by saying, "If Freemasonry were not a religion, such as you find in a church, what would have to be done to make it so?" He says, "Nothing would be necessary, or at least nothing but to add more of the same."[43] Coil reminds Masons that, "The fact that Freemasonry is a mild religion does not mean that it is *no* religion."[44]

If anyone still doubts that Freemasonry is a religion, we can think of no one better to quote than Albert Mackey, who in *Mackey's Revised Encyclopedia of Freemasonry* writes:

> We open and close our Lodges with prayer; we invoke the blessing of the Most High upon all our labors; we demand of our neophytes a profession of trusting belief in the existence and superintending care of God; and we teach them to bow with humility and reverence at his sacred name, while his holy law is widely opened upon our altars. . . . *It is impossible* that a Freemason can be "true and trusty" to his order unless he is a respecter of religion and an observer of religious principle.[45]

If you are a Christian involved in the Lodge, how can you in good conscience continue to practice false religion? As God's Word emphasizes:

> For what do righteousness and wickedness have in common? Or what fellowship can light have with darkness? What harmony is there between Christ and Belial? What does a believer have in common with an unbeliever? What agreement is there between the temple of God and idols? For we are the temple of the living God. As God has said: "I will live with them and walk among them, and I will be their God and they will be my people. Therefore come out from them and be separate," says the Lord (2 Corinthians 6:14-17 NIV).

Question 13

Does Freemasonry conflict with other religions such as Christianity?

As we have noted, though many Masonic authors state categorically that Freemasonry *is* a religion, they go on to claim that Masonry in no way conflicts with other religions. For example, Mackey in his encyclopedia has written:

> The *religion* of Freemasonry is not sectarian. It admits men of every creed within its hospitable bosom, rejecting none and approving none for his peculiar faith. It is not Judaism, though

there is nothing in it to offend the Jew; it is not Christianity, but there is nothing in it repugnant to the faith of a Christian. Its religion is that general one of nature and primitive revelation handed down to us from some ancient and patriarchal priesthood—in which all men may agree and in which no men can differ.[46]

This statement reveals that Masonry does have a problem with biblical Christianity. The reason is because the Bible says, "And there is salvation in no one else [other than Jesus Christ]; for there is no other name under heaven that has been given among men, by which we must be saved" (Acts 4:12).

It is nonsense to say a Christian can hold to two different religious beliefs at the same time, especially when they conflict. The Masonic Lodge says it is acceptable for men to worship God outside of Christianity. Jesus disagrees. He said, "I am the way and the truth and the life. No one comes to the Father except through me" (John 14:6 NIV).

Jesus Christ teaches that He is the way to God—not Masonry, that He is the truth—not Masonic religion, and that spiritual life is found only in Him—not in Masonic doctrine and Ritual (John 14:6). In John 15:4,5 (NIV), Jesus teaches, "Remain in me, and I will remain in you. No branch can bear fruit by itself; it must remain in the vine. Neither can you bear fruit unless you remain in me. I am the vine; you are the branches. If a man remains in me and I in him, he will bear much fruit; apart from me you can do nothing."

If a person agrees with the teaching of the Masonic Lodge, he logically must deny Christ. A person is forced to choose between the Lodge and Jesus. He cannot hold both at the same time.

In conclusion, we have clearly documented that Masonic authorities themselves say Freemasonry *must* be considered a religion because it fits any standard dictionary definition of "religion." We've also seen that Freemasonry does teach, through its emblems, its working tools, and its Ritual, how a man may go to heaven—which means Masonry has its own plan of salvation. We have noted Masonry has a distinct creed, its own confession of faith, a definite theology, and a specific Ritual of worship. Its symbols are comparable to those symbols found in any church.

Henry Wilson Coil in his 15,000-word article proving Freemasonry *is* a religion correctly concludes: "Nothing herein is intended to be an argument that Freemasonry ought to be religion. Our purpose is simply to determine what it has become, and is."[47]

Freemasonry obviously *is* a religion. Whether you are a Christian, a Jew, or of another religious persuasion, if you are also a member of the Lodge, do you realize that you are actively participating in a conflicting religion? If so, then how can you also participate in the religion of Freemasonry?

14

Where Does the Masonic Ritual Conflict with the Bible?

In the following six questions we will examine the religious teachings of Masonry and compare them with the teachings of the Bible. Remember that it is the *Ritual* of Masonry that is the supreme authority.[48] Individual Masons may disagree among themselves on various issues, but they may not disagree with the Ritual. And again, while there may be minor variations in the Ritual from state to state, these are largely insignificant. All Masonic Lodges accept the same basic interpretation of the Ritual that we will give.

During Masonic ceremonies various symbols are employed. Different symbols are used to identify the same idea or teaching—for example, both the compass and a sprig of acacia can symbolize immortality.[49]

Masonic authorities universally acknowledge the importance of the Masonic symbols. Roberts admits, "Symbolism is the life-blood of the Craft. . . . It is the principal vehicle by which the ritual teaches Masonic philosophy and moral lessons."[50] Mackey confesses, "To study the symbolism of Masonry *is the only way* to investigate its philosophy."[51] In the questions below we will show how the symbols and rituals of Masonry teach things that are contrary to Jesus Christ and the Bible.

Question 14

The Masonic Lodge teaches that all men including Christians live in spiritual darkness until they enter and become members of the Lodge. Is this biblical?

The Masonic Lodge teaches the nonbiblical view stated above in the first three degrees of the Blue Lodge, especially in the Entered Apprentice degree where the candidate is told he will now be brought out of darkness and into the light. This teaching can also be seen from the fact that *light* is the first and most important symbol in Masonry.[52] For the Mason, light symbolizes the seeking of truth. It is the goal of Masonic Ritual to bring the ignorant or unenlightened candidate to "Masonic Light."[53] Only Masonry brings light to the candidate, therefore only the Mason knows the truth.[54] This means all non-Masons exist in spiritual darkness.

Proof that Masonry teaches this concept can be found by examining the Ritual of the first degree of Masonry. In the first degree, each candidate is instructed, "You have long been in darkness, and now seek to be brought to light." In the Ritual, when the candidate stands at the anteroom door, he knocks three times. On the other side of the door, the Junior Deacon also knocks three times and opens the door. He then says, "Who goes there?" The answer given by his conductor (the Senior Steward) is given in the Ritual itself:

> Mr. [Peter Smith], who has long been in darkness, and now seeks to be brought to light, and to receive a part in the rights and benefits of this Worshipful Lodge, erected to God. . . .[55]

During our telecast, former Worshipful Master Jack Harris quoted Albert Mackey, who held the highest positions Masonry has to offer. Mackey was a thirty-third degree Mason and Secretary General of the Supreme Council of the Thirty-Third Degree Scottish Rite, a position he held for a great many years. In his book, *The Manual of the Lodge*, Mackey describes the candidate who seeks to enter the Masonic Lodge:

> There he stands without [outside] our portals, on the threshold of his new Masonic life, in darkness, helplessness and ignorance. Having been wandering amid the errors and covered over with the pollutions of the outer and profane world, he comes inquiringly to our door, seeking the new birth, and asking a withdrawal of the veil which conceals divine truth from his uninitiated sight.[56]

But how can any Christian take the first degree of Masonry and say that he has "long been in darkness, and now seeks to be brought to light"? Is it really true that Christians are still in darkness and the only way they can enter the light is to join the Masonic Lodge? When you became a Christian, weren't you rescued out of darkness? Let's look at what the Bible says.

Jesus said, "I have come into the world as a light, *so that no one who believes in me should stay in darkness*" (John 12:46 NIV, emphasis added). He also said, "I am the light of the world. Whoever follows me will *never walk in darkness*, but will have the light of life" (John 8:12 NIV). Here Jesus teaches that *He* is the Light. He teaches that believing in *Him* removes spiritual darkness; He does not teach that any *ritual*, Masonic or other, removes darkness.

Colossians 1:12-14 (NIV) says, "Giving thanks to the Father, who has qualified you to share in the inheritance of the saints in the kingdom of light. For *he has rescued us from the dominion of darkness and brought us into the kingdom of the Son he loves*, in whom we have redemption, the forgiveness of sins" (emphasis added).

Another example is Ephesians 5:8, where the apostle Paul writes, "For you were *once darkness, but now you are light* in the Lord. Live as children of light (for the fruit of the light consists in all goodness, righteousness and truth) and find out what pleases the Lord. *Have nothing to do with the fruitless deeds of darkness, but rather expose them.* For it is shameful even to mention what the disobedient do in secret" (Ephesians 5:8-12 NIV, emphasis added).

Jesus and the Bible plainly teach that any person who believes in Him is no longer in darkness. If you are a Christian, how then could you enter the Masonic Lodge and swear that you are still in darkness and seeking light? In the first degree of Masonry, didn't you say that which is directly contrary to what your Lord and the Scriptures teach?

In Henry Wilson Coil's *Masonic Encyclopedia* he writes, "Light is everywhere the symbol of intelligence, information, knowledge, and truth and is opposed to darkness which symbolizes ignorance and evil. So, in the ceremonies, the candidate is said to be brought from darkness to light."[57]

But if Coil is right, then no Christian should take the vows of the Lodge, confessing that he does not have the truth and is living in spiritual ignorance and evil. The Scriptures clearly state that Christians "are *not* in darkness" and are "all sons of the light and sons of the day. We do not belong to the night or to the darkness" (1 Thessalonians 5:4,5 NIV, emphasis added).

How can a Christian participate in rituals and promote another religion that denies and opposes the teachings of Christ? Jesus Himself asks, "And why do you call Me, 'Lord, Lord,' and not do what I say?" (Luke 6:46).

Question 15

Masons teach and believe in a universal Fatherhood of God and brotherhood of man. Is this biblical?

The Masonic Lodge teaches the nonbiblical view stated above in their first, second, and third degrees, but especially in the prayer of the Entered Apprentice and during their ceremony in the third degree concerning the legend of Hiram Abiff.[58] Specifically, the Masonic Lodge teaches its belief in the unity and universality of all men as "one family" accepted by God regardless of race, religion, or creed.[59] This Masonic teaching sounds good to most people. But if we examine it carefully, does the Bible really teach the concept of the universal Fatherhood of God and brotherhood of man, so that all men are automatically sons of God? Does the Bible teach that all men are in good standing before God even if they are ignoring God's Son?

The Bible does *not* teach any of the above, but Masonry *does*. During the ritual of the first three degrees, every Mason is introduced to the Masonic teaching concerning the Fatherhood of God. For example, in his discussion of the ritual encompassing the Masonic legend of Hiram Abiff, Allan E. Roberts in his *The Craft and Its Symbols: Opening the Door to Masonic Symbolism* instructs new candidates that "through these teachings the Mason will put into practice the brotherhood of man under the Fatherhood of God. In doing so, he will develop his character and personality in the image of the Great Architect of the Universe."[60]

Every man who has gone through the first degree of Freemasonry remembers the following prayer. It can be found in the *Standard Masonic Ritual and Monitor* of every state for the first degree (Entered Apprentice) of the Blue Lodge:

> Vouchsafe Thine aid, *Almighty Father of the universe*, to this our present convention; and grant that this candidate for Masonry may dedicate and devote his life to thy service, and become a true and faithful brother among us! Endue him with a competency of thy divine wisdom, that, by the secrets of our art, he may be better enabled to display the beauties of brotherly love, relief, and truth, to the honor of thy holy name. Amen.[61]

Masonic authority Carl Claudy admits that this prayer, at the start of the Masonic journey, forms the foundation of the Craft: "Among the most beautiful of Freemasonry's symbols, these express at the very beginning the fundamental principle of Freemasonry: the Fatherhood of God, and the Brotherhood of man."[62]

The Masonic temple itself is said to symbolize the idea of the harmony between the Fatherhood of God and brotherhood of man. For example, "The temple that the Craft is building is the unification and the harmonizing of the entire human family. This is summed up for us in the well-known lines: 'God hath made mankind one vast brotherhood, Himself their Master, and the world His Lodge.' "[63] God Himself is said to be the ultimate "W.M. [Worshipful Master] working through His supervising Master Masons."[64]

But the Bible does not teach the universal Fatherhood of God (that all Masons are in good standing with God and a part of His Lodge) and brotherhood of man (that all men can live in harmony even though they hold different religious beliefs). Scripture clearly teaches that sinful men only become children of God and attain favorable standing before Him when they place their faith in Jesus Christ as their Savior.

The following Scriptures prove that, apart from Christ, men may be the creation of God, but they are not the *spiritual* "sons" or "children" of God.

> But *as many as received Him*, to them He gave the right to become children of God, even to those who believe in His name (John 1:12, emphasis added).

> [Jesus said] If I speak truth, why do you not believe Me? He who is of God hears the words of God; for this reason you do

not hear them, *because you are not of God* (John 8:46,47, emphasis added).

The apostle Paul describes the condition of all men before God prior to their faith in Christ:

> And [you] were by nature *children of wrath,* even as the rest. . . . Remember that you were at that time *separate from Christ . . .* and strangers to the covenants of promise, *having no hope* and *without God in the world* (Ephesians 2:3,12, emphasis added).

> [Men] being darkened in their understanding, *excluded from the life of God,* because of the ignorance that is in them, because of the hardness of their heart (Ephesians 4:18, emphasis added).

> But if anyone does not have the Spirit of Christ, *he does not belong to Him* (Romans 8:9, emphasis added).

> Whoever believes in the Son has eternal life, but whoever rejects the Son will not see life, *for God's wrath remains on him* (John 3:36 NIV, emphasis added).

In Jesus' prayer to His Father, He describes the world's natural condition: "The world has *not* known Thee" (John 17:25, emphasis added). The Bible also teaches that someday Christ will return, "dealing out retribution to those *who do not know God . . .*" (2 Thessalonians 1:8, emphasis added). When Masonry teaches that all men are already saved because of the Fatherhood of God and brotherhood of man, they are effectively inhibiting and preventing Masons from coming to a personal knowledge of Jesus Christ and having their sins forgiven. In this sense, Masonry is unbiblical (John 3:16).

In the above verses, notice first of all that if Jesus gives to those who believe on Him the right to become children of God, then all men were not children of God before that. This means that men are not *born* children of God, as Masonry teaches, and that God is not the Father of all men—spiritually or relationally.

Why? It seems Masonry has forgotten or ignores the account of man's Fall in Genesis—of Adam and Eve in the garden. The Bible teaches that man, through disobedience to God, sinned and broke his spiritual relationship with God. All men, although created by God, are not in a right relationship with God. Proof of this can be found in the book of Acts where we read, "The God who made the world and all things in it . . . is Lord of heaven and earth. . . . Being then the offspring of God . . ." (Acts 17:24,29). Notice that because God is the Creator, all men may be said to be His children, His offspring, in the sense of His *creating* them. But they are not His children *relationally or spiritually.* Here is the problem. Look at what God says to His children. God now "commands all people everywhere to repent" (Acts 17:30 NIV). Repentance means we must be willing to turn away from our beliefs and reliance on self and turn to and fully rely upon Christ's salvation provided for us.

How is it possible for a Christian to promote and defend a false teaching which says that all sinful men regardless of their relationship to Christ will go to heaven? The Scripture says a Christian should know better.

The Scriptures instruct Christians to proclaim that only through Christ will men receive forgiveness of their sins and be able to go to heaven. Jesus said: "I am the way, and the truth, and the life; no one comes to the Father, but through Me" (John 14:6).

Question 16

Masonry teaches that the God of the Bible is the God of the Masonic Lodge. Is this true?

Masonry teaches at least three things about its God.

1. The Masonic God is called the Great Architect of the Universe (G.A.O.T.U.) but must remain undefined.
Coil's Masonic Encyclopedia states the following about God:

> Men have to decide whether they want a God like the ancient Hebrew Jahweh, a partisan tribal god, with whom they can talk and argue and from whom they can hide if necessary, or a boundless, eternal, universal, undenominational, and international Divine Spirit, so vastly removed from the speck called man, that he cannot be known, named or approached. So soon as man begins to laud his God and endow him with the most perfect human attributes such as justice, mercy, beneficence, etc., the Divine Essence is depreciated and despoiled.... The Masonic test is *a Supreme Being*, and any qualification added is an innovation and distortion.... Monotheism... violates Masonic principles, for it requires belief in a specific kind of Supreme Deity.[65]

At one level, Masonry teaches that its God must remain undefined and unknowable. In keeping God undefined and unknowable, Masonry believes it can then "accept" all men's ideas of God. Masonry believes that by leaving God undefined, it can claim that it accepts the God of the Muslims, Hindus, Buddhists, Jews, Mormons, etc. What Masonry means is that its "boundless Divine Spirit" is really the one true God that all men worship.

But this is completely false and is actually dishonest. The God of Masonry does have certain characteristics—he is single (unitarian, not trinitarian), deistic,[66] the "Life Force of Nature,"[67] and his secret name and true nature are described by reference to ancient evil and pagan gods and beliefs.[68]

The simple fact is that the God or gods of Buddhism, Hinduism, Islam, Judaism, Christianity, Animism, and all the other religions of the world are *not* the same God. To say that all gods are the same or that all religions teach the same fundamental truths is intellectual schizophrenia, *disrespect* for each and all religions, and *deception* to those to whom one teaches such falsehood.

Concepts of God throughout the world all conflict and disagree. For example, the God of Christianity, *Jehovah*, is infinite, personal, triune, loving, and holy. The deity of the Muslims, *Allah*, is unitarian (not triune); he is merciful, but he is not necessarily loving or holy. The deity of the Hindus, *Brahman*, is impersonal and monistic (neither unitarian nor triune) or polytheistic (a belief in thousands of finite gods, both good and evil). Buddhism is either polytheistic (believing *Buddha* is God and that there are hundreds of other good and evil gods) or completely *nontheistic*, claiming *there is no God*. Buddhism replaces God with a confusing state of being called *Nirvana*. Mormonism is different from all the above in that it is *henotheistic*—accepting belief in one central deity (*Elohim*) but accepting many other deities as well. (See Part 1.)

Masonry is wrong in teaching that all religions ultimately have the same concept of God. Masonry is also wrong in teaching that the God of all religions is the Masonic deity.[69] The gods of the above religions are not the same. All the above religions teach that God is either personal, impersonal, holy, evil, unitarian, trinitarian, monistic, infinite, finite, loving, not loving, existent, nonexistent, etc.

So when Masonry claims that the God all men worship is the God of Masonry, this can't possibly be true. Masonry has a *distinct* concept of God that *disagrees* with almost all of these other religions' specific concepts of God.

If we compare the God of the Bible with the God taught in the Masonic Lodge, we are faced with irreconcilable differences. As Martin L. Wagner has correctly stated, "This Great Architect as conceived by Freemasons is not identical with the Jehovah of Christianity, but . . . is another and distinct entity."[70] He says they "are entirely separate and different, mutually exclusive and no syncretism can harmonize them."[71]

Masonic authority Albert Pike admits, "If our conceptions of God are those of the ignorant, narrow-minded, and vindictive Israelite . . . we feel that it is an affront and an indignity to him [God], to conceive of him as cruel, shortsighted, capricious, and unjust; as a jealous, an angry, and vindictive Being."[72]

Pike later referred to the ignorance and stupidity of most Christians and confessed: "The God of nineteen-twentieths of the Christian world is only Bel [Baal], Molach, Zeus, or at best Osiris, Mythras or Adonai, under another name, worshipped with the old pagan ceremonies and ritualistic formulas. . . ."[73]

When Masons claim that the Lodge is "tolerant" of all faiths and accepts the God that all men worship, it is really engaging in dishonesty. The truth is that Masonry does not accept the God of any religion but changes each religion's belief in God into the strange, distinct Masonic view of God as the Great Architect of the Universe (G.A.O.T.U.).[74] Masonry falsely *claims* it is tolerant of other beliefs in order to attract men of different religious beliefs into becoming Masons. In actuality, a true Mason must forfeit his own religious beliefs in who God is and accept the new God of Masonry.[75]

2. God's secret name is "Jahbulon."

The Masonic Lodge teaches in the Royal Arch degree that it knows the true name of God. The candidate is instructed that from now on the true name of God is Jahbulon.

The candidate is clearly instructed in his Masonic manual that the term "Jahbulon" is a composite term for Jehovah (Jah), Baal (Bul or Bel), and "On," a possible reference to the Egyptian god Osiris.[76]

Masonic authorities such as Coil[77] and the *Masonic Ritual and Monitor*[78] admit that "Bul" or "Bel" refers to the Assyrian or Canaanite deity Baal and that "On" refers to the Egyptian deity. Wagner reveals the Masonic goal in this pagan trinity:

> In this compound name an attempt is made to show by a co-ordination of divine names . . . the unity, identity and harmony of the Hebrew, Assyrian and Egyptian god-ideas, and the harmony of the Royal Arch religion with these ancient religions. This Masonic "unity of God" is peculiar. It is the doctrine that the different names of gods as Brahma, Jehovah, Baal, Bel, Om, On, etc., all denote the generative [phallic] principle, and that all religions are essentially the same in their ideas of the divine.[79]

But to equate Jehovah with the pagan god Baal—a god so evil that he led the Israelites into human sacrifice and other terrible vices—is blasphemous. Anyone who studies how evil Baal was in the Old Testament can see this clearly.[80] For example:

> They forsook all the commands of the Lord their God . . . they worshiped Baal. They sacrificed their sons and daughters in the fire . . . and sold themselves to do evil in the eyes of the Lord, provoking him to anger (2 Kings 17:16,17 NIV).

> They built high places [altars] for Baal . . . to sacrifice their sons and daughters to Molech, though I never commanded, nor did it enter my mind, that they should do such a detestable thing . . . (Jeremiah 32:35 NIV).

> Among the prophets . . . I saw this repulsive thing: They prophesied by Baal and led my people Israel astray (Jeremiah 23:13 NIV).

Baal was so evil a deity that to find the name of the one, true, holy God, Jehovah, linked with Baal and Osiris in the rites of Masonry is blasphemous. God says, "Those who honor Me, I will honor" (1 Samuel 2:30).

117

The apostle Paul writes, "To Him [God] be honor and eternal dominion" (1 Timothy 6:16). If you are a Christian, according to Scripture is it honoring to God to participate in a rite that maligns His divine name by combining it with the names of evil gods? Didn't God's severe judgment fall upon Israel because she combined worship of Jehovah with the worship of Baal and other pagan gods? Didn't God's judgment fall because of teachings like those found in Masonry? As former Past Master Mason Edmond Ronayne confesses: "The very religious philosophy and false worship which caused Jehovah to destroy His own temple, and banish into captivity His ancient people, are precisely the same philosophy and worship which modern Masons profess shall fit them for the glories of heaven."[81]

3. Masonry teaches that its God is not the Christian God.

Masonry teaches that God is one person only (unitarian),[82] while Christianity teaches that God is triune, not unitarian. An article by G. A. Kenderdine, "The Idea of God in Masonry," cited in the Masonic magazine *The New Age* on pages 269ff. states, "Masonry holds and teaches that with all and above all there is God, *not* essentially a Christian Triune God."[83]

Masonry teaches that God is an amalgamation of all gods: "[The Mason] may name Him [God] as he will, think of Him as he pleases; make Him impersonal law or personal and anthropomorphic; Freemasonry cares not.... God, Great Architect of the universe, Grand Artificer, Grand Master of the Grand Lodge above, Jehovah, Allah, Buddha, Brahma, Vishnu, Shiva, or Great Geometer...."[84] But the Bible teaches that the Christian God alone is the one true God—He is not an amalgamation of all gods:

> O Lord, the God of Israel, there is no god like Thee in heaven or on earth... (2 Chronicles 6:14).

> I am the Lord, that is My name; I will not give My glory to another (Isaiah 42:8).

> Acknowledge and take to heart this day that the Lord is God in heaven above and on the earth below. There is no other (Deuteronomy 4:39 NIV).

4. Masonry also denies the biblical teaching on Jesus Christ.

Albert Pike taught that Masonry held that Jesus Christ was only a man and not God:

> It reverences all the great reformers. It sees in Moses, the Lawgiver of the Jews, in Confucius and Zoroaster, in Jesus of Nazareth, and in the Arabian Iconoclast, Great Teachers of Morality, and Eminent Reformers, if no more....[85]

Masonry claims that it does not offend a Christian's belief about Jesus Christ. For example: "We do not say to Christians that Christ was a mere man, whose life's story is only a revival of similar older [pagan] stories. To do any of these things would be irreverent. We utter no such words."[86] But Masonry *does* teach that Jesus Christ was merely a man.[87] The important Masonic Ritual called the Maundy Thursday Ritual of the chapter of Rose Croix states officially, "We meet this day to commemorate the death [of Jesus], not as inspired or divine, for this is not for us to decide."[88]

In his spiritual darkness or ignorance, an individual Christian Mason may choose to believe that Jesus was God and Savior of the world, but this is not Masonic truth. Those who consider themselves enlightened Masons hope that their unenlightened brethren will realize that all specific dogmas about Christ are in error. As Clausen emphasizes, it is important to "strip from all religions their orthodox tenets, legends, allegories and dogmas."[89] This is why the Masonic scholar Albert Pike asserts that Jesus was "a great teacher of morality"—but nothing more.[90]

So it is neither fair nor true for Masons to say that Masonry does not offend Christians by teaching that Jesus was only a man. This is exactly what it teaches. Why does Masonry say that Christ was only a man and thereby offend the beliefs of Christians? It does this because it does not wish to offend the religious sensibilities of those Masons who are members of other faiths which deny that Jesus is the only incarnation of God and Savior of the world. For example, the unique nature and mission of Christ is denied by Hindus, Buddhists, Muslims, Jews, etc. In order to not offend these people, Masonry offends Christians.

This is why nowhere in Masonic literature will you find Jesus called God or said to be the world's Savior who died for man's sin. To portray Him in such a light would "offend" men, and Masonry wishes to offend no one. The necessity for this approach can be found in the fundamental doctrines or Landmarks of Masonry (the Fatherhood of God, the brotherhood of man, and the immortality of the soul, Masonically interpreted). These doctrines *presume beforehand* that there is neither reason nor necessity that Jesus should be unique either as to His Person (God) or His mission (Savior). Thus, Masonry teaches that man already has a perfect standing with God. All men and women are guaranteed eternal life regardless of their personal religious beliefs. As a result, there is no need for God to incarnate (Philippians 2:1-8) in order to die for the world's sin (1 John 2:2) because the teachings of Masonry *assume* all people are saved or redeemed to begin with.

This is why Masonry completely excludes all particular biblical teachings about Christ such as His incarnation, redemptive mission, death, and resurrection. In fact, there is no biblical truth about Jesus Christ that is affirmed by Masonry as one of their Landmarks. This is why former Mason Edmond Ronayne confesses:

> Freemasonry "carefully excludes" the Lord Jesus Christ from the Lodge and chapter, repudiates his mediatorship, rejects his atonement, denies and disowns his gospel, frowns upon his religion and his church, ignores the Holy Spirit, and

sets up for itself a spiritual empire, a religious theocracy, at the head of which it places the G.A.O.T.U.—the god of nature— and from which the one only living and true God is expelled by resolution. . . .[91]

The Bible clearly teaches that Jesus Christ is God:

> In the beginning was the Word, and the Word was with God and the Word was God. . . . And the Word became flesh, and dwelt among us . . . (John 1:1,14).
>
> Looking for the blessed hope and the appearing of the glory of our great God and Savior, Christ Jesus (Titus 2:13).

Because Jesus Christ is God, He will one day judge all the world, including all Masons and other men:

> For not even the Father judges any one, but He has given all judgment to the Son, in order that all may honor the Son, even as they honor the Father. He who does not honor the Son does not honor the Father who sent Him (John 5:22,23).
>
> But when the Son of Man comes in His glory, and all the angels with Him, then He will sit on His glorious throne. And all the nations will be gathered before Him; and He will separate them from one another, as the shepherd separates the sheep from the goats. . . . Then the King will say to those on His right, "Come, you who are blessed of My Father, inherit the kingdom prepared for you from the foundation of the world." . . . Then He will also say to those on His left, "Depart from Me, accursed ones, into the eternal fire which has been prepared for the devil and his angels." . . . And these will go away into eternal punishment, but the righteous into eternal life (Matthew 25:31-34,41,46).
>
> And there is salvation in no one else; for there is no other name under heaven that has been given among men, by which we must be saved (Acts 4:12).

All of these teachings of Jesus in the Bible prove that Masonry is wrong in its teaching about Jesus Christ. How then can a Christian who claims to believe in Jesus as his Savior continue to support the false religion that denies his Lord? Did not Jesus Himself say, "Why do you call Me, 'Lord, Lord,' and not do what I say?" (Luke 6:46). Did not even Jesus warn, "But whoever shall deny Me before men, I will also deny him before My Father who is in heaven" (Matthew 10:33)? And did He not say, "Not every one who says to Me, 'Lord, Lord,' will enter the kingdom of heaven; but he who does the will of My Father who is in heaven" (Matthew 7:21)?

Masonic Ritual and oath demands that the Christian Mason's first allegiance is to Masonry, not to Jesus Christ. Who then is the "Lord" of the Christian Mason?

In conclusion, Masonry is opposed to the Christian God. One of the leading Masonic scholars, Albert Pike, describes Freemasonry as follows: "Masonry, around whose altars the Christian, the Hebrew, the Moslem, the Brahmin, the followers of Confucius and Zoroaster can assemble as brethren and unite in prayer *to the one God who is above all the Baalim....*"[92] Notice that the term "Baalim" which refers to the false gods and idols that men worship[93] is also applied to the Christian religion. That means Christianity is considered to be as false a religion as all the rest.

Masonry only claims to be tolerant of the concepts of God found in other religions. In reality, it sees them as inferior to its own concept of God.[94] But then how is it possible for a Christian to support Masonry when it denies the true God, blasphemes Him, and leads people to worship a false God? Christians are exhorted to "live a life worthy of the Lord and . . . please him in every way . . . growing in the knowledge of God" (Colossians 1:10 NIV). They cannot do this by remaining members of the Masonic Lodge.

If Jesus came back today or you died and faced Him, how would you explain to Him why you continued to uphold the beliefs of an organization that rejects and denies Him?

Question 17

The Masonic Lodge teaches that the Bible is only a symbol of the will of God and not to be literally obeyed. Is this true?

On the Masonic altar lie the square and compass and the Volume of Sacred Law. The Volume of Sacred Law is a *symbol* for the will of God.

Masonry has at least four distinct teachings about the Bible.

1. *The Bible is a piece of Lodge furniture,* a great "light" upon which the candidate obligates himself to Masonry.[95]

2. *The Bible is only a symbol of the will of God.* Masonry teaches that the actual contents of the Bible are *not* the Word of God. In *Coil's Masonic Encyclopedia* we read, "The prevailing Masonic opinion is that the Bible is only a symbol of Divine Will, Law, or Revelation, and not that its *contents* are Divine Law, inspired, or revealed. So far, no responsible authority has held that a Freemason must believe the Bible or any part of it."[96]

3. *The Bibles of other faiths are equally valid for the Mason. Mackey's Revised Encyclopedia of Freemasonry* states:

> The Bible is used among Freemasons as a symbol of the will of God, however it may be expressed. Therefore, whatever to any people expresses that will [of God] may be used as a

121

substitute for the Bible in a Masonic Lodge. Thus, in a Lodge consisting entirely of Jews, the Old Testament alone may be placed upon the altar, and Turkish Freemasons [Muslims] make use of the Koran. Whether it be the Gospels to the Christian, the Pentateuch to the Israelite, the Koran to the Mussulman, [sic; Muslim] or the Vedas to the Brahman, it everywhere Masonically conveys the same idea—that of the symbolism of the Divine Will revealed to man.[97]

4. *The Bible is only a part of the "revelation" of God.* In the Holman "Temple Illustrated Edition of the Holy Bible" Masonic leader Reverend Joseph Fort Newton wrote:

Thus, by the very honor which Masonry pays to the Bible, it teaches us to revere every book of faith . . . joining hands with the man of Islam as he takes oath on the Koran, and with the Hindu as he makes covenant with God upon the book that he loves best. . . . [Masonry] invites to its altar men of all faiths, knowing that, if they use different names for "the nameless one of a hundred names" they are yet praying to the one God and Father of all; knowing, also, that while they read different volumes, they are in fact reading the same vast Book of the Faith of Man as revealed in the struggle and sorrow of the race in its quest of God.[98]

In conclusion, virtually all Masonic authorities "establish three things: 1) that the Bible is only a symbol, 2) that a Mason is not required to believe its teachings, and 3) that some other book may be substituted for it."[99]

By contrast, this is what Jesus and the apostles taught about the Bible:

He who rejects Me, and does not receive My sayings, has one who judges him; the word I spoke is what will judge him at the last day. For I did not speak on my own initiative, but the Father Himself who sent Me has given Me commandment what to say, and what to speak . . . (John 12:48-50).

All Scripture is inspired by God and profitable for teaching, for reproof, for correction, for training in righteousness; that the man of God may be adequate, equipped for every good work (2 Timothy 3:16,17).

How can a Christian Mason, who claims to believe that the Bible is the literal Word of God, help to promote an organization that denies the Bible is God's Word and denies Jesus' teachings on the Bible? Scripture tells us we are to live "worthy of the God who calls you into His own kingdom and glory" (1 Thessalonians 2:12).

Question 18

The Masonic Lodge teaches that salvation and residence in the "Celestial Lodge Above" may be gained by Masons doing good works. Is this biblical?

By many different symbols Masonry teaches a doctrine of "works salvation"—that by personal merit and works of righteousness, the Masonic initiate will become worthy of salvation and eternal life. The candidate is told again and again that God will be gracious and reward those who build their character and do good deeds.

For example, the symbol of the "Sword Pointing to a Naked Heart" is said to "pointedly remind us that God will reward us according to what we do in this life."[100] In a similar fashion, the All-Seeing Eye, which symbolizes God, "pervades the inmost recesses of the human Heart, and will reward us according to our merits."[101]

The white apron or lambskin is "a symbol of Innocence, Purity, and Honor."[102] This is because, "The Lamb has in all ages been deemed an emblem of innocence. The lambskin is therefore to remind you of that purity of life and conduct which is *so essentially necessary* to your gaining admission to the Celestial Lodge Above, where the Supreme Architect of the universe presides."[103] This same teaching is found in the Holman edition of the Holy Bible that is published for Masons.[104] Mackey states of the apron: "The pure, unspotted lambskin apron is, then, in Masonry, symbolic of that perfection of body and purity of mind which are essential qualifications in all who would participate in its sacred mysteries."[105]

The compass, the sprig of acacia, the scythe, and other symbols are all said to symbolize the immortality of the soul.[106] All of this is why Jack Harris concluded:

> In all the rituals that I taught for eleven years, Masonry did teach how to get to heaven. They taught it with the apron that I wore, by my purity, life and conduct. They taught it in the Hiram Abiff legend of the third degree [symbolizing] the immortality of the soul. Through all their writings they say they are teaching the immortality of the soul to the Mason. But the Word of God tells me that the only way to have immortal life is through the Person of Jesus Christ. Never at any Masonic ritual did they point out that Jesus is the way of salvation.[107]

This is why Albert Pike says, "We must have faith in ourselves. . . ."[108] And this is why the charge to the Master Mason at his raising states, "Let all the energies of our souls and the perfection of our minds be employed in attaining the approbation of the Grand Master on high, so that when we come to die . . . we gain the favor of a speedy entrance to the Grand Lodge on high, where the G.A.O.T.U. forever presides, and where, seated at his right hand, he may be pleased to pronounce us upright men and Masons, fitly prepared [for heaven]."[109]

If you were to hear all of this in the Lodge, wouldn't you think that Freemasonry is clearly teaching that *you* can go to the "Celestial Lodge Above" if you live a pure and honest life? Isn't that "works" salvation? And if you're a Christian, when the Lodge teaches a man that by his good life and by his good deeds God will admit him into heaven, isn't that contrary to your Christian teaching?

In conclusion, there is absolutely no doubt that Masonry teaches that a Mason will inherit eternal life by his conduct and his personal merit. Masonry thus teaches a system of salvation by personal merit and good works. This concept of salvation is one which the Bible calls "another gospel." It is so contrary to God's way of salvation that Scripture places it under a divine curse (Galatians 1:6-8).

The following Scriptures give the biblical position on how a man gains eternal life:

> To the man who does not work but trusts God who justifies the wicked, his faith is credited as righteousness (Romans 4:5 NIV).

> For by grace you have been saved through faith; and that not of yourselves, it is the gift of God; not as a result of works, that no one should boast (Ephesians 2:8,9).

> And this is the testimony: God has given us eternal life, and this life is in his Son. He who has the Son has life; he who does not have the Son of God does not have life (1 John 5:11,12 NIV).

All of these verses in the Bible teach that salvation is a *gift* of God. Salvation comes solely by the grace [unmerited favor] of God, not by anything we can do to earn God's favor or by personal righteousness. By being a part of the Lodge, a Christian Mason is supporting "another Gospel," a false system of salvation that lies to people about how they may be saved.

If you are a true believer in Jesus Christ realizing this, shouldn't you obey the biblical admonition in 2 Corinthians 6:17 (NIV): "Therefore come out from them and be separate, says the Lord"?

Question 19

If a Mason has sworn allegiance to the Lodge, should he break his oaths?

God tells us to "have nothing to do with the fruitless deeds of darkness, but rather expose them. For it is shameful even to mention what the disobedient do in secret" (Ephesians 5:11,12 NIV).

But once a person is already a Mason, what should he do if he realizes that Masonry is wrong and sinful? What can someone do who has already taken the oath "for all time"?[110] Is that person bound to keep his oath? Here is what the Bible advises you to do:

> If a person swears thoughtlessly with his lips to do evil or to do good, in whatever manner a man may speak thoughtlessly with an oath, and it is hidden from him, and then he comes to know it, he will be guilty in one of these. So it shall be when he becomes guilty in one of these, that he shall confess that in which he has sinned. He shall also bring his guilt offering to the Lord for his sin which he has committed. . . . So the priest shall make atonement on his behalf for his sin which he has committed, and it shall be forgiven him (Leviticus 5:4-6,10).

The Bible tells every person that if he swears an oath, if the implications are hidden from him, when he understands the implication and finds himself guilty of offending God's moral law, then he is guilty, and is to confess that he has sinned and to repent.

In the Old Testament a person was to go to the priest and confess that he had sinned and offer a sacrifice for atonement. Today, a Christian is to come to his High Priest, the Lord Jesus Christ, who has died on the cross for his sin; he is to acknowledge that he is guilty of swearing wrongly and repent of his oath, ask for forgiveness, and acknowledge that he will obey God in following the truth.

The Bible says, "If we confess our sins, he is faithful and just and will forgive us our sins and purify us from all unrighteousness" (1 John 1:9 NIV).

It is the duty of every Christian to break and renounce any evil oath that binds him to disobeying God. By taking the Masonic oaths, a person swears to uphold Masonry and all its teachings (whether he knows all of them or not). Swearing to uphold all that is included in the Masonic oaths is sinful, unscriptural, and should not be a part of the Christian's life for the following reasons:

1) They make a Christian man swear by God to doctrines which God has pronounced false and sinful. For example, Masonry teaches the false doctrine of "the Fatherhood of God," whereas Jesus taught that only to those who receive Him, who believe in His name, "He [gives] the right to become children of God" (John 1:12).

2) The Christian man swears to accept and promote the Masonic lie that Jesus is just one of many equally revered prophets in the world. He does this when agreeing that all religions can lead a man to God. But the Bible records Jesus' true words: "I am the way, and the truth, and the life. No one comes to the Father but through Me" (John 14:6).

3) The Christian swears that he is approaching the Lodge while in spiritual ignorance and moral darkness, when the Bible says Christians are children of light and are indwelt by the Light of the world. The Bible says, "For you were once darkness, but now you are light in the Lord" (Ephesians 5:8 NIV).

4) The Christian falsely swears that the God of the Bible is equally present in all religions. But the Bible says, "I am the first and I am the last, and there is no God besides Me" (Isaiah 44:6).

5) By swearing the Masonic oath, Christians are perpetuating a false gospel to other Lodge members who look only to the gospel of Masonry to get them to heaven. But the Bible says, "But even if we or an angel from heaven should preach a gospel other than the one we preached to you, let him be eternally condemned!" (Galatians 1:8 NIV).

The Scripture warns:

> Do not be yoked together with unbelievers. For what do righteousness and wickedness have in common? Or what fellowship can light have with darkness? What harmony is there between Christ and Belial? What does a believer have in common with an unbeliever? What agreement is there between the temple of God and idols? For we are the temple of the living God. As God has said: "I will live with them and walk with them, and I will be their God, and they will be my people. Therefore come out from them and be separate," says the Lord. "Touch no unclean thing, and I will receive you" (2 Corinthians 6:14-17 NIV).

It is clearly the Christian's duty to break and renounce any evil oath that binds him in sin: "Have nothing to do with the fruitless deeds of darkness, but rather expose them" (Ephesians 5:11 NIV). Every Christian Lodge member should renounce his Masonic oath and confess it as a sin to his Lord. The Lord promises to forgive each one who will do so. ("If we confess our sins, He is faithful and just to forgive us our sins . . ."—1 John 1:9.) In this way the Chrisitan will stop adding his influence to the sins of the Lodge whose false religion results in the damnation of so many souls (John 3:18,36; 8:24; 12:48, cf. 3:6-8).

Right now confess to God that you have ignorantly taken a vow against Him and His teachings and ask His forgiveness. Then notify your Lodge in writing that you have decided to leave the Lodge. Tell them you believe that their teaching and their vows are not biblical, and as a Christian you can no longer participate according to 2 Corinthians 6:14-18 and Ephesians 5:8-17.

Conclusion

If you are a Mason or a Christian Mason, what should you do?

We have proven that Masonry is a religion. Masonry is a religion with specific teachings on specific topics which conflict with other religions. In particular, Masonry conflicts with Christian teaching.

A Mason who is not a Christian needs to ask himself the following: If Masonry *is* a religion, is it the *true* religion? Will it *truly* lead me to heaven? Does it *truly* honor and glorify God? Or has Masonry merely invented a new God and a new religion in order to defend the particular beliefs of Masonry?

In his encyclopedia, Coil confesses that *if* the idea that Masonry alone will get one to heaven is "a false hope," then Masonry should abandon that hope "and devote its attention to activities where it is sure of its ground and its authority."[111] But where *is* Masonry's authority?

Only the revealed Word of God, the Bible, can tell us the truth about God, about Jesus Christ, about ourselves, about salvation, and about life after death. Since Masonry denies God's Word on these subjects, how can it logically claim to be true? ("No lie is of the truth"—1 John 2:21.) But if Masonry is *not* true, how can you as a Mason continue to promote what is not true?

The bottom line for the Mason who is not a Christian is this: If Masonry is true, then he should follow Masonry and promote its teachings. But if Masonry rejects and opposes the truth—if it denies God and His Word, if it denies God's Son, if it denies God's plan of salvation, and if it offers men a false hope—then the Mason must leave Masonry and instead follow the truth of God.

Does the Mason who is not a Christian really desire to take the chance that he will discover that Masonry was not God's truth after it is too late? Or is he now willing to make an investigation of this matter?[112]

Jesus taught, "I am the way, and the truth and the life. No man comes to the Father but through Me" (John 14:6); and "This is eternal life: that they may know Thee, the only true God, and Jesus Christ whom Thou hast sent" (John 17:3). The Bible further teaches, "And there is salvation in no one else; for there is no other name under heaven that has been given among men, by which we must be saved" (Acts 4:12).

If you are convinced that you are a sinner, Jesus died and paid for your sins on the cross. If you are willing to confess your sins to Him and trust Him to make you a Christian, you may do so by saying the following prayer:

> Lord Jesus, I know now that Masonry does not bring honor to You. I confess that I am a sinner. I believe that Christ died for my sins on the cross. I receive Him now as my Savior and ask Him to give me the resolve and strength to turn from what is evil and to live a life that is pleasing to Him.

What of the Christian Mason? The Christian Mason also must decide. We have proven beyond any doubt whatsoever that Masonry is opposed to the one true God, it is opposed to the teachings of the Bible, it is opposed to the person and work of Jesus Christ, it is opposed to salvation by grace, and it is opposed to every major Christian doctrine. How then can a Christian possibly join in, live by, and promote the teachings of Masonry?

Jesus Himself warned, "Beware of the false prophets. . . . Not every one who says to Me, 'Lord, Lord,' will enter the kingdom of heaven; but he who does the will of My Father who is in heaven. . . . Every one who hears these words of Mine, and does not act upon them, will be like a foolish man, who built his house upon the sand. And the rain descended, and the floods came, and the winds blew, and burst against that house; and it fell, and great was its fall" (Matthew 7:15,21,26,27).

Christian Masons must decide today whether they will remain Masons and deny their Lord, Jesus Christ, or whether they will do the will of their Father in heaven and leave Masonry. Centuries ago the prophet Elijah challenged the people of God who had forsaken the true God and fallen into the grievous sin of idolatry. He warned them, "How long will you hesitate between two opinions? If the Lord is God, follow Him; but if Baal, follow him" (1 Kings 18:21).

This question remains true for Christian Masons today. If the Lord is God, then follow *Him*. Do not maintain the hypocrisy of claiming to be a Christian while living your life in an organization that denies everything Christian. Either follow God or follow Masonry. Either live as a Christian or live as a Mason. Jesus Himself warned: "These people honor me with their lips, but their hearts are far from me" (Matthew 15:7,8 NIV).

If you are a Christian and right now you would be willing to leave the Lodge and obey your Lord, you may say this prayer:

> Dear Jesus, I confess that I have sinned against You in supporting the unchristian teachings of the Lodge. I now ask Your forgiveness and that You would give me the strength to live my life for You and to forsake the Lodge. Help me also to pray for and be a witness to my friends in the Lodge.

The decision you have just made is a hard one to make. Friends may not understand. You may be laughed at or threatened. If you are, remember this: You are in good company. Jesus said:

> Blessed are those who are persecuted because of righteousness, for theirs is the kingdom of heaven. Blessed are you when people insult you, persecute you and falsely say all kinds of evil against you because of me. Rejoice and be glad, because great is your reward in heaven, for in the same way they persecuted the prophets who were before you (Matthew 5:10-12 NIV).

Finally, many pastors, elders, and deacons have no problem with accepting Masons as Christians and granting them positions of teaching and leadership in the local church. We urge such persons to reexamine this practice. Why? Because Masons are sworn to uphold the beliefs and practices of Masonry, which are contrary to Christianity.[113] How can such men be put in positions of leadership and authority when the Bible says, for example, "Deacons, likewise, are to be men worthy of respect, sincere. . . . They must keep hold of the deep truths of the faith with a clear conscience. They must first be tested; and then if there is nothing against them, let them serve as deacons" (1 Timothy 3:8-10).

PART FOUR

CULT WATCH

THE NEW AGE MOVEMENT

Answers to the 30 most frequently asked questions about the New Age Movement

15

Introduction
to the
New Age Movement

The purpose of this unit is threefold: 1) to provide reliable information in brief and popular language on the New Age Movement; 2) to challenge readers to critically reexamine their own worldview; and 3) to express love for those we would like to be our friends by sharing our concerns as to the nature and implications of this topic.

A New Age follower was once quoted in the *New Age Journal* (March, 1978, p. 81) as saying, "I think one of the greatest faults that exists in the spiritual [New Age] movement is that people are not willing to look at what is going on and say maybe it's wrong." We have examined the literature of the New Age Movement in depth and are seeking to give straight answers from the perspective of biblical revelation, believing that an unbiased examination of the historical, biblical, and logical evidence almost compels one to acknowledge its truth. No one should be unconcerned about the truth even if it is difficult or unpopular. As Samuel Johnson said, "It is more from carelessness about truth, than from intentional lying that there is so much falsehood in the world."

It is our desire to speak on issues that are complex, and to deal with ultimate questions that are very important. Indeed, a correct assessment of these issues may mean the difference between physical or spiritual life and death.

Why? Let us illustrate. A lion is an extremely powerful animal. As long as a lion is caged, it presents no danger to mankind. No man in his right mind would walk into the den of a hungry lion. If he did, he would be seriously injured or killed. Once within the lion's territory, the man would be subject to both the lion's attention and its wishes. In the spiritual world, there is a territory of the lion. It is the realm of the occult. Today unfortunately, men do not believe the lion exists or, if they do, they do not recognize him. Yet men are encroaching upon his realm, drawing his attention, placing themselves at his mercy. The Bible warns, "Be sober, be watchful. Your adversary the devil prowls around like a roaring lion seeking someone to devour" (1 Peter 5:8).

At times our brief question-and-answer format has required that we be less detailed than we would wish. For individuals who wish more information, we suggest they consult the recommended reading found at the end of this book.

16

New Age
Influence

Question 1

What is the New Age Movement?

Definition: The New Age Movement (NAM) is a title that refers to a worldview or philosophy of life that many people hold. The NAM can also be properly called a religion because it is based on religious views; for example, New Agers hold to pantheism, a belief that everything is a part of God. That is, God is all, and all is God. They believe that every man is part of God, even though those outside of the NAM might not realize it.

Through mystical experiences, or while participating in techniques which alter one's state of consciousness, people are powerfully persuaded that the religious worldview of the New Age is true.

An example of this is Shirley MacLaine. During a mystical experience in a hot tub, here is what she said she was led to believe, "My whole body seemed to float. Slowly, slowly I *became* the water . . . I *felt* the inner connection of my breathing with the pulse of the energy around me. In fact, I *was* the air, the water, the darkness, the walls, the bubbles, the candle, the wet rocks under the water, and even the sound of the rushing river outside."[1]

Such mystical experiences have led New Agers to believe they truly are one with the universe and are part of God. It has also led them to believe they have uncovered "human potential," an alleged divine power within themselves that, they think, exists in all men.* New Agers want to help

---

* See Part 7, Questions 6,10.

133

everybody discover this power and experientially realize they are one with God. Once people have the mystical experience, New Agers expect that people will live out their new worldview. This would mean striving for world unity and peace and then using their new powers to bring it about.

Many New Agers describe encounters with spirit guides or spirit beings. These spirit beings depict themselves as good spirits who claim to be people who have died and now reside in the spirit world to guide and help others spiritually.

The New Ager's interpretation of these mystical experiences, higher consciousness, spirit beings, etc., differs from the interpretations of orthodox Christianity. Orthodox Christianity has come to the conclusion that New Agers have embraced a mixture of Eastern religious beliefs along with many forms of the occult, such as "channeling," or spirit-possession. It is our belief that the dramatic out-of-the-body experiences, extrasensory knowledge, and the mind trips given to New Agers during their altered states of consciousness are typically experiences given by demons to fool people into believing New Age philosophy. (See Parts 5 and 7.)

For example, people in hospitals sometimes see huge rats or pink elephants that scare them. No one doubts they are really seeing these things, but the visions are a false reality. Likewise, the demons can give wonderful visions and experiences in order to fool people into believing a false religious view of the world. That these beings are evil spirits can be documented from psychology, history, religion, and the experience of many New Agers. (See Ch. 20 and Parts 5,7.)

In 1 Timothy 4:1 we read, "The Spirit clearly says that in later times some will abandon the faith and follow deceiving spirits and things taught by demons."

In John 8:44 Jesus stated, "The devil . . . is a liar and the father of lies."

In 2 Corinthians 11:14 we read, "For Satan himself masquerades as an angel of light."

In brief, orthodox Christianity views the New Age Movement as a false religious worldview, motivated and taught by Satan's demons masquerading as benevolent spirit guides concerned with the welfare of humanity.

Question 2

Why is the New Age Movement important?

The New Age Movement is important because of its current potential for influence at all levels of society—in education, health, psychology, the arts, business, industry, government, religion, science, and entertainment.[2]

According to Marilyn McGuire, executive director of the New Age Publishing and Retailing Alliance, there are some 2500 occult bookstores in the U.S. and over 3000 publishers of occult books and journals.[3] Sales of New Age books in particular are estimated at $1 billion a year.[4] This makes the New Age Movement a multibillion-dollar industry, and such industries receive the attention of corporate America and those in power.

Famous entertainers are being influenced by the New Age and they in turn influence many people in America. Helen Reddy, Marsha Mason, Lisa Bonet, Tina Turner, and musician Paul Horn are only a few of the entertainment industry's New Age converts.[5] Shirley MacLaine's books and televised miniseries "Out on a Limb" introduced millions of people to New Age occultism and spirit contact.

Many other famous personalities have appeared on Phil Donahue, Oprah Winfrey, and other major talk shows endorsing spirit guides and/or the New Age. Entity-channel teams, comprised of mediums and their spirit guides, have become local and national radio and television personalities. For example, on July 25, 1986, actor and convert Michael York appeared on the Merv Griffin Show with Jach Pursel who channeled "Lazaris" before an audience of millions. Merv Griffin himself commented "many of our top stars are now consulting the entity" ("Lazaris"). Actress Sharon Gless who plays "Cagney" on the hit TV series "Cagney and Lacey" won a 1987 "Emmy" for her role on the series. In her acceptance speech, she told tens of millions that her success was due to "Lazaris." Linda Evans of "Dynasty" fame and Joyce DeWitt (formerly of "Three's Company") follow the guidance of another spirit being, "Mafu," channeled by housewife Penny Torres.[6]

Occult filmstrips are promoting seances and necromancy (contacting the dead) in some elementary schools;[7] Tarot card readings are offered at a McDonald's Restaurant;[8] university students are turning out by the thousands to hear guest lectures on the occult.[9] There is also a new faith emerging in "scientific mysticism," or the mixture of the occult and science, and occultic New Age themes are impacting many sectors of society.[10]

In brief the NAM is important because it is shifting the way Americans think away from Judeo-Christian values to the practices of the occult.

Question 3

Who are some of the leaders in the New Age Movement?

Shirley MacLaine is the most visible of New Age proponents; her televised mini-series reached millions and apparently inspired thousands to take up channeling. Her 1987 nationwide seminars were attended by some 14,000 people.[11] She has begun a 300-acre spiritistic retreat center in Crestone, Colorado, that will make channelers (those whom spirits speak through) available for any and all visitors.[12] Although she rejects the title of leader or guru, the Los Angeles Times Magazine titled her "the super saleswoman for a fast growing New Age Movement."[13]

A brief listing of some New Age notables would include New Age theorist and "transpersonal" psychologist Ken Wilbur, dubbed by some "the Einstein of consciousness research,"[14] ("transpersonal" psychology seeks, for example, to blend Eastern religion and modern psychology).[15]

Medium Ruth Montgomery was once a tough-minded journalist who was an agnostic. She converted to the New Age and became a major popularizer of its teachings. She has now written books on the New Age, UFOs, contacting the dead, and related subjects. Marilyn Ferguson is one of the spiritual leaders of the New Age and wrote the bestselling book *The Aquarian Conspiracy: Personal and Social Transformation in the 1980's* (J.P. Tarcher, 1981). She is also editor of the *Brain-Mind Bulletin* and the *Leading Edge Bulletin* which discuss the scientific and social advances of the New Age.

Other influential New Agers include Werner Erhard, founder of est (Erhard Seminars Training), Fritjof Capra, a physicist who is author of the New Age texts *The Tao of Physics* and *The Turning Point*, and Carlos Castaneda, a UCLA anthropology student whose studies led him into the occult. He is the author of the multimillion-selling series of books on sorcery, such as *The Teachings of Don Juan: A Yaqui Way of Knowledge*. Benjamin Creme is the self-proclaimed forerunner of a New Age guru, Maitreya. He is also author of *The Reappearance of the Christ and the Masters of Wisdom*. John Lilly and Charles Tart are pioneering scientific researchers of altered states of consciousness, and Robert Muller, assistant to the secretary general of the United Nations, is the author of *New Genesis: Shaping a Global Spirituality*.

There are several major institutions of the New Age. One is Esalen in Big Sur, California. It appears as if almost every major figure in the New Age has been to Esalen or been influenced by it.[16] Another major institution would be the many New Age publishers, such as Shambala of Boston and J. P. Tarcher of Los Angeles, who are providing the intellectual underpinning for the New Age. Famous New Age doctors include Norman Shealy, author of *Occult Medicine Can Save Your Life*; Robert Leightman, who "channels" many of the famous dead, and mystic W. Brugh Joy, author of *Joy's Way*. World renowned gurus of the NAM include Bhagwan Shree Rajneesh, Swami Muktananda, and Sri Aurobindo among others.

Although there are scores of influential human guides of the New Age Movement, it is the spirit world, over the last two decades, which has provided the groundwork and the most potent leadership behind the scenes. These spirits have, through human agents, produced hundreds of texts with millions of copies of their books in print. Two modern mediums in particular may be considered important catalysts for the current revival of "spirit-written" books. In the 1960's and the 1970's both Jane Roberts and Ruth Montgomery crossed over to the large publishing houses. Between them, their two spirit guides, "Seth" and "Lilly" respectively, have penned almost 30 texts for several major publishers. They not only broke the mold, they set a trend. When Richard Bach's *Jonathan Livingston Seagull* (also dictated by an entity) broke all publishing records since *Gone with the Wind* and made the bestseller list for over two years, the die was cast. Over 25 million copies of the book have been sold worldwide. Today, the sheer number of titles of "spirit-written" books in print is unprecedented.

Question 4

What are the basic beliefs of the New Age worldview?

The NAM can be summarized in four basic beliefs: 1) that all true reality is divine ("God is all; all is God"); 2) that personal "enlightenment"is important (since men exist in a state of ignorance as to their divine nature); 3) that altered consciousness, psychic powers, and spirit contact are the means of such enlightenment; and 4) that in many quarters social and political activism is needed to help "network" (organize) people of like mind to produce a united world—socially, economically, religiously, and politically.

While there are wide variations of belief in the NAM, there is a broad consensus on the main points: the nature of God (God is impersonal), man (man is part of God), the predicament of man (ignorance of his divine nature), and the solution to human problems (accepting New Age beliefs and practices).

The basic New Age worldview that "all is God" is why actress Shirley MacLaine could stand before the Pacific Ocean, arms outstretched and chant, "I am God, I am God, I am God."[17] This is why the Eastern gurus claim they are God—and so is everyone else. For example, guru Sathya Sai Baba states that "... You are the God of this universe."[18]

Question 5

What moral consequences logically follow anyone holding a New Age worldview?

Believing that everything is God does have consequences. In the area of morality, the NAM worldview is an occultic view which teaches that evil is really an illusion and that belief in an absolute morality is wrong. This is why guru Bhagwan Shree Rajneesh states: "I don't believe in morality" and "I am bent on destroying it"; "to emphasize morality is mean, degrading, it is inhuman."[19] Since God is all in Eastern thinking, He includes both good and evil. Since God is impersonal, He therefore cannot be concerned over right or wrong. Thus, whatever is, is right. In fact, once a person realizes and accepts his own godhood, then by definition whatever he does is good, even if it is evil. This is why Rajneesh again states, "My ashram [spiritual community] makes no difference between the demonic and the divine."[20] This is why Swami Vivekananda can say, "Good and evil are one and the same."[21] Although the Bible teaches "Thou shalt not kill" (Exodus 20:13), Swami Vivekananda says, "The murderer too is God."[22] And Rajneesh even says, explaining the Bhagavad Gita (a Hindu holy book), "Kill, murder, fully conscious, knowing that no one is murdered and no one is killed."[23]

Thus we see how the basic worldview of the NAM ("all is one") is able to pervert so important a topic as moral values. Although many other areas could be discussed, we mention that the New Age worldview is also a comprehensive worldview. New Agers want to reinterpret all fields of knowledge to harmonize with New Age belief, including physics, psychology, biology, religion, and sociology. The reason for this is because their mystical experiences have persuaded them this is necessary, not only because these mystical experiences have revealed the "true" interpretation of these disciplines but because this will help educate people toward New Age thinking. This is why their library consists of revelations from the spirit world on these subjects.[24]

For example, these spirits teach that true science is both material and spiritual because of things such as ESP and psychic healing. Thus, the discipline of parapsychology (the scientific study of the occult) helps to align general science with Eastern and occult views. (See Ch. 35.)

The bottom line is that there are very few areas the NAM leaves untouched.

Question 6

Why are nonreligious people (scientists, atheists, rationalists, etc.) embracing this new religious view?

One reason is that regardless of personal belief, men are nevertheless spiritual beings created in the image of God (Genesis 1:27; Ecclesiastes 3:11). As such, they require some kind of spiritual reality to provide a true basis for meaning to life.

An illustration of how nonreligious scientists may become disenchanted with science and open the doors to New Age religion is found in Stanislav Grof's text *Ancient Wisdom and Modern Science*, where leading scientists have blended modern science with ancient occultism.[25] This text and many like it reveal that hundreds of scientists and academics are leaning toward the New Age. Also many of them admit they have turned to Eastern gurus and/or have become practicing disciples of various occult traditions. These scientists have joined the NAM because they are attracted to the New Age idea of an inner divine potential within man and because they see "proof" of this in the occult power they are experiencing. These scientists say they cannot find meaning in life through a purely material science, and they choose not to investigate it in Christianity, but they believe they have found this meaning in the NAM. As a result they have integrated science with occultism, often leading to an Eastern religious view of reality. In the process they have distorted science and made it a religion. For example, some leading scientists now state that because of their conversion to the NAM, they have changed their mind as to the nature of the universe. What they once believed was a real world is now seen as an illusion. What they used to think was an illusion (occult views of the universe) is now seen as a reality. It is this "reality" which they intend to investigate.[26]

Question 7

What are mystical experiences?

Mystical experiences are very important in the New Age Movement, especially because they tend to confirm New Age beliefs. In the NAM, mystical experiences are most frequently induced by various means (yoga, meditation, drug use) often bringing contact with spirits. A mystical experience usually involves a misperception of physical or spiritual reality.

For those who aren't already believers in an Eastern worldview, the mystical experiences are important because they seem to bring all the proof that is needed to persuade. Thus, in the NAM the mystical experience conclusively persuades that "all is God" and "God is all," and that men can tap a reservoir of inner divine power. Besides the feelings of the divine oneness of all things, common mystical experience involves a feeling of going beyond matter, time, and space which is often perceived as illusion. Mystical experiences also produce various behavior and attitude changes that reflect New Age beliefs. In addition the experience of spirits or unusual energies is common.[27]

From a biblical point of view, these experiences are dangerous and to be avoided because they lead people to contact the spirit world, to believe in occult philosophy, and to develop psychic abilities. They may also lead to spirit possession. (See Ch. 36.) These experiences cause people to wrongly believe they are inwardly God and therefore prevent faith in Christ as Savior. They cannot be divine, no matter how divine they appear.

17

New Age Practices and Goals

Question 8

What are some of the "new" occult techniques and practices of the New Age Movement?

There are hundreds of different practices in the NAM such as meditation, channeling, psychic healing, the use of "magical" objects, and various "holistic" therapies such as acupressure, homeopathy, etc. There are scores of cults and new "therapies" which also use these practices. The Rajneesh sect alone uses dozens of different methods to attain its goals of drastically changing human consciousness.

These practices have been developed from the teachings of many ancient cultures and may have been blended with the exercises of modern occultism. In addition, recent developments in psychology, technology, and medicine offer the NAM new options for altering consciousness (such as biofeedback).

We will discuss two of the most popular New Age practices, both of which are related to spiritism—channeling and using crystals as sources of occult power.

Question 9

What is channeling?

Channeling is a New Age term for spirit possession—a willing human "channel" or medium relinquishes his mind and body to an invading spirit who then possesses and controls that person for its own purposes, usually as a mouthpiece for the spirit's own teachings. Some of the more prominent spirits with current nationwide influence are "Lazaris," "Mafu," "Seth," "Saint Germain," and "Ramtha."[28] Overall, it can be documented that there are hundreds of spirits claiming responsibility for New Age books and their message has reached millions of people. In Los Angeles alone there are now an estimated one thousand channelers.[29] (For an analysis of the nature of these spirits, see Question 26 and Part 5.)

Major spiritistic revivals are not new in America; for example, they occurred in 1848 and in 1876. Judging from the tens of thousands who have taken up this practice in recent years, we are currently in the early stages of another revival. Thus, spiritism has become big business. New Age educator and psychologist Jon Klimo observes that "cases of channeling have become pervasive"; scores of new and old channeled books are being rushed to print and numerous guidebooks exist for spirit contact.[30] New magazines such as *Spirit Speaks* are devoted solely to channeled revelations,[31] and profits from channeled seminars, tapes, and books alone range from 100 million to 400 million dollars a year.[32]

For example, Jach Pursel channels "Lazaris" (the entity unexpectedly possessed him one evening during meditation and began speaking through him). A weekend seminar with "Lazaris" (through Pursel) will cost $275 per person with 600 to 800 people in attendance or $200,000 per weekend. At almost $100 per hour for a private sitting, "Lazaris" still has a two-year waiting list. His audiotapes sell at $20 per set, videotapes at $60. "Lazaris" may also be contacted by phone at $53 per half hour charged to your Mastercard or Visa.[33]

A recent prestigious poll reported that 67 percent of Americans now believe in the supernatural, and that 42 percent "believe they have been in contact with someone who died."[34] Thus the stage has been set for a revival of spiritism that could dwarf earlier eras. Some have asserted that channeling will one day be "bigger than fundamentalism."[35] Regardless, spirit contact has become, in many quarters, a socially acceptable practice—and the spirits have served notice that they intend to influence our future.

Question 10

How has channeling influenced the church?

Spiritism has, unfortunately, influenced the church. Many professing Christians fail to see anything wrong or unchristian in channeling. For example, Laura Cameron Fraser, the first woman Episcopal priest of the Pacific Northwest, chose to resign as rector of her church rather than renounce her faith in a channeled spirit named "Jonah."[36]

To cite one of many illustrations of such influence in the church, a number of spiritistically-produced texts have ignorantly been accepted by some Christians because they sound spiritual or claim to be inspired by God or Jesus. These include the devotional text *God Calling* (Revell Publishers, edited by A. J. Russell) which has been on the evangelical bestseller list for several years.[37] Many people are surprised to discover that Richard Bach's *Jonathan Livingston Seagull* was also on the evangelical bestseller list, in spite of its Eastern teachings. It was also inspired by supernatural sources.[38] Another illustration is the three-volume *A Course in Miracles*. This text by Helen Schucman has sold in the hundreds of thousands and has recently found an interested and expanding audience within Christianity.[39] Both *God Calling* and *A Course in Miracles* claim to be written by Jesus, which is impossible because these books deny the biblical Jesus and contradict the Bible.

The most obvious reason for Christian acceptance of such material is the fact that biblical ignorance and worldliness are common among Christians. The church is failing to educate her people properly in these areas.

Question 11

What dangerous potential lies ahead for America if we continue to follow "channelers"?

If the trend continues, the spirits could, through human mediums, offer actual classes on television and videotapes. The more powerful "channelers" would have live trance interviews or be "taped-in-trance" and the material played back on educational television or through other media. To millions of Americans the spirits are already accepted as "wise," instructive, and as entertaining as human teachers. If hundreds of millions of dollars are now being spent to listen to spirits on cassette and video, this means the age of electronic spirit contact is already here. If there is a large enough audience and sales potential, television programs offering the spirits as "entertainment" may not be far off.

Even the spirits themselves are actively promoting the idea of "educational" spiritism. Consider the following statement by the spirit being called "Mentor" who speaks through Meredith Lady Young. The spirit has reached thousands through mediumistic seminars conducted before large audiences. Ms. Young stated that "Mentor" told her "it will not be long, 50 years perhaps, before 'channeling' will be considered the norm rather than the exception . . . humankind will enter the New Age of awareness, learning to integrate the mystical and the practical. One's 'teachers' or 'spirit guides' will be as common as one's professors at a university. The professor will teach mathematics and the spiritual 'teacher' will enlighten."[40]

Question 12

Why are crystals being used by New Agers?

New Agers believe their impersonal God exists as an energy that is vibrating everywhere in the universe. If one wants to get into harmony with this energy, New Agers believe they may do so through certain objects that vibrate in harmony with God. We are all familiar with the TV commercials in which the singer hits a high note and the sound waves vibrate a crystal glass and break it. New Agers believe crystal rocks vibrate to the energy patterns of God and can help a person feel and use this energy. New Agers have found that by meditating and holding crystals or being in their presence powers are sometimes released. One major use involves the alleged focusing or directing of crystal energy for specific purposes, such as psychic healing, contact with spirits, or developing higher consciousness and psychic powers.

In essence, New Age crystal use is the modern equivalent of what missionaries deal with in occultic societies—the practice of using magic charms and other occultic objects believed to possess supernatural power for either good or evil use.

The objects themselves have no power. However, when used for occult purposes, they can become vehicles for spirits to work through, much like common wood (divining rod, Ouija board), cards, or sticks (Tarot cards, I Ching). (See Part 7, Questions 6,10).

Question 13

Are New Age beliefs and practices really based on spiritism?

To put it simply, the teachings of the New Age are the teachings of the spirits. What the New Age teaches and believes is what the spirit world has revealed and wishes men to believe. Many of the practices are also based upon instructions received from the spirit world. In other words, the New Age teachings and practices are not simply the enlightened discoveries of men, but more precisely the deliberately revealed teachings of the spirits that men have adopted and utilized. They merely appear to be enlightened teachings because the spirits use psychological principles and spiritual language, they speak of God and love, and they satisfy many of the genuine desires of fallen man. They provide practices which confirm the "truth" of the New Age worldview to the individual convert. Nevertheless, the spirits have given such teachings and practices for the express purpose of deceiving men under the pretense of loving God and helping men evolve spiritually toward "their true destiny." The Bible is clear at this point; there are teachings given to man by deceitful spirits and they influence both the church and society.

> The Spirit clearly says that in later times some will abandon the faith and follow deceitful spirits and things taught by demons (1 Timothy 4:1).

> And no wonder, for even Satan himself masquerades as an angel of light (2 Corinthians 11:14).

The spirits are coming out of the closet in force, in numerous disguises, doing all they can to spread the teachings of the New Age and similar themes. Again, this is often their stated purpose—to help mankind usher in "the New Age."

Yet these spirits are in fact the personal, malevolent spirit beings that the Bible classifies as "unclean spirits" or demons. They are the underlying power behind "modern" New Age practices and teachings. The basic reason that people cannot bring themselves to accept this conclusion is because the spirits disguise their motives and deceptively appear as good and friendly beings. Thus, most persons trust the spirits' claims about themselves. In return they receive blessings from them in the form of exciting revelations, blissful experiences, loving encounters, help and encouragement, protection from dangers, and assurances about their own divinity. But in assuring men and women that they are divine, the motive of the spirits seems evident—to insulate people from biblical salvation. If man's only problem is ignorance of his divinity, as the spirits teach, then what men really need is re-education concerning their true nature, not salvation from their sins and faith in Christ. But what if men are not divine? And what if God teaches that apart from Christ, no one can inherit eternal life? "And this is the testimony: God has given us eternal life, and this life is in His Son. He who has the Son has the life; he who does not have the Son of God does not have life" (1 John 5:11-12, cf. John 3:18,36). In our next chapter we will compare and contrast New Age teachings and those of Christianity. (See also Part 7, Question 5.)

18

The Theology of the New Age

Question 14

What are the religious beliefs of the New Age Movement?

In general, the religious views of the NAM are:

- God—an impersonal all-pervading energy.

- The Holy Spirit—an energy that can be used creatively or psychically.

- Jesus Christ—a New Age teacher and illustration of an enlightened individual who realized He was God.

- Man—inwardly good and divine; thus he carries within himself all that he needs for time and eternity.

- Salvation—development of psychic powers and higher consciousness. This is achieved by looking inside one's self and practicing New Age techniques to develop psychically and finally attain awareness of personal divinity.

- Sin—ignorance of personal divinity manifested in errors of consciousness.

- Death—the moment one hopes to experience a merging with God, the-all pervading energy of the universe. This only comes if personal transformation or enlightenment has been obtained.

- Satan—normal consciousness—man existing in his state of unrealized potential.

- Heaven—Hell—good or bad states of consciousness in this life.

In the New Age, God is impersonal and is one and the same as the universe. Technically, many in the NAM believe in pantheism.[41] In Christianity, God is the personal Creator who is separate, distinct, and over His creation. In the New Age, man is only a part of an impersonal God. As such, man shares God's essential nature. In Christianity, however, God specifically created man as other than Himself. Because of man's rebellion against God, he is separated from Him. According to the New Age, man must transform himself. He does this by changing his consciousness and actualizing his divine nature. In doing so he supposedly becomes aware of his inner divinity. According to Christianity, Jesus Christ alone is the Savior and reconciles man to God. In the New Age, salvation is by personal effort and works. Man must use a variety of Eastern or occultic techniques and apply these to his mind, body, and spirit to obtain "enlightenment." In Christianity, salvation is by God's grace and not by man's work. Man must receive God's gift by placing his faith in Christ and turning from sin. Salvation is not something earned by personal merit (Ephesians 2:8,9).

Question 15

Does the Bible say anything about the teachings and practices of the New Age Movement?

The Bible has much to say about the practices and teachings of the NAM. Specifically, the Bible teaches that spiritism and other occultic practices of the NAM are displeasing to God, inviting His judgment, for example:

> Exodus 20:3 (cf. Psalm 96:4)—"You shall have no other gods before me. You shall not bow down or worship them. . . ."
>
> Deuteronomy 18:9-12 (cf. 2 Chronicles 33:6)—"Let no one be found among you . . . who practices divination, or sorcery, interprets omens, engages in witchcraft, or one who casts spells, or who is a medium, or spiritist, or who consults the dead. Anyone who does these things is detestable to the Lord. . . ."
>
> 1 Corinthians 10:20 (cf. Psalm 106:34-40)—"The sacrifices of pagans are offered to demons, not to God, and I do not want you to be participants with demons."

In essence in these verses the Bible is condemning any involvement with spirits or demons.

The pantheistic teachings of the NAM are also rejected by Scripture. The Bible teaches that the eternal infinite God created a finite universe from nothing (Genesis 1:1; Nehemiah 9:6; Psalm 33:9; 148:5; Hebrews 11:3) and that it is both real and good (Genesis 1:31). God is not "one" with the universe (Isaiah 45:18,22). He is separate and over it.

The Bible teaches that both wisdom and knowledge come by non-mystical means (Proverbs 1; 1 Timothy 4:10-16; 2 Timothy 2:15; 3:14) and rejects the New Age idea that so-called "higher" knowledge is available in mystical states of consciousness. Revealed knowledge of God and spiritual truth come from God Himself who is Truth, who "cannot lie" (John 14:6; Titus 1:2), by means of verifiable divine revelation (2 Timothy 3:16, 17), not spiritistic imitations that give false information (1 Timothy 4:1; 1 John 4:1).

The Bible teaches an absolute morality that is based on God's character and His revealed Word (1 John 1:5; 2:29; 3:4). This rejects the NAM teaching of a morality based on personal preference which can lead to a potentially destructive approach to personal living and ethics.

Concerning knowledge of God, the Bible teaches that God is infinite (1 Kings 8:27; 1 Timothy 6:15,16), personal (Isaiah 43:10-13; 44:6-9), loving (1 John 4:8), holy and immutable (Psalm 55:19; Malachi 3:6; Hebrews 13:8; James 1:17). On the other hand, the NAM teaches that God is impersonal, and therefore should properly be referred to as an "It" like the "Force" in the Star Wars movies. The NAM God cannot love, is not holy, and cannot think or be merciful. "It" just is.

The Bible teaches that Christ was unique in nature as the only incarnation of God and the Savior of the world (John 3:16,18; Philippians 2:1-8; 1 John 2:2). He will return visibly and personally (Matthew 24:29-38; Acts 1:11). The Bible rejects the NAM teaching that Christ was merely an enlightened master or spirit guide.

The Bible teaches that sin is real (1 John 1:8-10), that sin separates an individual from God (Isaiah 59:2; Revelation 20:12,15), and that Christ died to forgive human sin (John 3:16; 1 Peter 2:24). This contrasts with the NAM which teaches that sin is an illusion (or mere ignorance of one's own perfection) and that Christ did not die for sin, but merely revealed the way to higher consciousness.

In the Bible, salvation, occurs when a man repents and receives by faith Christ's provision for his sin. Salvation is an instantaneous free gift received by grace through faith in the sacrificial death of Jesus Christ (Romans 11:6; Ephesians 2:8,9; John 6:47; 1 John 2:25; 5:13). This rejects the NAM view that salvation ("enlightenment") is a lengthy process of realizing one's own divinity. This is not a gift, but is achieved by personal effort and merit as in yoga meditation. The Bible teaches a real heaven or hell is the destination for all individuals after their lifetime (Matthew 25:46; Philippians 3:20,21; Hebrews 9:27; Revelation 20:10-15; 21:1–22:5). This rejects the NAM teaching of reincarnation throughout endless numbers of lifetimes. Thus, the Bible and the NAM disagree on many basic beliefs about God, salvation and the spiritual life.

Question 16

Do New Age writers use Christian words and refer to Jesus Christ and the Bible?

The NAM does use Christian words, does refer to Jesus Christ and quotes Bible verses, but this does not make it Christian. In fact it is anti-Christian. Merely using Christian words is no guarantee that Christian definitions are being given to those words. The words in the Bible come to us fixed and clearly defined by their cultural setting. The New Age redefines biblical words to fit its own ideas and distorts their intended meaning. As a result, the New Age does not allow the Bible to speak for itself.

The same is true for many groups which outwardly appear Christian, yet whose teachings are not (for example, Jehovah's Witnesses, the Church of Jesus Christ of Latter-day Saints [Mormonism], the World Wide Church of God [Armstrongism], The Way International [Victor Paul Wierwille], the Unification Church [Sun Myung Moon] and others).[42]

It should also be pointed out that the NAM which offers a sincere, although distorted, view of Christianity in some quarters offers the persecution of Christians in other quarters. A thorough reading of New Age literature will show that some New Agers sanction the persecution of Christians. They do so on the basis of the need to remove those who may refuse to accept or attempt to "prevent" a spiritual uniting of humanity.[43] This is one of the darker aspects to the NAM, yet it is consistent with the overall worldview of the NAM. If true globalism—or world unity—is eventually to be a reality, then by definition all dissenting voices must either be converted, silenced, or removed. That, of course, is the "rub"— the New Age of love and harmony may have to be repressive for a time to usher in their version of peace on earth.

Nevertheless, we wish to carefully emphasize the following: First, that not all New Agers are advocating the persecution of Christians. Second, that unfortunately there are some parts of the NAM which do.

Question 17

Why are some people in the New Age Movement antagonistic to Christianity?

Given the teachings of the NAM, the rejection of Christianity is quite logical, although not all in the New Age are openly hostile to the Christian faith. Indeed, many members come from nominal Christian backgrounds or are liberal Christians and for this reason are seeking to combine Christianity and the New Age. Nevertheless, there are those who have openly asserted that it was their dislike for orthodox Christian faith which led them into the NAM. As with certain secular philosophies, they found the NAM attractive simply because it rejected Christian faith and promoted freedom from the Christian God. In addition, some who are fanatically committed to the NAM and are also familiar with Christian teachings are openly antagonistic to Christianity because they realize that the Christian faith is a formidable barrier to New Age views ("all is one," spiritual evolution, salvation by personal merit, etc.) and to New Age goals (occult enlightenment, globalism, etc.). This is why Rajneesh, for example, says that "the greatest deception is the deception of devotion to God."[44] He recognizes that belief in the Christian God is harmful to his own interests. These individuals have labeled Christianity an "enemy" of mankind and in the tradition of those like the founder of the Theosophical Society, Helena P. Blavatsky, have attacked and ridiculed it. They do so because like, the Marxists of today, they recognize the Christian faith for the genuine threat that it is.

Question 18

How can we tell that the New Age Movement is influencing the Christian church?

We have already seen that some Christians are purchasing spiritistic books in large numbers (why Christian publishers would print and distribute such books in the first place is hard to fathom). Christians are also dabbling in various forms of mysticism, Eastern meditation and religion, parapsychology, visualization and positive thinking, and other New Age practices. For example, few Christians know that Napoleon Hill's book *Grow Rich with Peace of Mind* came from the "Ascended Masters" or spirit beings. Hill said that unseen spirits hovered about him and claimed that the "Ascended Masters" gave him the materials in the chapters of his book.[45] Hill joined with Clement Stone and coauthored a book using the same philosophy to develop the idea of a positive mental attitude known as PMA. Norman Vincent Peale picked up parts of New Age philosophy (which can be seen in some of his books)[46] and, through evangelical "positive thinkers," these ideas have come into the church. (See Part 8.)

It is interesting that even positive thinker Robert Schuller advocates a form of Eastern meditation which brings a person into the "alpha state." He also discusses the benefits of Eastern mantras.[47]

The influence of the NAM among Christians can also be seen in an issue of *Yoga Journal*. In one issue two persons who claim to be Christians, practice "yoga, T'ai Chi and akido" and state that Christians "stand to gain by learning discipline and spiritual awareness from the East" and the NAM. These men discuss their Eastern "introspective" form of meditation where they have learned to look within "to discover spiritual realities." They have taught two-month seminars on this meditation (which they claim is Christian) at their "conservative evangelical church" and they offer seminars on such meditation at other Christian churches.[48]

Another example is therapist E.S. Gallegos who works at a Lutheran Family Service counseling center and is coauthor of *Inner Journeys: Visualization in Growth and Therapy*. He offers the church a therapy incorporating occult theory and technique (shamanism) with visualization and modern psychology.[49]

Finally we note that parapsychology (the scientific study of the occult) is influencing the Christian church in a variety of ways. (See Chapter 35.) For example, a major Christian text on psychology gives qualified endorsement to such topics as psychic healing, parapsychology, and automatic writing.[50]

Question 19
Why is Christianity susceptible to New Age ideas?

Christians are being influenced by the NAM principally because of ignorance of biblical teachings and lack of doctrinal knowledge. Because of America's emphasis on materialism, commitment to Christ as Lord in every area of life is sadly lacking. This brings disastrous results. Unfortunately there are Christians who "love the approval of men rather than God" (John 12:43); who integrate the world's ways with their Christian faith (James 1:27; 1 John 2:15; 4:4), or who are ignorant of the extent of spiritual warfare (Acts 20:28-34; 2 Corinthians 4:4; Ephesians 6:12-18; 2 Peter 2:1; 1 John 4:1-3).

These sins of American Christianity open us to false philosophies such as the NAM. There are always some Christians who will actively embrace their culture. Whether they attempt to learn from it intellectually or borrow from it spiritually, or relish the enjoyment of worldly pleasures and pastimes, or attempt some kind of social reform along nominal Christian lines, the result is that their Christian faith becomes diluted or absorbed by an initially appealing but alien culture. This means that to the extent America turns to the New Age, to some degree there will be Christians who will adopt New Age practices or beliefs.

Question 20
What can concerned persons do about the New Age Movement?

The church needs to have a higher degree of commitment to Christ as Lord in every area of life, to studying and living the Bible's teachings, and to learning apologetics (Christian evidences).* We need to take sanctification (growth in obedience to Christ) more seriously, recognizing that because the world's ways are so ungodly the Bible warns us that "friendship with the world is enmity toward God. Therefore whosoever will be a friend of the world is the enemy of God" (James 4:4).

As a Christian, this is what you personally can do. First, you can become informed about the New Age (see Recommended Reading). Second, you can "contend earnestly for the faith which was once for all delivered to the saints" (Jude 3) and "sanctify Christ as Lord in your hearts, always being ready to make a defense to everyone who asks you to

---

* See e.g., J.I. Packer, *God's Words* and *Knowing God;* Francis Schaeffer, *True Spirtuality* and *He Is There and He Is Not Silent* and Henry Morris, *Many Infallible Proofs.*

give an account for the hope that is in you, yet with gentleness and reverence" (1 Peter 3:15). You can "examine everything carefully" and actively critique what is not sound, being "wise in what is good, and innocent in what is evil" (1 Thessalonians 5:23; Romans 16:19). Third, you can effectively prepare for spiritual warfare (Ephesians 6:10-18) and use the Bible intelligently, "for the Word of God is living and active and sharper than any two-edged sword, and piercing as far as the division of soul and spirit . . . and able to judge the thoughts and intents of the heart" (Hebrews 4:12). You can also encourage your pastor to speak forcefully about these issues from the Bible.

How can you deal with your friends who have joined the NAM? First realize that you are not just dealing with man's philosophies which can be countered with human arguments. You are dealing with demonic deceptions that require prayer, patience, and the Word of God. These false philosophies and practices will have the devil's power behind them, which is why they cannot be effectively defeated by human means alone. Thus, you should meet these problems with earnest prayer which "can accomplish much" (James 5:16), with patience and courage (Joshua 1:7; 2 Timothy 2:24-26), and with the power of the Holy Spirit and the Word of God. You should also love others and be careful to respect those who disagree with you, for in this way you will prove to the world you are truly a disciple of Christ (John 13:35; 1 Corinthians 10:24,33; 13:13).

19

Related
Philosophies
and Issues

Question 21

Is holistic health related to the New Age Movement?

The holistic health movement may be considered the "medical" arm of the NAM. The ideas of the NAM have invaded the medical world through a variety of unsound and/or potentially occultic practices such as Applied Kinesiology ("muscle testing"), Homeopathy (a diluting of certain essences for medical treatment), Iridology (the alleged medical diagnosis by inspection of the iris), Therapeutic Touch (an Eastern form of psychic healing and "laying on of hands"), and dozens of other unproven treatments.[51*]

In general, most holistic therapies are unscientific in nature and as such potentially dangerous when it comes to life-threatening illness. Using a treatment that has no power to cure can be deadly in the wrong situations. What then about reports of genuine cures? The reports of genuine cures are not so much related to the individual "treatments" used; rather, many times it totally depends on the psychological factors involved. Finally, it must not be forgotten that some treatments work because of the occult power behind them, but which also have unfortunate spiritual consequences.

---

* See also John Ankerberg, John Weldon, *Can You Trust Your Doctor? The Complete Guide to New Age Medicine and Its Threat to Your Family*, Wolgemuth & Hyatt 1991, for a more complete analysis.

How can one tell if a treatment is occultic or based on true medicine? The basic question one should ask is whether or not a given practice can be scientifically replicated or whether it is just another form of mystical experience.

In *New Age Medicine*, authors Paul Reisser, M.D., Terri Reisser, and John Weldon list the following important cautions about New Age medical practices: Beware of therapies which claim to manipulate "invisible energy"; beware of those who seem to utilize psychic knowledge or power; beware of a practitioner who has a therapy with which no one else is familiar; beware of someone who claims that his or her particular therapy will cure anything; beware of someone whose explanations do not make sense; beware of therapies whose only proof consists of the testimonies of satisfied customers; beware of therapies which rely heavily on altered states of consciousness; and finally realize that sincerity is no guarantee of legitimacy.[52]*

Question 22
What is parapsychology?

Parapsychology is the scientific study of occult phenomena. Parapsychologists study such things as mediumism, poltergeists or "troublesome ghosts," and psychic healing. The claims made by many parapsychologists that they do not study occultic phenomena are basically false. An examination of the literature in the field, including the publication and research reports of the scientific laboratories reveal that parapsychologists study occult phenomena although they may redefine it in more neutral or scientific terms. In fact, for 130 years mediumism has been the mainstay of parapsychology, even within periods of lessened interest in that particular subject. God's warning in Deuteronomy 18 applies to both the professional and nonprofessional investigator of occult phenomena.[53] (See Chapter 35.)

Question 23
Is there a New Age conspiracy to control the world?

An examination of New Age writings reveals that many people in the NAM have as their goals: 1) a one-world government; 2) a one-world economic system; 3) a one-world culture, where all education, religion, and races are joined in harmony; and 4) a god-like world ruler who will Help to implement these changes.[54] What makes these ideas desirable is that the world is fragmented by regional wars and nationalism, by competing ideologies such as Marxism and capitalism, by races, by various monetary standards, and by many conflicting world religions. Thus, it is

---

* See note at bottom of page 152.

the hopelessness of the world that gives New Age ideals their power. Many see New Age ideals as a logical necessity. This is why Robert Muller, the assistant secretary-general in charge of coordinating 32 specialized agencies and world programs of the United Nations, has written *New Genesis: The Shaping of a Global Spirituality*. He believes that a united world is not only possible, it is necessary.[55] Many others who recognize these same problems are also working for a united world. Their ideas of a world of unity, love, and brotherhood are widely and openly endorsed. Therefore to label the NAM a "mass conspiracy" is not correct.

Even if man could succeed in uniting the world and solving many of its problems, there are two vital issues which are never addressed by humanists and New Agers working for a new world. These are the power of sin within the human heart and the reality of the devil and his power over man's affairs. Both human sin and demonic power are ridiculed and ignored by those who believe that man alone can usher in a New Age. Men who are imperfect, indeed often evil, and who, by rejection of God, place themselves under the devil's power (2 Corinthians 4:4) can never achieve a true millennium. Thus, God teaches that some of the ideas for a united world will eventually be used for evil purposes.

For now we believe it is better to limit the use of the word conspiracy to the spirit realm. The NAM does contain the seeds for a conspiracy, but so have many other movements in history. If at some time America opens itself up to the NAM, and it sweeps the world, then the spiritual powers behind it may take advantage of this movement for more profound purposes. Biblically we know it will be the devil using unsuspecting men and women as his agents, conspiring behind the scenes to control the world. We also know that one day he will succeed (Revelation 12:9; 13:8,12-17). To what extent the NAM will take part in fulfilling this underworld conspiracy remains to be seen.

Question 24
Is the New Age Movement related to modern psychology?

To varying degrees, certain schools of modern psychology are supportive of New Age philosophy and practice. Some of these schools are the Humanistic, the Jungian, the Transpersonal (stressing Eastern psychologies), and literally scores of unconventional "fringe" psychotherapies. Thus, aspects of psychology are uniting to encourage confidence in the exploration of the mind to bring about the mystical experiences associated with the East and the occult. In fact, many are increasingly viewing psychology as the most promising bridge to ancient occult wisdom. As they do so, psychology is becoming a principal vehicle for expanding New Age influence in our culture.[56] (See Chapter 23, Question 13; Chapter 25, Question 16; Chapter 37).

Question 25

Is the New Age Movement related to witchcraft and Satanism?

There are similarities between the doctrines of the NAM and witchcraft and Satanism. Although they are by no means identical, there is general agreement among them that "all is one," "all is God," and that we are our own gods. There is also agreement on the personal use of both occult power and the spirit world. And there is an agreement on the rejection of absolute morality, including Christian values.[57] (See Part 7.)

This is why many witches have stated that they welcome the New Age Movement; it not only reflects their views of the world, it also makes it easier for other people to accept witchcraft and to even become witches themselves. Thus, guru Bhagwan Shree Rajneesh states that witchcraft constitutes "one of the greatest possibilities of human growth."[58]

Because of the NAM there is a revival not only of witchcraft but of all forms of occultism in our country, including Satanism. Investigative reporter Maury Terry has documented that there exists a satanic network crisscrossing the nation. This satanic network has apparently influenced Charles Manson, the "Son of Sam" killer David Berkowitz, and other serial killers—and is responsible for a large number of clandestine murders of innocent persons.[59] Although most New Agers would strongly object to any connection between Satanism and the New Age, even some Satanists recognize there is a connection. Thus, for example, former military colonel and Satanist, Dr. Michael Aquino, high priest of the church of Set, in response to the question "Is Satanism the same as the New Age?" could only say "Yes, but I would say we have a more precise grasp of what it actually is we are looking at here . . . of what is actually happening here [in the New Age]."[60]

Thus, there are connections between the NAM and witchcraft and Satanism even though this fact is not recognized by most people.

20

Analysis
and Critique

Question 26

What evidence would lead a thinking person to conclude spirit guides are dangerous?

An important question to consider is, Even though these spirits appear to be so helpful, kind, and wise, what is the real motive behind their behavior? New Agers firmly believe these spirits are highly advanced spiritual "Masters" who have come to instruct humankind and prepare the way for the coming New Age. Thus, by definition, the NAM believes the teachings of the spirits are good, even divine.

To the contrary, however, we will present evidence to show the teachings of these spirits are not divine. Rather, the teachings of the spirits are immoral, antisocial, unbiblical, and prejudiced against Christ. Each person should ask, "Is it logical that good or divine spirits would teach lies?" Men and women worldwide usually consider Christ as good and His teachings as beneficial. Why would "good" spirits adamantly be opposed to Him and consistently lie about His teachings? It must be admitted that it is at least a possibility that these are not good spirits but evil spirits who are masquerading as helpful beings. Could their real purpose be to appear helpful and give mystical experiences only to deceive men spiritually?

In brief, the evidence demonstrates that these "loving" spirits with their endless disguises (from "angels," to "aliens," to "nature spirits") fit the category of the demonic. It can be shown that these spirits promote sin and immorality, endorse occultism, and some even promote perverse rituals such as necrophilia or sex with corpses.[61] They also pervert and distort biblical truth, reject Christ and hate the God of the Bible, and purposely deceive those who listen—sometimes with sadistic intent.[62] If the above can be demonstrated, as it can, what other conclusions may we arrive at other than these creatures are deceiving spirits? (See Chapters 34,36.)

Consider the teachings of the spirit entity "Emmanuel" as found in the text by Pat Rodegast titled *Emmanuel's Book*. Morally, Emmanuel teaches the permissibility and desirability of divorce (in "incompatible" marriages); the possibility of "open marriage" (adultery); the permissibility of abortion ("a useful act" when done "with willingness to learn" for "nothing in your human world is absolutely wrong"); and homosexuality and bisexuality as normal behavior (even in full recognition of the AIDS plague).[63]

Emmanuel also demeans political leaders as ignorant and sick and teaches that the six million Jews who perished in the Holocaust really chose to be murdered in order to grow spiritually. Thus, Emmanuel says that Hitler and Stalin should not be condemned too severely, for they also are part of God.[64] Are these the kinds of moral codes man should live by? Are they good ethical teachings in any sense? Can they be considered socially constructive? Are these ideas what we would expect from morally pure, divine, or highly evolved spiritual beings? Or, on the other hand, are they what we would expect from evil spiritual beings? The fact is that Emmanuel's teachings are not the exception; they are merely representative of hundreds of other spirits' teachings.

In general all the spirits agree theologically, which is very interesting. Emmanuel, along with other spirits, teaches that God and man are one (see Genesis 1–3); that faith in God is unnecessary (see Hebrews 11:1); that Christ is man's "higher self" (see John 3:16,18; Philippians 2:1-9); and that death is "absolutely safe," merely a change without judgment (see John 3:36; Hebrews 9:27; Revelation 20:10-25).[65]

Here are some other typical New Age beliefs that Emmanuel and other spirits teach—"all is one," there is no good or evil, cosmic evolution through reincarnation, one-worldism, contact with alleged extraterrestrials, the importance of spirit contact, etc.[66] In light of this evidence, what do you conclude are the motives of the spirits?

Question 27

Are New Age mystical experiences really spiritual traps?

Today there exists a great misunderstanding in the area of psychic phenomena, mystical experiences, and the occult. They are all viewed as good, progressive, and of divine origin. In the future they are expected to be part of the natural and normal aspect of human evolution or potential. These are assumed to be not only "good" but "safe" activities. Usually the harmful realities are learned too late because our society rejects the idea of demonic powers who purposely deceive by masquerading as good.

People in the New Age have no idea that their new spiritual practices may be involving them with demons. For example, Johanna Michaelsen once believed she was serving God and Jesus by working for a psychic surgeon. At times she experienced great joy and peace through her New Age practices. Her spirit guide even claimed to be Jesus. In the process of becoming a Christian she discovered that this spirit guide had purposely deceived her and was a demon. She recalls, "Murderous demonic rage had been the spirits' reaction to my potential decision to accept Jesus Christ of Nazareth as He is, rather than as I had come to think He should be."[67]

Doreen Irvine realized the same truth. As a practicing witch who used psychic powers, she believed they were only part of everyone's "human potential." One day she discovered that the real power came from evil spirits. She came to realize they actually dwelled within her—something she had never known. She observes, "Now I was no stranger to demons. Had I not often called on them to assist me in rites as a witch and Satanist? [Now] for the first time I knew these demons were within me, not outside. It was a startling revelation . . . they actually controlled me."[68]

Finally, medium Raphael Gasson said that his spirit helpers tried to kill him when he decided to leave them and turn to Jesus Christ. He states, "As a former Spiritualist minister and active medium, it is possible for me to say that at the time of my participation in the Movement, I actually believed that these spirits were the spirits of the departed dead and that it was my duty to preach this to all those with whom I came into contact day by day. It was my earnest desire that mankind should accept this 'glorious truth' and find joy in the knowledge that there was no death."[69] Yet Gasson went on to say his very own spirit guide "attempted to kill me when it became obvious that I was out to denounce spiritualism."[70]

From this one can see that, initially at least, the New Age convert may encounter many exciting and joyful experiences. This is what the spirits desire to give because they lead people deeper into New Age philosophy and practices. But once a person is truly "hooked," the picture may change drastically. What New Agers must consider is that they may themselves be part of a spiritual "con." If a swindler is clever enough, his victim will joyfully hand over his entire life's savings. It is only too late that he discovers his loss. New Agers are trusting their minds and bodies to spirit beings they know little about. If these spirits are demons, logically what do you think will be the consequences? (See Chapters 26,36.)

Question 28

Where are the ideas of the New Age Movement leading America?

The New Age Movement is already having a significant impact on America. This can be seen in the classification of spiritual teachers. Because of the New Age, many are being classified as spiritual leaders and teachers who are really occultists. They are occultists (even if they reject the label) because of their involvement with spirits, who influence and/or control them.

The very fact that such leaders typically go through an occult training in the process of becoming leaders; the fact that they are using spiritual (occult) power; the far too numerous admissions of their having spirit guides—these considerations in light of the biblical data (2 Corinthians 4:4; Ephesians 2:2; 1 John 5:19) lead us to conclude such religious leaders are spirit-influenced and sometimes demonized.[71] (See Chapter 36, Question 16.)

These teachers are swaying millions of people. What this means is that millions of Americans are being influenced by the very spirits who instruct such teachers. It means our nation is in the process of accepting what the Bible calls demonization and we are doing it on a significant scale.

However, the experience of demonization in America is not necessarily the same as the illustrations of demon-possession in the New Testament. Today's Americans enter into these experiences voluntarily and interpret them as having positive spiritual value. A good example of this is people who are practicing channeling. Time and again in the autobiographies of such persons, we discover that the process of spirit possession is an essentially "positive," pleasurable, life-changing, and power-inducing experience.[72] This is initially true as the spirits seem to want to make a good impression. In the long run, however, it is another story entirely. (See Part 5.)

The New Age revival also has brought about cultural, societal, and family changes. Ideas have consequences, and philosophies and practices such as the idea that "all is one" (monism), the rejection of absolute morality, belief in reincarnation and the practices of spirit contact, divination, psychic development, etc., are changing the way people treat each other. In addition, it must be remembered that God judged and destroyed the Canaanite civilization explicitly for the idolatrous and occultic practices they had employed (Deuteronomy 18; Joshua 1–3). In light of this, do you think America is asking for God's judgment?

Question 29

What should people who are encountering spiritual difficulties in the New Age do?

Spiritual problems have become so widespread that "helping organizations" have been formed to deal with the crises that are occurring. The spiritual difficulties people are encountering send them to New Age counselors.

But the basic problem with New Age counseling is an incorrect diagnosis of the problem and thus an incorrect treatment. The concepts of "occult bondage" and demon-possession are not even considered.[73]

In fact, New Age counselors typically encourage the very occult practices that give birth to the problems. Their fundamental premise is that spiritual crises are really part of each person's spiritual journey and, therefore, something good. These experiences need not be avoided, they only need to be handled correctly. In brief, the goal of New Age counseling is to successfully inform and safely integrate these harmful occult experiences into a person's life.

What are some of the experiences that New Age counselors are trying to integrate into people's lives? Some people in the NAM are encountering frightening and unexpected psychic powers, hallucinations, abrupt possession by spirit entities, psychic attacks, and the often uncontrollable and painful kundalini arousal. Others are encountering severe depression or suicidal tendencies.[74] (See Chapter 36.)

In evaluating the problems that come with New Age practices, two facts are important to consider. First, not one in a thousand persons in the New Age ever expected to encounter such alarming experiences. These seekers did not know that these experiences came with the territory. Had they known, New Age practices would certainly have been avoided. Secondly, New Age counseling cannot truly help a person when it encourages the very ideas and practices that are the source of the problems to begin with. Because these experiences are occultic and represent contact with demonic powers, the end result of "properly integrating" such experiences may, from a Christian point of view, be merely a "properly integrated" yet demonized individual who is convinced he is advancing spiritually.

The New Age practitioner who wants deliverance from these problems, who wishes to "turn off" the switch, is left with a dilemma. The New Age has no "off" switch and the person may be left at the mercy of spirits and forces that will not leave him alone.

Abstinence is the only safe recommendation because occult practices open the door to demonic deception, manipulation, and possession. Once forbidden practices are engaged in and encountered, a person may only be delivered though the power of the biblical Jesus Christ. These New Age practices and powers must be renounced (Luke 13:3; James 4:7,8), the sin of involvement repented of and confessed to God (1 John 1:9), and Christ must be received as personal Savior and Lord (John 1:12). Any experience of hindrance should be resolved with constant prayer (1 Thessalonians 5:17), Bible study (1 Thessalonians 5:21,22; 2 Timothy 2:15), and responsible Christian counseling.[75]

Question 30

What does God's Son, Jesus Christ, offer to New Agers looking for answers?

Jesus Christ offers those in the New Age the opportunity to be loved by "the only true God" (John 17:3) and to know and love Him in return.

Everyone wishes to believe in something that in the end will be proven true. The truth that Jesus is God's Son can be proven by biblical prophecy, by His life and miracles, and by His resurrection from the dead. No other religion or religious leader gives such proof.* The New Ager must choose between the New Age and Jesus Christ. The Bible tells us all are sinners and that our sin has separated us from God. Unless we accept God's remedy, that separation will continue on into eternity, which Jesus called hell. But God does not desire that any should perish but that all should come to repentance (2 Peter 3:9). Because of His "great love" for us (John 3:16; Romans 5:8; Ephesians 2:4) Christ died to pay for our sin in order that he could forgive us our sin through faith in Him (John 5:24). Part of God's glorious salvation that Jesus Christ offers us is genuine eternal life, not endless reincarnations which promise only more lifetimes of pain and suffering. The Bible says, ". . . God has given us eternal life, and this life is in his Son. He who has the Son has the life; he who does not have the Son of God does not have the life" (1 John 5:11,12).

If you are not a Christian, it is eternally important that you make a decision for Jesus Christ with your mind, heart, and will.

The Bible teaches:

1. Romans 3:23—All have sinned and fall short of the glory of God.

2. Romans 6:23—The wages of sin is death—eternal separation from God.

3. Romans 6:23—The free gift of God is eternal life provided by the death of Christ on the cross (1 Peter 3:18).

4. Luke 13:3—To receive this gift you must be willing to repent; that is to confess you are a sinner and be willing to turn away from the sins of your life and follow Christ.

5. John 1:12—You must receive Christ personally.

Do you desire to know the living God? Are you willing to acknowledge your sin before Him and to receive His Son? If you are, John Stott recommends the following prayer.

> Lord Jesus Christ, *I humbly acknowledge* that I have sinned in my thinking and speaking and acting, that I am guilty of deliberate wrongdoing, and that my sins have separated me from Your Holy presence, and that I am helpless to commend myself to You;
> *I firmly believe* that You died on the cross for my sins, bearing them in Your own body and suffering in my place the condemnation they deserved;

---

* See John Ankerberg, John Weldon, *The Case for Jesus the Messiah: Incredible Prophecies That Prove God Exists* and *Do the Resurrection Accounts Conflict? And What Proof Is There that Jesus Rose from the Dead?* (Chattanooga, TN: Ankerberg Theological Research Institute, 1989).

I have thoughtfully counted the cost of following You. I sincerely repent, turning away from my past sins. I am willing to surrender to You as my Lord and Master. Help me not to be ashamed of You;

So now I come to You. I believe that for a long time You have been patiently standing outside the door knocking. I now open the door. Come in, Lord Jesus, and be my Savior and my Lord forever. Amen.[76]

If you prayed this prayer, there are several things you can do to grow in the Christian life. Start reading a modern-translation Bible and find a good church that honors Christ. Tell someone you have just become a Christian so they may pray for you and encourage you in your new life with Christ, for remember, in Christ "are hidden all the treasures of wisdom and knowledge" (Colossians 2:3) and "In him and through faith in him we may approach God with freedom and confidence" (Ephesians 3:12).

PART FIVE

CULT WATCH

SPIRIT GUIDES

*How to avoid
the seduction of
the spirit world
and demonic
powers*

21

Introduction to Spirit Guides

This unit discusses a subject of great relevance. This is the increasingly popular phenomenon of what may be termed voluntary spirit-possession or "channeling." Channelers claim a spirit actually enters their body and speaks as a spiritual "guide" through them. The key issue is: Exactly who or what are these spirit guides?

Many ideas, even bizarre ones, have been considered. Are they merely the hallucinations of the mentally unstable, as doctors say? Are they parts of the unconscious mind available to us all, as some psychologists say? Are they creatures from the future, or are they from civilizations deep in space, as some scientists say? Are they reflections of a divine aspect to man—a "higher" self that is now emerging as part of a dramatic leap in human-kind's spiritual evolution, as some ministers say? Are they genuine spirit beings such as angels, the dead, or the "gods" and nature spirits of various religious traditions, as the channelers say?

Or are they another category of "entity" entirely—the demons mentioned in the Bible?

The biblical view is rarely examined by those who study psychic phe-nomena. Parapsychologist (one who scientifically studies the occult) Alan Gauld refuses even to discuss the theory of demons because he says it is "now so rarely put forward that I shall nowhere consider it."[1] Those involved in studying channeling might be expected to have a natural bias against believing in the demon theory because it would implicate them with a view scorned by their associates.

Nevertheless, if one looks for a theory to explain all the facts, the demon theory cannot be ignored, whether or not it is personally appealing. Even William James, one of the great pioneers of Western psychology, once stated during his own investigations into channeling (then termed "mediumism"):

> The refusal of modern "enlightenment" to treat "possession" as a hypothesis to be spoken of as even possible, in spite of the massive human tradition based on concrete human experience in its favor, has always seemed to me a curious example of the power of fashion in things "scientific." That the demon-theory . . . will have its innings again is to my mind absolutely certain. One has to be "scientific" indeed to be blind and ignorant enough to suspect no such possibility.[2]

Again, if there is even a slight possibility these spirits are demons, the reader should be concerned. If it is probable they are such, the question of involvement with them is settled. We invite the reader to examine the logical evidence which has caused many others with us to conclude that the spirits of channeling are not who they claim.

22

Channeling:
Its Influence
and Reality,
and the Need
for Discernment

Question 1

What is channeling?

"Channeling" is a "New Age" term for spirit-possession. This occurs when humans willingly give their minds and bodies to spirit beings. These spirits enter and control people and use them to give spiritual teachings or other information. When spirits use the mouth and speak out information, this is called channeling.

Question 2

How popular is channeling in America and around the world?

In America there are thousands of channelers. Millions of followers seek out the channelers for advice or read the literature given by the spirits through their channelers.[3] Based on the sales of channeled literature, tapes, and seminars, channeling in America is a hundred-million-dollar-a-year enterprise.[4] Some have referred to America's growing interest in channeling as having "epidemic" proportions.

If we consider this phenomenon historically, we may understand the dangers of channeling and its potential to shape our future. For example, in 1851 there were an estimated 1200 mediums in Cincinnati, Ohio alone, as well as hundreds of mediums in other major cities.[5] By 1855, America boasted several thousand mediums and some 2 million followers.[6] These channelers and their followers undergirded an entire century of para-psychological research (the scientific study of the occult) in our country.[7]

This research, in turn, helped to pave the way for the modern occult explosion.[8] (See Chs. 33, 35.)

Today, Los Angeles is estimated to have about 1000 channelers,[9] indicating that we are at the beginning stages of another revival of interest. But the spirits today are turning to highly sophisticated marketing techniques through radio, television, and video.[10] In addition, the endorsement of channeling by famous television and movie stars is making the practice socially acceptable. Examples of stars who have this kind of influence are Shirley MacLaine, Linda Evans (of "Dynasty"), Michael York (of "Romeo and Juliet"), and others.[11]

Actress Sharon Gless, who played "Cagney" on the hit TV series "Cagney and Lacey," won a 1987 "Emmy" for her role on the series. In her acceptance speech, she told tens of millions that her success was due to "Lazaris," a spirit-entity who speaks through medium Jach Pursel.

The popularity of channeling can also be seen through new retreat centers and workshops around the country. In both, people are taught how to open their minds and bodies to the spirits to become channels themselves. In these retreat centers and workshops, live teaching sessions are taught by the spirits themselves, motivating people to start study groups, research centers, and magazines devoted solely to the study or development of channeling.[12]

Another area showing the popularity of channeling is its growing influence in the sciences and other disciplines. The spirits are speaking out of their human hosts, giving information which is applied to theories in psychology, to the practice of medicine, to the investigation of parapsychology, to the study of physics, to the application of sociology, and to the development of new ideas in theology, archaeology, and other disciplines.[13] In New York, spiritism has been used for several years as an adjunct to psychotherapy in some New York community mental health centers.[14]

Not only in America is channeling popular, there is an increasingly visible channeling movement emerging throughout the Western World, including Canada, England, and West Germany.[15] Brazil boasts over 1 million channelers or spiritists of various types with tens of millions of followers.[16] All in all it is safe to say that the influence of spirits speaking out of people will be with us for decades to come—and its fruits will affect the lives of our children.

Question 3

Why is an ancient occult practice so exciting and attractive to modern twentieth-century Americans, even including skeptics?

People today have a great need to find meaning in life. They have discovered, often painfully, that it cannot be found in a material view of reality alone. Even skeptics desire to know the answers to questions like, "Who am I?" "Why am I here?" and "What happens when I die?" Whether or not they admit it, the thought of life being no more than a few years of pain and pleasure replaced by eternal nonexistence is frightening to people. Men know they are more than the end product of hydrogen atoms and blind chance. And they are clearly searching for answers.

Modern man sees channeling as the proof of the deeper answers to life. Channeling seems to answer questions about the nature of reality (Is it spiritual?), the nature of death (Is it the end?), the nature of human potential (Is it unlimited?), and the nature of the self (Is it divine?). Thus, channeling powerfully persuades by claiming access to the very spirit world which can provide answers. The spirits are giving information which deceives men into thinking they are in contact with men who once lived on the earth, who died, and who now exist happily in the afterlife. The spirits claim that through death they have found the answers to life and the knowledge that all men will live forever. The spirits claim to speak with certainty about the nature of God, the purpose of life, and about what happens at death. They claim there is no hell and that God and heaven are not as the Bible has stated.

Channeling thus provides a false answer to modern man's need for religious experience. He is deceived into thinking such contact with the spirits gives meaning to his life and soothes his fears of death.

Think for a moment about what races through the mind of a person powerfully confronted by spiritism. It is like a blind person who suddenly is given his sight. Instantly, all is changed as he sees a new world of great wonder waiting to be explored. Likewise, the person encountering what he believes are genuine spirits of the dead believes death is no longer the end, the moment of absolute loss, but merely the beginning of a joyous new existence of literally unlimited possibilities.

People are deceived into thinking there is no hell to worry over, only the unending potential for advancement. The spirits do more than persuade; they exert great power over both the minds and hearts of men. This is the appeal of channeling.

Question 4

Who are the channelers?

Channelers come from all walks of life. They include clerks and scholars, artists and businessmen, truck drivers and Ph.D.'s, scientists and grade-school dropouts, business executives and housewives. They come from all races, nationalities, cultures, and creeds. Some are atheists (initially); others are religious. Except when in a trance and possessed, they look and act normally.

Channelers often channel more than one spirit. Well-known channelers and their main spirit guides include the late Jane Roberts and "Seth." "Seth," through Roberts, produced around 25 different books, which together have sold millions of copies. Another channeler was the late Helen Schucman. Schucman and her spirit guide "Jesus" are the author of the bestselling *A Course in Miracles*. (See Question 14.) Another channeler is Ruth Montgomery. Her spirit guide is "Lilly." They have

169

written numerous bestsellers on New Age topics. Another is Kevin Ryerson and his spirit guide "John," one of actress Shirley MacLaine's favorite channelers.[17] Ryerson is one of the more articulate channelers and has appeared on dozens of radio and TV shows. On these shows he offers live interviews with his spirit guides.[18] Another channeler is J. Z. Knight who channels "Ramtha." Knight claims she is a former fundamentalist Christian. Knight has sold almost a thousand hours of "Ramtha's" video and audiotapes. Like many channelers, she is now a multimillionaire.[19] Another channeler is Jach Pursel who channels "Lazaris." He runs a multimillion-dollar corporation entitled "Concept-Synergy." This corporation is dedicated to making Lazaris' teachings available to thousands of other people.[20] Lazaris' teachings have been especially popular among Hollywood movie stars.[21] But Lazaris' influence is not restricted to Hollywood. Amazingly, such diverse groups as Mennonites, Mormons, and Catholic nuns also testify to their following Lazaris' teachings.[22] (In Question 14 we briefly examine the religious views of some of these spirits.)

Question 5

What evidence would lead people to conclude channeling isn't all fraud and fantasy?

Many converging lines of evidence suggest the reality of another dimension of spirits who may be contacted by the proper occult methods. First, the belief in spirit contact is universal. It has occurred in all countries of the world throughout human history. This is documented by a great body of research. One study of nearly 500 modern societies revealed that 74 percent accepted the reality of not just spirit contact but of actual spirit-possession.[23] Something must account for so universal a belief. The skeptic who claims that such spirits do not exist holds his view in spite of this evidence.

Second, all major world religions have taught the reality of a spirit world. For example, Hinduism, Buddhism, Christianity, and Islam all believe in a world of good and evil spirits that may interact with men.[24]

Third, possessed people during channeling are sometimes able to give knowledge of the future and describe events taking place in another room or on the other side of the world. In other words, they exhibit knowledge, power, and abilities which they do not have when they are not in a trance.[25]

Fourth, exorcism cannot be adequately explained without assuming the reality of possessing spirits. Jesus Christ Himself believed in the reality of a dimension of demonic spirits and personally cast them out of individuals.[26]

All of this is evidence for the reality of spirits.

Question 6

Why does it matter who or what these spirits are as long as they help people?

Discovering their identity is vital. If they are evil beings, then even their "helping" is a deception. No matter what we think of them, it will change neither their nature nor their goals. If we view them incorrectly, we will be at their mercy. To misidentify a poisonous snake as a rope may be deadly. Thus, how we view these spirits is important. It is our interpretation as to their nature that will determine our personal response to them. If they are delusions, we will seek to help those suffering from them with medical assistance. If they are part of the unconscious mind or human potential, they will be sought out by those desiring to explore the powers of the mind. If they are angels or other benevolent spirits, or the human dead, they will be sought out for their spiritual wisdom or insights into life's great mysteries. Indeed, if these spirits really are highly advanced beings or the human dead, there is no reason not to seek their wisdom, for they may prove a genuine boon to human welfare. This is the standard argument. Nevertheless, if they are demons and irretrievably evil, to seek them out is foolish. Those who do so would sooner or later become their victims. Thus, identifying exactly what is happening in channeling is essential. For example, the fins of both sharks and dolphins are similar. What at first appears to be a playful dolphin could in reality be a deadly shark. To play in the water when only fins are visible could prove fatal.

Question 7

Should people trust the spirits speaking through channelers?

First of all, it must be stated there are both fake and real channelers. For example, in Question 26 we discuss channeler M. Lamar Keene who was a fake pretending to channel the dead to make money. But it is interesting to note that many genuine occultists such as channelers, shamans, psychics, mediums, and gurus have testified to the fact the spirits sometimes have deceived them. These occultists say the spirits imitate good spirits but actually trick, lie to, or injure their hosts. Occultists have found the spirits can imitate virtually anyone or anything with ease. Thus, Satprem, a disciple of occultist and Hindu guru Sri Aurobindo, states what all occultists know—that the spirits "can take all the forms they wish."[27]

The harrowing experience of astral traveler Robert Monroe is typical. In one of his many out-of-the-body experiences, he relates that he was repeatedly and viciously attacked by evil spirits. At one point in the fray, two of them instantly turned into exact images of his two daughters, emotionally throwing him off balance in his fight against them.[28] If occultists testify that the spirits have deceived them and that the spirits take different forms and they have taken these different forms for evil purposes, then it only seems reasonable that the spirits should not be trusted.

Another example of this is the famous medium Emanuel Swedenborg. He spent an entire lifetime associating with spirits. In the Western world perhaps no one else has had more experience with the spirit world than he. Yet Swedenborg cautioned that these spirits were so cunning and deceitful that it was almost impossible to determine their true nature. As an occult authority Swedenborg warned people that the demonic spirits are gifted actors and routinely imitate the dead. Thus, in a frightening way Swedenborg continues to caution people by saying,

> When spirits begin to speak with a man, he ought to beware that he believes nothing whatever from them; for they say almost anything. Things are fabricated by them, and they lie. . . . They would tell so many lies and indeed with solemn affirmation that a man would be astonished. . . . If a man listens and believes they press on, and deceive, and seduce in [many] ways. . . . Let men beware therefore [and not believe them].[29]

Unfortunately, despite all his cautions, Swedenborg himself fell prey to deceiving spirits by thinking his God had given him permission to contact the spirit world. Swedenborg ignored God's warning in Scripture against all forms of spirit contact (Deuteronomy 18:9-12). The reason Swedenborg ignored God's warning is that he believed "good" spirits had taught him the truth. Yet the "church" Swedenborg founded as a result of these "good" spirits has ever since promoted spiritistic revelation that is among the most antibiblical and anti-Christian material ever printed.[30]

So, can spirits speaking through channelers be trusted? If evil spirits do exist, and occultists tell us it is impossible for them to distinguish the good spirits from the evil ones, who is safe? They need some objective standard by which to test them. Channelers admit they do not have an objective standard. Therefore, their trust in the spirits is blind. Furthermore, if these spirits are demons, they could mask their evil intent for years and no one would be the wiser.

The Bible teaches that is exactly what is happening (2 Corinthians 11:14; 1 Timothy 4:1). In many cases the true goal of the spirits is to give false teachings, the consequences of which are learned too late or fearfully realized after death (Proverbs 16:25; Matthew 24:24; John 8:24,44; Galatians 1:6-8; 1 John 4:1; Revelation 16:14).

Even bad men succeed in masking their true intentions to deceive others. We cite Jim Jones as an illustration. Rev. Jones made many claims to being a minister of God. He was engaged in numerous "good works" through his church. But all along many signs were present that something was seriously wrong with Mr. Jones. Authoritarianism, intimidation of others, physical abuse of children, and irrational acts existed side-by-side with the "good." But Jones had power and charisma. He had an "explanation" for the evils and the failures. As a result many chose to ignore the warning signs and to believe he really was a good man sent of God. The end result was tragedy for over 900 people. The same type of situation exists with the spirits. They claim to be good. They claim to be representatives of God. But the warning signs are there. (See Question 24.)

Is it impossible to think that spirits could never mask their true intentions, like Jones? Yet in occult cases that have been researched, red flags have appeared (for those willing to see them) showing that the spirits' natures are evil. Even doing their best to imitate good, these spirits appear to have a difficult time suppressing their desires to harm man. Perhaps this is why the spiritists themselves sometimes suspect the motives of their contacts. Anyone reading what occultists say will conclude the fact that the spirits bring as much pain and suffering into their host's life as they may safely explain away. The spirits are master psychologists with long experience in dealing with human nature. The spirits know what they can get away with and how to cover their tracks. And the spirits have been doing it for thousands of years. People who would never trust a stranger are trusting strange spirits by the thousands. Yet there are dozens of points of similarity between spiritism (or channeling) on the one hand and the phenomena of demonism on the other. This includes the demonism of China, India, Japan, and other countries as well as the demonism of the Bible.[31] Thus, those who trust the spirits do so even though the entire history of spiritism is littered with evidence that these beings are demons.

Sometimes the spirits claim to be "angels" sent from God. They claim to bring divine revelations. But these entities cannot be true angels. Biblical angels are holy and godly; the entities behind the modern "angelic" revelations are neither. In the Bible true angels glorify Christ and give revelations that are scriptural. Modern "angels" deny Christ and give revelations contrary to Bible teaching. Judging from their recorded appearances in the Bible, we see that biblical angels usually operate "behind the scenes"; communications are rare and brief; and they do not seek glory for themselves (Hebrews 13:2). This is in contrast with the modern "angels" who operate in the open and seek to maintain communication in the manner of spiritistic contacts in general.

The Bible admonishes us to "test the spirits" (1 John 4:1). This is more important than ever, especially in the church.

23

The Characteristics
and Worldview
of Channeling

Question 8

What happens during channeling?

When a channeler goes into a full trance, it is as if he is falling backward into a deep sleep. Both his facial muscles and lips twitch as the invading spirit begins to gain control over the person. Once the spirit is in possession of the body, changes in breathing occur and the person's facial features and expressions are different, sometimes greatly different (for example, the late Jane Roberts). What can be most noticeable is when the voice changes; for example, a feminine voice becomes deep and masculine.[32]

The person who is possessed by the spirits may describe it as similar to an alcohol blackout or to what occurs in hypnosis. The person loses consciousness. Later he awakens. He is told he has said and done things he would not normally have done—yet he remembers absolutely nothing. He is told there was a total takeover of his individual personality. He became like a puppet under the control of a greater power.

Full trance-channeling may involve anything that is normally done in the body, from writing to painting, to singing and dancing, to composing music, to counseling or teaching others.[33]

There are two basic kinds of channeling—intentional and spontaneous. In "intentional" channeling the person actively seeks to be possessed by the spirits. And the spirits usually wait for that person's permission to enter the body. On the other hand, in "spontaneous" channeling the spirits simply take control when they please. The channel is at their mercy.

174

Yet even intentional channels may suddenly find themselves at the mercy of their formerly polite spirit guides.[34]

Channeling can involve different forms; for example, one form may involve complete loss of consciousness and another may involve partial loss of consciousness. Thus, there is full trance-possession with total loss of consciousness, and light-to-moderate trance-possession, in which the channeler retains full or partial awareness of his surroundings. In addition there is "sleep" channeling where the spirits teach or influence mediums during their sleep or in their dreams. Another form is known as "automatism" where the spirit seems only to control part of the body such as the hands in automatic writing or painting. There is "clairaudient" channeling where the medium only hears the words dictated by the spirits. There is "clairvoyant" channeling where the spirits put certain images, pictures, or symbols into the mind of the person. There is also what is termed "physical" channeling where the spirit uses the medium to affect or alter the environment. For example, the spirits either through a medium or on their own may materialize images of dead people (called "ectoplasmic manifestations"); they may move or levitate objects or imprint them with messages or pictures, or they may transfer objects from one location to another (known as teleportation).[35]

Remember, it is clear that whatever power the medium uses comes only as a result of his contact with the possessing spirit. It is universally recognized that apart from these spirits, the channelers have no power.[36] (See Chapter 33, Question 6.)

Question 9

How are people used by the spirits to become channelers?

Once the proper "invitation" is given, a spirit may unexpectedly take over a person at any time. There are no rules. Millions today are giving out such invitations ignorantly, with little idea of just who may arrive. One of the easiest ways to encounter the spirits or to be possessed by them is to deliberately seek altered states of consciousness. There are hundreds of such methods, including drugs, meditation, yoga, and hypnosis.[37] Channeling is also developed by direct contact with the spirit world through Ouija boards[38] and attending seances.[39]

Question 10

Who do the spirits claim they are?

The spirits claim to be many things. Judging from their own teachings, by far the most common assertion is that they are the spirits of the human dead. A recent prestigious poll revealed that over 40 percent of all American adults—approaching half the nation—claim to have been in contact with someone who has died. Of these, 78 percent claimed they saw, 50 percent heard, and 18 percent claimed to have talked with the dead.[40] From this it is clear the spirits most often claim they are human spirits who have survived physical death. They also claim they can reveal important information to men that will hasten their spiritual growth. Further, the spirits claim they are more evolved than we are because they have lived through many lifetimes and discovered the secrets of life and death. The spirits claim that if enough people will listen to them, they can even help to bring a worldwide spiritual awakening. This will produce a New Age of peace and harmony.[41]

We should also keep in mind that the spirits will also appear in the form most desirable or interesting to the one they are seeking to contact. For example, the spirits claim to be extraterrestrials (including Martians and Venusians), various gods of ancient or modern cultures (or God Himself), Jesus Christ, ascended masters, "group beings," angels, and nature spirits. By doing this, they know they will spark the interest of the people they are contacting. They may also claim to be various aspects of the human mind or the "collective" mind of humanity (some of the terms used here include the Creative Unconscious, the Higher Self, the Oversoul, the Super-conscious Mind, the Universal Mind, and the Collective Unconscious). They also claim to be the Holy Spirit, troubled ghosts, the spirits of animals and plants (dolphins, trees, flowers), multiple human personalities, the inhabitants of mythical cultures (Atlanteans, Lemurians), and even a possible alien computer that exists in the future.[42] Critics, realizing that some people are claiming to channel dolphins, the spirits of fruits and vegetables and even computers from the future, have come to conclude the sanity of the nation is at risk.

Question 11

What possible reason would spirits have for imitating the dead?

The Bible tells us there are such things as "unclean spirits" or demons. These spirits are so evil they will never be redeemed: These spirits already know they will eventually be consigned forever to a place Jesus called hell (Matthew 8:29). The Scriptures lead us to conclude the real motive of the spirits is to take as many men to hell with them as possible by preventing their salvation (John 8:44; 2 Corinthians 11:3,4,13,14; Hebrews 2:14; 1 Peter 5:8). If these spirits really are the human dead, then men can only conclude the dead are free to roam and, therefore, God has not judged them at the moment of death as the Bible teaches (Luke 16:19-31; Hebrews 9:27; 2 Peter 2:9). If, as the spirits say, the dead are not judged, then human sin is not an offense to God requiring separation from Him (Isaiah 59:2). If sin does not separate man from God, then Christ did not have to die for man's sin (1 Peter 2:24; 1 John 2:2). According to the spirits' views, this means man's faith in Christ as Savior from sin is unnecessary (John 3:16). And if men never trust Christ and receive Him as their Savior, then at death they go to judgment and the demons have achieved their goal (2 Thessalonians 1:8-10). To help them deceive men, the spirits enthusiastically teach what their presence as the dead implies—they teach there is no judgment and Christ did not die for our sin. In fact, these demons teach that all men are divine and as such do not even require salvation. The only things they recommend are minor adjustments in man's thinking. In this way the spirits have tricked men into rejecting what the Bible teaches about God, Christ, the death of Christ, man's sinful condition, the necessity of salvation, final judgment, and hell. (See Chapter 34, Question 9.)

Question 12

Why are spirits contacting men?

They claim they are here to help us. Again, most spirits claim to be the human dead. They claim they have come back to convince men and women not to fear their eventual death. Because the spirits say they are just normal men who have died, they claim they can offer us the truth about what will happen when men die.

They also claim they are here to enlighten us spiritually. They say that the purpose of life is to realize our true divine nature—that we are God. The spirits teach that the cause of humanity's problems is really ignorance of its divine nature, not human sin. They say that men need to accept the fact that they are part of God if human problems are ever to be solved. Beliefs like salvation, sin, guilt and judgment are worn out concepts, and according to the spirits, must be discarded. The spirits promise there is no hell. For example, the spirit "Emmanuel" who possesses Pat Rodegast states: "Death is perfectly safe."[43] The spirits also teach that all men will reincarnate until they achieve perfection. In brief, the spirits agree on the nature and destiny of man.

There is also agreement on the importance of occult practices and the necessity of widespread contact with the spirit world. Also, the spirits are in total agreement that Jesus Christ is not the Savior of the world. (The Bible teaches He is.) Most interestingly, the spirits are in agreement that the idea of the devil and demons are merely human inventions. (The Bible teaches the devil and demons are real.)

Question 13

Why do many channelers say their spirit guides are part of their unconscious mind?

Many channelers claim their spirit guides are a part of their "creative unconscious." They say this because they are uncomfortable with the idea that real spirits are actually possessing them. Channelers find it easier to believe the spirits are merely part of the newfound powers of their own mind or human genius. To deceive men, the spirits often go along with such labels.

Interestingly enough, modern parapsychology (the scientific study of the occult) has provided much support to relabel the activity of these spirits. Again, the spirits who desire to possess men find the relabeling of their activity to be good. Men who would never permit themselves to be possessed by spirits, might welcome the "scientific"-sounding idea that they are really contacting their own alleged "higher consciousness" or "divine mind." Once the spirits' activity is masked under the disguise of psychic powers, or the powers of the unconscious mind, their activity becomes unrecognizable for what it really is: true spirit contact. What is frightening here is that both the scientific community and psychics are redefining something supernatural and alien as really being something natural and human.[44] (See Part 7, Questions 6,9–13.)

In his classic book *The Screwtape Letters*, Oxford scholar C. S. Lewis astutely portrays two devils talking to one another and planning their strategy:

> Our policy, for the moment, is to conceal ourselves. Of course this has not always been so. We are really faced with a cruel dilemma. When the humans disbelieve in our existence we lose all the pleasing results of direct terrorism, and we make no magicians. On the other hand, when they believe in us, we cannot make them materialists and skeptics. At least, not yet. I have great hopes that we shall learn in due time how to emotionalize and mythologize their science to such an extent that what is, in effect, a belief in us (though not under that name) will creep in while the human mind remains closed to belief in the Enemy. The "Life Force," the worship of sex and some aspect of Psychoanalysis may here prove useful. If once we can produce our perfect work—the Materialist Magician, the man, not using, but veritably worshipping, what he vaguely calls "Forces" while denying the existence of "spirits"—then the end of the war will be in sight.[45]

Today even psychology is using its influence to promote the activity of spirits in nonthreatening psychological language. For example, we now have past-life therapy, inner-counselor therapy, transpersonal psychology, transcultural psychiatry, metapsychiatry, and shamanistic counseling, all of which involves or may verge on spiritism. Again, it is clear that certain concepts in modern psychology are becoming a major tool for camouflaging the demonic and expanding its influence in society under another name. Proof of this is that virtually every occult power or spirit manifestation has been "explained" psychologically or parapsychologically, or endorsed humanistically as the "new powers of the mind." And once psychology redefines these spirits as the hidden potential of the human mind, the goal of therapy will be to successfully tap into these new powers.[46] This approach agrees with the stated purposes of many of the spirits themselves who say their goal is to "empower" people to get in touch with their own "intuition," "higher Self," "creative sub-personality," or "divine potential," so that in the future *everyone* will become a channel for something.[47] In essence, the spirits desire man to view their activity as nothing more than the normal workings of the human mind. What they desire is invisibility.

24

The Theology
of
Channeling

Question 14

What are the religious views of the spirits?

First, we will present a brief summary in which we compare the spirits' views with Bible teaching. Then we will quote the spirits themselves from channeled literature to document their teachings.

God

The spirits teach that God is an impersonal force (an "It"), like electricity. It (God) has power but it cannot love. The Bible teaches that God is a personal, holy, and loving God (John 3:16).

Jesus

The spirits teach that Jesus is an ascended master or a man just like us. The spirits say that Jesus has died and has now evolved to a higher state of existence just like others. The Bible teaches that Jesus is fully man and fully God in one person. He is the only and unique Son of God (John 1:1; Philippians 2:1-9; Titus 2:13).

Man

The spirits teach that man in his true nature is perfect and one essence with God. The Bible teaches that man is a created being who sinned by disobeying God, resulting in his being separated from God's fellowship (Genesis 1:27; 3:3-8).

Sin

The spirits teach that sin is merely ignorance of one's own deity or "errors" of consciousness. The Bible teaches that sin is disobedience of God's law (1 John 3:4; 5:17).

Salvation

The spirits teach that salvation involves realizing that one is already God. Each man must accomplish this for himself by practicing various occult techniques. The Bible teaches that salvation involves receiving the gift of forgiveness of sins from God. Salvation has been provided for man by God's grace and is received by man through faith in Christ's death for us (Ephesians 1:7; 2:8,9).

Death

The spirits teach that at death there is no judgment. It is merely a transition into the spirit world. The Bible teaches death brings judgment and entrance either into an eternal heaven or hell (Matthew 25:46; Hebrews 9:27).

Satan

The spirits teach there is no devil. The Bible teaches that Satan and his demons are real (Matthew 4:1-10; 8:16; 17:18).

Now we will cite the words of the spirits themselves concerning their religious teachings. As you read them carefully, ask yourself some questions. Are these teachings good or evil? Are they true or false? Are they what we would expect from deceitful demons or truly good spirits?

Teachings of the Spirits[48]

1. "Ramtha"—The spirit speaking through medium J. Z. Knight in *Ramtha, Voyage to the New World* (Ballentine, 1987); citations are listed by pages.

> **"Ramtha's" teaching on God:** Ramtha teaches the Christian God is an "idiotic deity" (p. 219); ". . . God, the principal, is all things. . ." (p. 250).

> **"Ramtha's" teaching on man:** "You are *God*" (p. 61); "God the Father is you" (p. 136); "Everyone is what you call a psychic. . ." (p. 139); "Love yourself. . . live in the moment, to exalt all that you are" (p. 149).

Spirit Guides

"Ramtha's" teaching on sin: "... There is no such thing as evil" (p. 60); "...For 2,000 years we have been called sinful creatures... [but] we are equal with God or Christ" (pp. 180-181).

"Ramtha's" teaching on salvation: "Do not preach to this world... the world doesn't need saving—leave it alone" (p. 130); "Relinquish guilt... do not live by rules, live by feelings.... You are the Lord of Hosts, *you* are the Prince of Peace" (p. 149); "Now to become enlightened is to make the priority of enlightenment first—the priority of love of Self *first*" (p. 227).

"Ramtha's" teaching on death: "God has never judged you or anyone" (p. 62); "No, there is no Hell and there is no devil" (p. 252).

"Ramtha's" teaching on Satan and demons: "Devil? I looked far and wide for the creature... I found him nowhere [but] I found him thriving in the hearts of frenzied entities in a fervor of madness to save the world from its sins.... That is where he is. [Do] you understand?" (pp. 252-253). "... The devil is not really evil... because he's really God... who else would he be?" (p. 251).

2. **"Jesus"**—The spirit who worked through medium Helen Schucman in *A Course in Miracles* (1977); citations are listed by volume and page.

"Jesus' " teaching on God: "The recognition of God is the recognition of yourself. There is no separation of God and His creation" (1:136).

"Jesus' " teaching on Jesus: "There is nothing about me [Jesus] that you cannot attain" (1:5); "Christ waits for your acceptance of Him as yourself" (1:187); "Is [Jesus] the Christ? O yes, along with you" (1:83).

"Jesus' " teaching on man: "God's Name is holy, but no holier than yours. To call upon His Name is but to call upon your own" (2:334); "You are the Holy Son of God Himself" (2:353-54).

"Jesus' " teaching on sin: "...Sin does not exist" (3:81); "Sin is the grand illusion... joyously [release] one another from the belief in sin" (1:375, 377-78); "See no one, then, as guilty... [within all men] there is perfect innocence"; "No one is punished for sins [and you] are not sinners" (1:88).

"Jesus' " teaching on salvation: "[Divine] forgiveness, then, is an illusion..." (3:79); "[It is] a terrible misperception that God Himself [judged] His own Son on behalf of salvation.... It is so essential that all such thinking be dispelled that we must be sure that nothing of this kind remains in your mind. I was not 'punished' because you were bad" (1:32-33, 87); "A sense of separation from God is the only lack you really need to correct"; "Salvation is nothing more than 'rightmindedness' . . ."; ". . . you are one with God" (1:11,53; 2:125); "Do not make the pathetic error of 'clinging to the old rugged cross.' . . . This is not the gospel I . . . intended to offer you" (1:47).

"Jesus' " teaching on death: "There is no death, but there is a belief in death" (1:46); "Death is the central dream from which all illusions stem" (3:63).

3. **"Seth"**—The spirit speaking through Jane Roberts and written down by her husband in *Seth Speaks* (Prentice Hall, 1972); citations are listed by pages.

"Seth's" teaching on God: God is "All That Is" (p. 405).

"Seth's" teaching on Jesus: "He [Jesus] will not come to reward the righteous and send evildoers to eternal doom" (p. 389).

"Seth's" teaching on sin: "A strong belief in such [concepts of good and evil] is highly detrimental . . ." (p. 191).

"Seth's" teaching on salvation: ". . . The soul . . . is not something you must save or redeem, and it is also something you cannot lose" (p. 89).

"Seth's" teaching on Satan and demons: ". . . The devil is a projection of your own psyche . . ." (p. 7); ". . . There are no devils or demons . . ." (p. 405).

4. **"Lilly"** and other spirits channeled through medium Ruth Montgomery. (Note: Some of the following statements are Montgomery's although they reflect the teachings of the spirits which she has adopted as her own belief.)

The spirits' teaching on God: "God is the name of What Is" (R.M., *Here and Hereafter*, Fawcett Crest, 1968, p. 74).

The spirits' teaching on man: ". . . God wishes that it [psychic ability] be utilized and developed to the fullest potential" (R.M., *A Search for Truth*, Bantam, 1968, p. 160); ". . . We are God . . ." (R.M., *A World Beyond*, Fawcett Crest, 1972, p. 12).

The spirits' teaching on death: "There is no such thing as death" (Ibid., p. 66); "God punishes no man." (R.M., *Here and Hereafter*, p. 174).

The spirits' teaching on Satan and demons: "I have seen no signs of a devil on this side of the veil ['veil' here means death]" (R.M., *A World Beyond*, p. 64); "The devil was not a person ever..." (Ibid., p. 65).

5. **Various spirits** who allegedly knew Jesus on earth written through medium Kahlil Gibran in *Jesus, the Son of Man* (New York: A. A. Knopf, 1959); citations are listed by pages.

The spirits' views on God: "Israel should have another God..." (p. 32).

The spirits' views on Jesus: "Jesus the Nazarene was born and reared like ourselves.... He was [only] a man"; "Jesus was a man and not a god.... It's a pity his followers seek to make a god of such a sage" (pp. 43, 109, 113).

Now consider the content of what you have just read. Do these spirits deny there is a devil when Jesus taught that Satan was a real, personal being (Matthew 4:1-10)? Do the spirits endorse the occult when God forbids it (Deuteronomy 18:9-12)? Why do you think the spirits claim men are not sinners when all men know in their hearts they are? Why do the spirits teach that God is impersonal when God has revealed Himself in the Bible as a personal Being? Why do the spirits teach man to be selfish when such behavior is universally condemned? Why do the spirits deny that Christ died to forgive men's sins when Christ Himself taught this was the very reason He came (Matthew 20:28)? Why do the spirits claim Jesus was simply a man when all the evidence proves He was God-Incarnate, the only begotten Son of God? He Himself taught this (John 3:16; 5:18; 10:30; 14:6). Why do the spirits say men are God, when we know *we* are not God? Why do the spirits deny the existence of evil when its reality is obvious to all? The point is this: The religious teachings of the spirits are exactly what one might expect from demons. The irony is that the very theory that is most probably true, that Satan and demons do exist, is the one most rarely considered when evaluating these entities.

Question 15

What does the Bible say about channeling?

The first historical incidence of channeling is recorded in the Bible in Genesis, Chapter 3. There in the Garden of Eden the devil used the serpent as a "channel" to trick Eve (Genesis 3:1-5; 2 Corinthians 11:3; Revelation 12:9). Through channeling, the devil deceived man into doubting God, with serious consequences. Significantly, there are compelling reasons for believing that the basic reality of channeling that is suggested here has never altered, either as to its 1) origin (the devil or demons); 2) result (spiritual deception which undermines trust in God); 3) consequences (divine judgment, see Genesis 3:13-19; Deuteronomy 18:9-13). Channeling is thus condemned in the Bible as an evil practice before God. It is rejected because it is a form of spiritism which involves contact with demons and the spreading of their false teachings.

The Bible further teaches that "in later times some will fall away from the faith, paying attention to deceitful spirits and doctrines of demons" (1 Timothy 4:1). Spiritistic teachings pervert the nature of God, lie about Christ, and distort the way of salvation. Those who trust spiritistic teachings face judgment at death. On the authority of one no less than Christ Himself we discover that hell is a real place (Matthew 25:46; Luke 16:19-31). The demons who assure men that sin is not real and hell does not exist are bringing eternal ruin to those who trust them.

The Bible instructs man to reject every form of spiritism as something evil and an encounter with lying spirits. Channeling is a form of spiritual warfare with the souls of men at stake (2 Corinthians 4:4). This is why both channeling itself and following the teaching of the channelers are condemned in Scripture as rebellion against God and as courting His judgment. An example of this is King Manasseh of Judah in ancient Israel. "He practiced witchcraft, used divination, practiced sorcery and dealt with mediums and spiritists. He did much evil in the sight of the Lord, provoking Him to anger" (2 Chronicles 33:2-6). Likewise in Deuteronomy 18:9-12 God warns His people that "There shall not be found among you anyone . . . who uses divination, who practices witchcraft, who is a spiritist, or who calls up the dead. For whoever does these things is detestable to the Lord. . . ." The phrase "who is a spiritist" clearly condemns all aspects of channeling.

25

Channeling and Related Issues

Question 16

Is there any relationship between hypnosis, multiple personality, and channeling?

First, hypnosis is an altered state of consciousness that may open people to the entrance of spirits. In fact, many mediums first trained for spirit contact through the practice of hypnosis.[49] Historically, hypnosis has had a long history of occult associations, from yoga to mesmerism. To us, hypnosis' therapeutic value is debatable (not because it is never helpful but because of other concerns for which there are still no answers). And quite clearly, there is an obvious occult use of hypnosis so caution is urged.[50] For example, as already stated, many mediums admit their first spirit contact took place under hypnosis. Others have used hypnosis as a means of developing psychic powers. The simple truth is that the state of hypnosis is an especially useful state of mind for anyone who has wanted to learn channeling.[51]

The relationship between multiple personality and channeling presents a dilemma because these conditions can be difficult to distinguish.

Here is an example of the relationship that may exist between channeling and multiple personality. One or two additional personalities (called multiple personality) may be explained as a consequence of the natural breakdown of the human mind. Childhood abuse is apparently so frequent in such cases that this trauma may explain many (or most) of them. However, the cases of dozens or scores of personalities as the 92 personalities cited in the book *When Rabbit Howls* (written by the "entities" themselves) are often close enough to classical spiritism that possession by truly supernatural beings may explain some of these cases more adequately.[52] In fact, there are even a number of secular researchers of multiple personalities who admit that in many cases they are dealing with spirit-possession and not true multiple personality.[53] What is disturbing is that multiple personalities that appear to result from simple spirit-possession are being treated as a fascinating new area of human potential and scientific exploration. The medical goal today is to "integrate" the multiple personalities back into one original personality. Doctors seek to help patients accept their different personalities and permit them to continue to inhabit their body—perhaps under the leadership of the "dominant" personality. If these multiple personalities are really different spirits, then professional psychologists, who believe they are helping people, are really helping them to accept their own demonization. Some psychologists even refer to the multiple personalities as separate beings, literally as "entities," because this is exactly how these personalities act.[54] A biblical example of "multiple personality" that was certainly demonic was the Gerasenes' demoniac in Luke 8:28,30.

Question 17
What else is channeling related to?

The practice of spiritism does not arrive in a clearly marked package today. Often one needs to look beneath the surface of a given practice or phenomenon to uncover the spiritistic roots or source of power. Examples of this are most near-death experiences,[55] water and other dowsing,[56] UFO's,[57] aspects of parapsychology,[58] some forms of mysticism,[59] and many forms of "spiritual" healing and holistic health practices.[60]

Channeling sometimes bears a relationship to mental illness. One discovers many mental patients who are mentally ill precisely because they are demonized.[61] This is born out by the research of German psychiatrist and parapsychologist Hans Bender who coined the term "mediumistic psychosis";[62] by theologian and psychologist Kurt Koch;[63] and by clinical psychologist and Swedenborgian Wilson Van Dusen, who has examined thousands of patients and noted the parallels to spiritistic experiences and phenomena.[64]

Question 18
Are cults related to channeling?

There is a direct relationship between the origin of hundreds of cults and the phenomenon of channeling. Channeling is how they began, and the reason for this is a logical one. To illustrate, after Japan was dramatically defeated in World War II, the people's faith in the divine status of the Japanese emperor was shattered. A spiritual vacuum arose that was filled by scores of new cults, many of which began powerfully through spirit contact and channeled messages.[65] One such example of this was the

Odoru Shukyo sect begun by Kitamura Sayo in 1945. Sayo claimed, characteristically, that a Shinto deity "took possession of her" to give divine revelations.[66]

In the United States we have experienced a similar situation. This has occurred through the impact of secularism and other humanist beliefs which for millions has resulted in the loss of faith in God. This resulted in a spiritual vacuum—and vacuums are always filled by something.

In this case the vacuum was filled by hundreds of American cults and sects that are related to or involved with channeling.[67] In America some educators go so far as to assert that channeling "appears to be an essential element in the origins of virtually all of the great spiritual paths."[68]

But why should this be true? The reason is simple. Channeling and religion go hand in hand because the purpose of the spirits is to provide men with a religious belief that insulates against belief in Christ.

The Bible teaches, "The whole world lies in the power of the evil one" and that Satan "blinds the minds" of unbelievers (2 Corinthians 4:4; 1 John 5:19). False religion is one way to accomplish this goal.

A quick examination of religions in our world today that are associated with channeling include Islam, Hinduism, Buddhism, Shinto, and Animism.[69] In addition, some Eastern sects or cults have developed in America at least in part as a result of channeling. Among the gurus are Paramahansa Yogananda (Self-Realization Fellowship), Krishnamurti, Rajneesh, Sri Chinmoy, and Ram Dass, to name just a few.[70]

Other new religions and cults in America that are related to channeling are Alice Bailey's *Lucius Trust*, Paul Twitchell's *Eckankar*, David Berg's *The Children of God* (the Love Family), Sun Myung Moon's *Unification Church*, Rudolph Steiner's *Anthroposophy*, Earlyne Chaney's *Astara*, Elizabeth Claire Prophet's *Church Universal and Triumphant*, Guy Ballard's *The Mighty I Am*, Joseph Smith's *Mormonism* (the angel "Moroni"), Mary Baker Eddy's *Christian Science*—again, just to name a few.[71] When one stops to think about it, isn't it amazing that all of these religions have been touched by channeling? It is sobering indeed to realize that all of these religions have been influenced by channeling when the God of the Bible absolutely forbids it.

Question 19

What is Eckankar?

Eckankar is a controversial and anti-Christian religious sect begun in 1964 by occultist Paul Twitchell. Among its teachings are the ideas that the Christian God is the "devil" and that Jesus is a son of the devil.[72] It is actually an offshoot of Hinduism. It is also an occultic teaching stressing out-of-the-body experiences called "Soul Travel." It openly stresses the beneficial results of spirit contact. As such, Eckankar claims it is the conveyor of spiritual wisdom that has been revealed by ascended masters or spirit beings who live in other dimensions. Eckankar believes it is the oldest religion on earth and was begun by a former inhabitant of the planet

Venus whose name was "Gakko" and who came to earth six million years ago.[73]

Although Eckankar claims to be unique, Paul Twitchell (the founder of Eckankar) actually acquired some of the teachings of Eckankar from a Hindu school. This group of teachings, called "Surat Shabd Yoga," was systematized in India by Sawan Singh (died 1948) in his Radhasoami Beas sect. It was continued by Kirpal Singh (died 1974) in his Ruhani Satsang sect (into which Twitchell was initiated in 1955) and it was popularized in America by Dr. Julian Johnson in his book *The Path of the Masters* (1939).[74]

With Paul Twitchell's unexpected death in 1971, Darwin Gross became the leader or "living Eck Master" of Eckankar. In 1981 Gross appointed Harold Klemp as "living Eck Master," but a few years later Gross himself was excommunicated from Eckankar. This brought an extensive and embarrassing legal battle between himself and the organization. Today Klemp remains the spiritual head of Eckankar.

Since shortly after its inception Eckankar has been embroiled in controversy amidst charges that it is a religion based upon fiction and deception.[75]

Question 20

What are some of the serious concerns a student of Eckankar must face?

The student of Eckankar is placed in a "no-win" situation. First, at least two studies have been done which leave no doubt that Twitchell plagiarized the basic beliefs of Eckankar from the writings of Julian Johnson.[76] Second, it can easily be pointed out that Eckankar is riddled with massive internal contradictions in theology and basic teachings. In brief, it has become impossible for a disciple in Eckankar to know what are the "true" doctrines he is supposed to believe.[77] Third, on many issues Eckankar speaks out of both sides of its mouth, publicly denying what it privately affirms. For example, Eckankar publicly teaches all religions are good, but privately teaches its *chelas* [students] that Christianity is inferior and satanic.[78] Fourth, it can be clearly proved that Eckankar has engaged in a protracted cover-up of its true history.[79] Fifth, Eckankar believes their God encompasses evil and is imperfect.[80] Sixth, researchers of Eckankar have cited additional issues to be part of the tragedy of Eckankar. Such charges include embezzlement, spiritual authoritarianism, personal harassment, practicing black magic, making questionable moral decisions, and suggesting myth and fantasy are historic facts, which make it impossible for Eckankar to be considered a legitimate or valid religion.[81] In addition to dangerous occultic practices (mediumship, spiritism, magic, astral travel, etc.),[82] which are hazardous to the well-being (spiritual and otherwise) of the *chela*, or Eckankar disciple, the disciple must ignore his own conscience if he chooses to remain in Eckankar.

In summary, Eckankar, like many modern cults, is a religion of highly questionable origins, involving deception, contradiction, and dangerous practices.

26

An Analysis
and Critique
of Channeling

Question 21

What is the source of power behind channeling?

Channelers admit they have no power or abilities apart from their spirit guides. This admission is consistent with biblical teaching on the subject (Acts 16:16-19; see Chapter 33, Questions 6,10). As is clear by now, the source of power in channeling is the spirit beings referred to in the Bible as "unclean spirits" or demons who have Satan as their leader. In spite of their claims to want only to help mankind, these spirits continually reveal their true demonic nature by what they say.

There are many in the world today who disagree. One such example is channeling advocate and psychologist Dr. Jon Klimo. He says those who say that these spirits are demons and evil beings are doing positive harm to the welfare of humanity. Klimo proposes that an occult revival is good and something that mankind needs. (See Chapter 36.) It is to be achieved "with less guidance than ever before . . . from the churches of organized religion."[83] Klimo writes, "To the extent to which they [the churches] brand and prohibit channeling as demon worship and consorting with 'unfamiliar spirits,' they will be abdicating what should be their role: to help us reconnect ourselves in our own way with our common Source as underlying Reality."[84] In other words, "to return to the truth of truths . . . that we are God."[85]

But what if Klimo's spirits really *are* demons? Will they not be harming mankind? What if it is a *lie* that men are God? What if a person believes this not knowing that God says such a belief can result in his eternal damnation? What if the logical, historical, and biblical evidence all point to this conclusion? What if those who say these spirits are man's helpers do so merely because this is what they want to believe is true—that it is they who are unwilling to face the facts? What if those who believe these spirits are part of their "higher mind" are wrong? Sometimes it is easy for people to discard facts for personal preference. Famous writer Colin Wilson suggests the possibility of a realm of evil spirits and has questioned the reluctance of many to accept the spirits for what they are—real spirits.

> Why do we try so hard to find a theory that rules out living forces? It is as if a doctor tried to find a theory of disease that made no use of the concept of germs. Why do we experience a certain unwillingness to entertain this hypothesis of "discarnate entities"?... [It is because] there is an unwillingness to introduce a frightening unknown factor into our picture of the universe.[86]

The demon theory is often rejected because most people simply refuse to believe in the reality of personal spiritual evil *directed at them*. Yet this is exactly what the Bible teaches is true and why we are warned to "be on the alert" (2 Corinthians 4:4; 1 Peter 5:8).

It is the spirits' consistent teaching throughout human history which has condemned them and revealed their true identity. Their teachings are amoral and opposed to human welfare. They are liars and vehemently opposed to the God of the Bible.

Question 22

What additional evidence would lead a thinking person to conclude that demons actually exist?

There is a great deal of evidence for the existence of the evil beings the Bible refers to as demons.

We can suggest the following reasonings which infer the possibility of a real devil and the reality of spiritual evil: 1) the consensus of history and religion, 2) the testimony of active occultists, 3) the phenomenon of spirit-possession, 4) the authority of the Bible and the testimony of Jesus Christ, and 5) the odd prejudice against historic biblical Christianity which has been displayed in all spiritistically inspired literature.

Reasoning 1: The consensus of history and religion is an impressive one. Belief in a world of evil spirits has been with man throughout his history. It has been an accepted truth for most people in most times and cultures, whether ancient or modern (Assyrian, Babylonian, Celtic, Egyptian, Greek, Hebrew, Indian, African, Muslim, Roman, Tibetan, Persian, Chinese, Buddhist, Hindu, Christian, Jain, Japanese, Slavic, etc.).[87] In light of so vast a testimony from history, culture, and religion, can anyone credibly remain skeptical about a real devil and the reality of spiritual evil in the world?

Reasoning 2: The testimony of occultists themselves, whether magicians, psychics, channelers, mediums, or Satanists indicate they are very much aware of the reality of spiritual evil, however they may choose to define it. Many of them believe in literal evil spirits and have had personal encounters with them. Such encounters leave little doubt as to their malevolent nature.[88]

Reasoning 3: Another line of evidence involves the experience of demon-possession, which occurs in nearly every culture and religion, ancient or modern.[89] Former witch Doreen Irvine declares, "Demon-possession is real, very real, and is increasing at an alarming rate in this present day and age."[90] Naturally, the very act of a spirit invading and controlling a person implies, even demands, hostility and malice. And it is usually the occultist who gets possessed. In his text *People of the Lie,* psychiatrist M. Scott Peck, author of the bestselling *The Road Less Traveled* observes, "It seems clear from the literature on possession that a majority of cases have had involvement with the occult—a frequency far greater than might be expected in the general population."[91] (See Question 5.)

Reasoning 4: A fourth reason suggesting the reality of a real devil is the Bible. Because the Bible is the Word of God, what it says about the existence of a personal devil is obviously true; therefore in light of the abundance of data supporting its claim to divine inspiration, we may assume its statements about Satan are reliable. If one believes in the truth of the Bible, then it is impossible to doubt the reality of the devil. Jesus Christ Himself believed in the reality of Satan and demons. And no one else could speak with more authority. No one else in history directly claimed to be God (John 5:18; 10:30; 14:9) and proved the truth of His claim by literally rising from the dead (Matthew 20:18,19; Luke 1:1-4 with John 20:24-28; Acts 1:3).[92]* (See Chapter 34, Question 7.)

Reasoning 5: Finally, the teachings of the spirits *universally* oppose the Bible. The most logical explanation for their single-mindedness is that they are the very spirits that the Bible exposes as demons.

In addition some of the most brilliant minds of our modern era have accepted the reality of demons. The brilliant Christian apologist C. S. Lewis said in regard to their existence, "It seems to me to explain a good many facts. It agrees with the plain sense of Scripture, the tradition of Christendom, and the beliefs of most men at most times. And it conflicts with nothing that any of the sciences has shown to be true."[93] Lawyer and

---

* See John Ankerberg, John Weldon *Do the Resurrection Accounts Conflict? And What Proof Is There That Jesus Rose from the Dead?* (Chattanooga, TN: Ankerberg Theological Research Institute, 1989).

theologian Dr. John Warwick Montgomery asserts, "The problem involved in determining whether demon-possession occurs and whether witchcraft works is absurdly simple. The documentation is overwhelming."[94] He also states, "There is overwhelming extra-biblical data and empirical confirmation of the scriptural claims" regarding the existence of a personal devil and demons.[95]

In brief, when one considers not only the divine authority of the Bible and the testimony of Christ who, as God, was also an infallible authority, but also the consensus of history and religion, the testimony of active occultists, the phenomenon of possession, and the hostility to biblical revelation displayed in spiritistic literature, one is hard-pressed to maintain simply that demons do not exist. In the end, one either trusts the spirits and ignores the facts—or one trusts the facts and ignores the spirits.

Question 23

Do demons have a plan for men's lives?

The principal goal of a demon is spiritual deception which is camouflaged or invisible. They are masters of impersonating those who have died. The Bible tells us demons are personal evil beings from another dimension who would seek to camouflage themselves for hidden purposes. The disguises range from promoting themselves as myth to the opposite extreme of promoting themselves as the ultimate reality, or God Himself. And, indeed, the majority of people in our culture either believe that Satan does not exist or that psychic powers, contacts with spirits, and channeling spirits are actually divine practices and represent contact with God.

In the world today most men recognize the existence of evil, but few men recognize the existence of the devil who accounts for much of that evil. The devil can get us thinking about our own self-interests so that we are not concerned with the state of our soul. The end result is that this is the greatest threat any person can face (Matthew 16:26; Luke 12:20). In brief, we see that in the world today we may believe in a thousand little evils, but we do not believe in the one evil (Satan) that is responsible for many of them. Our greatest danger is when we do not recognize a threat that outweighs every other threat.

The Bible warns us of the devil's techniques and goes all the way back to "Day One" (2 Corinthians 2:11; 11:3; Ephesians 6:11). The Bible reports the devil lied to man in the garden in two ways. First, he told man, "You shall be as God." Second, he promised, "You shall not die." Isn't it interesting that his spirits have not deviated from their master's first lies? If channeled beings are not demons, then the consistency and persistence of these themes throughout the history of spiritistic revelations is nothing short of amazing. Not only is this amazing—but why would channeled spirits who have always been hostile to the Bible still use the very lies the Bible reports Satan used back in the garden?

What can you say to the unbeliever who does not accept the Bible as authoritative in his life and who views the story of Adam, Eve, and Satan in the garden as just another myth? Consider the following:

1. Why is it that channeled spirits who are usually considered to be "good" beings model their teachings on what so many modern men believe is a false myth?
2. Why would good spirits want to identify themselves in any way with the most terrible and despicable spirit-being in the Bible?
3. Could it be that these spirits have not changed their message because that is their message, has always been their message, and because what the Bible says is true?
4. Further, to the person who does not believe the Bible, how could the Bible accurately describe what these spirits say?
5. Finally, why is it that many former occultists who have been deeply involved with the spirits have said that the only way to escape from those spirits is through the Christ of the Bible?

Question 24

What evidence would lead a thinking person to conclude that the actions of the channeled spirits suggest their nature is evil?

The entire history of the influence of these beings upon humanity suggests their nature is evil. That these spirits are evil can be documented from history, religion, psychology, and especially from the experiences of channelers themselves as we will see in our next two questions. Because channeling is contact with demons, it is an evil practice by itself, and it is also one that leads to countless other evils. Among these are immorality, crime, fraud, and physical and spiritual destruction. We saw earlier that the spirits whose teachings reject God and lie about Christ cannot be considered good.

Professor Edmund Gruss mentions several cases of murder committed on the advice of the spirits. In one case a 15-year-old daughter murdered her father. In another case a 77-year-old man was literally forced to kill his wife in self-defense because she believed the lies the spirits told her about his unfaithfulness.[96] There are many such cases. John Weldon talked with a serial killer whose "religious commission" was to travel the countryside murdering people his spirit guide told him "deserved to die." (The spirits always provided a way for him to dispose of the body safely so they could not be discovered.) Historically the spirits have caused the murder of hundreds of thousands of children and adults through human sacrifice[97] (including, probably, the recent Atlanta child murders);[98] they have helped start revolutions (including the Mexican Revolution of 1910);[99] and their teachings have sapped the moral strength of countless numbers. They have done this by leading men to commit evil acts which they otherwise would not have committed.

Jesus Himself called the devil "a liar and a murderer" from the beginning (John 8:44). Those who play into his hands can expect great promises and excitement to begin with, but little else than deceit and destruction in the long run. (See Chapter 36.)

On a more practical level, if the channeled revelations suggesting "there is no death" become widely accepted, then people may become more open to death itself. In addition there are spiritistically engineered revelations from thousands of "near-death" experiences extolling the glories of death and the afterlife. Some people who have had a heart attack or been involved in a near-fatal car crash have had an out-of-the-body experience where they encountered a "being of light," the dead, and feelings of great peace and love. Almost all of them say they regret being "brought back" and they look forward to death with great expectation.

The combination of channeled revelations about death and the near-death experiences may lead to an increase in suicide or euthanasia. Consider one incident. San Francisco is a city known for both its romance and its perversions. In San Francisco, "the man and woman kissed each other time after time, then turned their backs to the bay and, holding hands, tumbled backward off the Golden Gate Bridge to their deaths." The man left a suicide note in his car that indicated he had been "called" to enter the "other world." The note ended: "I love you all; wish I could stay, but I must hurry. The suspense is killing me."[100] The suspense killed him all right.

Channeling teaches this life is not the end (annihilation) and that there is no judgment. If this life is simply too difficult or unpleasant, why *not* take the easy way out? Why not enter a world you have been promised is far more glorious? Death, after all, is claimed to be a friend. In fact, the spirits often encourage this. We have read innumerable cases where the "loving" spirits have deliberately induced emotional dependence upon their advice and then at a moment of weakness encouraged their contact to "come join us" and commit suicide.[101] And this has been occurring for decades, probably even centuries. In the 1920 text *The Menace of Spiritualism*, case after case of tragedy is listed. The foreword by Bernard Vaughan, S.J., states,

> This very morning I heard of a girl, who being told in a seance by her deceased lover that he would not live on the other side without her, drowned herself to join him, not, I fancy, in heaven....[102]

Question 25

Do channelers ever suspect the spirits may not be who they claim?

Many channelers seem to have periods of genuine doubt as to the nature of these beings. A more objective assessment might indicate they are merely manipulated to perform the occult work of otherworldly entities of dubious character and highly questionable intent. Too often the spiritist's faith is one whose entire basis is founded upon a naive trust undergirded through a romance of emotion and experience.

Nevertheless the channelers do have their doubts. These doubts are carefully handled by the entities themselves. For example, one of Elisabeth Kubler-Ross' spirit guides, "Salem," "proved" he wasn't a demon to a skeptical priest by allowing himself to be soaked with "holy water"—while in fully-materialized form. He was supposed to disappear but didn't, thus "proving" he was not a demon.[103]

Mohammad was not certain if he was possessed by a jinn (an Islamic demon) in receiving the revelations of the Koran, but was persuaded otherwise.[104]

When unbiblical revelations started coming from Edgar Cayce's unconscious trance sessions, the famous seer openly wondered if "the devil might be tempting me to do his work by operating through me when I was conceited enough to think God had given me special power." After his first unbiblical reading on reincarnation he replied, "If ever the devil was going to play a trick on me, this would be it."[105] J. Z. Knight who channels "Ramtha" went through a period where she felt he might be a demon but was eventually persuaded to trust him.[106]

Another example is Uri Geller, famous for bending spoons and knives by psychic power. Both Geller and his teacher, parapsychologist Andrija Puharich, M.D., had an uneasy feeling that there was something "funny" or "wrong" about their spirit contacts. They suspected they were being "played with" and wondered if the entities themselves were unstable.[107] There are many other cases where channels have been uneasy or apprehensive over the exact nature of their encounters.

Question 26

Are there actual cases where channeling has become destructive?

As an introduction, consider the case of Bill Slater, head of BBC television drama. One evening, after attending "an impromptu seance" with a Ouija board, he went home. In the early hours of the morning:

> I found myself half-awake, knowing there was some kind of presence massing itself on my chest; it was, to my certain knowledge, making every effort to take over my mind and body. It cost me considerable will-power to concentrate all my faculties to push the thing away, and for what seemed like twenty minutes this spiritual tussle went on between this awful presence and myself. Needless to say, although before going to bed I had felt perfectly happy and at ease with a very good friend, in a flat I knew well, I was now absolutely terrified—I have never known such fear since. I was finally able to call my friend's name; he woke up, put on the light, and was astonished to find me well-nigh a gibbering idiot. I have never since had any psychic experience.[108]

Spirit Guides

Besides the above flirt with the demonic, there are many cases where occultic activity has directly resulted in the destruction of human life. It is not just that there are a few cases; the fact is there are thousands of them littered throughout the history of religion, occultism, spiritism, and para-psychology—mental illness, suicide, physical crippling, blindness,[109] death. People who would never think of playing Russian roulette with a gun, even once, or who would never deliberately take a dangerous drug, have a very good reason for their decisions. The odds of disaster are too high. Yet the odds of harming oneself from occultic practices are apparently just as high or higher.[110] What is amazing is that the evidence is there for all to see and yet it is ignored.

In the Bible, demons are presented as inflicting numerous physical and psychological ailments upon their victims. Many of these parallel today's cases of channeling. While it must be stressed that most illness is not demonically wrought, the array of symptoms suggest the possibility of a virtual monopoly over the workings of the human mind and body: skin disease (Job 2:7), destructive and irrational acts (Matthew 8:28; Luke 8:27), deafness and inability to speak (Mark 9:25; Luke 11:14), epileptic-like seizures (Matthew 17:15; Mark 9:17; Luke 9:39), blindness (Matthew 12:22), tormenting pain (Revelation 9:1-11), insanity (Luke 8:26-35), severe physical deformity (Luke 13:11-17), and other symptoms. Demons can give a person supernatural strength (Luke 8:29) or attempt to murder him (Matthew 17:15,18).

Not unexpectedly, there are numerous accounts of mediums, channelers, and occultists or those who frequent them suffering physically in a variety of ways from their practice (ill health, alcoholism, spirit attacks, early deaths, etc.).[111]

Most people do not know the famous medium Arthur Ford became a morphine addict and alcoholic, which caused him no end of grief much of his life.[112] Bishop Pike died a tragic death from his involvement in spiritism.[113] Medium Jane Roberts died at the young age of 55. Others became addicted to drugs.[114] Medium Edgar Cayce, a large man of 6' 2", died in misery weighing a mere 60 pounds, apparently physiologically "burned out" from giving too many psychic readings.[115] The biography on Cayce by Joseph Millard reveals the extent of suffering Cayce's occult involvement cost him—from psychic attacks to mysterious fires, the periodic loss of his voice, erratic personality changes and emotional torments, constant "bad luck" and personal setback, and guilt induced by psychic readings that ruined other people's lives.[116] Many channelers seem to succumb to various vices later in life, from sexual immorality[117] to numbing their conscience,[118] to alcoholism and drug addiction,[119] to crime and worse.[120]

M. Lamar Keene spent 13 years among professional mediums as a famous (although fraudulent) medium. In his public confession, *The Psychic Mafia*, he observes,

> All the mediums I've known or known about have had tragic endings. The Fox sisters, who started it all, wound up as

alcoholic derelicts. William Slade, famed for his slate-writing tricks, died insane in a Michigan sanitarium. Margery, the medium, lay on her deathbed a hopeless drunk. The celebrated Arthur Ford fought the battle of the bottle till the very end and lost.... Wherever I looked it was the same: mediums, at the end of a tawdry life, dying a tawdry death.... I was sick and tired of the whole business—the fraud bit, the drug bit, the drinking bit, the entire thing....[121]

Spiritist and guru Sri Chinmoy, a spiritual advisor at the United Nations, observes, "Many, many black magicians and people who deal with spirits have been strangled or killed. I know because I've been near quite a few of these cases."[122]

Dr. Kurt Koch observed after 45 years of counseling the occultly oppressed that from his own experience "numerous cases of suicides, fatal accidents, strokes and insanity are to be observed among occult practitioners." And that "anyone who has had to observe for 45 years the effects of spiritism can only warn people with all the strength at his disposal."[123]

In addition, over many years, the very act of channeling itself appears to have a destructive effect upon the human body. It is as if there is a type of, for lack of a better word, "psychic vampirism" at work which slowly eats away at a person's physical constitution.[124] Time and again in the lives of psychics, mediums, and spiritists we have observed the power of the spirits in holding their captives to do their will (2 Timothy 2:24-26). When one attempts to suppress their channeling or mediumship, for example, the result will frequently be symptoms of disease or other serious problems, forcing a return to the practice.[125] What is doubly tragic is that for all these people it started out so good, so promising. Consider the case of "Carl" as a final illustration.

Carl was a qualified psychologist with a degree in physics and a personal interest in religion (especially Christianity) and parapsychology (the scientific study of the occult; see Chapter 35). In fact, he became a leading parapsychologist. His personal psychic abilities amazed not only himself but those who knew him. He was enormously excited by Aldous Huxley's *Doors of Perception*; what Huxley achieved by drugs Carl was certain he could achieve by psychic means: that, and perhaps more. Although fascinated by Christianity, Carl was convinced that the modern churches were corrupting the original teachings of Christ. Hence he sought "true Christianity" through occult means.

Consumed with a desire to find "original Christianity," he became personally involved in reincarnation research and astral travel. As his studies and involvement in the psychic world continued, he explored realm after realm. He was bright and enthusiastic, not to mention careful. Most of all he was *certain* he was on the road to vast personal discoveries. He had, in his view, all the right motives—and talent, abilities, and opportunities to complement them.

Eventually a mid-Western university offered Carl a professorship and allowed him to both teach and continue his experiments, which provided numerous psychic and mystical experiences. Gradually, however, Carl admitted to himself that some deep alteration was taking place inside of him.[126] He had earlier encountered some gnawing doubts about the fundamental nature of his spiritual path but he suppressed them because they were too uncomfortable in their implications. Any doubt as to what kind of spirit was leading him could mean a total revision of his work; it could even mean resigning his professorship and renouncing his parapsychological research.[127]

Giving up his research would have been costly, but after years of painstaking effort, benevolent motives, and great enthusiasm, Carl became consumed by forces so evil he ended up as an incoherent vegetable requiring exorcism and 11 months of hospitalization.

His eventual renouncement of all study and research in parapsychology was deplored by fellow colleagues who never learned the real reason for his strange disappearance from the community. He finally had to conclude,

> Solemnly and of my own free will I wish to acknowledge that knowingly and freely I entered into possession by an evil spirit. And, although that spirit came to me under the guise of saving me, perfecting me, helping me to help others, I knew all along it was evil.[128]

Question 27

What logical evidence would lead channelers to acknowledge their own peril, and what can channelers do to escape the consequences that must befall them?

We believe we have already presented sufficient evidence to show that these spirits are demons and that, as such, the life of the channeler is at risk. Certainly his spiritual life is at risk. Those who have been involved in channeling need to acknowledge their peril—as well as their responsibility to others they may think they are helping. (See Chapter 36.)

The Bible commands and warns us to "test the spirits" (1 John 4:1). If the spirits' teachings do not agree with the Word of God, then no matter what one thinks or feels, they cannot be from God. If they claim this, then they are lying. There is only one path of safety for a channeler—repentance from sin and faith in Christ.

Question 28

Have any channelers turned to God from channeling?

Victor Ernest, author of *I Talked with Spirits*, Raphel Gasson, author of *The Challenging Counterfeit*, and Ben Alexander, author of *Out from the Darkness*, are three public examples of individuals who came to recognize that the spirits they thought were their guides and friends were, in fact, evil spirits bent on their destruction. They were delivered from their power, not without struggle, by the only effective method available—a complete renouncing of their practices before God and a turning to Christ as personal Lord and Savior.[129] (See Appendix C.)

God teaches these practices will destroy you in the long run. They may seem helpful now, but appearances can be deceptive. There are many things in life which begin good and end tragically. Test the spirits to see if they are of God (1 John 4:1). Examine our arguments. If there is even a chance we are correct, then you owe it to yourself, to your family, to your friends, and to your clients to be certain the spirits are not deceiving you. The following prayer is suggested for those who have been involved in channeling.

> Dear God, these spirits are not of You and I ask for Your protection from them. I confess my sin of seeking what You have forbidden and I renounce these spirits and all involvement with them. I ask Jesus Christ to enter my life and to be my Lord and Savior. I recognize this is a solemn decision that You take very seriously. I believe that on the cross Jesus Christ died for my sin and I receive Him into my life now. My commitment to You is that I will follow Him and not the spirits. I ask for Your help in doing this. Amen.

If you prayed this prayer, there are several things you need to do to grow in the Christian life. Start to read a modern-translation Bible and find a good church that honors Christ. Tell someone you have just become a Christian so they may pray for you and encourage you in your new life with Christ. (Sometimes, unfortunately, Christians may not understand your experiences; persevere until you find a Christian friend who can pray with you and help you grow spiritually.) And remember, Jesus Himself said, "All authority has been given to Me in heaven and on earth. . . . I am with you always, even to the end of the age" (Matthew 28:18-20).

Conclusion

For anyone who may be unnecessarily concerned over the influence of the demonic in your life we encourage you to remember that although spiritual warfare exists, the devil and his demons are subject to the authority of God and present no danger to the average Christian seeking to do God's will (see Ephesians 6:11-13; James 4:7; 1 John 4:4). For the non-Christian (or Christian) involved in any form of the occult, there must be an immediate ceasing of all activity and a turning of one's life over to Christ as Lord. Dr. Kurt Koch's book *Occult Bondage and Deliverance* (Kregal, 1972) contains valuable insight for those seeking deliverance and in Appendix C we have supplied some of his recommendations.

CULT WATCH

ASTROLOGY

---

*What the
Bible, science,
and common sense
tell us
about Astrology*

27

Introduction to Astrology

Why is an evaluation of astrology an important topic in the 1990s? Astrology is important because national opinion polls consistently reveal that literally tens of millions of Americans believe in astrology. One Gallup poll indicated that at least 10 percent of evangelical Christians also believe in astrology. The subject of astrology is important because of the great number of people who trust their lives to astrologers.

Astrology plays a leading role in the dissemination of occult practice and philosophy within our culture. If astrology is one of the most subtle and effective introductions to the world of the occult, then anyone concerned about the occultic revival in our country should also be concerned about the practice of astrology.

In our full-length book *Astrology: Do the Heavens Rule Our Destiny?* (Harvest House, 1989), we document eight converging lines of evidence to show that the real source of power behind the effective astrologer is often the spirit world. If spirits are the power behind astrology, then the acceptance of astrology in American society indicates that millions of people are being influenced by the spirit world through this form of divination alone. Unfortunately, according to the Bible, this means that people are really being influenced by evil spirits (demons).

These demons are lying spirits whose hidden motives are to ruin men and women spiritually (see the material on Spirit Guides and on the Occult elsewhere in this text).

Why should anyone trust these conclusions? What makes us qualified to examine astrology and evaluate the practice, philosophy, and implications of astrology?

First, we have studied spiritistic phenomena for two decades; our acquaintance with astrology has enabled us to thoroughly assess its spiritistic aspects.

Second, we have seven graduate degrees in areas such as comparative religion, biblical studies, sociology, cultic studies, theology, church history and the history of Christian thought, and apologetics. This academic background enables us to assess astrology from many vantage points, including its relationship to Christian belief.

Third, in conducting our research we had many talks with professional astrologers. For example, we attended the July 4–8, 1988, Fiftieth Anniversary Convention of the largest and most influential of American astrological organizations, the American Federation of Astrologers. At this conference, we distributed questionnaires, conducted interviews, and had numerous discussions with practicing astrologers, among them leading American and European astrologers. We also attended many astrology classes.

Further, we were involved in a national, televised debate with two astrologers: Terry Warneke, a professional astrologer with an M.S. degree in astronomy, and psychic Maxine Taylor, the first vice-president of the American Federation of Astrologers.

Finally, we have read or consulted over 300 sources relevant to astrology, including 200 serious astrology texts.

The *Encyclopedia Britannica* observes that astrology has had a significant impact on numerous civilizations throughout history. Former Chief of Staff Donald Regan's *For the Record: From Wall Street to Washington* and nationally known astrologer Joan Quigley's *What Does Joan Say?: My Seven Years as White House Astrologer to Nancy and Ronald Reagan* reveal that astrology has recently influenced the highest levels of American government. With the dramatic influence of astrology in our own culture, and the fact that worldwide approximately one billion people believe in astrology, no one today should be uninformed about this important subject. (Readers who desire additional information may wish to consult our full-length book, *Astrology: Do the Heavens Rule Our Destiny?*)

204

28

The Claims,
Basic Terms
and Influence
of Astrology

Astrology was once again in the headlines. Not as in 1975 when 192 leading scientists, including 19 Nobel prize winners, publicly disavowed it.[1] This time astrology was in the headlines because of the influence it had achieved at the highest level of national government, the White House. The unforeseen result has been a literal flood of new public interest in astrology. According to Chief of Staff Donald T. Regan's text *For the Record*, the influence of astrology at the White House extended to "every major move and decision."[2]

Question 1

What is astrology?

Astrology is a belief system based on the assumption that the stars or planets (as interpreted and configured by the astrologers themselves) mysteriously influence the lives of men. Astrology teaches that this influence begins at birth and continues throughout a person's life. Thus the *Shorter Oxford English Dictionary* defines astrology as "the art of judging the occult influence of the stars upon human affairs."

The following are representative definitions of astrology that are given by astrologers themselves:

1) "Astrology is the study of the heavens . . . and the influence they exert upon the lives and affairs of humanity."[3]

2) "Astrology is the science of certain cryptic [hidden or mysterious] relations between the celestial [heavenly] bodies and terrestrial [earthly] life."[4]

3) "Astrology is the science of life's reactions to planetary vibrations."[5] ("Vibration" here is something mysterious that supposedly works like the moon's gravity influencing the ocean tides on earth.)

4) "Astrology is the system of interpreting *symbols* [heavenly bodies that are assigned names and influence by astrologers] correlated to human behavior and activities."[6]

There are many kinds of astrology: 1) *Ancient* astrology was practiced by the Babylonians. They taught that the planets were gods and as such the planets ruled and influenced life on earth (some occult groups using astrology today have similar beliefs); 2) those holding to *material* astrology believe that "emanations" or "influences" from actual planets in our solar system rule or affect life on earth; 3) those who believe in *symbolic* astrology teach that the stars and planets are only *symbols*. They go on to assume that there is a mysterious "magical correspondence" revealed by the symbols which influences life on earth.

There are many other kinds of astrology each with different assumptions. Nevertheless, here we have three kinds of astrology with three different sets of assumptions. The planets are either: 1) gods, 2) impersonal heavenly objects, or 3) just symbols. Yet all three claim they are responsible for producing the same conclusion: Whatever the planets are, they influence life on earth. But as Bertrand Russell once observed, when two views both claim to be true but contradict each other, one or the other may be true, but they both can't be true at the same time. The same can be said about astrology. Logically, the different kinds of astrology can't all be true when they contradict each other. It remains to be seen if any one of them is true.

Question 2

How does astrology supposedly work?

Astrology supposedly "works" by the planets or stars affecting our lives. The main tool astrologers use for interpreting this alleged influence on our lives is the astrological chart, called a *natal* [birth] *horoscope*. (Strictly, the term *horoscope* also involves the interpretation [delineations] of the chart, although the terms "chart" and "horoscope" are used interchangeably.) This chart calculates the exact position of the heavenly bodies at the moment of birth, usually from the baby's first breath. The baby's first breath is crucial with most astrologers because they accept a premise of magic called "correspondences" (that everything in the heavens is correlated to everything on earth; thus, events in heaven parallel events on earth). Thus, for them the child's first breath permanently "stamps" him with the corresponding heavenly stamp or pattern existing in the sky at that moment. It is this unique, impressed pattern stamped upon the child that astrologers believe determines one's character and ultimately his destiny.

For some astrologers the "permanent stamp" is the influence sent out by the heavenly bodies absorbed by each of us as we draw our first breath at birth. Some astrologers say these heavenly bodies send out influences which forever determine up to 80 percent of our potential personality and destiny.[7] ("As above, so below," is the ancient expression of this principle.)

For still other astrologers, the heavenly stamp is not claimed to correspond to the actual planets. It is assumed to correspond to mysterious influences that astrologers interpret by their symbols. Nevertheless, one way or the other, for our entire lives, astrologers claim that the heavenly planets continue to influence us in predictable ways based upon our original pattern at birth.

In addition to the birth horoscope, astrologers use "secondary" charts. For example, a *mundane* chart will examine the fortune of cities, states, or countries. An *electional* chart is drawn up to decide the best time to undertake some activity. The *horary* chart is composed to answer questions on any given topic. Why are all these secondary charts important? Because the heavens are in motion. Astrologers say that since the planets change their positions in the heavens, it is necessary to have new charts made to determine their current influence on us. These secondary charts (called *progressed horoscopes* and *directed horoscopes*) give us more specific information to relate to our birth chart. This additional information supposedly reveals to us how we are likely to act and choose at any given time.

Thus a chart may be drawn at any particular moment of time by astrologers to determine particular heavenly influences that may affect us. The information received supposedly helps the client to make decisions in such areas of life as love and relationships, family, financial matters, occupation, etc.

Whether or not the stars or their magic symbolism really influence us, one fact should be clear. Once we accept the premises of astrology, it does not matter. Astrology does indeed exert a powerful influence but it is because of the person's belief in astrology itself, not the influence of the stars. For example, the power we grant to the astrologer to accurately interpret the alleged heavenly pattern or influence acting upon us is a dramatic yielding of the direction of our lives. For many people, no major decision will ever be made without first consulting an astrologer. Also, merely because astrology *claims* to reveal the future, it will always have power, for the desire of many to know the future cannot be underestimated.

Astrologers claim to be able to predict both the heavenly influences on our lives at the present moment and for the future. These two powerful categories of motivation (decisions about the present and information concerning the future) that lead people to astrology are also discussed in the Scriptures. God gives guidance for responsible decision-making concerning the present moment. He also promises to help us in the future (Psalm 46:1; 48:14; 73:24; Matthew 6:25-34; 28:20; Philippians 4:1-20; Hebrews 13:5). If a person has a choice between going to an omniscient, infallible counselor or a fallible human being, would it be logical to choose the latter? If one can go to a loving and trustworthy source, why go to an unproven and questionable counselor? God has a proven record—astrology does not, as we will soon see.

Question 3

What are the basic terms and concepts necessary to understand astrology?

Why is astrology so often confusing to the average person? It is because of its complexity and the many unfamiliar words which astrologers use.[8] The following definitions and concepts are basic if one is to understand astrology.

The *Zodiac* is an imaginary "belt" of sky containing the 12 astrological signs or constellations around which the ancients built imaginary human and animal figures. (The Zodiac and the constellations are both imaginary geometric configurations.)

The *signs* are the "signs of the Zodiac" also known as "Sun-signs." Everyone is born under one of these 12 signs or constellations (Pisces the fish, Leo the lion, Gemini the twins, Taurus the bull, etc.).

The *houses* are the 12 sections of the Zodiac which together symbolize every aspect of life. The planets move through the houses; thus, when a planet falls into the sphere of the given house, it comes under its respective influence. The astrologer plots all of these factors and more on a chart. This chart is called a *horoscope*.

The *horoscope* is a "map" of the heavens at the moment of the birth of a person or any specific time thereafter. On this chart, an astrologer plots the positions of the "planets," "signs," and "houses" for a given moment. The chart is then interpreted by numerous complex rules, many of which vary greatly from one astrologer to another.

A mental picture might be helpful in understanding the basic ideas of astrology that we just defined. But we should first understand that the "world" of astrology is based upon an ancient view of the universe, not a modern scientific one. The ancients constructed their view of the universe based entirely on how things *appeared*. Thus looking up at the sky at night, it appeared as if the stars and planets moved along the inner surface of a great hollow globe, a celestial sphere. The sun, moon, and planets appeared to revolve around the earth, etc.

Now imagine a huge glass ball with a thin white belt encircling it. According to astrology, the *glass ball* is the *celestial sphere*. The *white belt* encircling the glass ball is the Zodiac. Divide the *white belt* into 12 sections. Each of these sections is given a name. The name is of a symbolic animal or man representing the imaginary *constellations* known as Aries the ram, Virgo the virgin, Leo the lion, Gemini the twins, etc. These symbols of animals and men are called the *"signs of the Zodiac"* or the "Sun-signs." This is what is meant when people say, "my sign is 'Libra,' 'Pisces,' 'Aries,' 'Gemini,' " etc.

If one could look inside this glass ball and see a tiny green marble at its center, this would be symbolic of the *earth*. And if one divides all the space inside the glass ball into 12 sections, these sections would represent what the astrologers call "houses." These sections would start at a point in the middle of the glass ball (the green marble—the earth) and extend out to the

Zodiac or the encircling white belt. However, these 12 house sections are spaced differently from the 12 Zodiac sections along the white belt. Inside the glass ball the astrologers place the Sun, Moon, and eight other planets. As these planets move, they move through the 12 sections on the white belt, the Zodiac, and also enter and pass through the 12 different sections of space called the houses.

In addition to all of this, astrologers believe that each planet "rules" or especially influences different signs of the Zodiac. For example, Mercury rules or influences Gemini and Virgo, whereas Venus is said to rule or especially influence Taurus and Libra.

One more important term used by astrologers must be defined. Astrologers use the word "aspect." Aspect refers to the angles between the planets as seen or plotted on a horoscope chart. Certain angles are interpreted as good and some angles are bad. For example, two planets angled at 90 degrees to each other (called a "square") supposedly exert a bad influence. However, two planets angled at 120 degrees to each other (called a "trine") supposedly exert a very good influence. But it is more complicated than this. Astrologers also must take into consideration whether the planets are "good" planets or "bad" planets. The words "good" and "bad" as referring to angles or planets has been defined by the astrologers. But why are these angles and planets logically defined as good or bad? Even the astrologers don't know; they simply accept them and point to their astrological tradition that has been passed on for centuries. To be fair, some astrologers would say these definitions are the result of thousands of years of observing human experience. But no one has accurately recorded 4000 years of human experience. And if they had, why are there so many conflicting astrological theories?

To show how subjective astrological interpretation is, ask any astrologer how he knows the different houses represent different things. For example, how does he know that the first house represents personality, the second house money, the third house communication, the eighth house death, the tenth house occupation, etc.? Astrologers have designated many different aspects of life to each of the different houses. The question is, "On what basis do they logically do this?" Again astrologers claim this information comes from 4000 years of human observation. But again, such observation has never occurred and if it had, then astrologers should agree with each other on their interpretation. Astrologers may also say these meanings were derived from numerology—from the meanings allegedly inherent in numbers which were then related to astrological theory. But if these meanings were derived from numerology, we still cannot explain a logical reason why such a system should be true or valid. In addition, to show the extent of disagreement, astrologers do not even divide the houses in the same manner. This means that a given house for one astrologer may be a different house for another, and therefore entirely different influences would be suggested.⁹

Also by determining when a planet crosses or "transits" a specific point on the horoscope chart, the astrologer feels he can advise a client as to "favorable," "unfavorable," or cautious times concerning a given activity. Thus, just as there are good and evil planets and angles, there are good and bad days for undertaking certain activities. This was why Hitler planned his war strategy by the stars and why even some American presidents have sought the advice of the stars as to the planning of their activities.

Question 4

How influential is astrology today?

Astrologers West and Toonder believe that astrology now "enjoys a popularity unmatched since the decline of Rome."[10] Science writer and engineer Lawrence E. Jerome makes the astonishing claim that at least one *billion* people around the globe "believe in and follow astrology to some extent."[11] Bernard Gittelson is a New Age human behavior researcher and former public relations consultant representing the West German government, the European Common Market, the U.S. Department of Commerce, and other major clients. He calculated that the circulation of newspapers and magazines carrying astrological columns in the United States, Europe, Japan, and South America totaled over 700 million or three-fourths of a billion.[12]

In the United States, the interest in astrology has fluctuated but remained high. For example, in 1969 *Newsweek* estimated there were 10 million committed believers in astrology and many more dabblers. In 1975 a Gallup poll indicated over 32 million Americans believed "that the stars influence people's lives" and in addition that many of them consulted their daily or weekly horoscopes.[13] Not only that, but estimates of the number of astrologers ranged as high as 10,000 full-time and 175,000 part-time.[14] Ten years later, a Gallup poll in 1984 revealed that among teenagers (aged 13-18), 55 percent believed in astrology. This figure was up from 40 percent in 1978. A 1988 Gallup poll indicated 10 percent of evangelicals believe in astrology.[15]

Today in the West, astrology is the subject of over 100 magazines, and the topic of millions of books in print. Since 1960 the annual production of new titles has doubled every ten years.[16]

Astrologers claim "there is no area of human experience to which astrology cannot be applied."[17] Many occult practices (numerology and Tarot cards) have logical connections to astrology; many world religions and religious cults (Hinduism and Theosophy) have their own brands of astrology; and astrologers have even attempted to integrate many of the sciences (medicine and psychology).[18]

Proof for the astrologer's claim that there is no area of human experience to which astrology cannot be applied can be seen by checking your local bookstore. For example, the smallest sampling of astrology titles indicates its potential for wide applications: *Your Dog's Astrological Horoscope; Your Baby's First Horoscope; Astro-power at the Racetrack; The Teenager's Horoscope Book; Cat Horoscope Book; Pluto: Planet of Magic and Power; Chinese*

Astrology; Cooking with Astrology; Diet and Health Horoscope; Earthquake Prediction; Medical Astrology; The Astrologer's Guide to Counseling; Horoscope of Murder; Find Your Mate Through Astrology; Astrology and Biochemistry; Astrological Themes for Meditation; Sex Signs; An Introduction to Political Astrology; Astro Numerology; Stock Market Predictions; Homosexuality in the Horoscope; The Astrology of I Ching; Sex and the Outer Planets; From Humanistic to Transpersonal Astrology; Financial Astrology; Astrology and the Edgar Cayce Readings; Aztec Astrology; Astrology and Psychology; Woman's Astrology; Esoteric Astrology; Hindu Astrology; Astrology and Past Lives; Astrology: Key to Holistic Health; Astrology, Alchemy and the Tarot; Asteroid Goddesses; Astrology of Theosophy; Astrology in the Bible; Horoscope of Canada; A Guide to Cabalistic Astrology, etc.

Research scientist Geoffrey Dean estimates there are as many astrologers in the Western world as there are psychologists.[19] And over 80 percent of all U.S. newspapers now carry horoscope columns.

Astrology today also can boast an impressive list of "who's who" believers. Today a few notables include: Prince Andrew and Fergie, Princess Diana, Hollywood stars Robert Wagner, Phyllis Diller, Jill St. John, Angie Dickinson, Lauren Bacall, Goldie Hawn, Olivia Hussey, Rona Barrett, Olivia Newton-John, Debbie Reynolds, Joan Collins, Liza Minnelli, Arlene Francis, Jane and Peter Fonda, and many others.[20]

Today astrology is offered for credit on some high school and college campuses.[21] Some corporations seek astrological advice for major decisions and overall, astrology is estimated to be anywhere from a $200 million to a one-billion-dollar-a-year industry.[22] In fact, a cable news network (CNN) report cited astrologers who claim that "at least 300 of the Fortune 500 [companies] use astrologers in one way or another."[23]

Question 5

Why is astrology so popular?

Astrology is popular because it claims to provide important information that people want to know. Astrology claims to provide people with information that will: 1) protect them, 2) bring them success, 3) guide them, 4) predict their future, and 5) help them understand themselves.

Astrology offers people the belief that they can "control" their own destinies, and it also provides them a ready-made justification for failure or sin. Astrology offers the false hope that through the "knowledge" of the stars, one can manipulate people or events for his own welfare or selfish desires. Astrology specializes in answering almost all the questions people ask concerning the future. In fact, it claims to offer power over life and death, love, sex and relationships, money and finances, personal health and happiness, etc.

Above all, astrology sells hope—and today people need hope desperately! In every age of social breakdown, the masses of people have turned to the occult and superstition for solace and counsel. Today is no exception.

In conclusion, astrology is popular because it claims to offer people hope through the knowledge of the manipulation of the influences of the planets and stars. With this secret knowledge, people believe they have greater control over themselves as well as present and future circumstances.

Question 6

Can newspaper horoscopes be dangerous?

The first horoscope column appeared in the *London Sunday Express* in 1930.[24] In the next 50 years, horoscopes were slowly incorporated into 80 percent of American newspapers, that is, into 1250 out of 1500. Most professional astrologers complain that these columns are vastly oversimplified at best and "utter nonsense" at worst.[25] This is true even though professional astrologers often write these columns (such as Sydney Omarr and Carroll Righter). It is also true that professional astrological organizations give seminars on how to write the columns.[26]

Most newspaper editors reject astrology and seem to believe that horoscopes are simply an amusing pastime for their readers.[27] But are the conclusions of these editors true? Could it be true that modern newspapers are being socially irresponsible for the following reasons?

1) Newspaper horoscopes seem to bear at least some responsibility for the modern revival of interest in astrology.[28] The law of averages tells us that a certain number of these very general "predictions" found in America's newspapers will come true, or will be interpreted as coming true by the people who read them. One can only wonder how many people have turned to astrology after months or years of reading their horoscopes. Even the occult encyclopedia *Man, Myth and Magic* stated: "The daily forecast and the feature articles in magazines have persuaded countless thousands that the 'stars' may conceivably influence human destinies. . . ."[29]

2) Astrology has been shown to be both false and dangerous.[30] Obviously to encourage something that is untrue, irrational, and superstitious is not in society's best interest.

3) Astrology is a proven occult art. By virtue of its many connections to numerous other forms of occultism (such as witchcraft and spiritism), astrology is a potential introduction to a much wider practice of occult activity. Newspapers would not think of carrying columns giving advice on witchcraft or spiritism but they do not hesitate to offer astrological "counsel." In conclusion, astrology leads to occult involvement. Occult involvement has been proven dangerous[31]* and is condemned by God (Deuteronomy 18:9-12; Isaiah 47:13; 1 Corinthians 10:20).

For these reasons and more, it is therefore irresponsible for newspapers to continue carrying astrological columns.

---

* See Chapter 36.

29

Astrology
and the Occult

Question 7

Is astrology related to the occult?

We may define the occult, in general, as the attempt to secure forbidden supernatural power or knowledge. The Christian believes that this occult knowledge and power come from spirit beings that the Bible calls demons.[32] Astrology is related to the occult in four major ways. First, astrology itself is defined by *Webster's Dictionary* as an occult art. As such it employs occult practices such as divination. Divination may be defined as "the art of obtaining secret or illegitimate knowledge of the future by methods unsanctioned by and at variance with the holiness of God" and which involves contact with evil spirits.[33]* Second, astrology appears to work best when the astrologer himself is psychically sensitive, what most astrologers would term "intuitive." Third, prolonged use of astrology often leads to the development of psychic abilities.[34] Fourth, due to its history and very nature, astrology often becomes the introductory course to a wider spectrum of occult practices. All of this points to the fact that the very practice of astrology is a foundational occult art and that the practitioners (astrologers) open themselves up to becoming involved in other occult practices.

Nevertheless modern astrology wishes to be seen as scientific. As a result, we are told that as a system of belief it has nothing whatever to do

---

* See Part Seven, Questions 6–11.

with the occult and that the astrologer himself need not be psychic at all, although he may be "intuitive." An example of this is leading astrologer Carroll Righter who "feels strongly that astrology should not be considered [part of] the occult."[35] Because of his practice as an astrologer, "he regards himself as a scientist...."[36] Another influential astrologer, Charles E. O. Carter, claims "astrology does not involve any form of psychism..."[37] thus showing his aversion to the occult. Practicing astrologer Colette Michaan states "astrology is magical only in the sense that insight is magical."[38]

These quotes remind us of the pronouncements of the parapsychologists who similarly claim that when they study psychics and mediums they are only studying "natural" and "normal" human powers—nothing occult, supernatural, or spiritistic. But such claims are false whether made by parapsychologists or astrologers. In Part Seven we show that parapsychologists unwittingly have opened themselves to demonic powers under the guise of studying latent human abilities.[39] If astrologers wish to truly be seen as scientific, it is natural to expect they would not admit to the occult nature of their craft. But instead we could expect them, like parapsychologists, to define their craft in modern scientific and psychological terms. But have astrologers misstated the case? Can it be documented that astrology by nature is part of the occult? Finally, is there a connection between the astrologer and psychic abilities?

From its inception, astrology has been tied to the world of paganism, magic, spiritism, and the occult and this remains true today. For example, in examining two dozen "channeled" books (revelations given by a spirit possessing someone's body), astrology was accepted or endorsed in almost all of them.

Proof that the spirits (demons) are clearly interested in promoting astrology can be seen in the following two examples.[40]

First, one of the spirits who communicated through mystic and occultist Alice Bailey (founder of Lucius Trust) telepathically transmitted many books to her, including *Esoteric Astrology*.[41] A second example is Edgar Cayce, who was a powerful medium. Throughout most of his life the spirits speaking through him endorsed the practice of astrology. The 14,000 readings Cayce gave in trance are considered the largest single body of psychic information in the world. Over 2500 of them dealt with what were termed "life readings" and "almost all [of them] refer to past incarnations and specific astrological or planetary influences bearing on the present."[42] When asked if it was right and proper to study astrology, the spirits that spoke through Cayce said "very very very much so."[43]

The spirits are not the only occult connection to astrology. In terms of occult realities, astrology and the occult go hand in hand because they are fundamentally inseparable. There are historic ties between the rise of astrology on the one hand and the corresponding turning to the occult on the other. It is also true that where there has been the rise of the occult there has also been a corresponding turning to astrology. For example, Helena P. Blavatsky was a potent medium and virulent antagonist of

Christianity. She founded one of the most influential occultic movements in modern Western culture, known as the Theosophical Society. Astrologers West and Toonder have pointed out the influence of Theosophy on the modern American revival of astrology: "It is to Ms. Blavatsky and the Theosophical Movement she founded that astrology owes its revival.... Theosophy, in one blow . . . inspired a renewed and serious inquiry into astrology, first in England, then not long after in Germany, France and America."[44] (Actually it was Theosophy and two other occult societies— Rudolph Steiner's Anthroposophy, and modern Rosicrucianism—which are responsible for America's renewed passion for astrology in the twentieth century.)

Next, it can be noted that most occultists use astrology and that many astrologers practice other occult arts. For example, astrologer Daniel Logan admits he is involved with mediums and spirits;[45] astrologer Marcus Allen has a spirit guide and studies yoga, Zen, Tibetan Buddhism, and Western magical traditions, etc.[46]

And it is not surprising that both astrologers and occultists admit that astrology is a pillar of occultism. In his *A Manual of Occultism*, astrologer "Sepharial" states: "The astrologic art is held to be the key to all the occult sciences."[47]

In her book *My Life in Astrology*, famous witch Sybil Leek states, "Astrology is my science, witchcraft is my religion. . . ."[48] She calls the horoscope "a magical document."[49] She also claims astrology is "a vital tool" for using magic and observes its connection to numerology, phrenology, palmistry, and witchcraft.[50]

In her *An ABC of Witchcraft Past and Present*, witch Doreen Valiente observes: "Astrology . . . is another of the fundamentals of magic. It is studied by witch and magician alike."[51] Thus, when "a witch wants to select an herb to use for a magical purpose, she has to use one whose astrological rulership [remember the planets rule the signs] is correct for the work in hand . . . the Moon rules psychic things, and an herb of the Moon, mudwort . . . is used to make an infusion or tea which many believe is an aid to clairvoyance."[52]

Some astrologers admit that astrology is an occult practice. For example, the field of "humanistic" and "transpersonal" astrology combines astrology with Eastern philosophy, the occult, and Jungian psychology. Theosophist Dane Rudhyar is the leader in this field. In his book *The Practice of Astrology* he states that "the astrologer has authority as one who deals understandingly and effectively with . . . the occult." He then says "astrology is threshold [by this he means occult] knowledge."[53]

Henry Weingarten is a leading astrologer, director of the National Astrological Society in New York, and author of the multivolume series titled *The Study of Astrology*. In his studies he has concluded that astrology is related to palmistry, numerology, and Tarot cards. He also admits "almost all occultists use astrological timing [that is, the best time as set by astrology] in their work."[54] Then he quickly adds, "Most astrologers are not occultists." When Weingarten claims that most astrologers are not occultists, he allows his philosophical "slip" to show.

Not only do many astrologers and virtually all occultists admit that astrology is part of the occult, but so do objective scholars who have studied the subject. Richard Cavendish was the main editor of the 24-volume encyclopedia entitled *Man, Myth and Magic* and also *Encyclopedia of the Unexplained: Magic, Occultism and Parapsychology*. He was educated at Oxford University and is considered a leading authority on the history of magic and occultism. In his book *The Black Arts* he observes: "Astrology is essentially a magical art . . . astrological considerations have always been extremely important in magic . . . some magical textbooks classify the 'spirits' . . . in terms of their planetary affiliations."[55]

In his definitive study of sixteenth- and seventeenth- century English occultism, *Religion and the Decline of Magic*, Oxford-educated historian Keith Thomas documents the strong intellectual and practical links between magic, divination, astrology and witchcraft.[56] He shows that much of occultism is actually undergirded by an astrological worldview. He also documents that some medieval astrologers claimed to get their knowledge of astrology from the spirit world. For example, he mentions a spirit named "Bifrons" that made men "wonderfully cunning" in the subject of astrology.[57]

In *Astrology Disproved*, science writer and engineer Lawrence Jerome concludes that of all the occult "sciences," astrology appears most scientific but is really "nothing more than a magical system for controlling others."[58] He states, "Astrology, then, has played a major role in all the magical 'sciences': alchemy, black magic, the conjuring of spirits, necromancy, and even in the simpler magical practices such as the use of talismans."[59]

Trial lawyer and philosopher Dr. John Warwick Montgomery asserts that astrology is "found virtually everywhere occultism is to be found."[60]

Other scholars believe that among certain people, astrology provides a logical connection for a conversion to the occult practice of Satanism. In "Magical Therapy: An Anthropological Investigation of Contemporary Satanism" sociologist Edward J. Moody explains there is a certain psychological need for control and power in many whom (because of their disposition) he classifies as "pre-Satanists." He shows how this need naturally finds its expression first in astrology. It then logically progresses into Satanism which claims to provide a "more powerful means of control" of one's fate. Everyone should take notice of Moody's frightening conclusion that "those who eventually become Satanists usually have begun with astrology. . . ."[61]

In summary, if astrologers say their craft has no associations to the occult, they are either uninformed or they are lying.

Question 8

Do some astrologers claim to use psychic abilities?

The attempt to maintain a scientific image and to avoid the occult image of their practice requires most modern astrologers to stress the "objective" nature of interpreting their chart or horoscope. For example, astrologers enjoy informing the public that astrological information is so objective that they can look up chart information in the "standard" manuals of astrological interpretation (for example, what Pluto in the seventh house means). This sounds good but hardly makes astrological interpretation objective.

Astrology is anything *but* looking at facts to make authoritative interpretations. There is obviously a great deal of subjective and "intuitive" assessment by each astrologer in explaining a horoscope for a person. Many astrologers, who care little about maintaining a scientific image, admit astrological practice often utilizes or requires a *psychic* sensitivity. (The *Oxford American Dictionary* [1982] defines psychic as that which is "concerned with processes that seem to be outside physical or natural laws, having or involving extrasensory perception or occult powers.") This shouldn't surprise anyone. After all, astrology is defined even by *Webster's Dictionary* as an occult art. It is also a fact of research in this area that continued occultic practice and use eventually tend to develop psychic abilities in a person.[62]

Right at this point, some astrologers play word games. They say they are merely developing and using the "intuitive" powers which lie dormant in everyone. Astrologers have adopted the modern myth promoted by parapsychologists (those who scientifically study occult phenomena) that everyone has psychic potential.* As a result, they may claim they are not engaging in anything supernatural or "psychic." Yet, when pressed, the astrologers we contacted admitted that "intuitive" and "psychic" were one and the same word for them. These astrologers prefer the word "intuitive" because for many people the term "psychic" has too many negative occult connotations, while the word "intuitive" is far more neutral, positive, and universal to people's ears. Thus, just as the old negative terms of mediumism and spiritism have often been replaced with the modern New Age term "channeling," the old occultic term psychic has for many people now been replaced by the new word "intuitive." For example, psychic researcher Bernard Gittelson talked to "dozens of astrologers" and observed, "Though many adepts [experts] feel *psychic* to some degree, most spoke of their *intuitive* senses without necessarily calling themselves *psychic*"[63] (emphasis added).

The question that must be answered is, "Are *all* astrologers psychic?" Truthfully, even though all astrologers practice an occult art, this does not mean every astrologer is necessarily psychic. It is common knowledge that there are standard "cookbook" methods for interpretation of astrological charts that anyone can buy. But some astrologers do openly classify themselves as "psychic astrologers." And one astrologer even went so far as to tell us that all *genuine* astrologers were psychic by definition. Yet some astrologers never seem to develop psychically, and others may require

---

* See Part 7, Question 6,10,12,13.

years to become psychic. However, we believe the vast majority eventually do. One former astrologer believes that because of their abilities, all true astrologers are sooner or later subject to spiritistic inspiration, whether or not they are personally conscious of being psychic.[64]

For example, when interpreting the chart, astrologers may feel mild to strong "impressions"; they may notice they are "led" to certain data, or find themselves saying something unexpectedly. Information derived in this way turns out to be highly important to the client and may involve information about the client that the astrologer could not possibly have known. Yet, the fact is that many spiritists are guided by their spirit guides in a similar manner. Thus Robert Leichtman, M.D., states of his spirit guides: "What they did was to give me a whole bunch of ideas. And of course I thought, well, my mind has suddenly become brilliant. It was already great before, but now it is absolutely brilliant. I was getting all kinds of ideas from time to time and of course, the spooks [spirits] said they were giving them to me [but at first I didn't believe it]."[65]

It is hardly surprising that many astrologers would seek to develop themselves psychically, for astrologic philosophy encourages this. For example, "the Piscean is [told he is] highly intuitive, and can develop psychic and mediumistic abilities."[66] Astrology teaches that when "Pisces is on the ascendant and Aquarius rules the twelfth house," this can indicate a high degree of psychic potential.[67] Any number of different combinations of astrological interpretations may encourage an astrologer or his client in the direction of psychic development. Famed astrologer Sydney Omarr admits that "with Uranus in the fifth house" he had to find outlets for his "need for expression" and these were "magic, the occult . . . palmistry, numerology, psychic phenomena."[68] Some astrologers associate the planets Uranus, Neptune, and Pluto with development of psychic potential.[69] In addition, the public is told that if the Moon, Mercury, or Venus are in the twelfth house; if the Moon is in Sagittarius or Aquarius; if Mars and Jupiter are in Cancer; or if there is a Jupiter-Saturn conjunction in Taurus, all of these can indicate mystical, psychic, or intuitive potential.[70] And these are only some of the total possible combinations that may indicate this.

That astrology often does depend upon psychic ability is recognized both by occult authorities and astrologers themselves. In *The Occult: A History*, Colin Wilson observes that astrology, like palmistry ". . . depends upon an almost mediumistic faculty."[71] The occult encyclopedia *Man, Myth and Magic* refers to astrologers who excel at horoscope interpretation as having "highly developed intuitive powers."[72] Humanist astrologer Michael Shallis believes astrological knowledge comes through intuition.[73] Astrologer Julien Armistead says, "I don't think you can read an astrological chart if you're not intuitive."[74] Astrologer Charles Jaynes claims he does "not think a non-intuitive astrology works very well at all, because it *can't*"[75] (emphasis added). But astrologers Jane Gosselin and Julien Armistead candidly admit they do use psychic abilities to interpret the chart.[76] Dr. Ralph Metzner, a famous explorer of consciousness through drugs and the occult, observes in his *Maps of Consciousness* how the astrologers' psychic processes may work:

> Astrological horoscope casting is in one way a framework for intuitive perception. I know of one clairvoyant astrologer who simply looks at the actual horoscope diagram and then begins to "see" the inner life, the thought forms, and emotional patterns of her client, almost as if she were gazing into a crystal ball.[77]

It must be pointed out that some astrologers clarify the source of their intuition and psychic ability. For example, astrologer Marcus Allen has written *Astrology for the New Age: An Intuitive Approach*. In this book he thanks "my spirit guide for his insight and clarity and presence."[78]

So what we have seen here is that despite the many claims to being scientific, astrologers often admit their practice involves psychic abilities, and some even admit to having spirit guides. Of course, not all astrologers would admit to having a spirit guide. But isn't it interesting that those who do not admit to having spirit guides have the same powers as those who do?*

---

* See our *Astrology*, pp. 201-256.

30

Astrology
Versus
Christian Belief

Question 9

What do astrologers think about God?

If an astrologer claims to be a Christian, attends church and reads his Bible, and claims that his practice of astrology is compatible with his Christian belief, would you believe him? Is there any conflict between Christian belief and astrology? What would you say to Christian laymen who think there is nothing wrong with checking their horoscope each day? In reading and asking practicing astrologers to put their beliefs about God in brief form, most would say something like this: For them, the idea of pantheism (all is God; God is all) defines their belief in God. Others say they are not opposed to belief in God, in whatever shape or form a person wishes to believe. What is clear is that almost 100 percent of the astrologers do not arrive at their views of God from reading the facts of the Bible.

The astrologer who has formed his view of God from data other than the Bible has a different God than the biblical God. He is more in agreement with the common view that teaches "the Fatherhood of God and the brotherhood of man." Whether you are an atheist, Hindu, Buddhist, or Moslem or hold to almost any view of God at all does not bother them. As long as anyone allows astrology, they do not care what they believe about God. This is the view of God they accept. However, astrologers are opposed to believing in a God who defines certain actions and deeds as being wrong—as sinful—and obviously astrologers are opposed to someone who believes in a God who condemns the practice of astrology. And finally, like the majority of people in the world, they do not accept the views of our Lord Jesus Christ who said, "No one comes to the Father except through me" (John 14:6). That is, they don't believe that Jesus is the Savior of the world who forgives their sins by His death on the cross and our faith in Him (John 3:16; 5:24; 6:47).

Many astrologers define God in such a way that their belief easily blends within an occult view of the world. For example, for the majority, God is seen existing as a divine power and in some sense all life and all Nature are seen as divine.[79] This is why witch-astrologer Sybil Leek writes, "God is in everyone," including nature, and she sees no conflict in using astrology as a major means of practicing witchcraft.[80] Another astrologer states that astrology is an "affirmation of the Divine order in the universe" which enables one "to align oneself with the energies of Nature" and realize that the "planets are our sources of energy...."[81] Another astrologer states that true astrologers are spiritually oriented "healers" who know that they are "only the channel through which the Power [inherent in creation] flows" and "but a channel through whom the energies can flow."[82] Unfortunately, when astrologers look to nature and the creation for divine wisdom or empowerment, "nature" often becomes a "smoke screen" (a disguised worldview) that allows spirits or demons to provide occult powers to the astrologers. This power includes revelation, the "intuition" to give startling true information about a person from the horoscope. Again, when astrologers give this kind of information, it is very similar to what happens when spiritists give information to people through the power of their spirit guides.

In addition, astrology really rejects God for His creation. Both the idea of a personal creator God and man's responsibility before Him are abandoned. The result is that men are no longer responsible to God, but only to themselves and to some impersonal force.

In conclusion, astrology rejects the biblical teaching on God and adopts occultic views which give to God's creation the glory due to God alone. As Dr. Robert Morey states, "It is idolatry to ascribe to the stars that which belongs *only* to the God who created them."[83]

Question 10

What does astrology believe about Jesus Christ?

It is clear that astrology is willing to accept every view of who Jesus Christ is except the view that Jesus Himself taught and what the Bible teaches. The second thing to be noticed is that astrologers typically adopt an occultic view of Christ (for example, that Jesus the man was reincarnated on the earth and that "Christ" is our "higher self"). Note two leading astrologers' views of Jesus Christ. Ronald Davison is "England's foremost living astrologer" and has been editor of *The Astrologers Quarterly* since 1959. He states, "The story of the most perfect Being whoever incarnated on earth tells of the ultimate sacrifice on the cross... for the purpose of paying off any remaining debts [karma] of his own to the past...."[84] Notice that this prestigious astrologer believes Jesus was just another spirit who was reincarnated on the earth. Davison sees Christ's death on the cross as necessary for paying the price of His own "sins" (*karma*).

Marcus Allen is another example of a professional astrologer who teaches an occult view of Christ. He believes Christ is now everyone's higher occult self. Thus he states, "Christ had all seven ancient planets . . . all conjunct in Pisces . . . so he was the supreme, the ultimate Pisces . . . and so he initiated the Age of Pisces which is now coming to an end with the dawning of the Age of Aquarius, which is initiated by the second coming of the Christ Life within *all* of us. . . . In the Age of Aquarius, everyone is the Avatar, everyone is tuned into their higher self. . . ."[85]

What Allen is saying is that Jesus Christ was the supreme illustration of the Piscean temperament or personality. However, what Allen believes is that since the Age of Pisces is now passing and the Age of Aquarius is started, the Second Coming of Christ is the beginning of a period of higher "consciousness" for all men. In other words, this professional astrologer concludes that Christ Himself, through His "return," is equal to the emerging occult consciousness of all humanity. This view is in conflict with what the Bible teaches. The Scriptures teach that Jesus Christ is fully man and fully God in one person, the only begotten Son of God and Savior of the world, who will return someday physically and visibly to the earth (Matthew 24:1-35; John 1:1; 3:16; 10:30; Acts 1:11).

Question 11

What does astrology believe is man's basic problem and its solution?

Most astrologers believe the problem of man is that he is out of harmony with the divine forces and energies of the universe. He must become united with this harmony. And therefore, for many astrologers, salvation is not forgiveness from sin (most astrologers do not believe in sin in a biblical sense) but rather an enlightenment as to the underlying divine pattern they say governs the universe. "Salvation" is becoming aware of the powerful effect of these celestial patterns. Many astrologers believe that through a "higher consciousness," which is supposedly a joining with the divine evolutionary "impulse," that this will eventually bring a mystical Oneness with what they call "God" or ultimate reality. Astrologer Dane Rudhyar has written of the one who accepts astrology, "He learns to identify his consciousness and will with the 'celestial' patterns and rhythms." He goes on to say that the person "becomes one with the principles of universal order, which many call 'God.' "[86]

On the other hand, the Bible teaches that we are rebellious creatures who willfully ignore God and commit endless sins. Salvation is a free gift that delivers us from God's wrath against our sin and is based on our believing Christ died for us and receiving this gift by faith (John 3:16; Romans 5:1-10; Ephesians 1:7; 2:8,9; 1 Peter 2:24).

In addition, most astrologers also believe in reincarnation (one survey revealed about 75 percent of astrologers believe this).[87] Reincarnation teaches that over many lifetimes men will die and come back to life and eventually evolve back into the state of their original oneness with God. Astrology is seen as a guide and a tool to enlighten men during each life to avoid adding more *karma*, thus quickening the day when they will attain their true divine nature. However, The Bible teaches we do not have an endless number of lifetimes to perfect ourselves; we have only one lifetime in which to decide either to accept God's forgiveness or face His righteous judgment after death (Hebrews 9:27; Revelation 20:10-15).

Question 12

What does the Bible say about astrology?

The Bible teaches that astrology is not only a futile (worthless) activity, but an activity so bad that its very presence indicates God's judgment has already occurred (Acts 7:42,43). As both a philosophy and practice, astrology rejects the truth concerning the living God and instead leads people to dead objects, the stars and planets. As it mocks idols, the Bible mocks astrologers and their practice (Isaiah 47:13).

However, this has not prevented most astrologers from claiming the Bible favorably supports astrology. Jeff Mayo, founder of the Mayo School of Astrology, states, "the Bible is full of astrological references."[88] Joseph Goodavage, author of *Astrology: The Space Age Science* and *Write Your Own Horoscope*, claims that "the Bible is full of" the philosophy of astrology.[89]

Astrologers "justify" such statements in the same way many cults quote the Bible as evidence for their own false and unbiblical teachings. They twist the Scriptures until they teach something contrary to the Bible.[90] Any Scripture which refutes such false teachings is simply ignored, misinterpreted, or deleted. It can be proven that every single biblical text that astrologers quote to prove the Bible supports astrology has been either misinterpreted or misapplied.[91*] Just as oil and water do not mix, the Bible and astrology are utterly irreconcilable. Even non-Christians admit there is a "permanent ideological wedge between the two beliefs."[92]

Christianity has historically been opposed to astrology for three biblical reasons. First, the Bible explicitly rejects astrology by name as a futile (worthless) practice. Proof of this is Isaiah 47:13,14 where God states, "All the counsel you have received has only worn you out! Let your astrologers come forward, those star gazers who make predictions month by month, let them save you from what is coming upon you. Surely they are like stubble; the fire will burn them up. They cannot even save themselves. . . ." Here we can see that first, God is condemning the counsel of the Babylonian astrologers. Second, God says their predictions based on the stars will not save them from what is coming: divine judgment. Third, God says the counsel of the astrologers is not only worthless to others but it cannot even save the astrologers themselves. (See also Deuteronomy

---

* See our *Astrology*, pp. 119-156.

4:19; 17:1-5; 18:9-11; 2 Kings 17:16; 23:5; Jeremiah 8:2; 19:13; Ezekiel 8:16; Amos 5:26,27.)

The second biblical reason Christianity has historically opposed astrology is because God forbids occult practices. Astrology is basically divination. Divination is defined by *Webster's New Collegiate Dictionary* (1961) as "the act or practice of foreseeing or foretelling future events or discovering hidden knowledge." In *Webster's New World Dictionary* (1962) it is defined as "the art or practice of trying to foretell the future or the unknown by occult means." Because it is an occult art, God condemns divination as evil and as an abomination to Him and says it leads to contact with evil spirits called demons (Deuteronomy 18:9-13; Acts 16:16-19; 1 Corinthians 10:20).

Finally, the Bible rejects astrology because it leads people to the horrible transference of their allegiance from the infinite God of the universe to the things which He has made. It is a bit like ascribing all the credit, honor, and glory to the masterpieces of art themselves, completely forgetting the great artist who made them. No astrologer, dead or living, would have ascribed the works of Rembrandt or Picasso to the paintings themselves, yet they routinely do this with God. And yet God is infinitely more worthy of honor than men, a God who "made heaven and earth" and in whose hands is their very life's breath (Genesis 1:1; Daniel 5:22,23).

Question 13
Does the book of Daniel support the practice of astrology?

Astrologers often say the book of Daniel is proof of God's acceptance of astrology. First, they say this is true because God made Daniel the head of the astrologers and magicians in Babylon (Daniel 2:48). Second, if he was the head of all the Babylonian "wise" men, he must certainly have been proficient in astrology, for Babylon was widely known for its astrological practices. But this is not true. Why? The first reason this is not true is that the biblical account of Daniel explicitly attributes all of Daniel's success to God alone, not to his alleged practice of astrology or to the stars (Daniel 1:17; 2:27,28; 4:17,18). Second, Daniel was a godly man who, according to his own testimony, abhorred the idolatrous and evil practices of Babylon (Daniel 1:8; 4:27). Third, it is unthinkable that God would permit Daniel to engage in the very practices for which the nation itself was now in judgment (astrology, idolatry, etc.). Fourth, proof that Daniel did not embrace astrology is seen in the fact that he pointed out the constant failures of the Babylonian astrologers compared with the true knowledge given by God. Far from endorsing astrology, Daniel rejected it and pointed to the one true God. Thus the entire book of Daniel reveals the uselessness of astrology. The astrologers had a failure rate of 100 percent when compared with the one true God (Daniel 2:27,28; 4:7; 5:7-9,12,13,17).

God was the One who was sovereign, but the Babylonian kings had turned to the stars for advice and ignored the true God. For example, in Daniel 5 He pronounces judgment upon the Babylonian ruler Belshazzar by stating, "But you his son, O Belshazzer, have not humbled yourself, though you knew all this. Instead, you have set yourself up against the Lord of heaven.... You praised the gods...which cannot see or hear or understand. But you did not honor the God who holds in his hand your life and all your ways" (Daniel 5:22,23). When divine glory and power are given to the "gods" of the heavens and not to the God who made the heavens, God says they have "exchanged the truth of God for a lie, and worshiped and served created things rather than the Creator—who is forever praised" (Romans 1:25). In fact this is the very reason why God's judgment comes. It comes because men ignore Him and suppress the truth in unrighteousness; thus "the wrath of God is being revealed from heaven against all the godlessness and wickedness of men who suppress the truth by their wickedness, since what may be known about God is plain to them, because God has made it plain to them. For since the creation of the world God's invisible qualities—his eternal power and divine nature—have been clearly seen, being understood from what has been made, so that men are without excuse. For even though they knew God, they neither glorified him as God nor gave thanks to him, but their thinking became futile and their foolish hearts were darkened. Although they claimed to be wise, they became fools and exchanged the glory of the immortal God" for false idols (Romans 1:18-22).

In other words, astrology is condemned in the Bible because its very practice indicates a form of idolatry already under divine judgment: "But God turned away [from them] and gave them over to the worship of the heavenly bodies" (Acts. 7:42,43).

In conclusion, astrology is rejected in the Bible because it 1) is futile and worthless, 2) constitutes involvement with occult powers, and 3) is a form of idolatry (exchanging the heavens for God). Thus it 1) has no power to save men from their sins, 2) opens men to demonic deception, and 3) robs God of the glory that is due Him.

Question 14

Is there such a thing as Christian astrology?

We have just seen that the Bible completely rejects astrology. Any comprehensive study of Christian history presents a strong testimony against astrology, despite astrologers' claims to the contrary.[93] The only brief period in which some in the church ever "embraced" astrology was a period in which the Bible itself was largely rejected and the church was full of evil practices, immorality, and paganism.[94]

In spite of all this, there are three categories of those who are astrologers and yet who claim the Christian faith: 1) those who claim to be Christians simply because they live in a "Christian" country or were raised in a nominal Christian environment, yet they have no association with any church or doctrinal faith whatsoever; 2) those who actively practice a pseudo form of Christianity and attend a church that is not biblical; and 3) those who say they accept biblical authority yet still practice astrology. However, one cannot *logically* hold to both Christianity and astrology. We shall now briefly examine these three categories.

Category 1—Many astrologers *claim* to be Christian, yet in reality they are hostile to Christianity! Dr. Robert Morey has observed, "Even though the majority of astrologers claim to be Christian, they are generally hostile to the teachings of historic and biblical Christianity."[95] These people who claim to be Christian would probably admit themselves they have a preference for occultism (however they define it) and that they are not *biblically* Christian.

Category 2—Then there are those with moderate-to-strong church affiliation who say they are Christians but nevertheless reject the Bible as the final authority in matters of astrology. Their faith is usually in God in a general sense. They do not admit to knowing God personally and show little interest in being born again (John 3:3-8). Since these people practice astrology and reject God's instruction on this topic, the following verses may apply to them. "They claim to know God, but by their actions they deny him" (Titus 1:16). Or, "If we claim to have fellowship with him yet walk in the darkness, we lie and do not live by the truth" (1 John 1:6). Or, "The man who says, 'I know him,' but does not do what he [God] commands is a liar, and the truth is not in him. But if anyone obeys his word, God's love is truly made complete in him. This is how we know we are in him: whoever claims to live in him must walk as Jesus did" (1 John 2:4-6).

It is sad to say that many Americans believe that psychic Jeane Dixon is a good Christian. Yet in her book *Yesterday, Today and Forever* she states she was guided by the "Holy Spirit" in integrating Christianity and astrology.[96] She claims:

> Some of my friends consider this a strange practice for a Roman Catholic. As I understand it, however, the Catholic church and many other religious bodies as well has never condemned the study of astrology.... I have never experienced any conflict between my faith and the guidance I receive from my church on the one hand and the knowledge I find in the stars on the other... actually, much of what I know about astrology I learned from a Jesuit priest, who was one of the best-informed scholars I have ever met.[97]

She relates that it was through a series of visions that she was led to adopt astrology. She says that from these visions, she discovered:

> the answer which could pull together the facts of Scripture and the data of astrology... now I understand why, in my vision, each apostle was associated with a different Zodiac sign; for each was being revealed to me as to the archetype of that sign. Each [apostle] embodied all the mental and emotional characteristics of his own segment of the Zodiac... that simple yet

profound truth was the message I received both through my meditations and in subsequent visions during the following weeks.[98]

She concludes:

Astrology fits into God's plan for mankind by helping us understand both our talents and our shortcomings. Being better informed about ourselves, appreciating our strengths and aware of our weaknesses, we will be much better equipped to turn everything we are [over] to the service of the Lord.[99]

(To understand why Jeane Dixon is wrong concerning her views on astrology, see the comments below in Category 3.) In continuing to discuss those who categorize themselves as Christian astrologers we must reluctantly admit that in spite of all the Bible says against astrology there have been a few true Christians who have embraced astrological views.

Category 3—Dr. John Warwick Montgomery refers to Lutheran scientists Tycho Brahe and Johann Kepler as Christian men who "were convinced that astrology was not incompatible with divine revelation."[100] A man wrote to us claiming to be a "Christian professional astrologer" and wanted us to know that he finds "no clear and specific injunction against astrology in the Bible." In presenting his defense to us he said, "True, astrologers are called to task for . . . misuse of their skills—as are prophets, priests and kings—but are not called to deny or shun the practice of those skills." He went on to say:

Indeed, *worship* of "the starry host" as it is translated in the NIV is forbidden to the believer; as is *worship* of money or "the king"; but a respectful *observance* and *stewardship* of economic and political forces is not only permitted, but required.

Scripturally, only if astrology is assumed to be divination can we find it placed off limits for God's people; and most astrological counseling is not divinatory in nature. Moreover, while the Scriptural warnings about divination read as though they were absolute, we find in comparing Scripture with Scripture that the Covenant People were divinely provided with an oracle, the Urim and Thummin, which was to be used *only at the hands of the member of the Covenant Community.*

The practical inference is that it is wrong for believers to enlist the skills of *unbelievers* when they wish to discern the will of God—with which I heartily agree; for to do so places one in spiritual jeopardy. [Emphasis added; in other words he believes Christians *are* permitted to consult Christian astrologers—such as this individual!]

It is my conclusion, therefore, that astrology—like any other human art or science, such as nuclear physics or psychotherapy, can be useful when carried on in submission to the Lordship of Jesus Christ; but is spiritually and psychologically dangerous when practiced in the spirit of the world, the flesh, or the devil.[101]

This is essentially the same argument "Christian parapsychologists" use. (Christian parapsychologists scientifically study the occult and, among other things, apply it to the church, cf. Chapter 35.) Like Christian astrologers they claim that the Old Testament condemnation of mediumistic and spiritistic practices (Deuteronomy 18:9-12) was only intended for those who misused these practices, but was not meant to condemn those who use such practices "ethically," "wisely," with good motives, and for God's glory.[102] However, Christian astrologers and parapsychologists ignore the fact that God specifically called these practices in and of themselves evil. God Himself failed to make any fine distinctions on such practices. Proof that there is no such fine line made by God as to Christian astrology or Christian spiritism is seen in the fact that God makes such fine distinctions when they are important. If Christian astrology or Christian spiritism *were* important to spiritual growth, we should expect that God would have made such a distinction. After all, God has done so in many other cases. For example, sex is glorified within marriage but condemned outside of marriage or among persons of the same sex. God also says that certain foods and drink are permissible in one situation, but not in another (Romans 1:26,27; 14:20; 1 Corinthians 6:18). The basic argument of the Christian astrologer is that astrology can be beneficial as long as one is not *worshiping* the stars (which would be idolatry) or engaging in *divination* ("the act or practice of trying to foretell the future by occult means"), but this is a false conclusion. It is a conclusion based largely upon pragmatism (if it works, it's okay). They say astrology "works" and is "helpful or useful," therefore, it should not be condemned. But if this reasoning is true, then why not try and strip all other forms of the occult of their divination and idolatry and, as Christians, simply glean their "wisdom" and practical uses?

But the arguments of Christian astrologers never address these eight important issues: 1) Can astrology really be separated from its occult connections?; 2) Are the basic premises and principles of astrology scientifically accurate?; 3) Can it be said that astrology is in any sense concerned with moral principles?; 4) Does Scripture really justify the practice of astrology for any purpose?; 5) What are the unforeseen risks or consequences of practicing astrology (see Question 23)?; 6) Why would God forbid astrology if it were really so helpful? After all, would God totally condemn any practice if it were even slightly good?; 7) Astrological "counseling" typically involves divination. For example, former astrologers like Karen Winterburn have told us that there is simply no way to do astrology, even astrological counseling, without engaging in divination. Also the "Urim and Thummim" were not to be used by the laity, nor are they in use today. The use of astrology in the church cannot be defended on the basis of the ancient and very selected use of these instruments; and 8) *Worship* is more than simply bowing down to something. It involves that which we serve and grant our *devotion* to, that which we praise and hold in awe, that which we acknowledge as directing our lives, and that which we reverence. Christian astrologers may not literally bow down to the stars, but neither do other astrologers. But both the heavenly objects and astrology itself fit the characteristics of worship in the lives of astrologers, Christian or not.[*]

---

[*] See our *Astrology*, pp. 141-156, 285-300 for a further critique of Christian Astrology.

31

Critical
Evaluation of
Astrology*

Question 15

Is the scientific evidence for astrology valid?

In the last question we answered the assertions of those who claim there is such a thing as Christian astrology. We will now examine the evidence from science that astrologers claim validates their practice. We attempted to secure the best scientific evidence available on behalf of the claims of astrology. For example, we contacted the largest and most scientifically oriented astrological society, The American Federation of Astrologers in Tempe, Arizona. This organization offers almost 1000 books for sale, over 600 tapes, and claims to be "the nerve center of astrology in America today...." The AFA also claims that for 50 years it has been the leader in "astrological education and research."[103]

But the literature they recommended as giving the best evidence for astrology was both disappointing and questionable.[104] The most important research they cited was the Gauquelin research which we will discuss. It must first be said that much of astrology is simply not scientifically testable because of the very nature of astrology. For example, it claims to be a practice based upon mystical influences and private, subjective interpretations of individual astrologers reading the horoscope. That is why (at these points) astrology can never be *scientifically* proven or disproven. Its phenomena lie outside the boundaries of science ("intuition,"

---

* For a more indepth treatment, see our *Astrology*, pp. 47-118, 175-256.

mystical planetary influences, symbolic correspondences, etc.). Nevertheless, both astrologers and scientific investigators of astrology agree there are definite astrological principles which merit scientific testing.[105] But if these prove false, and if the practical results of astrology are *better* explained by nonastrological data, then our only conclusion is that there is simply no evidence for the truth of astrology.

The overall evidence astrologers set forth to prove their case may be divided into three basic categories: 1) the general arguments, 2) statistical studies, and 3) practical results (the third issue is the most important and the one most often cited. For our critical analysis see Question 22).

First, the common arguments as put forth by most astrologers are examined by Kelly, et al., and summarized by research scientist Geoffrey Dean. Dean noted that Kelly, et al., said that none of these arguments cite *valid* reasons for belief in astrology. (Remarks in parentheses are theirs.)

1) Astrology has great antiquity and durability
   (So has murder)
2) Astrology is found in many cultures
   (So is a flat earth)
3) Many great scholars have believed in it
   (Many others have not)
4) Astrology is based on observation
   (Its complexity defies observation)
5) Extraterrestrial influences exist
   (None are relevant to astrology)
6) Astrology has been proved by research
   (Not true)
7) Nonastrologers are not qualified to judge
   (So who judges murder?)
8) Astrology is not science but art/philosophy
   (Not a reason for belief)
9) Astrology works
   (The evidence suggests otherwise)[106]

The second area of evidence astrologers set forth to prove the validity of astrology comes from certain statistical studies. We are unable to cite all major studies here, but we can briefly cite the negative results of four major studies. We may also state that *every* other study we are aware of encounters the same or similar problems as these.

Please note that the following studies have all been claimed as evidence or proof of astrology. Yet nothing could be further from the truth.

1) The *Mayo-White-Eysenck Study* attempted to determine if astrology could predict in advance whether the personality of adults would be introverted or extroverted. It was done with 2324 adults who had their extroversion/introversion scores tabulated on the Eysenck Personality Inventory (EPI). These scores were then correlated with astrological predictions. Their conclusion: *Marginal* (astrologers read "favorable") results

were obtained that could not be accounted for by chance alone. In five additional studies, three did not support these findings, two did. Finally, it was discovered later that the positive results could be adequately explained in a number of different ways, *without* recourse to astrological theories. Eysenck himself in later research (confirmed by other researchers) came to believe that "the entire astrological effect [of the original study] was due to the subject's expectation and familiarity with the characteristics associated with their Zodiac sign."[107] In brief, this study cannot be used as evidence for validating astrology.

2) The research involving the *Gauquelin "Mars" Effect* became a scientific study to test if the birth dates of 2088 sports champions were statistically significant according to "astrological" predictions. What researchers concluded was that a statistically significant number of sports champions were born when Mars was situated between the eastern horizon and the celestial meridian. This means that a correlation of 21.65 percent (of those sports champions born at the above time) existed against an expected chance correlation of 17.17 percent (the number of sports champions normally expected to be born).

The "Mars" Effect has never been absolutely confirmed in 20 years of subsequent studies. The most that can be concluded to date is "the success of replication [could these same statistics be confirmed?] is a matter of some debate."[108]

Significantly, even though Gauquelin's research is often noted by astrologers as confirmation of astrology, Gauquelin himself has done perhaps more definitive research than anyone else to disprove it. His work involved seeking out possible *cosmological*—not *astrological*—influences. (Gauquelin's so-called "neo-astrology" is not related to astrology proper and is still subject to debate.) Yet he has examined the claims of astrology and tested them in great detail. In one study he used 15,560 subjects to test the alleged influence of the Zodiac in relationship to professional success. Gauquelin concluded "the results were entirely negative."[109] When astrologers objected that "professional success" was "far too crude a criterion to reveal the astral subtlety of Zodiacal influences," Gauquelin established further elaborate testing to satisfy their complaints and substantiate his conclusions. (Note: Astrologers *do* claim the heavens influence the likelihood of professional success.) Nevertheless the astrologers said that Gauquelin should have tested not professional success but *personality*, and they claimed if he did so then he would have found a real influence. It is important to notice here that when data seemed to confirm astrology, the astrologers accepted the criteria of professional success for the sports champions, but when the same criteria disproved astrology, they rejected it. In spite of this, Gauquelin obliged the astrologers and tested personality traits with Zodiacal predictions. In his test, 52,188 personality traits were systematically collected from 2000 subjects. What did he find?—only that astrological predictions received "a fatal blow."[110]

Read almost any book by a scientifically minded contemporary astrologer and most likely you will find him citing Gauquelin's works as evidence for astrology. Yet just the opposite is true; Gauquelin himself never claimed to prove astrology. For example, Gauquelin has authored *The Scientific Basis of Astrology: Myth or Reality* (1973) and *Dreams and Illusions of Astrology* (1979). Listen to what Gauquelin himself forcefully stated about the scientific validity of astrology: "Every attempt, whether of astrologers or scientists to produce evidence of the validity of astrological laws has been in vain. It is now quite certain that the signs in the sky which presided over our births have *no power whatever* to decide our fates, to affect our hereditary characteristics, or play any part however humble in the totality of affects, random and otherwise, which form the fabric of our lives and mold our impulses to action. *Confronted with science*, modern and traditional astrology are seen to be imaginary doctrines"[111] (emphasis added).

3) The massive *Guardian-Smithers Study* tested 2.3 million people comparing occupations and Sun-signs. Although a *mild* correlation was noted, Smithers himself remained unconvinced. He concluded that most of the data "can be explained in other ways" (for example, seasonal factors, social habits, belief in astrology, etc.). Later, a further reevaluation of Smithers' research claimed design flaws. It was also noted that effects could be explained by additional nonastrological factors.[112]

4) *The National Enquirer* test examined 240 people and correlated their astrological sign and personality. They claimed to show that 91 percent of the people tested had their personality determined by their Zodiac sign. However, subsequent testing failed to substantiate the *Enquirer's* claims.[113]

In conclusion, the scientific evidence cited in favor of astrology turns out to be no evidence at all. Just the opposite is true—in fact, science disproves astrology.

Question 16

What is the scientific evidence against astrology?

The scientific evidence against astrology is extremely conclusive. Yet the response of astrologers to this fact is simply to ignore it. Astrology has always lived in its own private world, impervious to all assaults. As one critic remarked, "The situation is not helped by the typical astrologer's attitude toward factual evidence so well described by Levy (1982), [a man] who runs Australia's largest computerized chart calculation service: 'I often get the feeling, after talking to astrologers, that they live in a mental fantasy world, a kind of astrological universe where no explanations outside of astrological ones are permitted, and that if the events of the real world do not accord with astrological notions or predictions, then yet another astrological technique will have to be invented to explain it.' "[114]

Among astrologers there is a stubborn refusal to face the facts, and they often exhibit a fundamentally *irrational* approach. For example, note the comments of the chairman of the United Kingdom Astrological Association, who is critical of the astrologer's inclination for excuses. He is describing what an astrologer can do to "harmonize" astrological predictions with a person who does not match them. In this case below, he is describing a person who is very meek, but whom astrology predicts should be aggressive:

> If I found a very meek and unaggressive person with five planets in Aries, this does not cause me to doubt that Aries means aggression. I may be able to point to his Pisces Ascendant, or to his Sun conjunct Saturn, or to his ruler in the twelfth house; and, if none of these alibis are available, I can simply say that he has not yet fulfilled his Aries potential. Or, I can argue (as I have heard argued) that, if a person has an *excess* of planets in a particular sign, he will tend to suppress the characteristics of that sign, because he is scared that, if he reveals them, he will carry them to excess. But if on the next day I meet a very aggressive person who also has five planets in Aries, I will change my tune: I will say that he *had* to be like that because of his planets in Aries.[115]

Astrology is a modern myth that millions believe. Just as millions once believed the stars were gods, today millions believe the stars influence their character and destiny. Yet to date, dozens of tests have *failed* to prove astrology. The comprehensive nature of this scientific testing conclusively invalidates astrology. In the following questions, we will examine some of the tests for specific tenets of astrology.

Question 17
What have the tests for Sun-sign validity proved? (For example, are you a Pisces, Aries, or Leo?)

According to astrology a person's Sun-sign is said to have the greatest importance in determining his overall character.[116] One researcher's analysis of the content of astrological literature revealed 2375 specific adjectives for the 12 Zodiacal Sun-signs. Each sign was described by about 200 adjectives (for example, "Leo" is strong, domineering, tough—a born leader; a "Taurus" is indecisive, timid, insecure—not a leader). In this test, 1000 people were examined for 33 variables, including physical attractiveness, leadership ability, personality traits, social and religious belief, etc. The conclusion was that this test failed to prove any astrological prediction: "All of our results can be attributed to random chance."[117]

There was another test to find out if the planets influenced compatability in marriage. That is, was there any significant indication of numbers of couples who, because their signs showed they were "compatible," stayed married? Did those born under an "incompatible" sign get divorced? This study involved 2978 couples who got married and 478 couples who got divorced in 1967 and 1968. This test proved that astrological signs did not significantly alter the outcome of either group. Those born under the "compatible" signs married and divorced as often as those born under the "incompatible" signs.[118]

Astrologers claim that scientists and politicians are favored by one Sun-sign or another. That is, there is supposed to be a connection between a person's Sun-sign and his chances of success in a given profession. John McGervy, in doing research on this topic, compared birth dates of 16,634 scientists and 6475 politicians and found no correlation to substantiate the astrologers' claims. There can be no doubt the distribution of signs among these two professions was as random as for the general public.[119]

In conclusion, the scientific evidence today shows there is no validity to the astrologers' assertion that your Sun-sign influences your life.*

Question 18

What have the tests for horoscope validity proved?

At least seven independent studies have indicated that even with the best astrologers there is *little agreement as to the meaning* of a chart.[120]

In addition, seven other studies revealed that people who have horoscopes interpreted for them cannot tell the difference between a right chart and a wrong chart. That is, they are just as likely to identify someone else's horoscope rather than their own as being the one that they think "best" describes them. In other words, the tests showed that people were just as happy with wrong charts (someone else's chart) as they were with right charts. Thus, researchers found that the interpretations "fit" people even when the interpretation was from the wrong chart. (These results could *not* be explained away by astrologers blaming poor chart interpretation or by astrologers claiming the people lacked knowledge of themselves.)[121]

In fact, many tests reveal that people cannot even tell authentic charts from charts that have been deliberately *reversed*. People rated reversed charts just as highly as authentic charts. It is obvious that reversed charts are diametrically the opposite of authentic charts. Therefore, the conclusion people drew from these two horoscopes could not have been more wrong.

In conclusion, these tests show that people tend to accept *any* chart as valid for a variety of reasons (about 20)[122] wholly unrelated to astrological theory (such as gullibility, expectation, emotional need, etc.).[123]

And what's worse, researchers found that astrologers who used charts were no better in their judgments than those astrologers who did *not* use charts—who were just guessing. In fact, the research showed that astrologers who used charts made slightly *worse* judgments.[124]

Question 19

What have the tests for the influence of the Moon proved?

Over three dozen scientific studies have failed to indicate any "causal relationship between lunar phenomena and human behavior."[125]

---

* cf. Anthony Standen, *Forget Your Sun Sign*, Baton Rouge, LA, Legacy, 1977.

Question 20

What have tests for astrological predictions proved?

These tests have revealed that astrological predictions have an extremely high failure rate. For example, one large study examined over three *thousand* predictions by leading astrologers and leading astrology publications from 1974 to 1979. This study revealed a 90 percent failure rate in astrological predictions.[126]

The editor of *Free Inquiry*, Dr. Paul Kurtz, has written that "there have been exhaustive tests of astrological claims to see if they have any validity" and yet, despite the fact that astrologers claim to have a 4000-year record of success and that this record speaks for itself, "dozens of scientific tests of astrological columns, charts and horoscopes clearly contradict this claim."[127]

We may state fairly and accurately that it has scientifically been proven that the heavens do not influence us in the manner astrologers claim. To our knowledge, astrology has failed every test ever given.

Yet all of the scientific disproof of astrology still cannot explain how astrologers can sometimes provide true self-disclosures to their clients (information they have no way of knowing), or how in rare cases they are accurate in their predictions. As we shall see in Question 22, it "works" for reasons fully unrelated to astrology itself. Some of these reasons are natural ones and some of them are supernatural, but in no case are they astrological.

Question 21

What do astrologers believe about astrology?

It appears that as a whole, many or most astrologers do not think very highly of their craft or even of other astrologers. First, even some astrologers, admit that most other astrologers are frauds. John Townley, a respected U.S. astrologer with 20 years experience, admitted the following, "I would say that most of the accusers of astrology are probably correct. They think that astrologers are 100 percent charlatans, but I would bring it down to 90 percent. [They are] not necessarily . . . intentional charlatans. . . . [But] maybe 50 percent of the people are deliberately selling hokum straight ahead."[128]

Second, many astrologers admit to the reality of contradictory and false theories within astrology. For example, Kathleen Russo and Carolyn Burmingham, president and vice president of the Federation of Scientific Astrologers, admit that "Much of what has been proposed by astrologers in the past and today is without foundation. . . ."[129]

Third, astrologers themselves admit many interpretations of horoscopes are unfounded and uncertain. For example, astrologer John Addey admits, "So far as the practical rules of horoscopy are concerned there are a host of uncertainties—[concerning] the Zodiac, the houses, aspects—all [of them now] present intractable problems. . . ."[130] In addition, astrologer

Dr. W. M. Davidson wrote that astrology was largely a failure and that "many [of its] interpretations are just a mass of generalities, haphazard guesses. . . ."[131]*

Fourth, concerning scientific testing, Charles Carter, editor of *Astrology Magazine* and recognized as "one of the world's outstanding and most knowledgeable astrologers," states, "Statistical research, such as early astrologers could not carry out for lack of sufficient data, has [now] cast considerable doubt on the validity of portions of the rather incoherent mass of tradition that till recent years represented astrological science."[132] S. Best, the editor of *Correlation*, the scholarly journal of research into astrology, has concluded: "We really have no alternative. Either we put our house in order or someone from the establishment will sooner or later take great delight in doing it for us, or, alternatively, taking it apart brick by brick."[133]

In conclusion, to date we have found the scientific evidence against astrology is conclusive, and that astrology itself, according to astrologers, is in a state of disarray and confusion. These findings prepare us to examine what astrologers claim is the key "proof" of astrology—that "it works." But we must ask, if it is not true, how can it work?

Question 22

If astrology is false, how can it work?

Astrology works for reasons unrelated to astrology. Consider the dilemma of modern astrology. Every test given proves it is false. Astrology schools and theories contradict one another. Astrologers themselves are depressed over the state of astrology. The astrologer has no recourse but to claim that it *must* be true, since it works. Yet if we can show that it does not work for any reason related to astrology, then no astrologers can logically claim that it works because it is *true*. And if it is not true, then a massive campaign of consumer fraud is being foisted upon the public. If a man purchases a car that he is promised works on gasoline and yet it only works on nuclear power, he is up the proverbial creek.

Knowing *how* something works can be more important than knowing *that* it works. If astrology claims it works because of celestial birth patterns, and yet it only works because of reasons related to human psychology or, as we shall see, spiritistic deception, then the consumer has been deceived. He was promised objective knowledge of stellar influences to help him better live his life. In fact, what he got was a con that in the end opened him to the occult and other dangers. Astrology does not need to be true in order to work, but the reasons *why* it works make it potentially dangerous. If astrology is offering occultism to people in the disguise of celestial influences, it is both morally and spiritually dangerous. When astrologers offer "knowledge" of the future to people based on their unproven theories or under the guidance of spirits, people should be warned of the consequences.

---

* For a detailed analysis of chart interpretation see our *Astrology*, Chapters 4, 12-13, 15.

Astrologers see the arguments against astrology as no arguments at all because astrology seems to work and who cares if we can't explain *why* it works.[134]

If people knew astrology was false, and that it only worked by self-deception or demonic spirits, and that it was also dangerous, can we believe they would continue to consult astrologers?

It has been shown that psychological factors can account for a great deal of astrology's success.[135*] What about the supernatural spirits called demons? Are they related to the startling self-disclosures that are sometimes found in astrology? Psychic researcher Bernard Gittelson states:

> One friend of mine was amazed that on the first visit, her astrologer was able to pinpoint major life events, that the astrologer could never have known about, to specific two-week periods that occurred twenty years before they met. In other words, don't be surprised by what your astrologer knows about you.[136]

Consider the following assessment of a former professional astrologer:

> As we look honestly at astrology, we begin to see that adherents of this system—without knowing it—are banging on the door through which communication is established with knowledgeable yet deceptive spirit beings. Eventually that door opens. And that opening produces an appalling development in the adherent's life. He or she matures in the craft in a most unthought-of manner: as a spirit medium. Without contact with spirit beings, there would be no astrological self-disclosures. Or if they did come, [without spirit contact] it [supernatural information] would be almost entirely from guess work; [and] they [supernatural self-disclosures] would be very rare.[137]

But if it is not possible to distinguish between astrological self-disclosures and those given through the spirit world in general, then, in light of all that we have seen, it is more logical to conclude that these amazing disclosures derive from spiritistic sources—not from the stars. In addition, when astrology is seen to be an occult practice, often using or developing psychic abilities, and when we find the same tragedies and deceptions as found in spiritism, then how can we believe the astrologers when they say that it is merely the stars which are influencing us?

---

* For an analysis see our *Astrology*, Chapters 12-13.

Question 23

Are there dangers for those who believe in or practice astrology?

Some things work extremely well but are nevertheless quite dangerous: for example, guns, dynamite, and car bombs.

The dangers of astrology (and of all forms of divination) can be divided into six basic categories: 1) physical damage, 2) inducements to crime, 3) economic loss, 4) psychological damage, 5) spiritual damage, and 6) moral damage.*

1) *Physical damage*—For example, even some astrologers admit that because it is often quackery, "medical astrology is an area often fraught with many pitfalls."[138] Thus when an astrologer advises a client against his child's appendectomy and the child dies as a result, this is more than tragic.[139]

2) *Inducements to crime*—Dr. Kurt Koch observes that "astrology has been responsible for a number of suicides and murders."[140] He gives examples in his books concerning the evil effects of the suggestive nature of astrology. Thus astrological predictions or advice may cause people to do things they would otherwise never have done, and in some cases this has led to tragedy. For example, a woman murdered her son because an astrologer predicted he would have a life full of mental illness. The shattered mother went to jail; the astrologer went free.[141] The possibilities here are endless: A chart reveals a deformed baby, so an abortion results; a company may fail so the treasurer embezzles funds; etc.

We can only ask, How many crimes have been committed because of astrology?

3) *Economic loss*—With people asking astrologers for advice and counsel concerning financial investments and a variety of other economic decisions—such as gambling, weather prediction and crop yields, stock market fluctuations, etc.—there is plenty of room for financial loss or tragedy.

4) *Spiritual damage*—Since astrology is an occult practice (divination) condemned in the Bible, the worst damage an astrologer does is in helping to turn people away from God and Christ—to trust in a false religious philosophy. It not only prevents personal salvation, but opens the door to greater occult activity which may result in demonic involvement.

How does astrology lead people into the occult? A review of 14 "standard" astrological sources revealed three Sun-signs in particular that have occultic qualities—Pisces, Scorpio and Aries. Those born with these signs are supposed to be mystical, intuitive, psychic, spiritual, magical, clairvoyant, occultic, etc.[142] These persons are informed that they are *supposed*

---

* Also see our *Astrology, Chapter 16.*

to be psychic or have psychic tendencies. Will not many of these people who are told of their "spiritual" nature try to fulfill their astrological or karmic "destiny" and thereby enter the occult?

5) *Psychological damage*—When clients make major decisions on the basis of astrological predictions or calculations—decisions relating to health, family and children, business, employment, or future—then the door is open for potential tragedy. Such decisions are made upon an irrational and/or emotional basis only and not necessarily upon the basis of sound judgment or actual facts concerning the matter. Anyone claiming knowledge of the future is exercising an influence which can radically redirect a person's thinking. It may even lead some people into a decision-making process based on anxiety and the irrational. (When the element of demonic deception also enters the picture, one is more certain that harm will sooner or later result.)

"Astrological counseling" of sensitive people is fraught with potential dangers. What of those who are told they are born under Gemini, whose "influence" might result in split personalities? Will *some* Gemini who live under the burden of this knowledge be moved closer to the brink? What of those who try to live up to their "astrological nature" when it is really not *their* nature? What difficulties or problems might this present?[143]

Even professional astrologers admit the dangers here. Astrologer-psychiatrist Bernard Rosenblum, an advocate of counseling by astrology, nevertheless warns, "The bad reputation astrology must contend with is partly due to those astrologers who make definite predictions about people's death, divorce, or illness, and other statements that suggest the client must suffer the rest of his life with a difficult psychological problem in order to correct a karmic imbalance. Such astrologers are exhibiting arrogance and insensitivity in the extreme."[144]

Prominent astrologer Dane Rudhyar observes, "I have received many letters from people telling me how fearful or psychologically confused they have become after consulting even a well-known astrologer and being given a biased character analysis and/or predictions of illness, catastrophe, or even death."[145] Former astrologer Charles Strohmer admits, "Major sorrows came my way due to my involvement with astrology."[146]

Since most visits to astrologers concern issues that are of major importance to the client (for example, major decisions on money, health or illness, relationships, children, length of life or a spouse's life, etc.) the opportunities for deception are endless.

6) *Moral damage*—Astrology has no moral character. First, almost all astrologers reject any absolute standard of morality and prefer a "situation ethics" approach where moral decisions are determined subjectively—largely by the whim and preference of the astrologer. Astrologer Alan Oken states, "No Path is the True Path, for in the Absolute there is no Truthfulness or Falsehood, no right and no wrong, no yes and no no."[147]

Second, many astrologers deliberately reject moral values. For example, astrologer John Manolesco observes, "Religious and moral values are declining, the fiction of free will, moral obligation, [and of] immutable, eternal values has been exposed for what it is—myth."[148]

Third, astrologers choose not to morally educate the public. Jeff Mayo, founder of the Mayo School of Astrology, emphasizes, "It must be understood that astrology: Does not moralize; the birth chart indicates weakness or strength in this respect: choice of action is the individual's."[149]

Finally, the astrologer is responsible to no one but his own beliefs, and the impersonal stars which have little or no concern over his behavior. For example, the kinds of tragedies seen above are easily justified on the part of the astrologer by an appeal to his client's "karmic destiny." Whatever his client's sins or tragedies in this life, they are only the results of conditions in a past life which have "predestined" them. For example, a number of astrologers serve the homosexual community. They may casually advise a client as to the time of his next affair, or explain to homosexuals that their sexual preference was "determined" by the stars.[150] Even one astrologer admits that "people used it [astrology] so often as an excuse, a justification for their weaknesses and shortcomings...."[151]

Conclusion: Two Real-Life Stories

The fact is that astrological predictions can have tragic results in people's lives. For many, the astrologer is a "god" and his or her words have "divine" authority. Thus an astrological interpretation can, for many, be the equivalent of a personal revelation from God himself. Consider the following true stories that further compound the problem of astrological counseling. A young man consults an astrologer who informs him that the stars reveal he will marry young but that his first wife will not be the one "destined" for him. Only his second wife will bring him "true happiness." The man deliberately marries young in order to get his first wife, that is to fulfill the prophecy, so that he will not miss finding his second wife who alone will make him happy. His first wife is a very good and devoted wife and bears him three children. But after the third child is born, the husband abandons his wife and family and later obtains a divorce on the grounds of his own complicity. He marries the second wife whom he believes is the one the stars have destined to make him happy. Yet within a few months she joins a cult and has made his life utterly miserable and he divorces her.[152]

Thus a single astrologer with a single prediction brings pain and tragedy into the lives of six people—three adults and three children. Now multiply this prediction power by millions of astrological predictions and advice given every year and you can see the potential for disaster. Far too many tragedies are "arranged" by astrological predictions. The pattern is clear: 1) clients are amazed by accurate self-disclosures; 2) these self-disclosures generate *trust*; 3) trust leads to deception; 4) deception produces unwise or immoral decisions and actions; 5) bad actions bring ruin or destruction.[153]

A second illustration reveals not only how easily astrology becomes a vehicle for tragedy but the reality of spiritual warfare hidden beneath the surface. Here we see how astrology produces an irrational fear and despair. It also paralyzes initiative and sound judgment, and can lead to suicide if not prevented. A certain woman was engaged to be married and felt that seeking the advice of an astrologer might be useful. After drawing the horoscope, the astrologer predicted the following: "Your engagement will break up. This man will not marry you. You will not marry at all, but remain single." The woman was devastated. She was so much in love with her fiancé she could not bear the thought of losing him. She became paralyzed with fear. She continually worried that the engagement would break up, that she would never marry. She finally resolved to put an end to her life, but on the day she intended to kill herself, a friend of her fiancé was able to stop her. Upon the advice of that friend she went for pastoral counseling, revealed her plight, repented, and gave her life to Christ. Soon after that day, her fiancé also gave his life to Christ. Today they are married with several children and are quite happy. Nevertheless had it not been for Christ, the disaster which was set afoot by the astrologer could easily have happened.[154]

A Personal Word

If, as a Christian, you are now involved in some way with astrology, we would hope that the information in this book would cause you to stop your involvement.

There are two reasons why. First, as a Christian, your loving God warns you that astrology is one of Satan's philosophies, and we are not to seek information from such sources. As we have seen, evil spirits are the real power behind many astrologers. But second, the columns they write and books they author are also means to ensnare our minds and rob us of peace.

Ask the Lord to forgive you of your disobedience to Him and ask Him to supply all your needs. He will.

If you are wondering if you are a Christian, or you know that you never have placed your faith in Jesus Christ, we encourage you to receive Christ now. If you do want to receive Christ, just pray:

> Dear God, I ask Jesus Christ to enter my life and be my Lord and Savior. I recognize this is a decision that You take very seriously. I believe that on the cross Jesus Christ died for my sin and I receive Him into my life now. My commitment to You is that I will follow Him and not astrology. I ask for Your help in doing this. Amen.[155]

CULT WATCH

THE OCCULT

Answers to tough questions about spiritism, occult phenomena, & psychic powers

Once again that time of year has come wherein we are inundated with the dross of the Nazarene worshippers. One attitude that is constantly shoved down our throats, in addition to the phony cheer, is that this is a season for forgiveness and mercy. Here stands revealed one of the most insidious elements of the Christian creed. . . . Satanists reject mercy as a vile sham. The end times are here, the final days of the rule of the cross. The world will be swept by a wave of Satanic individuals who will stand forth to claim their birthright as humans, proud of their nature. Let those who are slaves grovel on their knees in the mud before the images of non-existent gods. The times demand the efforts of self-proclaimed Gods, who worship themselves and can produce results. . . . There will be room no longer for the coddling of vipers in our midst. . . . They shall be made to pay! The creed of the Nazarene, and his ilk, shall be trodden under cloven hooves! Which side shall hold your allegiance?

—Satanist Peter H. Gilmore
"Lex Talionis"
The Black Flame,
Christmas issue,
Vol. 1, No.3

32

Introduction to
the Occult

Of the various hazards that people face in a lifetime, from a broken leg to a car accident, some of the most serious dangers arise from enemies that are invisible—bacteria, viruses, etc. The AIDS epidemic has recently given everyone a new appreciation for the power of invisible enemies. We rarely see these invisible invaders; we see only their effects, the ruin they leave in their wake. A virus "tricks" the cell into believing that it is a "good" entity, so the cell lets down its defenses and "accepts" the invader. Only when it is inside is the virus discovered to be a Trojan Horse, an invading parasite which begins the process of destroying its host.

The occult revival in our land is a spiritual AIDS, an AIDS of the soul. In many ways occult activity is similar to an unperceived virus operating within the human organism: It may exist for some period without producing symptoms, or it may kill quickly. Whichever it does, it means certain death for those terminally infected and an uncertain and precarious existence for those who have the virus within them but are currently without symptoms. Apart from treatment, the occult will kill spiritually just as effectively as AIDS will kill physically. The only difference is that there is a cure for occult involvement: repentance and faith in Jesus Christ (see Appendix C).

What is incredible is not that millions of people have been harmed by occult activity but that the cultural myth continues to persist that the occult is either pure quackery, a harmless pastime, or a genuine spiritual quest. This myth is all the more amazing considering that psychics, occultists and former occultists, parapsychologists, psychic counselors, psychiatrists and psychologists, Eastern gurus, and theologians have issued stern warnings concerning the dangers of the occult: Our files contain over 100 pages of citations from such individuals.

Further, many people who do accept that dangers stem from the occult compound the problem by asserting that there is both a "dangerous" and a "safe" approach to the occult. These people feel that with sufficient caution and wisdom the occult may be pursued to great spiritual benefit.

Unfortunately, it appears that in nearly all forms of occult activity there is "something" in operation which binds a person to the occult, even when he or she wishes to be rid of involvement. A person may find his or her environment or circumstances manipulated to prevent his or her abandoning psychic activity; he or she may become sick and suffer from disease, have accidents, become suicidal, or actually be threatened by spiritual powers and entities. Dr. Nandor Fodor, author of the authoritative *Encyclopedia of Psychic Science*, observes that when spiritists and mediums attempt to suppress their activities or powers, the end result is illness and disease: "Curiously enough, mediumship, if suppressed, will manifest in symptoms of disease."[1]

Once the practices are accepted, the disease disappears. (The famous psychic Edgar Cayce is one prominent illustration.[2]) Former medium Raphael Gasson wrote of his own experience:

> Many have suffered greatly because they started investigating into this thing [mediumism] and have eventually been brought to distraction when they have attempted to free themselves from it. Homes have been broken up, suicide and lunacy have afflicted those who were once in it, and have dared to seek deliverance from its power. Those who have found that deliverance can only give thanks to God for His grace and mercy.[3]

Former leading European witch, Doreen Irvine, sold her soul to Satan with her own blood. Although she was eventually delivered, having 47 demons exorcised over many months, she encountered suicidal urges, depression, discouragement, horrible nightmares, and psychic attacks. She acknowledges, "I was tormented day and night, with very little let up."[4]

Before her conversion, she recalled that her "heart was filled with hate for anything Christian," but she eventually became convinced that the only possible way of deliverance was through the power of Christ.[5] "Far from being harmless" she wrote,

> Witchcraft and other forms of the occult are harming, yes, wrecking and ruining lives today, to an alarming degree— driving men and women to suicide, mental hospitals, utter fear, and a living hell. If people saw only half of what I've seen, they would think again before writing it off as a harmless craze.[6]

In this material we will examine the influence, nature, phenomena, and consequences of the modern occult revival.

33

The Occult:
Its Influence,
Phenomena,
and Philosophy

Question 1

Why is the subject of the occult important and how influential is it?

In the last 30 years America has experienced a major revival of the occult. One of the great modern scholars on comparative religion and occultism, the late Mircea Eliade of the University of Chicago, observes in his *Occultism, Witchcraft and Cultural Fashions*:

> As a historian of religions, I cannot fail to be impressed by the amazing popularity of witchcraft in modern Western culture and its subcultures. However... the contemporary interest in witchcraft is only part and parcel of a larger trend, namely, the vogue of the occult and the esoteric....[7]

Eliade is not alone in his assessment. Seminal author and authority on occultism Colin Wilson comments in *The Occult: A History*, "It would probably be safe to say that there are now more witches in England and America than at any time since the Reformation."[8] Nat Freedland writes in *The Occult Explosion*, "No modern, post-industrial society has ever experienced anything like this occult explosion."[9] C. A. Burland, a science and natural history writer with the British Museum for 40 years acknowledges that "at no time in the history of civilization has occultism and its various forms been so widely practiced as today."[10] Noted theologian Dr. Merrill Unger (Ph.D., Johns Hopkins University), the author of four books on the occult, confesses, "The scope and power of modern occultism staggers the imagination."[11]

In his *The Second Coming: Satanism in America*, acclaimed novelist Arthur Lyons discloses, ". . . satanic cults are presently flourishing in possibly every major city in the United States and Europe. . . . The United States probably harbors the fastest growing and most highly-organized body of satanists in the world."[12] Some details of this growing satanic network are revealed in award-winning investigative reporter Maury Terry's book, *The Ultimate Evil*. Terry warns:

> There is compelling evidence of the existence of a nation-wide network of satanic cults, some aligned more closely than others. Some are purveying narcotics; others have branched into child pornography and violent sadomasochistic crime, including murder. I am concerned that the toll of innocent victims will steadily mount unless law enforcement officials recognize the threat and face it.[13]

Unfortunately, Satanism, witchcraft, santeria, voodoo, and other "hard-core" forms of the occult are only the proverbial tip of the iceberg. If we were to consider the mediums, clairvoyants, psychics, channelers, spiritists, diviners, mystics, gurus, shamans, psychical researchers, Yogis, psychic and holistic healers, etc., only then would we have a better grasp of the actual size of the modern revival of the occult. UFO, near-death and past-life experiences; astral travel; astrology; mysticism; energy channeling; Yoga; psychic healing; Ouija boards; Tarot cards; contact with the dead; and a thousand other occultic practices dot the modern American landscape.

Not surprisingly, Gallup, Roper, and Greeley polls have indicated that tens of millions of people are interested in occult subjects or have had occult experiences.[14]

For example, a recent University of Chicago national opinion poll revealed that 67 percent of Americans "now profess a belief in the supernatural," and that 42 percent "believe that they have been in contact with someone who died."[15] Profits from "channeled" (spirit-originated) seminars, tapes, and books alone range from $100 to $400 million a year and, in the minds of some people, channeling may become "bigger than fundamentalism."[16] In his text *Channelling: Investigations on Receiving Information from Paranormal Sources*, New Age educator and psychologist Jon Klimo observes, "Cases of channelling have become pervasive."[17]

The late authority on cults and the occult, Dr. Walter Martin, estimated that over 100 million Americans were actively or peripherally involved in these areas.[18]

In spite of this, most people still do not recognize how drastically the 1960's revival of occultism has now changed American attitudes and culture. This revival undergirded the success of the New Age Movement in the 1970's and 1980's, which today constitutes a multibillion-dollar industry. It is also the supporting pillar for parapsychology, the scientific study of the occult which has had vast influence in modern society. The occult revival has also promoted the revival of occultic, Eastern religions such as Hinduism, Taoism, and Buddhism which now have 10 to 20 million followers. In addition, the occult has supported the burgeoning field of New Age Medicine which has also influenced literally millions of people.[19]

Unfortunately, a good portion of modern occultism in not necessarily evident at first glance. Perhaps most people would find it easy to identify the more blatant forms of the occult. But as it is filtered through the secularism of Western culture, it becomes more difficult to spot. Secularized forms of the occult have had considerable influence through psychology, medicine, education, arts and entertainment, business, and even science and theology.[20]

Occultists themselves are amazed at the modern revival. The well-known novelist and UFO contactee Whitley Strieber (*Cat Magic, The Wolfen*) is also the author of several bestselling books on his UFO experiences (*Communion* and *Transformation*). These texts detail his occult contacts with alleged UFO entities—entities which bear striking resemblance to demons.*

Nevertheless, Strieber has confessed that such UFO and other spiritistic encounters "have taken on an intensity never before experienced by humankind." He concedes that these supernatural entities are *demanding* communion with "the very depths of the soul."[22]

Another leading authority on spiritism, Spiritual Counterfeits Project cofounder Brooks Alexander, agrees. He observes, "Spiritism has moved beyond the weird and the supernatural into the normal and the mundane. Quietly, but convincingly, the entities have been serving notice that they intend to shape our future."[23] (See the unit on Spirit Guides elsewhere in this volume.)

The subject of the occult is therefore important—vitally important—because in one form or another almost everyone in our culture will sooner or later be exposed to the occult. And at that very point of exposure, a person's entire life path can be determined. Why? Because tens of millions of people are now vulnerable. They are searching for answers, some desperately. The occult claims it can provide answers. Occult practices seem to offer not only meaning and purpose in life, but powerful spiritual experiences as well. And such experiences are forceful persuaders. When people have such dynamic encounters with a supernatural reality, it can dramatically change their lives and perspective. Occultism is thus much more than a mere philosophy of life; it can become a commanding presence, having irresistible persuasion.

---

* John Keel, a prominent authority on UFO's, confesses, "The UFO manifestations seem to be, by and large, merely minor variations of the age-old demonological phenomenon," and "the manifestations and occurrences described in [the literature of demonology] are similar, if not entirely identical, to the UFO phenomenon itself. Victims of [demon] possession suffer the very same medical and emotional symptoms as the UFO contactees."[21] See Clifford Wilson, John Weldon, *Close Encounters* (1978) for data.

Everywhere today, people in the occult claim that their methods offer true spirituality, leading to a higher state of existence, and finally to ultimate Reality. But what if this assessment is wrong and the road of the occult really leads elsewhere? If the occult delivers, what exactly does it deliver? It is the purpose of this booklet to answer that question. We begin with a definition of the occult.

Question 2

What is the occult?

The English word "occult" comes from the Latin "occultus," meaning "to cover up, hide, or conceal." Below, we offer several definitions from various authoritative sources:

The *Oxford American Dictionary* defines the occult as:

> 1. secret, hidden except from those with more than ordinary knowledge. 2. involving the supernatural, occult powers. The occult [involves] the world of the supernatural, mystical or magical.[24]

Webster's Third International Dictionary (unabridged) defines the occult in the following manner:

> deliberately kept hidden. . . . of, relating to, or dealing in matters regarded as involving the action or influence of supernatural agencies or some secret knowledge of them.[25]

The *Donning International Encyclopedic Psychic Dictionary* defines the occult as:

> 1. (ancient) that which is hidden behind outer appearances and must be studied to be understood; that which is magical or mystical; only available for the initiates; a system of methods . . . to develop psychic powers; knowledge of the invisible world and its relationship to mankind.[26]

Encyclopedia Britannica defines and discusses occultism as follows:

> A general designation for various theories, practices, and rituals based on esoteric knowledge, especially alleged knowledge about the world of spirits and unknown forces of the universe. Devotees of occultism strive to understand and explore these worlds, often by developing the [alleged] higher powers of the mind. . . . Occultism covers such diverse subjects as Satanism, astrology, Kabbala, Gnosticism, theosophy, divination, witchcraft, and certain forms of magic.[27]

The Occult

Dr. Ron Enroth, professor of sociology at Westmont College at Santa Barbara, California, and an authority on new religions and cults, offers the following definition:

> The term refers to "hidden" or "secret" wisdom; to that which is beyond the range of ordinary human knowledge; to mysterious or concealed phenomena; to inexplicable events. It is frequently used in reference to certain practices (occult "arts") which include divination, fortune telling, spiritism (necromancy), and magic.
>
> Those phenomena collectively known as "the occult" may be said to have the following distinct characteristics: (1) the disclosure and communication of information unavailable to humans through normal means (beyond the five senses); (2) the placing of persons in contact with supernatural powers, paranormal energies or demonic forces; (3) the acquisition and mastery of power in order to manipulate or influence other people into certain actions.[28]

What all these definitions have in common is that they accurately understand the occult as involving 1) things normally invisible or "hidden," and therefore normally unavailable to people and 2) contact with supernatural agencies and powers.

But who or what are the "supernatural agencies and powers" that people involved in the occult contact? Deciding who these supernatural powers or entities are is of major importance. In fact, for those involved in the occult, nothing is more important.

Question 3
Are the supernatural entities and spirits of the occult who they claim to be, or are they something else entirely?

We do not think these spirits and entities are what they claim to be. It is, therefore, one purpose of this discussion to offer evidence for a biblical view of the occult. From this perspective, the occult involves various activities seeking the acquisition of "hidden" things—particularly supernatural power and knowledge—which are forbidden by God in the Bible. Such activities utimately bring one into contact with the spirit world which the Bible identifies as the world of demons under the power of Satan (see Questions 6-11). Thus, the philosophy derived from occult practices characteristically originates in or is compatible with the "doctrines [teachings] of demons" (1 Timothy 4:1).

No one involved in the occult (or considering involvement) can be unconcerned over such a possibility. If the evidence indicates that the biblical view is correct, then those who become involved in the occult may get more than they bargained for. (See Chapter 26, Questions 22-26.)

Question 4

What are some common occult categories and phenomena?

Occult phenomena are too comprehensive to begin to list. Consider Nandor Fodor's *Encyclopedia of Psychic Science*, *The Donning International Encyclopedic Psychic Dictionary*, and Leslie Shepherd's *Encyclopedia of Parapsychology and the Occult*. These three sources alone list some 7000 topics in some way related to the occult.

Nevertheless, in our critique of astrology *(Astrology: Do the Heavens Rule Our Destiny?)* we provided the following illustrations of general occult categories and phenomena.[29]

General Occult Categories

Magic
Sorcery
Satanism
Divination
Necromancy

Witchcraft
Voodoo
Spiritism
Astrology
Shamanism

Occult-Related

Parapsychology
Holistic health practices
Yoga
Visualization

Mysticism
Meditation [Eastern and Western occult traditions]
Hypnotism

Occult Phenomena

Ectoplasmic manifestations
Telepathy
Apportation
Poltergeists
Spirit possession
Levitation
Altered states of consciousness
Precognition
Most near-death experiences
Reincarnation phenomena (for example, hypnotic "past-life" experiences)

Materializations/apparitions
Telekinesis
Clairvoyance/clairaudience

Psychic transference of power
Polyglot mediumship
Spirit guides, fairies, nature spirits, UFO entities, ascended masters
UFO experiences

Occult Practices

Seances
Psychometry/radionics
Psychic diagnosis/healing/ surgery

Magic ritual, spells, curses, charms
Various "automatisms" (writing, typing, dictation, painting, etc.)

The Occult

Astral travel	Water dowsing
Pendulums	Crystal-gazing
Ouija board	Tarot cards
I Ching	Runes

Occult religions*

Rosicrucianism	New Age Movement
Theosophy	Scientology
Association for Research and Enlightenment (Edgar Cayce)	The Church Universal and Triumphant
Astara	Silva Mind Control
Children of God	Eckankar
Mormonism	Anthroposophy

Unfortunately, there are today a large number of occult practices and phenomena which have become redefined as natural human processes or actual divine practices. For example, psychic (supernatural) powers are redefined as "psychological" powers of the mind and psychic healing is reinterpreted as "divine" healing. It is this masking of fundamentally occultic realities as either human or divine which entices many people into entering a domain they would otherwise never think of entering.

Indeed, if people knew the true reality of occult practices—that they bring one into contact with genuinely evil entities who only feign love and concern and whose major purpose is their personal spiritual destruction—only a minute percentage of the most foolhardy would consider involvement. And yet worldwide, the number of people associated with these practices can be conservatively numbered in the hundreds of millions. That so many people accept a basically false view of the occult offers abundant testimony to the deceptive power of the devil and the spiritual underworld.

Question 5

What is the general underlying philosophy of the occult? What is the general underlying philosophy of Christianity? How do they differ?

The basic philosophy and premise of the occult is described by a specific term—"monism." Monism is defined as a "philosophical theory that everything consists of or is reducible to one substance."[30] *The Encyclopedia of Philosophy* observes that monism "is a name for a group of views in metaphysics that stress the oneness or unity of reality in some sense."[31]

There are different forms of monism. The occult may be described as a mystical form of monism which characteristically accepts some form of

---

* Almost all major religions and cults are occultic to one degree or another.

pantheistic belief. Pantheism teaches that everything is God. For example, as one text on magic teaches, "God and the universe . . . have always existed: visible and invisible, both make up the divine being."[32]

The modern influence of monism can be seen in that several major world religions are monistic. Hinduism and Buddhism are examples of world religions that reflect monistic teaching. In monistic Hinduism the one ultimate Reality is defined as "Nirguna Brahman." In monistic Buddhism, the one ultimate Reality is defined as an indescribable state of impersonal existence termed "Nirvana."

Christianity, on the other hand, is not monistic. Christianity teaches that an infinite-personal Triune God, who is Spirit (John 4:4), created the physical world distinct from Himself.* This idea that God made the universe apart from Himself is known as "religious dualism" and it stands in contrast with occultic monistic philosophy. Christianity does not teach that Reality is only one thing, but rather that Reality is composed of two things: Christianity teaches there is *both* an eternal spiritual Reality (a personal God) and a second Reality, the created universe, itself involving a material and spiritual realm of existence.

Occult monism claims, in contrast to Christian teaching, that "God" and the "creation" are ultimately the same thing—they are one in essence. Christianity maintains that because God created the world apart from Himself, God and the creation are *not* the same thing. The basic Christian doctrine which rejects monistic teaching is the biblical doctrine of *creation*.

In essence then, the occult, which is monistic, and Christianity, which is not monistic, are based on entirely different and opposing beliefs. The underlying premise of each system powerfully conditions how their proponents view God, man's relationship to God, the world, and man's place in the world. So let us further compare and contrast Christianity with the occult so the reader may understand how fully opposing these worldviews are.

In Christianity, God is personal. The material world is a real place created by God and distinct from Him. Man is a creation of God, made in His image, having as his ultimate purpose in life a loving, personal, and eternal relationship with his Creator.

But in the world of the occult, all of this is rejected. God is impersonal. The material world is ultimately a secondary or illusory manifestation of God. Inwardly, man is part of God, currently existing in ignorance of his divinity, whose ultimate purpose is a merging of his true nature back into impersonal Reality.

This is why the final goal of occult practice is to experience a condition of alleged spiritual "enlightenment" where one supposedly understands the true nature of Reality ("All is One") and one's proper place in the world (seeking a final reuniting with the One).

---

* For an excellent study, see Francis Schaeffer's, *He Is There and He Is Not Silent*.

The alleged truth of occult monism is "confirmed" through occult practices such as altered states of consciousness, magic ritual, spirit possession, drug use, meditation, or other means whereby monistic consciousness (the feeling that "All is One") is directly "experienced" and interpreted as "evidence" for the truth of one's occult philosophy.

It is the monistic premise of occultism that makes its philosophy so fundamentally anti-Christian. Dr. Gary North observes in his excellent evaluation *Unholy Spirits: Occultism and New Age Humanism*:

> Because God created the universe, there is a permanent, unbridgable gap between the ultimate being of God and the derivative being of creatures. There is a Creator-creature distinction. Though men are made in the image of God (Genesis 1:27), they do not partake of God's being. They are like God, but they are not of the same substance as God. There is no more fundamental doctrine than this one. Significantly, in every form of occultism this principle is denied, sometimes implicitly and usually explicitly. Satan's old temptation to man hinges on his denial and man's denial of the Creator-creature distinction....
>
> In direct contrast to the biblical view of man and God, the occult systems, from the magical sects of the East to the gnostics of the early church period, and from there unto today's preachers of the cosmic evolution and irresistible karma, one theme stands out—*monism*. There is no Creator-creature distinction. We are all gods in the making. Out of One has proceeded the many, and back into One are the many travelling.... It is such a convenient doctrine, for it denies any eternal separation of God and His creation and therefore it denies any eternal separation of saved and lost. It denies any ultimate distinction between good and evil, past and present, structure and change.... [It] leads to rampant immorality, and... to a dismissal of earthly affairs and earthly responsibility. The result... is moral nihilism.[33]

Of course, if one can indeed be a god, then to be as God and exercise one's divinity demands above all else the exercise of power—power over personal limitations, power over others (human and nonhuman), power over the creation, etc. Personal "realization" of one's godhood finds "confirmation" through the development of supernatural power over one's environment. In other words, occult practice develops occult abilities which "confirm" personal divinity outwardly in the acts of supernatural power. As one practicing occultist comments:

> The power that is used in magic is derived from the forces we have been describing and so comes from both within and

outside ourselves. It is formed by linking one aspect of the magician's personality with the corresponding aspect of the cosmic mind. This at once sets up a current of power which the magician can draw upon for his own purposes.[34]

The above brief discussion of the differences between Christian and occult philosophy reveals why occultism in all its forms is so fundamentally hostile to Christian faith.

Below we present a brief contrast between the worldview of the occult and that of Christianity:

Occult/Psychic Worldview

Pantheism-monism. Everything is divine. There is only one divine Reality (spirit).

God is ultimately impersonal.

Man is inwardly divine, one with God in essence.

Evil is an illusion, but ultimately in harmony with God (God is amoral)

Salvation or enlightenment is achieved through self-realization (awareness of personal divinity) by means of psychic practices.

Psychic powers normally result from psychic practices and are often used for personal profit or power.

Eternal cyclic incarnation or absorption into impersonal divinity (personal extinction).

Biblical Worldview

Traditional theism. God is the Creator, distinct from His creation (spirit/matter). (Genesis 1:1).

God is personal and loving (John 3:16).

Man is a creature, created in God's image, but not inwardly deity (Genesis 1:27).

Evil is a concrete fact, which operates in opposition to God's nature (God is holy) (1 Peter 1:14,15,3:12).

Salvation is based on the atonement (Christ's vicarious suffering and death for sin) and received as a free gift (by grace) through faith in God and Christ (John 3:16; 5:24; 6:47; 17:3). *Spiritual gifts* are distinct from and work in contrast to psychic powers. They are given by God to His people for service to others (1 Corinthians 12:4-11; 14:3).

Eternal heaven or hell. Personal immortality (Matthew 25:46).

What difference does all this make?

In occult monism, normal ways of thinking and perceiving are often rejected. Because "All is One," there is no ultimate distinction between good and evil, moral and immoral, right and wrong. True Reality is beyond these "illusory" categories. In other words, rape, theft, murder, etc., cannot finally be considered evil if evil itself has no final Reality. But who can say such thinking has no consequences? Charles Manson himself observed, "If God is One, what is bad?"[35] In the end, nothing evil is really evil.

But in the end, neither is anything ultimately good. Love, empathy, forgiveness, and truth cannot be considered "good" when "good" also has no ultimate Reality. In Question 17, we will supply specific illustrations of how occult monism can affect people's lives and the decisions they make.

Further, there is no such thing as genuine personality, either human or divine, because true Reality is impersonal. In other words, the personal God of Christianity plus all individual human personality is ultimately an illusion.

Finally, there is no final Creator/creature distinction because inwardly man's true nature is intrinsically united to the One impersonal divine Reality. Man is already God; he is simply ignorant of this fact until he becomes "enlightened" through occult practice.

It should be plain that whether we are Christians or whether we are occultists, the difference between these respective philosophies is both profound and important.

Question 6

Do all men have natural psychic ability or are psychic abilities mediated through spiritistic (demonic) power?

A very common occult practice involves the development of psychic abilities. Yet a great deal of confusion exists as to what psychic abilities are. Are they really latent human powers possessed by everyone? Most people who think so refer to the research of J. B. Rhine and modern parapsychology as having "proven" that psychic powers are natural abilities within all people. But this is not so (see Questions 10 and 12).

We believe that psychic powers are mediated through demonic ability. We think this because of the testimony of occultists themselves; those who claim psychic powers freely confess that apart from their spirit guides (demons who imitate helping spirits), they have no supernatural abilities. Shamans, Satanists, witches, mediums, channelers, psychic healers, and spiritists of every stripe freely concede that apart from their spirit helpers they are powerless to do the things that they do.

Michael Harner has been a visiting professor at Columbia and Yale. He teaches anthropology courses on the graduate faculty of the New School for Social Research in New York and is chairman of the Anthropology section of the New York Academy of Sciences. He is also a practicing shaman and author of *The Way of the Shaman*. He observes that the fundamental source of power for all shamans is the spirit world: "Whatever it is called, it is the fundamental source of power for the shaman's functioning. . . . Without a guardian spirit, it is virtually impossible to be a shaman, for the shaman must have this strong, basic power source. . . ."[36]

Concerning Hindu and Buddhist gurus, which incidentally have many characteristics in common with the shaman,[37] they too confess that their power comes from the spirit world. No less an authority than Indries Shah observes, "It is true that the Sadhus [gurus] claim that their power comes exclusively from spirits; that they within themselves possess no special abilities except that of concentration."[38]

Louis Jacolliot, a former Chief Justice of the French East Indies and Tahiti, confesses the same. In *Occult Science in India and Among the Ancients*, he observes that psychic forces are conceded to be "under the direction of the spirits."[39] Thus, the Indian psychics "produce at will the strangest phenomena entirely contrary to what are conventionally called natural laws. With the aid of spirits who are present at all their operations, as claimed by the Brahmans, they have the authority as well as the power, to evoke them."[40]

In his *Adventures into the Psychic*, seasoned psychic researcher Jess Stearn makes this common observation: "Almost without exception, the great mediums . . . felt they were instruments of a higher power which flowed through them. They did not presume to have the power themselves."[41]

In other words, people who have this power characteristically recognize it is not a natural human ability. In *Freed from Witchcraft*, former Satanist and witch Doreen Irvine confesses, "I had known and felt that [occult] power often enough, but I believed it was not a natural, but rather a supernatural, power working through me. I was not born with it. The power was not my own but Satan's."[42] Significantly, even as a Satanist and witch she did not know that she was possessed by numerous demons: "Now, I was no stranger to demons. Had I not often called on them to assist me in rites as a witch and Satanist? [But now] for the first time I knew these demons were *within* me, not outside. It was a startling revelation."[43]

Apparently then, even the most demonized individuals such as Irvine, who as noted earlier had 47 demons cast from her,[44] need not be *consciously* aware that spirits are indwelling them. If this is so, it may be logical to assume that many others who traffic in less virulent forms of the occult may also be possessed by demons and yet not know it.

Further, if such people are cleverly taught that their supernatural powers are "natural and innate," they will wrongly assume that their powers originate within them as some "natural" or evolutionary psychic ability. The fact that demons work through them will not only be hidden from them, but there will be a natural aversion to the very concept of demons because the concept of "natural powers" is infinitely preferable to the idea of collusion with evil, supernatural spirits. This is one premise of much occultism; that nothing is truly supernatural. In the end, everything is a "natural" part of the "creation." As one occult manual observes, "We will adopt the view that there is no such thing as the supernatural: whatever exists must be natural. . . ."[45]

Nevertheless, however occultists may choose to interpret their powers, they cannot escape the fact that it is really spirits that work through them. For example, consider the phenomenon of psychic healing, which many people consider a "natural" and/or "divine" ability. In his *Supersenses*, Charles Panati refers to the research of psychic researcher Lawrence LeShan who has observed Eastern and Western psychic healers firsthand. Panati states, "But if the healers he studied had one thing in common, it was that they all felt that they did not perform the healing themselves; 'a "spirit" did it working through them.' They felt they were merely passive agents. . . . All the healers he studied slipped into altered states of consciousness in order to heal."[46]

One of the most comprehensive collections of information on psychic healing is *Healers and the Healing Process*. This authoritative ten-year investigation observes,

> Any study of healers immediately brings the investigator face to face with the concept that spirit intelligences (variously referred to as guides, controls, or protectors) are working through the minds of healers to supply information of which the healer himself has no conscious knowledge.[47]

This study also noted that "the only large concentrations of healers seemed to be in countries where the belief systems involve what is generally known as spiritualism or spiritism."[48] For example, "in both Brazil and the Philippines the healers have developed almost entirely in the confines of spiritualistic communities."[49]

Similar citations could be multiplied indefinitely for all the different categories of occult practice. Whatever the person with psychic abilities calls them, it is the spirits and not the individual that are the true source of power.

The bottom line is this: Wherever psychic powers are found, the spirit world is also found. Further, apart from these spirit beings, those with psychic abilities claim they are powerless. What this tells us is that the only way psychic powers are generated is through some involvement with the spirit world, and that all men do *not* have the natural capacity for such abilities. If psychic powers were truly a human capacity, anyone could develop them. But again, the only people who develop such abilities are occultists who, through their occult practices, come into contact with the spirit world. As the vast majority of people have never developed these powers, it is not logical to think such powers constitute a "natural" human potential lying dormant within the race.

Consider the comments of Danny Korem, a world-class stage magician who has investigated or exposed a number of leading psychics. Responding to the question, "Do humans actually possess psychic powers?" he replied:

> If you mean by psychic abilities things the mind can do in and of its own ability, I say it's not possible. That's what you find when you investigate case after case after case. Tens of millions of dollars have been spent on research in this area and there has never been a verifiable demonstration of human psychic power.[50]

We see no evidence for natural or latent psychic powers. These powers are "potential" only to those who are tapping the powers given by spirits, whether or not such beings are perceived and whether or not they are conveniently redefined in terms of natural and neutral categories.

Nevertheless, some accept the possibility of a neutral, if quite limited, ESP faculty. They cite illustrations where a mother may sense her child's danger, apparently through ESP. But such a perspective could also assume a normal "link" between one human spirit and another. For example, a mother and child may be connected spiritually/genetically in an unknown manner entirely unrelated to ESP. If the Traducean theory of the transmission of the human spirit is correct, a child may be linked in some unknown fashion to its parents in ways beyond the biological, and this may hold true for all family members; the link decreasing in power as proximity to the original source decreases.

But even if true, this does not necessitate that we accept the view that man has latent supernatural powers. The fact that the body houses a living spirit, and that the mind is part of that spirit, hardly proves the human mind or spirit itself can perform genuine miracles. Further, we are ignorant of the exact "spatial" relationship existing between the material and spiritual worlds. If the spiritual world does interpenetrate the physical at some level, the fact of some unintended or accidental cross-overs might be expected. Thus, it is not surprising that the human spirit/mind may occasionally and innocently interact with or contact the environmental reality of the spiritual world. This could also be perceived as a form of ESP, but it would not be the same as having an inner-nature or "core" structure which is capable of supernatural powers. Further, cases where a mother senses danger to her child or similar incidents could also originate in God or from godly angels, rather than a genetically instituted spiritual linkage.

In conclusion, given the spiritual nature of man and the possibility of a spiritual dimension that interpenetrate the physical realm, it becomes difficult to prove even a small amount of natural or neutral ESP. But even if such exists, it is not the same thing as the psychic powers of occultists.

34

The Bible, Psychic Powers, Demons, and the Occult

Question 7

What does the Bible say about the devil?

The Bible has a great deal to say about Satan or the devil. The devil is seen to be an apostate angel who fell from heaven (Luke 10:18; Jude 6; Revelation 12:9). He is called the "tempter" (1 Thessalonians 3:5), "wicked," and "evil" (Matthew 6:13; 13:19), the "god of this world" (2 Corinthians 4:4), the "prince of this world" (John 12:31; 14:30; 16:11), "dragon," "serpent," (Revelation 12:9; 20:2), and a "liar" and "murderer" (John 8:44).

Further, the Bible asserts that Satan has a kingdom (Matthew 12:26) which is hostile to Christ's kingdom (Matthew 16:18; Luke 11:18), and that he rules a realm of demons or evil spirits (Matthew 9:34). He deceives the whole world (Revelation 12:9; 13:14), works in the children of disobedience (Ephesians 2:2), worked even among the apostles (Matthew 16:23; Luke 22:31; John 13:2), and opposes the people of God (1 Chronicles 21:1; Zechariah 3:2; Acts 5:3; 2 Corinthians 2:11; 1 Thessalonians 2:18). He even tried to gain the worship of God Himself in the person of Christ, an act suggestive of his mental imbalance, if not insanity (Mark 1:13; Matthew 4:1-10).

The Bible further teaches that Satan sows seeds of error and doubt in the church (Matthew 13:39), blinds the minds of unbelievers (Mark 4:15; Acts 26:18; 2 Corinthians 4:4), is capable of possessing men (John 13:27), has the power of death (Hebrews 2:14), and prowls about like a roaring lion seeking those he may devour (1 Peter 5:8). His key abilities are power, deception, and cunning. He has great power (2 Thessalonians 2:9) and his subtlety (Genesis 3:1) is seen in his treacherous snares (2 Timothy 2:26), wiles (Ephesians 6:11), devices (2 Corinthians 2:11), and transforming, impersonating abilities (2 Corinthians 11:14).

Christ appeared to destroy the work of the devil (1 John 3:8) who will soon be defeated (Romans 16:20) to spend eternity in hell along with those who follow him and reject Christ (Matthew 25:41; Revelation 20:10).

As we see, the biblical testimony concerning the existence of Satan is clear. Concerning the occultic idolatry of Israel, Psalm 106:35-40 observes:

> But they mingled with the nations, and learned their practices, and served their idols, which became a snare to them. They even sacrificed their sons and their daughters to the demons, and shed innocent blood, the blood of their sons and their daughters, whom they sacrificed to the idols of Canaan; and the land was polluted with the blood. Thus they became unclean in their practices, and played the harlot in their deeds. Therefore the anger of the Lord was kindled against His people, and He abhorred His inheritance.

As the above verse hints—and note the reality of the demonic behind idolatry—one reason for the danger of the occult is that it constitutes trafficking with the spiritual enemies of God (Deuteronomy 32:16,17). Scripture does acknowledge there is genuine power in the occult (Isaiah 47:9), but it is to be avoided because it is *demonic* power (Matthew 24:24; Acts 8:7; 13:6-11; 16:16-19; 19:18-20; 2 Corinthians 4:4; Ephesians 6:7-11,22; 2 Timothy 3:8). As Dr. Robert A. Morey observes,

> Data from Scripture, history and personal experience demonstrate that there is a Satan. He is a finite spirit being—i.e., a creature of pure energy not hindered by a physical body. Around him are gathered millions of other "energy beings" who can kill, mutilate or possess the bodies and minds of human beings. This vast horde of extradimensional energy-beings constitute the forces behind occult phenomena.[51]

In many cases, Scripture explicitly cites Satan or his demons as the reality behind occult involvement, idolatry, and false religion (Deuteronomy 32:16,17; Psalm 106:35-40; Acts 16:16-19; 1 Corinthians 10:19-21; 2 Thessalonians 2:9,10; 1 Timothy 4:1).

The reason is simple. Satan has as his purpose the denigration of God though the moral defilement and spiritual destruction of man, God's creation. Satan and his demons have a hatred for God and for God's unique creation, man (Luke 8:12; 13:16; Acts 26:18; Colossians 1:13). No one who has read the Gospels can fail to notice the warfare that exists between Christ and man on the one side and Satan and the powers of darkness on the other (Matthew 4:1; 12:24-28; Mark 5:1-15; Luke 7:21). The demons' animosity toward God and man never ceases, nor can it, for they are never to be redeemed. Hence, both God and man constitute the objects of their malevolence (Matthew 8:29; Jude 6; Revelation 20:10). For example, on endless occasions demons have attempted to murder those they have indwelt (cf. Matthew 17:15-18).

The only thing a man will ever receive from a demon is deception about what is important spiritually. Although they may feign almost any benevolent guise in order to accomplish their purposes, in their real nature demons have no sense of fairness or compassion and certainly no genuine love. They are selfish, evil, and in fact, sociopathic. For example, in the New Testament one demon literally begged Jesus, "Do not torment me," but it and its hosts acted oblivious to the fact that they had unendingly tormented the man that they were possessing (Luke 8:26-30; cf. 9:37-42).

Question 8

Is it wise to disbelieve in a personal devil?

In spite of this abundance of biblical testimony for the existence of a personal devil, many people continue to disbelieve in his existence. But if the devil really does exist, then denying his reality serves his purposes by making his activities invisible. If there is no devil, then everything the devil does is explained in other ways and the real nature and consequences of his activity remain hidden from us.

One of the greatest theologians of this century, Dr. J. I. Packer, asks the following question and supplies the answer:

> Was it rational and enlightened, as liberal theologians thought, to give up belief in the devil? Not particularly. The natural response to denials of Satan's existence is to ask, Who then runs his business?—for temptations which look and feel like expressions of cunning, destructive malice remain facts of daily life. So does hell in the sense defined by the novelist John Updike—"a profound and desolating absence" (of God, and good, and community and communication); and "the realization that life is flawed" (Updike goes on) "admits the possibility of a Fall, of a cause behind the Fall, of Satan. Belief in Satan is not illogical, for it fits the facts. Inept to the point of idiocy, however, is disbelief in Satan, in a world like ours; which makes Satan's success in producing such disbelief all the more impressive, as well as all the sadder....
>
> Satan is a person whom churches and Christians ignore at their peril.[52]

And indeed, millions of people in our culture believe either that Satan does not exist or that psychic powers and phenomena are in fact divine. Significantly, the spirits' own teachings also emphasize there is no devil: Virtually every revelation from the spirit world denies the reality of the biblical Satan and demons. They may accept evil *human* spirits in a post-mortem state who are supposedly "earthbound" and unhappy about it, but they never admit to the reality of themselves as the biblical fallen angels with Satan as their leader. (See Part 5, Question 14.)

Denis De Rougemont observes in *The Devil's Share: An Essay on the Diabolic in Modern Society*:

> What appears to be incredible is not the Devil, not the Angels, but rather the candor and the credulity of the skeptic, and the unpardonable sophism of which they show themselves to be the victims: the Devil is a gent with red horns and a long tail; now I can't believe in a gent with red horns and a long tail; therefore, I don't believe in the Devil. And so the devil has them precisely where he wants them. Those who stick to old wives' tales are those who refuse to believe in the Devil because of the image they form of him, which is drawn from old wives' tales.[53]

The devil is real, more real than most people will ever suspect. Again, the Bible warns that the devil is the enemy of all men, not just some men. He seeks to deceive unbelievers about the truth of salvation in Christ alone, and in various ways he seeks to deceive and neutralize the believer in Christ. His influence is evident both within and without the church.

All of this is why the Bible teaches that spiritual warfare is a reality and that supernatural manifestations are not to be accepted uncritically, but to be tested by the Word of God (Deuteronomy 13:1-5; 18:20-22; Matthew 24:24; Acts 17:10-12; 2 Corinthians 2:11; Ephesians 4:27; 6:10-18; 1 Peter 5:8; 1 John 4:1; Revelation 2:2).

Question 9

Are demons polymorphs (able to assume different forms), and what are poltergeists? What are the implications of the imitating capacities of demons?

As we have seen, the Scripture speaks of the reality of a personal devil and myriads of demons who have "great power" and who should be regarded as cunning enemies of all men (Isaiah 47:9; Matthew 6:13; 9:34; Luke 8:12; 13:16; John 8:44; 13:27; Acts 16:18; 2 Corinthians 2:11; 4:4; 11:3; Colossians 1:13; 2 Thessalonians 2:9; 2 Timothy 2:26).

One of the devil's key tactics is to masquerade as "an angel of light" or a servant of righteousness. Scripture states clearly that "Satan disguises himself as an angel of light" (2 Corinthians 11:14); that is, that he and his demons can imitate a good spirit or entity merely to suit their own evil purposes. Is it then logical or wise for those who contact the spirits to uncritically accept the spirits' claims to be divine entities, or to believe them when they claim that their true motives are to help humanity spiritually?

How can anyone logically do this when it is a fact that, throughout the history of the occult, men have recognized the endless morphology and mimicking capacity of the spirits? Occultists have long confessed the spirits can assume any shape, size, or appearance, including "gods," mythological creatures, animals, half-god/half-animal entities and half-man/half-animal beings. Demons can appear in forms from the strikingly beautiful to the hideously ugly. They can appear as men or women, fairies or elves, aliens or extraterrestrials, the dead or the living. Thus, according to Satprem, a leading disciple of the prominent occultist Sri Aurobindo, the spirits "can take all the forms they wish...."[54]

Poltergeists provide one illustration of the subtlety of demonic strategies. For demonologists of the sixteenth century, the phenomenon of the poltergeist was clearly diabolic. However, for more enlightented modern folk, poltergeists are harmless "ghosts" (alleged spirits of the human dead) that haunt houses. But in fact poltergeists are not the roaming spirits of the human dead. Rather, they are demons who imitate the dead for two distinct purposes: 1) denial of the biblical teaching on judgment and 2) the promotion of the occult. If the human dead are free to roam, as poltergeist incidents would seem to demonstrate, then the Bible is wrong when it claims that the spirits of dead men have been judged and confined and cannot return and contact the living (Hebrews 9:27; Luke 16:19-31; 2 Peter 2:9).

Further, those who are brought in to investigate poltergeist disturbances are typically occultists and supporters of the occult—mediums, spiritists, psychical researchers, parapsychologists, etc. Because such persons are usually able to "resolve" the disturbance (the spirits gladly cooperating behind the scenes), the entire episode grants the occultist spiritual authority and credibility. But as former mediums have testified, this is merely a ruse of the spirits to fool men into adopting unbiblical teachings—erroneous spiritual teachings that have harmful consequences. The story of former mediums Raphael Gasson in *The Challenging Counterfeit* (1969) and Victor Ernest in *I Talked with Spirits* (1971) are illustrative.

In addition, poltergeist phenomena often become the means of a person's conversion to the occult. The supernatural encounters are so startling and intriguing that witnesses and participants may become converted to a belief in the supernatural and may end up becoming involved in psychic investigation such as using Ouija boards or attending seances.

Also, poltergeists are clearly *not* "harmless ghosts." Besides the typical poltergeist activities such as throwing rocks, overturning furniture, wrecking kitchens, setting clothes on fire, soaking rooms with water, rearranging personal belongings, transporting items and babies, "there is also evidence that they do far worse things, seriously wounding and even killing people."[55]

Finally, of thousands of incidents recorded or investigated by Dr. Kurt Koch, a leading authority on the occult, in every case "occult practices lay at the root of the [poltergeist] phenomena."[56]

Given this ability of the spirits to assume virtually any shape and to take virtually any disguise, from angels to the human dead, how can any occultist or spiritist be certain that the spirits they contact are really who they claim to be? How can they be certain that the appearances of their "dead loved ones" in seances are not simply the clever tricks of demons to foster emotional trust and dependence?

The harrowing experiences of seasoned occultists like Robert Monroe are an illustration of the problems encountered in identifying the true nature of these entities. In one of his many out-of-the-body episodes, Monroe was viciously attacked by two evil spirits. At one point in the fray, he panicked and desperately attempted to remove himself from their torment. As he looked at them, they instantaneously turned into the images of his two daughters, attempting to throw him off balance emotionally in his fight against them. "The moment I realized the trick, the two no longer appeared to be my daughters. . . . However, I got the impression that they were both amused, as if there was nothing I could do to harm them. By this time, I was sobbing for help!"[57]

With abilities like this, where does one find a scorecard? Even the famous spiritist Emanuel Swedenborg had to confess a serious problem at this point. Though Swedenborg freely contacted the spirits, he cautioned others about the dangers of this. The spirits were, he warned, generally untrustworthy and only those who had, allegedly, received divine sanction (like himself) could "safely" communicate with them. Thus he warned:

> When spirits begin to speak with a man, he ought to beware that he believes nothing whatever from them; for they say almost anything. Things are fabricated by them, and they lie. . . . they would tell so many lies and indeed with solemn affirmation that a man would be astonished. . . . If a man then listens and believes they press on, and deceive, and seduce in divers [many] ways. . . . Let men beware therefore. . . .[58]

Even more disconcerting, according to Swedenborg, are demonic spirits that are gifted actors, who can impersonate anyone or anything, living or dead. They can convince their unsuspecting contacts that their communications come directly from deceased friends and relatives or from famous persons of the past.

In other words, no less an authority than Swedenborg himself confessed that the spirits were 1) untrustworthy liars and 2) deliberate deceivers and impersonators.

Swedenborg's cautions have rarely been heeded, of course, as virtually all magicians, spiritists, mediums, and occultists claim "divine sanction" and decide to trust the spirits regardless. But remember, the above statement did not come from a Christian believer but from one of the foremost occultists of this millennium. Further, his concerns *are* echoed by former modern mediums and spiritists who have found their once-friendly spirit guides, in the end, to be demonic spirits. The testimonies of Raphael Gasson, Victor Ernest, Johanna Michaelsen, and Ben Alexander are illustrative.[59]

Spirits who communicate with their human hosts may at first bring incredibly loving, blissful, and wonderful experiences to those they contact. They can literally fill a person's being with overwhelming sensations of peace and love. They can also be protective—as long as they are obeyed. And when behind the scenes they cause their hosts suffering, they justify it as necessary for their hosts' supposed spiritual purging and growth.

Invariably, however, in contrast to the love of God, the spirits' love is erratic and conditional—it is administered in strategically reinforcing doses as long as the host obeys. But let a person resolutely seek to end the relationship and he or she will soon discover how quickly a loving and benevolent spirit guide reveals its true nature as a malevolent demon.

From a biblical and historical perspective then, even though these spirits may appear good, kind, and concerned about us, all the available evidence points to their nature as being evil.

The paradox is this: The evidence of all forms of spiritism throughout history *proves* that the spirits cannot be trusted, yet millions of people *are* trusting them if for no other reason than the fact that they *are* spirits. And spirits, whatever their nature, are utterly fascinating to people who once believed that the physical universe was all that existed. Millions are turning to the spirits because they *seem* so "wise," "kind," and "loving"; the very thought of spiritual warfare, the very concept of evil imitating good, is fundamentally alien to the consciousness of millions of modern Americans. And for the spirits, this has resulted in a circus-like atmosphere in which the country has become a playground for demonism.

What is the evidence that all these "nice," "loving," "wise," and "witty" spirits that millions of people are trusting are really demons?

It can be proved that these entities with their endless wardrobes, who have an answer for every failure, *fit the category* of the demonic. It is their own teachings and actions which give them away. Oftentimes their actions are subtle, but nevertheless these entities can be proven to:

1. reject or hate God and Christ
2. pervert and distort biblical truths
3. purposefully deceive, even with sadistic pleasure
4. endorse occultism and perverted, evil forms of religion
5. promote sin and immorality
6. bring both evil and judgment upon their contacts
7. reject *only* the biblical faith.

In our files, we have hundreds of pages of documentation for these assertions. For example, the 70-odd books channeled by the spirit guides of Jane Roberts' "Seth," Ruth Montgomery's "Lilly," Robert Leichtman's multiple guides, Jack Pursel's "Lazaris," and Penny Torres' "Mafu" can be cited as illustrations.

The spirits accomplish all of the actions listed above under the pretense of loving both God and man, of achieving man's spiritual growth, of advancing human or cosmic brotherhood—and by means of endless other alleged benevolences.

267

If the above can be demonstrated, and it is our claim that it is demonstrated throughout the history of the occult, then what conclusion can we arrive at other than that these creatures are deceiving spirits—what the Bible identifies as demons? If all this is not what we should expect from demons, then what should we expect?

Is it not the nature of the intelligent yet evil or criminal personality to mask its true intentions, to deceive by imitating good, and even to appeal to the finer (or baser) instincts of men? If deception exists throughout the material world, on what basis can we assume it is entirely absent in the spiritual world?*

Think of the many criminal or evil personalities throughout human history. Was Hitler initially discovered to be evil, or was this realized too late? Was this mad man not capable of kindness, even love? Was he not a good father? Was he not an able politician? Was not his talk of peace among men praised by all, at least initially? But was not all of this merely a ruse to further the evil he had always intended?

Did not Jim Jones imitate a man of God, preach from a Bible, and speak and do many good things? Even to this day, does not Charles Manson continue to speak of love and compassion for all living things? What finally gave away all these human deceivers was their actions. Their words meant nothing once their actions were seen and the horrors understood.

It is the same way with the spirits—their *actions* always give them away. Do we really think that the devil himself, when necessary, will not speak of "loving God" and pronounce the sincerest of divine blessings upon his unsuspecting human contacts and agents? Do we really think that he and his minions will not do whatever is necessary to deceive their contacts and secure their intended goals? Yet beneath the surface lurks a "massive baleful intelligence that is ageless, that has witnessed cosmic creation, that is extremely powerful and extremely evil."[60]

Question 10

What biblical evidence exists that psychic powers are produced by demons and are not natural human capacities?

It is our conviction that not only the history of parapsychology and the occult (see Question 6), but biblical teaching as well (see Question 11), indicates that human nature is devoid of the supernatural capacities that many psychics and occultists claim. Nowhere in the Bible is man presented as having supernatural powers that originate from his own nature, and so any truly supernatural miracles performed by men or women must originate either from a divine or a demonic source—either from God and the good angels or Satan and the fallen angels (demons).

---

* For a fascinating study, see M. Scott Peck's *People of the Lie*.

268

This is why when we examine the Bible, we discover that the miracles done by believers are done entirely through the power of God or holy angels.*

Which biblical prophet was able to do miracles apart from God's power? Who were the disciples before Jesus gave them authority? Did any of them perform miracles? Even the greatest, most godly man alive, apart from Jesus, never did a single miracle (John the Baptist; Matthew 11:11; John 10:41). Likewise, the most dramatic miracle performer apart from Jesus was Moses. But Moses confessed that his power to perform miracles was not his own, but God's alone (Exodus 3:11,20; 4:1-17). Jesus Himself taught, "Apart from me you can do nothing" (John 15:5 NIV).

Further, note the thrust of the following Scriptures. Collectively, they imply that there is no latent psychic ability for men and women to develop.

In Acts 16:16-19 we find the story of the slave girl who had "a spirit of divination." Significantly, when the apostle Paul cast the spirit out of the girl, she lost her psychic powers. "And it [the spirit] came out at that very moment. But when her masters saw that their hope of profit was gone, they seized Paul and Silas and dragged them into the market place before the authorities." Now if this girl's powers were innate and natural, why did she lose them the very moment that the spirit was cast out of her? It would seem evident that the psychic powers came from the spirit, not the girl. For those who hold to biblical authority this single episode rejects the mushrooming claims in our day to allegedly natural, neutral energies or powers that can be developed by anyone.

Moses, the greatest prophet in the Old Testament, had no power except from God. As noted, Moses openly confessed the miracles he performed were not from his own hand. God Himself spoke specifically to Moses: "So I will stretch out My hand, and strike Egypt with all My miracles which I shall do in the midst of it" (Exodus 3:20; cf. Deuteronomy 34:11,12). "See that you perform before Pharaoh all the wonders *which I have put in your power*" (Exodus 4:21).

What was true for Moses was consistently true for every other Old Testament biblical prophet who performed miracles: Elijah, Elisha, Daniel, etc. (cf. Micah 3:8).

In the New Testament we find the same situation—apart from God the apostles had no power of their own. The apostles were "clothed with power *from on high*" by God the Holy Spirit (Luke 24:49; Act 2:4,43). For example, in the healing of the lame beggar in Acts 3:12, "When Peter saw this [the people's amazement over the miraculous healing], he replied to the people, 'Men of Israel, why do you marvel at this, or why do you gaze at us, *as if by our own power* or piety we had made him walk?'" (emphasis added).

---

* Even in the category of spiritual gifts, the nature of a gift implies a person does not possess it prior to its being given.

The apostle Paul and Barnabas reflected the same attitude. In Acts 14:11-15 we find the attempted worship of Barnabas and Paul by the crowd that had witnessed their miracles: "And when the multitudes saw what Paul had done... [they said] 'The gods have become like men and have come down to us....' [but Paul said] 'Men why are you doing these things? We are also men of the *same nature* as you....'" In Acts 10:26 Cornelius attempted to worship Peter after seeing his miracles, but Peter responded, "Stand up; I too am *just a man*." In Acts 4:29,30, Peter prayed, "Now Lord... stretch out *your hand* to heal and perform miraculous signs and wonders..." In Acts 14:3, "Therefore they spent a long time there speaking boldly with reliance upon the Lord, who was bearing witness to the word of His grace, *granting* that signs and wonders be done by their hands." In Acts 9:34, "And Peter said to him, 'Aeneas, *Jesus Christ* heals you....'" In Acts 19:11, "And *God* was performing extraordinary miracles by the hands of Paul...." In Romans 15:19, "In the power of signs and wonders, in the power *of the Spirit*...I have fully preached the gospel of Christ." Jesus Himself said in Luke 10:19, "Behold, *I* have given you authority... over all the power of the enemy...." Further, in James 5:17: "Elijah was a man with *a nature like ours*," but when he *"prayed earnestly"* a miracle *from God* resulted. (Emphasis added in the above verses.)

Similar verses declaring that divine miracles come from God and not from man are found in Genesis 41:16; Daniel 1:17,20; 2:27-30; Mark 6:7; Acts 15:12; 16:16; 19:11; Romans 15:19; and 1 Corinthians 12:9,10,28,30.

But if the Bible is clear that men have no supernatural powers, it is just as clear that the devil does have them and that he can perform true miracles (2 Thessalonians 2:9).

The evidence, then, would seem clear. Occultists themselves frequently admit they have no psychic abilities apart from their spirit guides. The Bible also testifies that men are without latent supernatural power and that miracles come from one of two sources: God or Satan. Finally, over a century of intensive parapsychological study has failed to produce any genuine evidence of latent psychic ability.

All of this seems to indicate that man is not the psychic and supernatural creature that many in the New Age and the modern revival of the occult claim he is.

Question 11

Are the biblical miracles in the same category as psychic powers and how do the gifts of the Spirit differ from psychic abilities? (See also the next chapter.)

Biblically, true miracles have certain characteristics. They are performed through the power of God to glorify Him, edify the church, and validate the gospel (Acts 14:3; Romans 15:19; 1 Corinthians 12:7, 14:12; Hebrews 2:4).

But there are also miracles performed through the powers of evil, sometimes by impostors of Christ, and wrought in support of false religion (Exodus 7:10-12,22; 8:7; Deuteronomy 13:1,2; Matthew 7:22; Acts

8:9-11; 2 Thessalonians 2:9; Revelation 16:14; 19:20). These miracles are not to be regarded (Deuteronomy 13:1-5), and they deceive the ungodly (2 Thessalonians 2:8-11; Revelation 13:14; 19:20).

In addition, biblically, the gifts of the Holy Spirit are clearly stated to be given by God to His church for God's purposes; by contrast psychic powers are received spiritistically and function in accordance with the devil's goals, such as the promotion of occult philosophy and practice. Even in the closest parallels between biblical miracles and demonic counterfeits, such as Paul's alleged "psychometry" (Acts 19:11,12) and Moses' "transmogrification" of sticks into serpents, the source of the miracle is nevertheless plain. In both Paul's and Moses' cases, the miracles validated the true God and His message, whereas psychic powers never validate God's message, but only an occult philosophy and practice (cf. Question 13).

35

Parapsychology and the Occult*

Question 12

What is parapsychology? Are its claims legitimate? Is it inextricably bound to mediumism and spiritism?

Parapsychology, or psychical research, is the "scientific" study of what is called "psi," a term that refers to psychic events and abilities and/or the energy through which they are accomplished. In modern parapsychology, psi is often viewed as either a "new discovery" or as evidence of man's sudden "evolving" to a supposedly higher level—an evolutionary "mutation in consciousness"—allegedly demonstrated through man's ability to perform psychically. Louisa Rhine (wife of the well-known "father" of modern parapsychology, J. B. Rhine) reflects the scientific, "new discovery" approach:

> One of the most significant advances of science is the discovery that psychic or psi ability is real.[61]

David Hammond, author and copublisher of *Psychic Magazine* (now *New Realities*), reflects the evolutionary view:

> What seems clear is that a giant leap forward in human evolution is being taken now. Evolution of the mind, along with the emergence of a psychic sense, has begun.[62]

---

* Some of the following material was adapted from coauthor Weldon's *Psychic Forces* (Global, 1987).

The Occult

Parapsychology holds to a basic premise concerning psychic abilities. It assumes that the psychic powers it studies reflect genuinely human potential—latent powers of the mind that anyone can unfold and learn to develop. The premise it holds to is that psychic abilities are solely *human* powers. Although undeveloped in most people, they are nevertheless natural and innate to all men and women. A standard resource, the *Handbook of Parapsychology* reflects such a view, referring to psychic powers as "potentialities of the race," "latent human possibility," and "slumbering abilities within the self."[63]

Many proponents view psychical research as a new and exciting frontier of human knowledge. However, it is not new, nor is it ultimately involved in advancing the cause of human knowledge. Even after 100 years of research, the "science" of parapsychology has yet to prove its basic premise—that psychic powers represent latent human abilities rather than spiritistic powers.

Nevertheless, the serious scientific research into parapsychology consistently attempts to draw a line between "the occult" on the one hand and "parapsychology" on the other. It apparently does so to convince us that parapsychology is a truly "scientific" field of study and is not involved with occultism. Below we present a different point of view:

The Claim of Parapsychology

1. Parapsychology involves a field of scientific study that is uninvolved in the occult.

2. Psi or psychic abilities are innate and natural human capacities that, given the proper training program, can be developed by anyone through proper instruction.

The Data

1. Parapsychology may use scientific methods, but it is not a science per se, nor is it uninvolved with the occult. It is an attempt at the classification and quantification of occult powers and abilities that have existed throughout history. This is why experimental parapsychology has largely failed to make psi a scientific realm of study: Occultic powers and abilities will always remain beyond the realm of true scientific investigation.

2. Psi abilities are not natural, human powers. The evidence reveals they are initiated by and related to the spirit world. Although we do not know exactly how spirits

operate in relation to psychic abilities, they are known to occur through one of three contexts: 1) hereditary predisposition, 2) an occultic environment and training program, or 3) transference from one occultist to another, usually during ritual initiation or at death.

3. Although the study of parapsychology can be dangerous, if we use caution, wisdom, and discernment, we can study this area effectively and without harm. (This is the view generally presented by parapsychologists in books such as Martin Ebon's *The Satan Trap: Dangers of the Occult.*)[64]

3. The study of parapsychology, in general, is consequential and to be avoided. Solely human discernment in this area is inadequate to deal with the spiritual complexities involved.

4. Parapsychology research—studying the psychic abilities of mediums, other spiritists, psychics, gurus, etc.—can produce a wide variety of benefits to man.

4. No benefits will come from parapsychological research. Rather, harm will come to those who personally involve themselves. Further, by helping to move society more and more into the occult, culture itself will progressively deteriorate with serious consequences in every area, including the spiritual, moral, and economic.[65]

5. The Bible contains hundreds of parapsychological events which can be cited to support the study of parapsychology. Further, the biblical record clearly indicates that the prophets, apostles, and Jesus Himself utilized psychic abilities and that all men have this power. (Christian parapsychologists especially promote this view.)

5. The Bible contains hundreds of supernatural events, but these supernatural events originate from one of two sources—God or Satan. Because psychic abilities represent occult rather than divine powers, the Bible opposes rather than supports the study and phenomena of parapsychology. Further, the

biblical record indicates human nature does not have supernatural capacities, and so all men do not have natural psychic power. The miracles of the prophets, apostles, and Jesus were accomplished by means of divine power working through them, not by their innate psychic ability (see Questions 10, 11).

6. From the viewpoint of Christian parapsychology, the church and all Christians should promote the study of parapsychology. The gifts of the Holy Spirit are none other than psychic abilities.

6. Christians are commanded to leave the occult alone entirely. The gifts of the Holy Spirit stand in opposition to psychic abilities. They arise from a different source and have a different nature and outcome (see Questions 11 and 13).

7. Parapsychology will advance the cause of true science.

7. Parapsychology is opposed to true science; where the study of the occult is interwoven with science, science becomes contaminated and distorted.

8. "Neutral," "unbiased," and "pure" scientific experimentation and research into parapsychology is of a different nature and higher quality than lay research in this area. Given such conditions, we can safely study parapsychology.

8. Scientific "neutral" experimenters are subject to the same hazards as others delving into this area and are not exempt from the laws of God which presuppose judgment upon those occultly involved.

9. Parapsychology largely involves the study of a neutral, natural, psychic energy, "psi."

9. Parapsychological events may at times utilize a natural energy (human or environmental, as possibly in the production of ectoplasmic phenomena or as in electromagnetism), but it is regulated and manipulated

275

by spirits. True psychic
powers are neither natural
nor neutral; they are un-
natural and used for pur-
poses contrary to God's will.

The claims made by parapsychologists that they are not occultly involved are basically false. Although the methods and sometimes approach
of study are different, an examination of the literature in the field, including the publications and research reports of the scientific psi laboratories,
clearly shows that parapsychologists study occult phenomena. Indeed, for
130 years, mediumism has been the mainstay of parapsychology, even
within periods of lessened interest in that particular subject.[66]

Parapsychology was initially founded on the study of spiritistic mediums and this dependence upon those with occult powers remains today.
Parapsychologists are forced to study those persons having occult powers
because normal people do not possess such abilities and therefore provide
nothing to study.

That parapsychology is undergirded by mediumism, spiritism, and
related practices is confessed by standard texts such as the *Handbook of
Parapsychology*, by leading parapsychologists such as Gardner Murphy,
and even by the father of parapsychology, J. B. Rhine himself.[67]

All the major early societies of psychical research were largely engaged
in mediumistic/spiritistic investigation or even composed of professed
mediums.[68] In 1869 the first serious investigation of spiritism was undertaken by the London Dialectical Society, which appointed six subcommit-
tees to investigate mediumship. In the 1870's the Phantasmological
Society at Oxford and the Ghost Society at Cambridge also studied mediumism. In 1874 the first public meeting of the British National Association
of Spiritualists commenced with most of the prominent spiritists of that
time as members. In 1882, with two-thirds of its membership comprised of
professed mediums, it became what is known today as the Society for
Psychical Research.

In essence, as psychical researcher D. Scott Rogo confesses, "The major
precipitating factor in the development of psychical research was the
Spiritualist movement. . . ."[69]

This is why no better definition has ever been proposed of parapsychology, or psychical research, than that put forth by one of the leading
psychical authorities of this century, Dr. Nandor Fodor, in his *Encyclopedia
of Psychic Science*. He defines psychical research as "a scientific inquiry into
the facts and causes of mediumistic phenomena."[70]

In conclusion, from its beginning over a century ago until the present,
the foundation and sustenance of parapsychological research has been
based upon the study of those with spiritistic powers. We emphasize again
that parapsychologists do not study normal people because normal people
are not psychic and there is, therefore, nothing to study. Parapsychologists
study only those who have occult powers—and such occult powers are
invariably associated with the spirit world.

Question 13

What is "Christian" parapsychology and is it a logically and biblically justified discipline?

So-called "Christian" parapsychology is the study of occult phenomena under allegedly Christian auspices and terminology. A partial list of organizations engaged in supporting Christian parapsychology includes: The Foundation for Christian Psychical Research of Ridgefield, Connecticut, publishers of *Soul Searcher* (the foundation holds to the Apostles' and Nicene Creeds); The Church's Fellowship for Psychical and Spiritual Studies in London, publishers of *The Christian Parapsychologist*; The Academy of Religion and Psychical Research, Bloomfield, Connecticut, publishers of *The Journal of the Academy of Religion and Psychical Research*; Spiritual Frontiers Fellowship of Independence, Missouri, publishers of *Spiritual Frontiers*; the Christian Institute of Parapsychology in Atlanta, Georgia, and several others.

In addition, numerous books by professing Christians have been published adopting a highly positive view of parapsychology, including E. Garth Moore's *Try the Spirits: Christianity and Psychical Research*, Charles E. Cluff's *Parapsychology and the Christian Faith*, H. Richard Neff's *Psychic Phenomena and Religion*, Morton T. Kelsey's *The Christian and the Supernatural*, and John J. Heaney's *The Sacred and the Psychic: Parapsychology and Christian Theology*.[71] Even though all these books actively support the occult in various ways, surprisingly, they are carried by many Christian bookstores.

Christian parapsychologists offer various arguments in defense of their practices. Below we present several examples.

The Reverend William V. Rauscher claims:

> A Christian who looks at parapsychology must have a very special fondness for its researches because the very things of which the Judeo-Christian tradition speaks involve psychical and parapsychological study.... Our theological seminaries face the very obvious and relevant task of including parapsychology in their curriculae.... We are not dealing with demons and witches, but with science, and with the deeper needs of the human soul, of which we still know too little.[72]

H. Richard Neff, pastor of a Presbyterian church in Maryland, argues:

> I cannot draw the line that consigns everything that people associate with the name of the Holy Spirit to the Kingdom of God, and everything associated with mediums to the realm of the devil. One must look at the results and ask if they are good or evil.[73]

J. C. Crosson claims, "If Christians warn against psi [psychic phenomena] as 'a thing of the devil,' better informed individuals may eventually question the responsibility of Christianity."[74]

The United Presbyterian Church's "Report on Occult and Psychic Activities," prepared by the Advisory Council on Discipleship and Worship, concluded that parapsychology was not occultic or demonic and that it could accept "an intelligent and concerned study of psychic phenomena as it relates to the well-being of the total person."[75]

But the arguments of the Christian parapsychologists are flawed in at least four ways. First, Christian parapsychologists ignore what God clearly says in the Bible. God condemns all involvement with occult practices because this constitutes participation with demonic powers. God never says these powers may be studied scientifically or that such practices are godly. God never implies it is permissible to study those with such powers, to encourage them to perform psychically, or to attempt to lend scientific credence to such practices. As we have seen, parapsychology basically involves the study of occultists—mediums, spiritists, psychics, etc. God clearly says these people and their practices are to be avoided (Deuteronomy 18:9-12) rather than sought out, investigated, and held up as alleged examples of human potential. Despite Rauscher's assertion, parapsychology *does* deal with, among other things, "demons and witches."

Second, Christian parapsychologists cannot biblically, logically, or historically justify their division of mediumism into supposedly "acceptable" and "unacceptable" categories. Christian parapsychologists somehow think that there are allegedly legitimate "spiritual" or "Christian" forms of mediumism. They contrast these with allegedly "unacceptable" forms—fraudulent, "carnal," or "unchristian" practices of mediumism. But which Christian parapsychologist has ever biblically demonstrated there exists such a category as "godly" or "Christian" mediumism?

When Christian parapsychology supports what it considers the "godly" practice of mediumism,[76] it ignores the fact that all mediumism is condemned by God Himself in Deuteronomy 18:9-11 and elsewhere. We agree with Dr. Koch, "I cannot believe that a Christian who has really given his life to Christ would be able to take part in parapsychological experiments involving mediums."[77]

A third problem with Christian parapsychology is seen in its worldview confusion. This often, but not always, involves a blending of occultism and Christian faith in both doctrine and practice. The end result is a distortion of biblical doctrine and Christian practice. For example, Jesus Christ is no longer seen as the unique Son of God and atoning Savior of mankind, but is perceived as a psychic, medium, or shaman whose supernatural miracles were performed through psychic ability.[78]

The fourth problem is that Christian parapsychologists assert the Bible offers evidence for the basic claim of parapsychology—that all man have latent psychic power. In other words, the Bible is so full of miraculous events performed by men that it allegedly offers a wealth of data for the existence of human psychic ability.

But in the end, this approach only confuses the work of God with the work of the devil:

- The biblical phenomena of prophecy becomes the occult art of precognition.

- Christian prayer becomes a form of occultic telepathy; answered prayer involves occultic miracles.

- Biblical revelation becomes a form of occultic clairvoyance.

- Divine healing becomes psychic healing.

- Theophanies/angelic appearances become mediumistic materialization phenomena such as ectoplasmic manifestations.

- Paul's experience in 2 Corinthians 12:1-4 becomes the occult phenomena of astral projection.

- Jesus' ascension into heaven becomes a form of spiritistic levitation and dematerialization.

- Philip's experience in Acts 8:39,40 becomes occultic teleportation or apportation.

However, if we examine the above identifications of divine miracles with their occult counterparts, it is not difficult to see we are dealing with fundamentally distinct phenomena. For example, we are told that the occult ability of precognition (knowledge of events that have not yet happened) is an allegedly human capability; but biblically, "Know this first of all, that no prophecy of Scripture . . . was ever made by an act of human will, but men moved by the Holy Spirit spoke from God (2 Peter 1:20,21).

Also, prayer is not telepathy. The occult phenomenon of telepathy—the direct experience of another's thoughts—is either a passive experience that happens to one human or is allegedly directed from one human to another. But biblically, prayer involves communication and fellowship with God. It constitutes the communication of men with God, not men with other men. Further, answers to prayer do not involve occult miracles. God is the One who answers prayer in a personal sense in accordance with His holy nature and sovereign purposes. But in the occult, "prayer" is neither petitionary nor personal; it is manipulative, requiring the proper mental state, occult formula, or ritual which forces the corresponding response or "answer" of spirits or alleged impersonal divine energies, as in psychic healing, psychokinesis, etc.

None of the supernatural experiences in the Bible should ever be equated with occultic phenomena. For example, teleportation or apportation is the spiritistic movement of people or objects to another location. Its purpose is to display the power of the occult and thereby lead men into false religion. Christian parapsychologists cite Philip's experience in Acts 8:39,40 as an alleged illustration of teleportation. But in Acts 8:39,40, Philip was supernaturally taken from Gaza to Azotus by the Spirit of God Himself for the express purpose of preaching the gospel. The experiences of occultic teleportation and that of Philip are different in 1) the source of the miracle—spiritism versus the Holy Spirit, 2) the purpose of the miracle—to display occult power or expand occult interest versus preaching the gospel, and 3) the result of the miracle—converts to the occult versus converts to Christian belief.

Nor was Paul's experience in 2 Corinthians 12 the occult phenomena of astral projection. Astral projection involves either mental manipulation by the spirits or the spiritistic removal[79] of the spirit from the body, allegedly to explore other spiritual realms and to converse with and receive revelations from the spirit world. Astral projection involves either spiritistically induced false experiences, replete with mental delusions (as in hypnosis), or actual spiritual experiences that involve contact with deceiving spirits. In either case the result is 1) engagement in spiritism and 2) removal of the fear of death by falsely assuming such an experience will be repeated when one dies.

Every astral projector has *the experience* of being literally detached from his physical body, whether the event is real or fabricated by manipulating the mind. But in Paul's case, he did not have such an experience. He clearly stated that he could *not* determine whether he was "in" or "out" of the body, hence, a different experience. Also, the event was initiated by God and took Paul to God at a very specific location, the third heaven. Paul did not flit about in astral realms talking to "ghosts," spirits, or "gods." Further, the apostle heard things he was not permitted to speak of; he did not return to broadcast the message far and wide as modern occultists do.

If we falsely interpret the Bible through the eyes of parapsychology, then virtually every biblical miracle becomes reinterpreted in light of the premises and phenomena of the occult. The end result is that the Bible becomes little more than a historic compilation of the supposed manifestations of psychic abilities latent in the human race.

But such a view has consequences. One result of confusing psychic powers and biblical miracles is that it lends credence to the occult abilities of mediums, spiritists, and psychics themselves. It justifies these occult phenomena as "divine" in that they are all finally *equivalent* to biblical miracles. After all, don't most psychics claim their powers are divine and that they originate from God? What better proof than to find these same powers in the Bible, among the prophets and apostles of God, not to mention Jesus Himself? Such an approach lends divine authority not only to occultists but to the teachings and philosophy of occultists as well. If the psychic's power comes from God, how can his or her teachings possibly come from the devil?

In conclusion, what we are dealing with in "Christian" parapsychology is a drastic worldview confusion, a blending of two fundamentally incompatible realms: the world of Christianity and the world of the occult. We are mixing apples and lemons. No one denies apples and lemons have similarities. Both apples and lemons are round, both have skins, both grow on trees, both can be eaten. But no one argues they are the same thing, in spite of such similarities. No one argues lemons should be eaten like apples. Apples and lemons grow on different trees, have different skins and tastes, different textures and colors. They are used for different purposes. Using lemons in a recipe calling for apples can ruin a good dinner. In essence, apples and lemons have different *natures*.

In a similar fashion, Christianity and the occult have different natures. To confuse their supernatural manifestations is dangerous. When it comes to the supernatural, Christian parapsychology has confused the outward similarities with fundamental differences in basic nature. Biblical miracles are *not* psychic powers; upon examination the surface similarities are seen to mask contrary natures that are irreconcilable:

Biblical Miracles	Psychic Powers
Source or Origin	
God or Angels (Psalm 78:11; Galations 3:5; Hebrews 2:2-4; Revelation 16:1-12; 18:1)	Satan or Demons (Acts 16:16-19)
Purpose or Goal	
(a) To display divine power and/or reveal or confirm divine truth (Exodus 4:5,29-31; 7:5; John 15:24; Acts 2:22)	(a) To display occult power, and/or reveal or confirm occult truth and thereby hide or counterfeit divine truth (Acts 8:9-11; 2 Thessalonians 2:9,10)
(b) To lead people to God, resulting in individual salvation (John 4:39; 10:38; 11:40-45; Acts 17:31)	(b) To deceive and to lead people to false gods (Deuteronomy 13:1-5) resulting in the destruction of the soul (Revelation 21:8)
Result or End Product	
To glorify God (Exodus 9:16; John 11:4, 40-42)	To glorify man or demons to the exclusion of God (Acts 13:8-12)
Quality of Miracle	
Excellent	Often poor and generally inferior.

36

What Are
the Dangers
of the Occult?

Question 14

How can we know when psychic experiences become dangerous?

Unfortunately, we cannot know when psychic experiences become dangerous. We can only say that they should not be sought. Brooks Alexander, senior researcher for Spiritual Counterfeits Project in Berkeley, California, made the following observation:

> Many people seem to have so-called "psychic" experiences without being emotionally or spiritually injured by them. At the same time it seems clear that the world of psychic pursuit and fascination is a demonic playground. How do we know the acceptable level of psychic involvement? We do not know. Each individual encounters the demonic danger at his own level of temptation—whatever that may be.
>
> The fact is that no one knows how demonic beings operate in relation to psychic phenomena. Therefore it is impossible to say that "X" amount of psychic involvement will result in demonic contact. We do not know where the line is drawn between dabbling and demonism, or between curiosity and commitment, nor do we know how and when that line is crossed. It may be that the question of "how much" has less to do with it than we think. I would suggest that the neural and mental pattern set up by psychic involvement provides an

interface with other forms of consciousness, which are extra-dimensional and demonic in nature. If that is the case, then psychic dabbling is a little like entering the cage of a maneating tiger. You may or may not be eaten, depending in part on how hungry the tiger is. The significant point is that once you enter the cage, the initiative passes to the tiger.[80]

It would appear that occult involvement is in many ways like other sins: the longer and deeper the involvement, the greater the risk. Perhaps for one person consequences could come sooner than for another. Thus a given activity or duration of activity in one context may not have the same effects in another context.

It must also be noted that the effects of psychic involvement may not be visibly discernible. They may be unseen, subconscious or incipient; for example, an indiscernible but increasing resistance to the gospel or the early imperceptible stages of psychological damage or demonization.[81]

Question 15

Are there physical and psychological dangers to occult practice?

It should be obvious that one reason the occult is dangerous is because it brings people into contact with demons who, despite their benevolent claim, have little love for men. In the Bible, demons are presented as inflicting numerous physical and psychological ailments upon their victims. While it must be stressed that most illnesses, mental or physical, are *not* demonically instituted, the array of possible symptoms cited in Scripture covers virtually all of the workings of the human mind and body: skin disease (Job 2:7), destructive and irrational acts (Matthew 8:28, Luke 8:27), deafness and inability to speak (Mark 9:25, Luke 11:14), epileptic-like seizures (Matthew 17:15, Mark 9:20, Luke 9:39), blindness (Matthew 12:22), tormenting pain (Revelation 9:1-11), insanity (Luke 8:26-35), severe physical deformity (Luke 13:11-17), and other symptoms. Demons can just as easily give a person supernatural power and knowledge (Luke 8:29) or attempt to murder him or her (Matthew 17:15).

Not surprisingly, there are many accounts of mediums, spiritists, and occultists—and those people who frequent them—suffering physically in a manner similar or identical to the symptoms described above.[82]

For example, the famous Russian medium Ninel Kulagina was the subject of repeated parapsychological experimentation. During some tests her clothes would spontaneously catch on fire and unusual burn marks would appear on her body. She "endured pain, long periods of dizziness, loss of weight, lasting discomfort," sharp spinal pains, blurred vision, and a near-fatal heart attack from her psychic activities.[83] Unfortunately, the heart attack was massive and left Kulagina a permanent invalid.

The infamous "black" occultist Aleister Crowley ended up in an insane asylum for six months after trying to conjure the devil. His attempts to conjure helping spirits often produced demons instead. His children died and his wives either went insane or drank themselves to death. Two biographers observe, "Every human affection that he had in his heart . . . was torn and trampled with such infernal ingenuity in his intensifying torture that his endurance is beyond belief."[84] Crowley's tragedy illustrates an important point, that even with great knowledge and expertise in the occult, one is still not safe. And if experts in the occult aren't safe, how can anyone else guarantee their own protection?

Further, tragic "accidents" and other injuries also happen to the psychically involved and sometimes to their families. No less an authority than Dr. Koch has observed that people under occult subjection and demonization "frequently are in fatal accidents. I have many examples of this in my files."[85] Elsewhere he observes, "I would like to point out that in my own experience numerous cases of suicides, fatal accidents, strokes and insanity are to be observed among occult practitioners."[86]

As we survey the world of the occult, it is easy to cite illustrations of such "accidents" and other consequences. The famous psychic surgeon Arigo died in a horrible car crash; the Russian occultist Gurdjieff nearly died in a car accident. Well-known parapsychologist Edmond Gurney, author of *Phantasms of the Living*, died a tragic death either by accident or suicide; "Christian" spiritist William Branham died from a car accident; occult guru Rudrananda died at age 45 in a 1973 airplane crash.[87]

The famous medium Eileen Garrett's parents both committed suicide; Krishnamurti's brother, Nityananda, died at age 25 and Krishnamurti himself experienced terrible demonization throughout his life. He suffered incredibly strange and agonizing torments as part of a transforming "presence" he called "the process."[88]

James I. Wedgwood, a Theosophy convert and leader of the Theosophically instituted Liberal Catholic Church, went mad for the last 20 years of his life—and we could mention scores of other illustrations. In our own studies, we have encountered heart attacks; epileptic seizures; mental derangement; strange blackouts; stomach, eye, and skin problems; and many other maladies from occult practices.[89]

During his lifetime, Dr. Koch counseled over 11,000 people[90] who had encountered problems arising from their occult practices. He observes of those who carry on an active occult practice, "The family histories and the end of these occult workers are, in many cases known to me, so tragic that we can no longer speak in terms of coincidence."[91] For those *passively* involved, he observes that "occult subjection has been seen in relation to psychological disturbances which have the following predominant characteristics:

a. Warping and distortion of character: hard, egotistical persons; uncongenial, dark natures.

b. Extreme passions: abnormal sexuality; violent temper, belligerence; tendencies to addiction; meanness and kleptomania.

c. Emotional disturbances: compulsive thoughts, melancholia; suicidal thoughts, anxiety states.

d. Possession: destructive urges, fits of mania; tendency to violent acts and crime. . . .

e. Mental illnesses.

f. Bigoted attitude against Christ and God: conscious atheism; simulated piety; indifference to God's Word and prayer; blasphemous thoughts; religious delusions.

g. Puzzling phenomena in their environment."[92]

Dr. Merrill F. Unger, author of four books on occultism and demonism, observes, "The psychic bondage and oppression that traffickers in occultism themselves suffer, as well as their dupes, is horrifying to contemplate."[93] Further,

> Both psychiatry and psychology recognize the adverse effects of spiritistic activity upon the mind. Symptoms of split personality appear after sustained dealings in the occult. Psychiatry defines the resulting disorder as mediumistic psychosis.[94]

Philosopher, trial attorney, and noted theologian Dr. John Warwick Montgomery has authored or edited several books on the occult and owns one of the largest private libraries of rare occult books in the country. He warns:

> There is a definite correlation between negative occult activity and madness. European psychiatrist L. Szondi has shown a high correlation between involvement in spiritualism and occultism (and the related theosophical blind alleys) on the one hand, and schizophrenia on the other. The tragedy of most sorcery, invocation of demons, and related practices is that those who carry on these activities refuse to face the fact that they *always* turn out for the *worst*. What is received through the Faustian past never satisfies, and one pays with one's soul in the end anyway.[95]

There are many ways to pay such a price. As noted, suicide is one risk for occult practitioners. Many times there is a deliberate attempt by the spirits to induce suicide in the unwary person. If the individual is trying to leave the occult, they are told they will never be able to do so and that the only escape is suicide. Some gurus have even taught that disciples who leave them will commit suicide as a natural consequence—the disciple's only choice is either to follow the guru or die.[96]

Other individuals become enamored with their spirit guides' blissful descriptions of the "wonders" and "pleasure" of the "next life" and are lovingly urged to "come join us." Liberal theologian and occult supporter Morton Kelsey observes, "Two researchers working with the problem of suicide in Los Angeles were amazed at how often, in the course of their interviews, people who showed suicidal tendencies refer to contact with the dead."[97] United Nations' spiritual adviser and spiritist guru Sri Chinmoy confesses that the spirits are cunningly evil. He observes that, in visions, they have even appeared to disciples in the actual form of their guru and instructed them to kill themselves in order to attain "karmic liberation" sooner.[98]

In light of all this, Jesus' condemnation of the devil as "a liar" and a "murderer from the beginning" (John 8:44) is highly accurate. Indeed, the devil's lethal methods and intent are evident throughout the inglorious history of the occult. Consider the case of Dr. Carl A. Wickland, M.D., a physician, accomplished spiritist, and researcher in psychology. His wife was a trance medium "easily controlled by discarnate intelligences."[99] For over 30 years Wickland communicated with the spirit world through her, recording her teachings. These were given in his *Thirty Years Among the Dead*.

Wickland became an acknowledged authority in the area of spiritism and the occult. Even Sir Arthur Conan Doyle, author of the Sherlock Holmes series and a noted convert to spiritism, said of Wickland, "I have never met anyone who has had such a wide experience of invisibles."[100]

Wickland's life was somewhat reminiscent of the great Emanuel Swedenborg, the famous spiritist of the eighteenth century. Though both Swedenborg and Wickland practiced spiritism extensively, both issued stern warnings about its dangers (see Question 9). Wickland observes that "a great number of unaccountable suicides are due to the obsessing or possessing influence of . . . spirits. Some of these spirits are actuated by a desire to torment their victims. . . ."[101]

According to his own extensive experience, he observed that spiritism frequently causes

> . . . apparent insanity, varying in degrees from a simple mental aberration to, and including, all types of dementia, hysteria, epilepsy, melancholia, shell shock, kleptomania, idiocy, religious and suicidal mania, as well as amnesia, psychic invalidism, dipsomania, immorality, functional bestiality, atrocities, and other forms of criminality.[102]

In fact, his book devotes entire chapters to the spirits' influence in fostering suicide, criminal practices, drug use, and other unsavory activities. He confesses, "In many cases of revolting murder, investigation will show that the crimes were committed by innocent persons under the control of disembodied spirits. . . ."[103]

Wickland is not alone in his assessment of the psychological dangers of occult practice. Some authorities think that a significant percentage of those institutionalized in mental hospitals may be suffering from mental illness induced by occult practice and/or demonization. Dr. Koch refers to a New Zealand psychiatrist who "claims that 50% of the neurotics being treated in the clinics in Hamilton are the fruit of Maori sorcery."[104] He also observes a Christian psychiatrist who believes that up to half of the inmates at his psychiatric clinic are suffering from occult oppression rather than true mental illness.[105]

Dr. Anita Muhl, an authority on the use of the mediumistic ability of automatic writing in psychotherapy, observes that automatisms "frequently precipitate a psychosis." She supplies many examples.[106] Roger L. Moore, psychologist of religion at Chicago Theological Seminary, observes that "there are haunting parallels" between the paranoid schizophrenic and the deeply involved occultist. He also observed at a four-day symposium of the American Academy of Religion, "Participation in the occult is dangerous for persons who are the most interested in it. ... A lot of them have become paranoid psychotics."[107]

All this proves that occult involvement carries both physical and psychological risk; indeed, no one familiar with the facts can deny it. But it also carries spiritual risk.

Question 16

Is demonization a very real possibility for those involved in the occult?

What is demonization? Dr. C. Fred Dickason, who has authored several books on demonology, provides the following discussion of the word's origin and meaning:

> The [Greek] verb *daimonizomai* means "to be possessed by a demon." The participle from the same root, *daimonizomenos*, is used twelve times in the Greek New Testament. It is used only in the present tense, indicating the continued state of the one inhabited by a demon, or demonized. ... Putting it all together, the participle in its root form means "a demon caused passivity." ... Demonization pictures a demon controlling a somewhat passive human.[108]

In essence, a demonized person is one who is under the direct influence or control of one or more demons. Symptoms of demonization are not present at all times and demons may, apparently, come and go at will. Nevertheless, it appears they usually prefer to stay within their host, even though the person may have no conscious awareness of this fact (see Question 6).

Unfortunately demonization, or inhabitation by demons who control a person to their ends, is an increasingly frequent occurrence in American society, and this is the direct fruit of our modern revival of occultism. Most people do not recognize how extensively demonization occurs in America. Former Satanist and witch Doreen Irvine confesses, "Demon possession is real, very real, and is increasing at an alarming rate in this present day and age."[109] The modern revival of channeling illustrates that literally tens of thousands of Americans are willing to open their minds and bodies to spirits, allowing the spirits to enter and possess them.[110] Noted psychiatrist M. Scott Peck correctly observes that it is usually the occultist who becomes possessed: "It seems clear from the literature on possession that the majority of cases have had involvement with the occult—a frequency far greater than might be expected in the general population."[111]

Still, many people today scoff at the idea of demon-possession. But this phenomenon is as old as man himself. Indeed, the documentation for its reality is impressive.

No less an authority than Dr. Montgomery asserts, "The problem involved in determining whether demon possession occurs and whether witchcraft works is absurdly simple. The documentation is overwhelming."[112] In a major text on altered states of consciousness, *Religion, Altered States of Consciousness and Social Change*, editor Dr. Erika Bourguignon observes that of 488 societies surveyed, fully 74 percent believed in possession by spirits:

> It will be noted that such beliefs occur in 74% of our sample societies, with a maximum of 88% in the Insular Pacific and a minimum of 52% in North America. The beliefs are thus characteristic of the great majority of our societies [on earth]. . . .[113]

In *The Devil's Bride: Exorcism Past and Present*, psychic researcher Martin Ebon confesses, "The uniform character of possession, through various cultures and at various times, is striking."[114]

We must ask ourselves how such a predominant belief originated, if not from the fact of spirit possession itself? And does not its uniformity suggest in Ebon's own words the possibility of a "universal presence of devils, demons or possessing spirits"?[115] John S. Mbiti observes in his *African Religions and Philosophy*, "Spirit possession occurs in one form or another in practically every African society."[116] The same holds true around the world.

Unfortunately, the fate of those demonized, whether voluntarily or involuntarily, is horrible to contemplate. These horrors are meticulously detailed in the history of the occult and parapsychology, in anthropological studies (shamanism), throughout mediumism and spiritism, and in numerous works on demon-possession.[117] Although many moderns scoff at the very idea of demon-possession, many occultists actually seek it for its "empowering" characteristics. Consider the following description of the occultist's possession by a possessing spirit during the Kabbalistic Master Ritual:

> At last—and he will certainly know when—the god-form will take control of him. To begin with, the adept will feel an exquisite giddiness somewhere at the base of his skull and

quickly convulsing the whole of his body. As this happens, and while the power is surging into him, he forces himself to visualize the thing he wants his magic to accomplish, and wills its success. He must put all he has into this and, like our friends the Bacchantes, must whip himself into a veritable frenzy. It is at this point that the force evoked will be expelled to realize the ritual intention.

As he feels the force overflowing inside him the adept, while still visualizing the realized magical intention, bids it go forth to fulfil his wishes. . . .

For some magicians the dislocation of reason [a temporarily cultivated madness] coincides with the moment of sacrifice. Others perform this sacrifice before proceeding to the climax of the rite, arguing that the vital energy discharged by the victim's blood assists the possessing entity to appear inside the [magic] circle. Traditionally, the victim's throat is cut. . . . More common . . . is the use of sex. . . . The outburst of power is effected at the same time as orgasm is reached, with possession occurring a few seconds before.[118]

Not surprisingly, there are serious moral and social consequences to the modern occult revival and some of these must briefly be noted as well.

Question 17

What are some of the moral and social consequences of occultism?

Occult philosophy is typically amoral, that is, it is not ultimately concerned with moral standards. This is why, for many people, occult practice becomes an addiction to evil. As Dr. Unger asserts, "People who deal in the occult are often found to be immoral."[119] Indeed, the sexual immorality alone is so pervasive and so perverted one simply cannot describe it. Sadomasochism, bestiality, necrophilia, snuff films, and worse are common in some occult circles. As Unger further observes, "For those who surrender themselves to worship and serve Satan, the moral degradation and perversion are horrifying. . . ."[120]

Former leading European witch Doreen Irvine recalls,

Lying, cheating, swearing, free lust—even murder—are condoned. . . . The chief Satanist didn't care about my prostitution. He believed the more evil he condoned or achieved on earth, the greater would be his reward. . . . I had witnessed evil and ugly orgies in the Satanists' temple, but I was to see far worse in the witches' coven. . . . All meetings included awful scenes of perverted sexual acts. . . . Many black witches were lesbians or homosexuals. Sadism was practiced frequently. . . . Imagine over 100 black witches all taking part in such perversions at the same time. . . . I practiced more wickedness in a single week than many would in an entire lifetime.[121]

Unfortunately, the methods of the occultists are generally pragmatic—whatever is effective in securing the desired end. This may include anything from the development of psychic power to voluntary spirit possession, from human sacrifice to other acts of deliberate evil, from temporarily cultivated insanity to acts of physical self-mutilation.

In other words, to secure occult goals, it is often vital to enforce a temporary destruction of conventional existence as a prelude to so-called spiritual "enlightenment." Time, space, reason, morality, and normal consciousness must all be "transcended." Occult states of consciousness, frequently leading to personal detachment and abandonment, are one principal method for so-called enlightenment. These states may be induced by drugs, sex, transfer of occult power, ritual possession, meditation, intense concentration, and other means.[122]

Many occult traditions, such as Tantrism, teach that those who desire spiritual "enlightenment" may actually participate in evil or criminal acts in order to personally understand and experience that evil is merely an "illusion." Hindu and Buddhist gurus often emphasize that Reality is amoral. This is why the prominent Indian guru Rajneesh taught, "Tantra is not concerned with your so-called morality. Really, to emphasize morality is mean, degrading; it is inhuman." He continued to emphasize that even evil was "good"—"EVERYTHING is holy; nothing is unholy"—including things like rape and murder. He also taught "God and the Devil are not two" separate things.[123]

In commenting upon the lesson of the Bhagavad Gita, a Hindu holy book, Rajneesh says:

> Even if you kill someone consciously, while fully conscious [i.e. enlightened] it is meditative. That is what Krishna was saying to Arjuna...Kill, murder, fully conscious, knowing fully that no one is murdered and no one is killed....Just become the instrument of Divine hands and know well that no one is killed, no one can be killed.[124]

Here Rajneesh is only echoing the amoral philosophy of many Eastern "gods" and gurus who preach occultic philosophy. The Hindu god Indra asserts in another Hindu holy book, the *Kaushitaki Upanishad* (3:1,2): "The man who knows me as I am loses nothing whatever he does. Even if he kills his mother or father, even if he steals or procures an abortion, whatever evil he does, he does not blanch if he knows me as I am."[125] In the *Bhagavad Gita* 9:30, the Hindu god Krishna declares, "Even if one commits the most abominable actions...he is to be considered saintly because he is properly situated," that is, in service to Krishna and in "higher" consciousness.[126]

In his commentary on the *Bhagavad Gita*, peacemaker Maharishi Mahesh Yogi, founder of Transcendental Meditation, observes that the central character of the *Gita*, Arjuna, must attain "a state of consciousness which will justify any action of his and will allow him even to kill in love in support of the purpose of evolution."[127] But we can just as easily switch from such Eastern religion to the philosophy of the Manson clan. Charles Manson once stated, "I've killed no one."[128] Manson family member Susan Atkins believed her murders were committed in love. "You really have to have a lot of love in your heart to do what I did to [Sharon] Tate." Clan member Sandra Good explained, "There is no wrong... You kill whoever gets in your way."[129]*

The antisocial orientation of many Eastern practices now employed in America is further revealed by Mircea Eliade in his *Yoga, Immortality and Freedom*:

> The tantric texts frequently repeat the saying, "By the same acts that cause some men to burn in hell for thousands of years, the yogin gains his eternal salvation...." The Brhadaranyaka Upanisad (V, 14,8) [teaches]... "One who knows this, although he commits very much evil, consumes it all and becomes clean and pure...."[130]

Further, in Buddhist Tantrism, the aspiring Buddha is permitted to lie, steal, cheat, and commit adultery and other crimes because in Tantra "all contraries are illusory, [therefore] extreme evil coincides with extreme good. Buddhahood [supreme spiritual "enlightenment"] can—within the limits of this sea of appearances—coincide with supreme immorality...."[131]

It is therefore not surprising that Eliade observes the following connections between European witchcraft and Tantric Yoga:

> All the features associated with European witches are— with the exception of Satan and the Sabbath—claimed also by Indo-Tibetan yogis and magicians. They too are supposed to... kill at a distance, master demons and ghosts, and so on. Moreover, some of these eccentric Indian sectarians boast that they break all the religious taboos and social rules: that they practice human sacrifice cannibalism, and all manner of orgies, including incestuous intercourse, and that they eat excrement, nauseating animals, and devour human corpses. In other words, they proudly claim all the crimes and horrible ceremonies cited *ad nauseam* in the western European witch trials.[132]

Indeed, there is little doubt that in America today hundreds and perhaps thousands of human sacrifices occur each year in occult rituals

---

* Eastern gurus may or may not advocate the practice of evil; the problem is that their monistic philosophy can logically lead to it, especially given the fact of human sinfulness and demonic reality.

throughout the country.[133] Psychologist Dr. James D. Lisle believes that in the case of various types of black magic such as Satanism and witchcraft, "You can never be sure a person involved in this won't step over the line into infant sacrifice or cannibalism. We have evidence that it happens."[134]

Further, a connection between serial killers and the occult is now beginning to emerge. Richard Ramirez, the alleged "Night Stalker" and prime suspect in 14 murders and almost 50 other felonies in California, appears to have been involved in Satanism; mass murderer David Burkowitz, the "Son of Sam killer," was also apparently a member of a satanic cult.[135] Even the Atlanta child murders may have combined voodoo, snuff films, pornography/prostitution, drugs, and ritual murder.[136]

In fact, murders are sometimes committed by occultists on the direct command of their spirit guides. Even Jim Jones, who engineered the slaughter of over 900 people in Jonestown, Guyana, also "believed that he was guided by a supernatural spirit."[137]

Of course, using supernatural powers to commit murder has a long and noble tradition in the occult, including witchcraft, Satanism, voodoo, shamamism, hex-death, etc.[138]

For example, the ABC News program "20/20" on May 16, 1985, ran a segment titled "The Devil Worshipers." It alleged that Satanism was "being practiced all across the country" with perverse and "hideous acts that defy belief" including "suicide, murders, and the ritualistic slaughter of children and animals."[139]

Consider one illustration. In 1974, Arlis Perry, a young Stanford University student, newly wed, and committed Christian, was kidnapped and horribly tortured and killed in a satanic ritual. She had apparently been witnessing to members of a Satanist group. As it turns out, Charles Manson and "Son of Sam" murderer, David Berkowitz, were also members of this group, apparently part of a linked nationwide satanic net-work.[140] In fact, Berkowitz himself "emphasized the hideous torture Arlis endured—indicating knowledge that went far beyond any newspaper account."[141] Berkowitz had smuggled a book out of jail, Peter Haining's *The Anatomy of Witchcraft*. On pages 114 and 115 of this book, he had written the following message on the top of the page: "Stanford University" and to the left, "Arils Perry, hunted, stalked and slain, followed to California."[142]

Today, a dozen books collectively present evidence that Satanism has now gained an impressive hold in America and, because it seeks to destroy the foundation of American social and moral values, constitutes a genuine threat to society. Among these books are Jerry Johnson's *The Edge of Evil: The Rise of Satanism in North America* (1989); Mark Bubeck, *The Satanic Revival* (1991); Arthur Lyons, *Satan Wants You: The Cult of Devil Worship in America*; and Dr. Carl Raschke's *Painted Black: From Drug Killers to Heavy Metal—The Alarming True Story of How Satanism Is Terrorizing Our Communities* (1991).

Again, in his *Second Coming: Satanism in America*, Arthur Lyons observed that satanic cults are "presently flourishing in possibly every major city in the United States and Europe.... The United States probably harbors the fastest growing and most highly organized body of Satanists in the world."

In *Cults That Kill: Probing the Underworld of Occult Crime*, award-winning investigative journalist Larry Kahaner chronicles interviews with police officials and occultists throughout America showing that occult crimes, including drug peddling, child abduction/rape/pornography/sacrifice/ and worse are now practiced in places across America. For example, Detective Pat Metoyar of the Los Angeles Police Department observes of those Satanists and other occultists who murder babies, "These groups don't always kidnap babies. Some have doctors within the group who will perform the birth and not fill out a birth certificate. Then when they sacrifice the baby, they are not really killing anyone who existed.... Before we say something like this [i.e., that testimony exists a child has been sacrificed], it has been verified with a minimum of five separate people who don't know each other, who have never spoken to each other. Minimum five people" (Larry Kahaner, *Cults That Kill*, p. 240).

The rationale for human sacrifice is discussed by Oxford-educated Richard Cavindish, a leading authority on the history of magic and occultism, in his *The Black Arts*:

> In occult theory a living creature is a storehouse of energy, and when it is killed, most of this energy is suddenly liberated.... The amount of energy let loose when the victim is killed is very great, out of all proportion to the animal's size or strength.... The spirit or force which is summoned in the ceremony is normally invisible. It can appear visibly to the magician ... by taking possession of one of the human beings involved in the ritual.... The most important reason for the sacrifice, however, is the psychological charge which the magician obtains from it.... It would obviously be more effective to sacrifice a human being because of the greater psychological "kick" involved.... there is a tradition that the most effective sacrifice to demons is the murder of a human being.... [when the sacrifice] is combined with the release of sexual energy and orgasm, the effect is to heighten the magician's frenzy and the supply of force ... still further.[143]

Consider the following description by a high-ranking member of the Rajneesh cult. After a Rajneesh disciple died of apparently natural causes, "We all suddenly felt ecstatic ... energy was so alive. We could feel it all around us: inside us, in the trees, in the air." One individual, at the exact moment of the disciple's death, felt "an incredible overwhelming energy [had] passed from her body into mine. I was filled with energy. It was like a total orgasm."[144]

It is experiences like these, apparently induced by demons who produce or manipulate occult energies, that may eventually lead to more powerful forms of occult practice—and finally to a descent into human sacrifice as a means of spiritual intoxication and/or advancement.

Unfortunately, several books could be written on the social consequences of occultism. Put simply, social disintegration is the result of a culture's wholehearted turning to the occult. America has now begun down this path. In essence, the occult's rejection of morality; its active promotion of drugs and perverted sexuality, including child molestation; its obsession with death; its glorification of demons; and its denial of cause and effect in the realm of ethics and medicine to name a few, all take a collective toll.

In his article "Satanism and the Devolution of the New Religions," Dr. Carl A. Rashcke, a Harvard Ph.D. and professor of religious studies at the University of Denver, ties together the interrelationships between Satanism, the new religions, drugs, and modern criminality. This article, along with many others, clearly reveals there are drastic social implications to occult activity.[145]

All of the above underscores the fact that there are serious moral and cultural consequences to occult practices, far more serious than many people imagine. Thankfully, several recent national symposia on the occult and criminality indicate there is an emerging awareness of some of these consequences. For example, from October 30 to November 1, 1990, North American Conferences of San Demas, California, sponsored a Las Vegas conference on "Occult Crime and Its Impact on Society." It noted, "One of the fastest growing areas of crime has been occult-related crimes, crimes so bizarre and heinous" that they simply cannot be believed, but for the "cold hard facts of police reports and documented evidence."[146]

Nevertheless, because of the secret nature of so much occult practice, the majority of criminal offenses relating to the occult are probably never uncovered. In many ways, only those who have been in hard-core occultism and then delivered from it have any idea of how horrible and antisocial these practices actually are.

What then is the conclusion of our study? Our conclusion is that our nation desperately needs reeducation concerning the facts on the occult.

PART EIGHT

CULT WATCH

FALSE TEACHING IN THE CHURCH

*What **you** need to know*

37

Introduction to
False Teaching
in the Church

The following material examines some of the false teachings in the church today. We state at the outset that we are careful to distinguish false teachings from false teachers. We do not say those listed herein are necessarily false teachers, but we are pointing out they are teaching false ideas. For us a *false teacher* is one who knows the truth and has deliberately turned away from it. On the other hand, *false teaching* is a mixture of truth and error. Thus, people may at the same time be encouraged and nourished by some things that are true but unknowingly accept error along with it. Unfortunately, sometimes even a small amount of error may be dangerous. Ninety-eight percent of rat poison is wholesome food. Only two percent is deadly.

In approaching this topic, we have been reminded of the illustration of Apollos in the book of Acts. There we are told that Priscilla and Aquila "took [Apollos] aside and explained to him the way of God more accurately" (Acts 18:26). Apparently Apollos was inadequately instructed in the things of God and therefore was teaching error without realizing it. However, he was willing to listen to their counsel even though he was highly esteemed and considered a great teacher in the church. As a result, both he and the church were greatly profited (verses 27 and 28).

We should hope that some of our highly esteemed Christian teachers would also listen to counsel and that, as a result, the church would be greatly profited.

In examining false teachings in the church, we, along with all other Christians, recognize that God has given us His Word, the Bible. All of us agree the Bible is an objective test, an absolute standard, for dividing truth from error. If we or anyone else interprets that standard wrong, then we are wrong, and the standard itself informs us we are wrong. We are not free to change the Bible. What matters is what God has said. The authority of God's Word stands over us and speaks truth to us. And God tells us to "contend earnestly for the faith which was once for all delivered to the saints" (Jude 3).

This is why God emphasizes the importance of personal study in His Word—so we can learn that standard thoroughly (2 Timothy 2:15; 3:14). God said that the noble-minded Bereans "[examined] the Scriptures daily, to see whether these things were so" (Acts 17:10,11). Our responsibility before Christ is to also "examine everything carefully; hold fast to that which is good; abstain from every form of evil" (1 Thessalonians 5:21,22).

Bible teachers should be aware of their responsibility to God to teach the Bible accurately. James says, "Not many of you should presume to be teachers, my brothers, because you know that we who teach will be judged more strictly" (James 3:1 NIV). This warning is necessary because Paul referred to some in the church who were "teaching things they should not teach, for the sake of sordid gain" (Titus 1:11).

We should not suppose that the errors taught in part of the body of Christ will never affect the rest of the body of Christ. As a little leaven leavens the whole lump of dough, in the same way the error of a teacher can be picked up and spread in many directions. The directions it takes are often unpredictable and surprising.

We should also realize that some of the teaching errors of today are really unchallenged errors of yesterday. And rarely will the church reap what it sows in the same season. Thus, the very problems that we address in this booklet are themselves the results of the sins of yesterday, and unless we repent, they will lead to problems for us all tomorrow. If the body of Christ, the church, is in some sense an organic unity, then what happens to one of us, in some way, affects all of us (Romans 12:5; 1 Corinthians 12:26).

Joshua chapter 7 provides a frightening illustration of how God has held His people collectively responsible.[1] In this chapter Israel was unexpectedly defeated in her attempt to conquer Ai. God said that the problem was, "The sons of Israel acted unfaithfully" (Joshua 7:1). But only one man had done wrong and stolen the gold items under the divine ban. Yet in God's eyes all of Israel had sinned. "Therefore the sons of Israel cannot stand before their enemies..." (Joshua 7:12).

The responsibility of the entire nation was called into account for allowing the conditions which permitted the transgression to begin with. Now let us apply this illustration to the church. If we allow false teaching to be taught in the church and do not correct it, we will all suffer for it. But there is a solution. If we place God first—not men or their ministries or their worldly philosophies and theologies, but God first—His Word and His glory—then God will spare us His discipline (1 Peter 4:17). If we repent, God will bless us.

38

Is There
a Conflict Between
Christianity
and Psychology?

Question 1

Do the claims of the Bible, Christian psychology, and secular psychology conflict?

To answer this question we must ask, "What does secular psychology claim, and what does Christianity claim?" First, secular psychology may be briefly defined as the study of why people are the way they are and how they change. But does this definition seem to invade an area the Bible claims is its domain? Please examine the claims of each category listed in the chart on pages 300 and 301 (note: space limitations require that we express this material in general terms).

1) Has God given His instructions for life?
2) What is the way or method to treat man's problems or the approach to therapy?
3) What is the extent of the Bible's authority?
4) What is the priority and value given to each body of knowledge?
5) Who knows man best?

As we see from the chart on the following pages, the Bible, Christian psychology, and secular psychology disagree on some very important issues.

The issues we are concerned about are: 1) What is legitimate and what is not legitimate in modern psychology and psychotherapy; 2) the problem and implications of modern psychotherapy replacing biblical counseling

Claims of the Bible	The Claims of Christian Psychology*	The Claims of Secular Psychology†
1) The Word of God is sufficient for everything pertaining to life and godliness. 2 Peter 1:3 NIV—"His divine power has given us everything we need for life and godliness through our knowledge of him."	1) Many new truths have been discovered through psychology that Jesus and Paul never stated.[2] This assumes there are foundational principles and important new truths pertaining to what man is and how to ultimately change his behavior that have not been revealed in the Scriptures. The issue is whether all of these "new truths" are valid. If some are, are they ultimately as helpful as responsible biblical counseling?	1) Divine revelation is a myth, even a harmful myth. There is no absolute truth from God about who man is or how he can change his behavior. Men must decide these issues for themselves on the basis of their own best interests. They must not look to a mythical God for help.
2) The Bible offers one comprehensive view of man and God's consistent plan or "therapy" for successful living. The Bible calls itself an instruction book for successful living. 2 Timothy 3:16 NIV—"All Scripture is God-breathed and is useful for teaching, rebuking, correcting and training in righteousness, so that the man of God may be thoroughly equipped for every good work."	2) Along with the Bible, most or all of secular psychology's techniques and theories *may be* incorporated into therapy.[3] This assumes the theories and techniques of secular psychology *are* helpful or unbiased. The issue is whether all of them really are helpful and are they really in agreement with Christian truth?	2) Pick one of 250 conflicting secular theories of human personality. Then choose one or more of 10,000 different techniques to apply your particular theory in counseling people. Have faith that the chosen theory and technique will lead the counselee to a life of success and happiness.
3) The Bible claims God has given us through Christ everything for life and godliness, including those areas of concern to modern psychology such as relationships, self-image, and personal behavior. (The book of Proverbs and Psalms; Jn. NIV 13:34,35; 14:27; 15:9; 16:27; Rom. 14:7; 16:19; 12:13; 1 Cor. 6; 10:24; 13:1,4-8; 15:33; 2 Cor. 7:6; Gal. 6:1-10; Eph. 4:4-6; Phil. 2:3; 1 Tim. 4:7; 1 Thess. 5:5-17; 2 Pet. 1:3-8; 1 Jn. 3:1; etc.)	3) In some areas modern psychology should be granted priority *over* the Bible. The Bible speaks primarily (or only) to the believer's spiritual life; modern psychology gives us the tools or knowledge for dealing with the more complex human problems.[4] This assumes the Bible does not deal effectively with many areas modern psychology deals with. The issue is whether this is true and whether psychological assumptions are permitted to sit in judgment over what the Scriptures say.	3) Modern psychology has discovered the "true nature" of man and offers the best solutions to his problems. The Bible is irrelevant, for the most part, to human living. Because man is basically good, not sinful or evil, the biblical view which teaches this is flawed or destructive and not to be trusted.

4) Christians are to seek God's wisdom above all else, including alleged human "wisdom." Christians are to rejoice in the truth, not in philosophical or psychological theories of questionable value.

Colossians 2:8 NIV—"See to it that no one takes you captive through hollow and deceptive philosophy, which depends on human tradition and the basic principles of this world rather than on Christ."

1 Thessalonians 5:21,22 NASB—"But examine everything carefully; hold fast to that which is good; abstain from every form of evil."

5) Because God created man, He knows who man really is, the true nature of man's problems, the proper solution to those problems, and what is best for man.

Psalm 139:1,3,13 NIV—"O Lord, you have searched me and you know me. . . . you are familiar with all my ways. . . . For you created my inmost being; you knit me together in my mother's womb."

Isaiah 45:12 NIV—"It is I who made the earth and created mankind upon it."

---

4) As a formal discipline, Christians may rejoice in the findings of modern psychology and utilize secular psychotherapy. Some Christian psychologists admit that Christian psychology is largely secular. Others go further and claim there is no difference.[5] This assumes that modern psychotherapy *has* been proven effective. The problem is that even secular authorities in psychology are criticizing the effectiveness of psychotherapy and challenging many of its assumptions.

5) The Bible needs modern psychology to explain what is best for man.[6] This assumes that for 1900 years the Bible was somehow deficient in helping men. It means that in some important areas God and Jesus left us incomplete until modern psychology arrived to tell us how best to live.

---

* We believe the term "Christian psychology" is really inappropriate if the majority of those who call themselves such actively endorse secular therapies of questionable value and ignore what God teaches on these subjects. Such individuals are more properly termed "psychologists" but not "Christian" psychologists. Even psychologist Gary Collins regretfully observes: "Many who call themselves Christian [psychologists] aren't much different from counselors who are blatantly secular" (Collins, op. cit., p. 169).

---

4) There is no divine wisdom. Modern psychology should not rejoice in the Bible but should replace the false and harmful assumptions of the Bible and Christian counseling with the truths of modern psychology. (Even many psychologists admit that much of secular psychology is anti-Christian.)

5) Psychology alone knows what is best for man. The domain of the psyche, the mind, and of human behavior is the sole domain of psychology. Corrupting influences, like the Bible, are to be shunned. [Note: Question 1 is not intended as a criticism of counselors who are genuinely biblical in their counseling and also employ insights from secular fields that are consistent with established biblical, medical, or scientific fact.]

in the church; and 3) the issues surrounding Christian psychology. One of the major issues here appears to be this: Are most Christian psychologists replacing biblical counseling with psychotherapies of questionable value? And if so, what are the consequences for the church at large?

We will cite some brief illustrations of the potential problem of uncritically accepting modern psychological theory.

Question 2

Was Carl Jung involved in the occult?

Though Carl Jung was a brilliant psychologist, it can be documented that he had a deep interest in the occult and strong dislike for the biblical God and historic Christianity. He is often seen as a friend of religion, even though he taught religion was no more than myth.[8] But there should be no doubt that he was an enemy of the church who has done it great harm. His theories have laid a strong intellectual foundation for the integration of psychology, religion, and the occult. In fact, Jung has done as much as anyone to promote the occult in the 20th century.[9]

Jung, for example, supported parapsychology (the scientific study of the occult), used mandalas (geometric forms for occultic meditation), and was a fortune-teller who used the I-Ching (a Chinese form of divination).[10] It has been shown that he was a spiritist (one who was in contact with spirits) and necromancer (one who received information from supposedly dead human spirits).[11] Through his writings we learn that he had a number of personal spirit guides which he often "internalized" (interpreted) as "normal" (psychologically normal) functions of his own consciousness.[12] In fact, at times he apparently became possessed by spirits who spoke out of him, just as in what is today called channeling.[13] He also used astrology, attended seances, and was a passionate advocate of Eastern religious belief.[14] His biographers revealed that he was ruled by whim, dream, and vision—and by the spirits from whom he derived much or most of his theories.[15] If you read his autobiography, *Memories, Dreams, Reflections*, you will find the details of his occult beliefs and experiences.[16]

All of this is important, as it is our view that many of his theories skillfully mask demonic realities, reinterpreting spiritistic activity as psychological phenomena. His view of the "self," his ideas on archetypes, the collective unconscious, synchronicity, and active imagination and individuation are now being used by some of his followers and many others to explain their occult or spiritistic experiences.[17] Jung used some of these theories to explain his own spiritistic experiences.[18] All of this documents that Jung was heavily involved in the occult and that his occult experiences shaped his psychological views.* (Pg. 303)

Question 3

How is Carl Jung's occultism influencing the church?

The theories of the world-famous psychologist Carl Gustav Jung have influenced some Christians' psychological thinking.[19] Also, Jung's theories have cultivated a particular "Christian" mind-set relating to powers of the mind. For example, some Christians use Jung's theories to stress the importance of subjects such as the unconscious mind, inner healing, dream-work, and visualization.[20]

Before embracing the psychological views of Carl Jung, Christians should exercise discernment for, after all, he admitted his involvement with spirits. He admitted his occult experiences "form the *prima materia* [basic material] of my scientific work."[21] And he scorned the God of the Bible and historic Christianity.[22]

How then can we turn to him for wisdom? It is clear and the facts show that Jung became an unwitting agent of the spirit world. He was simultaneously used to promote and mask its activities. In a scientific era which did not accept the reality of spirits, Jung "psychologized" them and promoted them as normal and natural components of the human mind. And the Christian church, which should have known better because of the revealed Word of God, was taken "captive through philosophy and empty deception, according to the tradition of men, according to the elementary principles of the world, rather than according to Christ" (Colossians 2:8).

Question 4

Should inner healing and inner guides be practiced in the church?

Inner healing is a form of counseling which seeks to correct the harmful memories of the past by reliving them in the present through visualization and other techniques, often using Jesus as an "inner counselor" or "inner guide." It is a method based largely upon the theories of Freud and Jung, and often the practices of religious mysticism.[23] It has come into the church through Jungian therapists and laymen such as Agnes Sanford, Episcopal priest Morton Kelsey (her pastor), John Sanford (her son), and John and Paula Sandford, Dennis and Rita Bennett, Paul Yonggi Cho, Father Francis MacNutt, and Ruth Carter Stapleton.[24] It has also entered the church through other Roman Catholic and Protestant charismatics and by some Christian psychologists and parapsychologists.

The problem with most inner healing† is that it is based upon an unproven assumption of an unconscious mind operating in a particular manner, in an alleged natural connection with, or as part of, God.[25] The unconscious mind has become the means to meet Jesus and be sanctified.

---

* Some claim Jung merely had a detached academic interest in studying the psychological aspects of the occult. Certainly his interest often was academic, but his purposes for studying and using the occult were not always clear. To separate Jung from the category of the occultist is not always easy. For example, many occultists stress the psychological importance of the occult and interpret occult phenomena along psychological lines just as Jung did. For both Jung and the occultist the occult is one means to self-insight and power. Whatever Jung's motive for studying the occult or interpretation as to occult phenomena the fact remains he engaged in a number of occult practices. His more "scientific" image results, in part, from keeping his occult views private for personal reasons [e.g., Kurt Koch, *Satan's Devices* (Kregel, 1978), p. 156].

---

† Inner healing approaches vary. See the critiques by Don Matzat and Spiritual Counterfeits Project listed in the Bibliography.

Besides opening Christians to the occultic theories of Jung, inner healing may open them to the occult itself via inner guides who are really demons. Even the September 1986 *Charisma* magazine published an article on inner healing which warned, "According to some, Eastern mysticism and even necromancy are infiltrating the movement in some quarters. 'I know this is going to offend some people,' says [Martin] Lynch cautiously, 'but it has to be said. We're starting to see a deification of the unconscious. It's a major problem.' Lynch, who is Roman Catholic, says that certain people 'tend to be susceptible to the teachings of Carl Jung. But Jung is a nemesis. He's anti-Christian. He was a gnostic and a purveyor of gnosticism.' "[26]

The problem of "inner advisors" so often found in Jungian psychology, inner healing, and in some Christian psychotherapy is that it is often indistinguishable from the contacting of spirit-guides in occultism.[27] Some inner "guides" may be either genuinely imaginative (as in dreams) or they may be spiritistic. Cultivating them may also progress from the purely imaginary to genuine spiritism. Thus, there is growing interest in what may be termed "imagination spiritism" where the imagination becomes the vehicle for spirit contact, whether deliberately sought or not (although often under another name).[28]

Mary Watkins is a psychotherapist who uses Jungian "active imagination" and inner dialogue with "guides" in her patients' therapy. In her book, *Invisible Guests: the Development of Imaginal Dialogues*, she sets forth her belief that psychotherapy should encourage the emergence of "imaginal presences" and that the patient can benefit by deepening his relationship with them.[29] She believes, along with Jung, that these psychic counselors are not spirits but are merely "indicative of the process of personification that occurs spontaneously in the unconscious."[30] In other words, these are seen as Jungian archetypes; yet both Jung and she directly experienced that these are autonomous "entities." Dr. Watkins admits, "The imaginal other may have as much autonomy as the so-called real others I meet in consensual space."[31] In his autobiography Jung describes one of his archetypes, "Philemon," as being "quite real, as if he were a living personality" and compares his experience with Philemon to the ancient practice of contacting a god. In fact, he admits both Philemon and another archetypal figure, "Ka," perfectly fit the category of spirit-guides.[32]

In our opinion, when the church accepts Jungian and other dubious methods, it is treading on potentially dangerous ground. What objective standards exist to discern imaginary inner guides from spirits who initially assume such a pose as a means of later contact or influence? (Such methods are, in fact, encouraged by the very spirit world which utilizes them because they help mask spirit contact under the guise of psychotherapy.)[33] The question must be asked, "Are some portions of the church by innocence or naiveté, at least in some cases, helping its own members to contact spirits?"[34]

39

What Do Christian Positive Thinkers Teach and Practice?

Question 5

What is Christian Positive Thinking?

Christian Positive Thinking (CPT) is a term that refers to a number of movements or philosophies advocated by those claiming it is Christian. Unfortunately, these teachings sometimes incorporate the findings of modern humanistic psychology and stress the powers of the mind. Their goal is to get people to believe in a new power. They claim this power will provide success, happiness, and abundance in life, and even allow some to perform miracles. Their emphasis is placed upon such conscious methods as exercising one's "faith," to develop a new outlook on life. Usually, faith is seen as a force or power which can be used to change one's environment (bringing financial or other success) or other people (as in physical healing), and as a by-product, such success will bring self-esteem and self-worth, changing the person. Many teach that exercising a belief in such a faith can even influence divine laws and force God to act on one's behalf.

Some of those stressing the powers of the mind, "faith," or Positive Thinking include: Robert Schuller—"Possibility Thinking"; Clement Stone—"Positive Mental Attitude"; Norman Vincent Peale, the modern "founder" of Positive Thinking; Oral Roberts' "Seed-Faith" principles; the teachings of Kenneth Hagin and Kenneth Copeland, also known as "Word-Faith" teaching; Paul Yonggi Cho, who stresses a health and prosperity gospel; and Charles Capps and many others who stress "Positive

Confession." The terms Positive Confession, Prosperity Thinking, Theology of Success Movement, or "name it and claim it" are all terms used to describe those stressing the powers of faith as a force to influence the environment or God.

This is *not* biblical faith. However, believing that our health and wealth are already present in the "spirit" world and that we can manifest this on the physical level by proper thinking ("faith") is a tenet of Science of Mind and occultism, not biblical faith. Perhaps one reason why some Christians are being deceived by cultism and occultism is because some principles of the health and wealth positive confession ideas are so similar to cultic and occult teaching.*

Question 6

Is CPT an issue of major importance in the church?

Most of the preachers of these messages are on television and many of them have worldwide influence. The key issues are, first, is the theology of CPT biblical? Second, do these practices conform to biblical instruction concerning human experience? If Positive Thinking is not based on fact, or if it is unbiblical, then the millions of Christians who follow these teachings are being given a substitute faith of questionable or harmful value.

For millions of people around the world, these Christian Positive Thinking programs are the only basis by which they know American Christianity or even Christianity at all. It is our view that these Positive Thinkers are presenting a distorted, unbalanced, and false Christianity around the world. Such "Christian" Positive Thinking will not stand the test of time precisely because it is more of humanistic faith than biblical gospel. People are becoming converted by the millions who may eventually fall away because they have embraced another gospel.

Question 7

Who are some of the well-known Christian "Positive Thinkers" teaching errors?

Space does not permit listing the scores of Christian teachers of humanistic psychology or questionable theology and practices. The major leaders we list below have dramatically molded the faith of literally thousands of churches and millions of Christian people. They may be cited as an illustration of the problems of this field in general:

Norman Vincent Peale has mixed humanistic psychology and occultic mental techniques with Christian terminology. For example, in his book

---

* For further information on positive confession and the occult see "Positive Confession: Part I," *News & Views*, June, 1988 and "Positive Confession Teachings and the Occult Part II," *News and Views*, July 1988 (Chattanooga, TN: Ankerberg Theological Research Institute) and McConnell, op.cit. passim.

Positive Imaging, he says you can send thoughts to hover over people's minds, eventually bursting in on them, compelling them to do things like write out checks for $5,000.[35] He has also written many forewords to books supporting psychic practices or teachers. See, for example, his foreword in Helen Keller's *My Religion,* where she testifies to her belief in the occultic practices and philosophy of the 18th-century medium Emanuel Swedenborg.[36]

Robert Schuller has replaced some important biblical doctrines with modern psychological concepts. This is clearly revealed in his books such as *Self-Esteem: The New Reformation* (see Question 10).

Oral Roberts claims that Jesus personally gave him the "Seed-Faith" principles. Ultimately, when one reads the Bible, Jesus denies many aspects of these principles (see Question 11).

Kenneth Copeland claims that he believes in and teaches the doctrine of the deity of Jesus Christ. Yet in the February 1987 *Believers Voice of Victory* magazine, he gives a prophecy of Jesus Christ where Jesus stated through him: "They crucified Me for claiming that I was God. *But I didn't claim I was God;* I just claimed I walked with Him and that He was in Me. Hallelujah. That's what you're doing" (emphasis added).[37] Copeland stands by this prophecy today. He must stand by it, of course, otherwise he is guilty of false prophecy. His response to critics is that he is not denying the deity of Christ, merely that Christ was saying through him that while on earth He never claimed He was God. But this is wrong. While He was on earth Christ did claim He was God (John 5:18; 10:30; 14:6; 20:28). Copeland has also taught that Christ was "born again" while in hell.[38]

Kenneth Hagin has taught that Christ did not specifically die for our sins, but instead experienced a sin nature like Adam's. While on the cross, the important thing that happened was that Christ accepted the sin nature of Satan in His own spirit. When He was in hell, Jesus became the first one ever "born again."[39]

Paul Yonggi Cho teaches we can "incubate" or unleash ideas (by thinking, visualization, and meditation) which will enter what he terms "the fourth dimension," a level of reality where our ideas can become successful manipulators of the physical world (see Question 14).

Robert Tilton misinterprets the biblical teaching concerning tithing and giving money for the ministry in his "Success in Life" programs. For example, like many other "faith" teachers, he teaches a hundredfold return on giving. If this principle is really true, then possibly he should give his money to poor people and thereby increase his wealth a hundredfold, no longer needing people to send him money.

Charles Capps and *John Osteen* teach a system of positive confession that has elements similar to pagan occultism and magic. There are "words of power" similar to magical spells which, once uttered, powerfully influence people or change reality.[40] The "confession of the mouth" (the spoken word) is the incantation which releases the power. In *Dynamics of Faith and Confession* (1983) Charles Capps redefines faith and makes salvation a ritual technique (pp. 83-87). He teaches the virgin birth was accomplished through Mary's positive confession. Here, he appears to teach that what Mary conceived by positive confession was not the eternal second person of the Godhead but the verbal power of God which became personified on earth as Jesus. "Jesus was the personification of God's Word on this earth. . . . Jesus in Word form was the creator of all things."[41]

Morton Kelsey, an Episcopal priest and Jungian psychologist, rejects biblical authority. Kelsey believes Jesus was a psychic and one of the greatest shamans (or witchdoctors) who ever lived. Christians are to be just like Jesus, that is, become psychics and shamans, following in His footsteps.[42]

Agnes Sanford was a Jungian, who believed that God could work through "good" spirits and the spirits of people who have died. She believed God used some mediums to heal people. Like modern channelers, she also believed that angels and dead saints could "speak and act in and through us." She accepted other occult teachings and practices and denied certain important biblical doctrines.[43]

E. W. Kenyon taught supernatural power is unleashed by the words we speak. Therefore he said, "You confess that you are perfectly healed while the disease is making full headway in your body." He would say that if you have to ask for faith, "all prayer for faith is nothing but unbelief."[44]

Napoleon Hill was a spiritist whose beliefs were derived from or influenced by the spirit world. For example, see his confession of this in his book, *Grow Rich with Peace of Mind*.[45] He is the grandfather of the Success/Positive Mental Attitude seminars taught widely to leaders in business and industry.

Jerry Savelle teaches, "If you will please God, you will be rich."[46]

Benny Hinn teaches that God wants to make us prosperous and that poverty is from the devil; "Do you know that confession activates heaven? Confession releases the spirit world. . . ."; Christians are "little gods on earth"; "your spirit-man doesn't have God . . . [it] is part of Him."; "The spirit-man within us is a God-man . . . say . . . 'I'm a God-man. I'm a sample of Jesus. I'm a super being.' Say it! Say it! . . . 'I walk in the realm of the supernatural.'" (Transcript of Nov. 6, 1990 and Oct. 20, 1990 TBN broadcast.)

The above is only a small sampling of errors that are being taught by Christian leaders in the Positive Thinking and Faith-Confession movements. In every case we know of, the root problem is either rejecting the Bible as a final authority or being ignorant of its teachings.

Question 8

Isn't Positive Thinking something good?

There are two things one must keep in mind. First, reading his Bible, the Christian knows he is made in God's image (as are all men) and therefore he is of immeasurable worth. Second, the Christian is forgiven all his sin—past, present, and future (Ephesians 1:7). He knows he is reconciled to God, justified (declared righteous by God), and is guaranteed a place in heaven (Romans 5:9-11; 1 Peter. 1:3-5). He knows God loves him because Christ died for him, and he has innumerable promises of God for comfort and encouragement in difficult times (Romans 8:28-39). Therefore, of all men on the earth, it is the Christian who should be most secure and confident. It is only the Christian who has a logical basis for being so positive.

The problem with CPT is that it often exchanges these great theological truths[47] (which alone give a logical basis for true self-worth) for nonbiblical beliefs. For example, a Christian who knows God's promises can approach the world with a positive outlook. He is positive rather than negative in his attitude because of what God has provided. On the other hand, in CPT, when a man generates a positive attitude 1) some say he forces God to act on his behalf; 2) others teach he unleashes powers to manipulate reality on his behalf; 3) still others teach he unleashes powers God has put in all of us that will bring us success or power.

The issue is not just a positive outlook on life, but whether or not that positive outlook is based on God and biblical truth or on humanistic wishful thinking mixed with some alleged power. For Positive Thinking to be of value, it must be based on what is really true and not on lies or fantasies.

40

Why Are
the Teachings
of Christian Positive
Thinkers False?

Question 9

What is "Possibility Thinking"?

"Possibility Thinking" is Robert Schuller's Christian form of Positive Thinking. He says, "I call it *possibility thinking*. Others call it faith."[48] In essence, he stresses developing Possibility Thinking by never verbalizing negative emotions. He also stresses conditioning the subconscious mind by programming positive thoughts into the conscious mind.[49] He apparently believes the conscious mind can be trained emotionally and neurologically (chemically) by Positive Thinking.[50] To Schuller, faith in oneself and self-esteem is vital to success. He believes that in each one of us there resides an inner reservoir of divinely implanted creative potential which we can draw upon. For example, he says, "Begin by believing that you possess latent gifts of creativity. You will respect, trust, and admire your own thoughts" and "let the Creative Mind of the universe inspire you." "Fill your life with the God Spirit and all kinds of power [will] break forth."[51]

One aspect of Robert Schuller's philosophy is called PTM or Possibility Thinking Meditation. In PTM he encourages Christians to use deep relaxation and meditation to enter the "alpha state."[52] He admits this method of meditation is similar to that taught by Eastern practitioners.[53] He is wrong in teaching that Transcendental Meditation, for example, is not religious or anti-Christian. It is both (see coauthor Weldon's book *The Transcendental Explosion* for documentation).[54] He is also wrong in teaching that the mantras with the "M" sound will help clear your mind from the distractions in the world.[55] Maharishi Mahesh Yogi himself has said the TM mantras are spiritual vehicles involving or invoking Hindu spirits or deities, which the Bible would identify as evil spirits or "demons."[56] Robert Schuller is also wrong in stating, "It is important to remember that meditation in any form is the harnessing, by human beings, of God's divine laws."[57] In fact, we have studied most major meditation systems in the world today and discovered they are not divine as he claims, but to the contrary they are clearly Eastern or occultic. They are used for occultic purposes, such as developing psychic powers or helping one realize one is God.[58] In essence, Schuller's "Christian" Possibility Thinking Meditation is a form of meditation which should be rejected by the church—not accepted by it or practiced as a means of spiritual growth.

Question 10

Has modern psychology influenced the religious views of Robert Schuller?

Modern psychology *has* influenced the religious views of Robert Schuller. He states that 1) "Christian theology has failed to accommodate" modern psychology; and 2) that Christian theology has failed to "apply [the] proven insights" of psychology to human behavior. Therefore, he believes what is needed is a "reformation of theology" along psychological lines.[59] Consider a few examples from his book *Self-Esteem: the New Reformation* (Waco, Texas: Word, 1982; citations are by page number).

Sin is redefined

Robert Schuller teaches "sin is any act or thought that robs myself or another human being of his or her self-esteem" (p. 14). Thus, "the core of sin is a lack of self-esteem" (p. 98). The Bible teaches something altogether different. Sin is transgression against God and His law, not against oneself (1 John 3:4). David said, "Against Thee, Thee only, I have sinned" (Psalm 51:4). Robert Schuller teaches: "Do not fear pride. The easiest job God has is to humble us. God's almost impossible task is to keep us believing every hour of every day how great we are as His sons and daughters on Planet Earth" (p. 57). The Bible teaches "God opposes the proud, but gives grace to the humble" and "pride goes before destruction" (James 4:6 NIV; Proverbs 16:18 NIV).

Salvation is redefined

Robert Schuller teaches "to be born again means that we must be changed from a negative to a positive self-image..." (p. 68). He teaches "pursuing possibility thinking is the way of the cross. Make no mistake about that.... The cross sanctifies the ego trip" (p. 75). He means that the hardships we experience will keep our self-esteem in check just like the cross Jesus died upon was God's method to keep Jesus' self-esteem in check. Does Schuller mean to say that Jesus didn't have a perfect humanity and required the humility of the cross to keep His self-esteem in check? The proper answer to that question is no. Jesus was in all points tempted as we are, yet without sin.

In contrast to Schuller's definition of the new birth given above, the Bible teaches that salvation is repentance from sin (and self) and faith in Christ for forgiveness of sins (Acts 26:18). As a result of being "born again," a true Christian will surrender his life to God and deny his own way. Thus, the Bible teaches that the way of the cross is self-denial, not Possibility Thinking (Matthew 16:24,25).

Unbelief is redefined

Robert Schuller teaches unbelief "is really a profoundly deep sense of unworthiness" (p. 15). Here, unbelief about man's value is one thing. But let's be clear. Unbelief in the Bible is mainly referring to man's rejection of God's gift of salvation, that is, belief in His Son Jesus Christ (John 3:36). This is what Schuller does not mention. In fact, where in the Bible does God ever mention that unbelief is man not thinking he has value? Where does the Bible say unbelief is a profoundly deep sense of unworthiness?

Hell is redefined

Robert Schuller teaches, "And what is 'hell'? It is the loss of pride that naturally follows separation from God. . . . The person is in hell when he has lost his self-esteem" (pp. 14,15). The Bible, however, teaches that hell is a real place of eternal torment, black darkness, and weeping and gnashing of teeth, not a state of mind (Matthew 25:46; Revelation 20:10-15; Matthew 13:42).

Evangelism is redefined

Robert Schuller teaches, "I do not think anything has been done in the name of Christ and under the banner of Christianity that has proven more destructive to human personality, and hence counter-productive to the evangelism enterprise, than the often crude, uncouth and un-Christian strategy of attempting to make people aware of their lost and sinful condition."[60] He also teaches "for the church to address the unchurched with a theocentric [God-centered] attitude is to invite failure in mission" (p. 12). The Bible, however, teaches that unless people are aware of their "lost and sinful condition" before a holy God (a "theocentric" attitude), they will never be saved (Romans 10:13-15). Schuller is wrong. Jesus said, "And repentance and forgiveness of sins will be preached in his name to all nations" (Luke 24:47 NIV).

Sanctification is redefined

Robert Schuller states, "God's ultimate objective is to turn you and me into self-confident persons" (p. 80). The Bible teaches God's ultimate purpose is to conform us to the image of Christ (Romans 8:29). In conclusion, the above views of Robert Schuller are not biblical and should not be accepted by the Christian church.

Question 11

Is Oral Roberts' "Seed-Faith" principle biblical?

To answer this we must first explain Roberts' "seed-faith" principle. It is a combination of elements of Positive Thinking psychology, "positive confession" based on divine "laws," and a "gospel" stressing "prosperity" or health and wealth.[61] Roberts believes that his "seed-faith" principle is something which Jesus Himself revealed to him. Roberts calls it a "blessing-pact covenant."[62] He claims this is "God's way of doing things through His Son Jesus Christ . . . and then through His followers, for the meeting of all our needs. . . ."[63] Roberts teaches that the first principle of "seed-faith" is that God is our Source of total supply. His second principle is giving, e.g., money. Giving is "the seed of faith itself" and this "seed" can then be directed by the giver to perform miracles. His third principle is to expect a miracle. Why? Roberts says it is because this is "God's way of doing things . . . [and it is] based on eternal laws . . . laws so exact and perfect they always work for you."[64]

Here is one of Roberts' illustrations of how giving money is the seed that produces miracles. In January of 1985 Oral Roberts sent out a letter informing his supporters that they could send for his "33 Predictions for You in 1985." These predictions were allegedly based on Roberts' exercising his "gift of prophecy" for them. The many recipients of his letter were instructed to expect "creative miracles" and money. The reader was urged to send a "seed-faith gift" which would help him get a "hundredfold return." But there was a catch. Roberts said, "If you neglect to pay attention to what He [God] is especially saying to you, then Satan will take advantage and hit you with bad things and you will wish that 1985 had never come."[65] What could you have concluded from these statements if you didn't want to send any seed-faith money?

Even Roberts' former daughter-in-law, Patti Roberts, now questions her involvement in Roberts' ministry. Besides guilt over the excessive wealth the Roberts' enjoyed, she noted "the seed-faith" theology that Roberts had developed "bothered me a great deal because I saw that, when taken to extremes, it reduced God to a sugardaddy. If you wanted His blessings and His love, you paid Him off. Over and over again we heard Oral say, 'Give out of your need.' I began to question the motivation that kind of giving implied. Were we giving to God out of our love and gratitude to Him or were we bartering with Him? . . . I believed we were appealing to their sense of greed or desperation. . . . I had a very difficult time distinguishing between the [Roman Catholic] selling of indulgences and the concept of seed-faith. . . ."[66] Patti Roberts felt Oral Roberts was a manipulative fund-raiser and she also had a problem with his priorities—the principles of seed-faith were given on every TV show, yet the gospel itself was rarely given.[67]

Our problems with Roberts' seed-faith principles are: First, the conversations Roberts had with Jesus are suspect. If Jesus actually intended these principles for all believers, then why didn't He put them in the Bible instead of waiting until Oral Roberts arrived on the scene in the 20th century? Has the Christian church from the time of Christ and the apostles to the present been left without these divine principles? If so, how did the church manage?

Remember, Jesus supposedly told Roberts the following four things. First, "I have come to remind men of this eternal law of sowing and reaping, or of giving and receiving."[68] Second, Roberts claimed "Jesus" told him that his principle of seed-faith was the deeper meaning of Matthew 17:20 ("If you have faith as a mustard seed...").[69] Third, Jesus included Galatians 6:7 ("Whatever a man sows, this he will also reap") as part of these principles.[70] Fourth, he explained that "Saint Paul stated the New Testament or New Covenant is based on seed-faith."[71]

But let's stop for a moment. Could Jesus have said these things? Is this what Paul meant? Paul did not even mention seed-faith, let alone say the New Testament is based on it. And according to the writer of Hebrews, the New Covenant is based on the Person and work of Christ Himself (Hebrews 9:15), not the principles of seed-faith giving, which will produce miracles for any giver.

Also, the Jesus that spoke to Roberts was mistaken about his "deeper meanings" in Scripture. This is serious, because often known cultists use "deeper meanings" to prove their unbiblical teachings or heresy in the same way.[72] The meaning of New Testament words can always be determined by checking a dictionary and by reading them in context. Before one applies Scripture, one must first determine its true meaning. And the one true meaning of Matthew 17:20 and Galatians 6:7 is *not* Oral Roberts' "seed-faith" interpretation, as any good commentary will show. The same can be said about the false interpretation of Galatians 6:9 stated by Roberts' "Jesus" ("Let us not become weary in doing good" NIV).[73] This is simply not a reference to seed-faith.

If we accept Roberts' claim of Jesus' additions or corrections to Scripture here, where do we draw the line? One may accept this teaching as a teaching of Oral Roberts. However, if one accepts the Bible as an authority, one cannot accept Roberts' statements as the teachings of Jesus Christ. Who, then, is really speaking to Oral Roberts? It is such a crucial question to determine who is speaking to Roberts that we present another illustration.

Jesus supposedly told Roberts that when the Bible records His statement, "It is more blessed to give than to receive" (found in Acts 20:35), that His actual words do not convey His true meaning. Jesus revealed to Roberts that, "I meant it is more *productive* to give than to receive."[74] Here we must ask, would the Jesus Christ of the Scriptures, who is the same yesterday, today, and forever and who "never changes" (Hebrews 1:12; 13:8; Malachi 3:6), be someone who would shift the meaning away from what Scripture actually records? Would the Jesus Christ of Scripture change His mind? If so, how many other verses require Jesus to give new interpretations to make them accurate? What does this do to the verbal inspiration of the Bible? The fact is that the Greek word for "blessed" (*makarion*) means "blessed," "fortunate," or "happy"—it does not mean "productive."[75] Does Roberts expect us to believe that Jesus Himself has completely changed the emphasis of His original meaning from the *joy* of giving to the *utility* of giving? The biblical Jesus said, "Freely you received, freely give" (Matthew 10:8). To lead men to expect an automatic financial return of a hundredfold simply because they gave their money is to corrupt the very purpose and nature of giving. To our way of thinking, this leads to old-fashioned selfishness; moreover, one wonders how many people have "given to get" and ended up in financial difficulty or ruin. If God does not work this way, and these seed-faith principles are really not biblical, then those who trust in them will find constant disappointment and question God's truth and loyalty.

Question 12

What is the "health and wealth" gospel?

The "health and wealth" gospel teaches that the human mind and tongue contain a "power." When a person speaks expressing his faith in supposedly divine laws, his positive thoughts and his positive verbal expression (such as, "I am healed of my heart attack") are supposed to produce a "divine force" that will heal, produce wealth, and influence the environment. According to the "health and wealth" teachers, God automatically responds and accomplishes what we command when we positively confess our needs and desires. The nonbiblical part of this teaching is that God is obligated to do what we decide. We are in charge, not God. Charles Capps and other "faith" teachers clearly state, "Words are the most powerful thing in the universe."[76]

The teachings and emphases in this movement vary, but in general there are at least five major tenets of the "health and wealth" or "faith" gospel.

1. Perfect divine healing was made available to all believers through the death of Christ. A person's healing is limited only because of his insufficient faith to receive it.[77]

2. It is God's desire that all believers prosper—financially, physically, and spiritually.[78]

3. A person must "claim" his health and wealth. He can do this immediately by believing he already has it and by positively confessing these conditions, even though all outward appearances seem to be different. When sense perceptions do seem to contradict health and wealth beliefs (such as when a person is not healed of his heart attack), our senses must be rejected and a person must live by "faith." The reason given is as follows: The mind is so powerful that "negative confession"

is just as potent a force as positive confession and therefore can become a destructive force.[79]

4. "Health and wealth" teachers often insist one must experience the "baptism in the Holy Spirit" which is usually evidenced by speaking in tongues.[80]

5. Many "health and wealth" teachers rely on "angelic" contact. They receive guidance and in turn command angels to do their will! "Angels" appear to be responsible for directing the ministries of several of the leading "health and wealth" teachers.[81]

"Health and wealth" or "faith" teachers often claim divine visions, divine inspiration, or divine interpretations of Scripture passages which give their teachings absolute authority. This is an especially serious claim and Christians need to examine it carefully.

Question 13

Do the "health and wealth" teachers claim their message is based on direct counsel from God?

Many of the leaders in this movement claim that God, Jesus, or angels appeared to them and taught them these ideas. But we must ask, "Are these revelations biblical if they condone actions that are unbiblical or foolhardy?" In fact, the supposedly divine visions, revelations, prophecies, and interpretations are often so false or unbiblical that one wonders if these visions are from their own mind or worse, from the devil. Time and again in almost all of the writings of the faith teachers we find superficial or false interpretations of the Bible, misapplication, or serious errors of logic.[82] This means that the "health and wealth" or "faith" teachers are in serious trouble. To start with, the Bible says that God is not the author of confusion or error (1 Corinthians 14:33; John 3:33; 17:17).

For example, "Jesus" told Charles Capps, "I have told my people they can have *what they say*, and they are *saying what they have*."[83] Does that make sense? Does it even sound like Jesus? Capps also states, "The Spirit of God spoke to me concerning confessing the Word of God aloud: where you can hear yourself saying it. He said, 'It is a scientific application of the wisdom of God to the psychological make-up of man.' "[84] Again, does this sound like something the Spirit of God would say?

Another example is Kenneth Copeland's "Jesus," who supposedly told him one must "believe that your words [Copeland's or any other Christian's] have power, and the things you say will come to pass. The result is that you can have whatever you say when you believe."[85] Does any Christian really believe Jesus said that in light of the Bible?

Still another example of one of these faith teachers claiming God spoke directly to him is Robert Tilton. He states, "The Spirit of the Lord has given me this [prosperity message] to share with you."[86]

Or Kenneth Hagin, who said, "The Lord spoke to me and said, 'Don't pray for money anymore. You have authority through my name to claim prosperity.' "[87] Kenneth Hagin promotes E. W. Kenyon's unbiblical and sometimes illogical text, *The Wonderful Name of Jesus*, by saying, "It is revelation knowledge. It is the Word of God."[88]

In Jerry Savelle's prosperity series we are told, "The revelation knowledge in this set was given to Brother Savelle *supernaturally by God*" (emphasis added).[89] Savelle himself tells us, "I was just sitting there, minding my own business . . . when suddenly the Lord appeared unto me. When he appeared, he said these words to me: 'Son, my people are in financial famine [in *America*??!] and I'm giving you the assignment to tell them how to get out.' Then He began to reveal to me the keys to deliverance."[90]

In summary you can see all these men claim direct counsel from God. But is this really true? The appearances of Jesus and angels, the words they spoke to these men—these do not sound like the biblical Jesus or the angels that speak for God in the Bible. God or Jesus would never encourage teachings that are unbiblical, unbalanced or illogical, or which could bring spiritual confusion or ruin into the lives of those who live by them.

If these visions and appearances are real and not inflated self-delusions, then they can only result from Satan appearing as an "angel of light" (2 Corinthians 11:14). It is the devil (and certainly not the above teachers) who desires to distort the Word, encourages spiritual excesses and illogical thinking, and brings difficulties or spiritual destruction into the lives of Christian people. (See our next question.)

Question 14

What are some illustrations proving the errors of Positive Confession?

Consider the following illustrations of Positive Confession belief. As you read them, ask yourself, "Would God reveal such teachings to His people for their welfare? Are these formulas or words found in the Bible? Are they based on trusting God or upon presumption? Are they reflecting the life and teachings of Jesus? Do they make sense, or are they irrational? Are they wise or foolish—or could they be dangerous?"

E. W. Kenyon

". . . When God imparts to us His nature, there comes with it all the attributes of [God] Himself. They are undeveloped but they are there lying latent in our human spirits."[91]

Kenneth Hagin

"Give what you *can't* afford."[92]

"God wants his children to . . . wear the best clothing. He wants them to drive the best cars, and he wants them to have the best of everything . . . just claim what you need."[93]

"Too few people today know that they can write their own ticket with God."[94]

Kenneth Copeland

"As a born again believer, you have the same spiritual capacity Jesus has."[95]

"Believers are not to be led by logic. We are not even to be led by *good sense*. . . . The ministry of Jesus was never governed by logic or reason."[96]

Charles Capps

"He [God] said, [to Capps] . . . I am not the one causing your problems. *You are under an attack of the evil one* and *I can't do anything about it*. You have bound me by the [negative] words of your mouth" (second emphasis added).[97]

"We have said, 'Oh, it looks like the wicked prosper.' Well, we said they were, that is one reason they are prospering."[98]

"In fact, I am convinced the only thing you can't have here on earth is the glorified body. You can have the kingdom [of heaven] and the benefits of it right here on earth."[99]

Robert Tilton

"[re: John 15:7] Jesus didn't put any limits on this. . . . You are wall-to-wall Jesus . . . the miraculous should be commonplace in every church . . . He [Jesus] was talking about demanding your rights and having restored back to you what the devil stole from man in the fall!"[100]

Paul Yonggi Cho

Dr. Cho pastors the world's largest church (600,000 members) and is one of the less extreme Positive Confession teachers. He claims God spoke to him and revealed his [Cho's] teachings, yet Cho teaches Christians a "law" of faith involving "incubating our subconscious" through visions, visualization (mental imaging directed toward a specific goal), and dreams.[101] According to Cho, our subconscious is our spirit and our spirit is linked to the fourth dimension, the spiritual world. Because the spiritual world is always forming and shaping the physical world, and because we are linked in our subconscious to the spiritual world, we have power to shape it, therefore also shaping this world.[102] Physical reality may be altered in accordance with the visualized desires. By picturing what we desire inwardly in our subconscious mind, we somehow enter and/or manipulate "the fourth dimension" (the spiritual world) in order to actually permit God to produce miracles for us in the physical realm, the third dimension. Thus, "what becomes pregnant in your heart and mind is going to come out in your circumstances. . . . Your word actually goes out and creates [reality]. God spoke and the whole world came into being. Your word is the material which the Holy Spirit uses to create."[103] Cho believes that genuine pagan miracles are part of the potential of the human spirit because by exploring and influencing the fourth dimension (the spiritual world) even unbelievers can change third dimensional reality since it is controlled by the fourth dimension. But unbelievers use the fourth dimension in an evil manner by Satan while believers use it by God and so "can have all the more dominion over circumstances."[104] The fourth dimension principle is the key to Cho's ministry and apart from manipulating the fourth dimension he believes we cannot be effective in evangelism.[105] Visualization is also held to be the secret of victorious praying. It is our mental power to alter the fourth dimension which produces effective ministry here on the earth.[106]

But did God ever teach these things in the Bible? Does God require of us a certain state of consciousness—or simple trust in Him? Do we have power over the creation or does God? Is visualization really the "deeper language" of the Holy Spirit?[107]

Cho has recently and correctly rebuked the American faith teachers for excesses and imbalance.[108] But in his book *Salvation, Health and Prosperity* he teaches that apart from knowing the truths of the threefold blessings of salvation, of health, and of prosperity as outlined in his book, we cannot properly understand the Bible. "Like blind men touching an elephant to comprehend its shape, those of us who read the Bible without this foundation cannot understand or interpret fully what we read."[109] He also teaches, "If Jesus is with us now, the same things which He did 2,000 years ago should appear daily in our lives. By this we can judge whether Jesus' sayings are true or not: if these things are not happening among us, the promises of Jesus have become empty words to us."[110]

Question 15

What logical consequences may follow those holding to a strict "health and wealth" gospel of Positive Confession?

Without the slightest hesitation we may say the health and wealth gospel of Positive Confession is a blight upon the church. It is a perverted gospel of cheap grace which reverses biblical values, produces fear and spiritual bondage or intimidation, holds out false promises, leads to false guilt and despair, in some people produces apostasy and in others results in personal tragedy.

For example, like Christian Scientists and Jehovah's Witnesses, some Christian parents accepting the faith teachings have let their own children die by withholding from them life-saving medication.[111] They have done this under the mistaken assumption that, in spite of evidence to the contrary, their child was divinely healed. Thus, to continue to give them medication would supposedly be a "lack of faith" in their divine healing. Does anyone need to be told that teachings which cause the deaths of others are not godly, no matter how godly they sound?

The problems and destruction already wrought by these teachings is considerable,[112] yet thousands of churches and millions of Christians continue to support these "ministries," while godly ministries suffer for lack of support. Why would some Christians continue to supply the very funds without which these ministries could not exist? Put simply, because they are promised what they want to believe. "For the time will come when they will not endure sound doctrine; but wanting to have their ears tickled, they will accumulate for themselves teachers in accordance to their own desires; and will turn away their ears from the truth, and will turn aside to myths" (2 Timothy 4:3,4).

41

Where Does the Bible Show That the Faith Teachers Are Wrong?

Question 16

Does the Bible really teach the "health and wealth" gospel of Positive Confession?

Positive Confession is not a biblical teaching and the scores of Scriptures used to support it are typically misinterpreted or misapplied. For example, in reference to Matthew 6:20 ("Lay up for yourselves treasures in heaven") we are told by Kenneth Copeland, "Jesus was not referring to when we get to heaven. He was teaching about God providing for us *now*."[113] Anyone who wishes to prove to himself how extensively such verses are taken out of context need only examine Positive Confession literature and then consult standard commentaries to prove their errors.

For example, 3 John 2 (that you may "prosper and be in good health") is a personal wish for Gaius, not a divine promise of money and health to every Christian. It was a standard greeting in antiquity and had nothing to do with money. How many of us would really end up "spiritually prospering" if we were rich? Likewise, Mark 10:29,30 ("the hundredfold return") is not literal but figurative since believers do not literally receive a hundred mothers and sisters and brothers as well. So why is it used literally only in reference to money? Also, Jesus says this is true only of those who have nothing now because they have left everything behind to follow Him, which is not true of most Christians. It is especially not true of the prosperity teachers who are generally very wealthy.

Instead of having the poor people send them money, if the hundredfold return is really true, why don't the prosperity teachers (such as Robert Tilton, Kenneth Hagin, Kenneth Copeland, Oral Roberts, Jerry Savelle, Charles Capps, etc.) send $100 to every person on their mailing list in order to get billions of dollars in return? But it doesn't seem to work that way.

The Bible, far from stressing the spiritual benefits of wealth, encourages us to be content with what we have. We are told, "Keep your lives free from the love of money and be content with what you have . . ." (Hebrews 13:5 NIV). In fact, it often warns about the perils of money. Jesus said, "You cannot serve both God and Money" (Matthew 6:24, cf. James 5:1-5). The apostle Paul "suffered the loss of all things" (Philippians 3:7,8). He was content to live in poverty, hunger, and to suffer need (Philippians 4:12). He also noted that most Christians were "poor" and "had nothing" (2 Corinthians 6:10). Paul said not wealth but "the sufferings of Christ are ours in abundance" (2 Corinthians 1:5). If these "prosperity" teachings really came from the Lord, why did the Lord Himself and His disciples end up poor and martyred?

Paul also said that greed was the same as idolatry (Colossians 3:5). The Bible teaches we are to place God's will first in our lives—not self-will. We cannot "write our own ticket with God." "And this is the confidence which we have before Him, that, if we ask anything *according to His will*, He hears us" (1 John 5:14, emphasis added). Even Jesus Himself, when He prayed for deliverance before the cross did not demand of God but said, "*If* you are willing . . ." (Luke 22:42 NIV, emphasis added). James taught that it was "arrogant" and "evil" to presume of the Lord. He said, "Instead you ought to say, '*If the Lord wills*, we shall live and also do this or that.' But as it is, you boast in your arrogance; all such boasting is evil" (James 4:15-16, emphasis added). Paul himself said, "If the Lord wills . . ." (1 Corinthians 4:19). He referred to those who supposed that godliness (religion) was a means of financial gain and he said, "For we have brought nothing into the world, so we cannot take anything out of it either. And if we have food and covering, with these we shall be content. But those who want to get rich fall into temptation and a snare and many foolish and harmful desires which plunge men into ruin and destruction. For the love of money is a root of all sorts of evil, and some by longing for it have wandered away from the faith, and pierced themselves with many a pang" (1 Timothy 6:7-10).

Question 17

Do Isaiah 53:4,5; Matthew 8:17; and 1 Peter 2:24 really teach that by the atonement of Christ we may claim physical healing?

Almost all the "faith" teachers and "faith" healers claim these verses *prove* that the atonement of Christ guarantees our physical healing. On the basis of these verses they teach that all we need do is "claim" our healing by "faith." But we disagree. The Bible and these verses do not teach that Jesus died so that all may "claim" divine healing now.

Let us examine these Scriptures to see if they are properly applied by the faith teachers. In Isaiah 53:4,5 it states, "Surely our griefs [the Hebrew word implies both physical sickness and the emotional and physical consequence of sinful behavior; cf. Ecclesiastes 6:2] He Himself bore, and our sorrows [or pains] He carried.... He was pierced through for our transgressions, He was crushed for our iniquities [sins]. ... By His scourging we are healed." In response to this verse we may state the following:

In English or Hebrew the word "heal" (in Hebrew, *napha*) may refer to either physical or spiritual healing. The context must determine if one or both meanings are meant. For example, in 1 Peter 2:24, Peter refers to spiritual healing (quoting the Greek Septuagint), and in Matthew 8:17, Matthew refers to physical healing (quoting the Hebrew Masoretic text).

Peter says of our spiritual healing, "He himself bore our sins in His body on the cross, that we might die to sin and live to righteousness, for by His wounds you were healed" (1 Peter 2:24). Peter stresses the spiritual aspect of the atonement of Christ. Nothing is said here about a believer's physical healing. On the other hand, Matthew does refer to physical healing. He says that Jesus physically healed those who were brought to Him, "in order that what was spoken of through Isaiah the prophet might be fulfilled, saying, 'He himself took our infirmities, and carried away our diseases'" (Matthew 8:17).

The question is, Do these verses teach that perfect physical healing is available to every believer if, by faith, he simply "claims" it? Since it is beyond doubt that Peter stresses the spiritual healing of the atonement, we only need concern ourselves with Isaiah and Matthew. We accept that Matthew applied Isaiah 53 to Christ's earthly ministry of healing. But we cannot accept that this example of Christ's ministry gives anyone permission to teach that all Christians should therefore claim their healing immediately. Why? Because in other scriptural accounts Jesus and the apostles did not teach this (Matthew 25:37-40; 1 Timothy 5:23; 2 Timothy 4:20). We do not believe that the apostle Matthew contradicted Jesus or the other apostles in this matter of the application of Jesus' healing ministry.

Also, Matthew is only pointing out that when Jesus was healing, this was another sign of fulfilled Messianic prophecy. In healing many people physically, Matthew realized Jesus fulfilled Isaiah's prophecy, thereby proving His rightful claim to be the Jewish Messiah (see Luke 7:19-23).

It's possible that Matthew's words could lead one to speculate that Jesus now provided healing for everyone, but such speculation can be seen to be false because Matthew himself specifically quotes Jesus against such a view.

In Matthew 25:37-40 Jesus Himself states He personally "expected" sickness and difficulty among believers ("[those] brothers of Mine," verse 40). Also the writings of the apostle Paul reject such speculation as can be seen in 1 Timothy 5:23 and 2 Timothy 4:20. For those who are following faith teachers and still not convinced, we submit the following additional evidence from Scripture proving this view is wrong. Many biblical persons who had great faith were sick and in spite of their great faith not healed, such as Elisha, Daniel, Lazarus, Dorcas, Paul, Timothy, Epaphroditus and Trophimus (2 Kings 13:14; Daniel 8:27; John 11:2; Acts 9:36,37; Galatians 4:13-15; Philippians 2:25-30; 1 Timothy 5:23; 2 Timothy 4:20).

False Teaching in the Church

When we read the scriptural letters of the apostle Paul, we find that physical pain and sickness were indications of God's gracious *work* in his life (2 Corinthians 12:7-10). Paul also boasted in his physical weakness, not in his power (2 Corinthians 11:24-30).

Our Lord Jesus Himself said that even physical blindness and death could be to God's glory (John 9:1-3; 11:4).

Job said, "Shall we indeed accept good from God and not accept adversity?" (Job 2:10). These verses and many others indicate that God does not expect every Christian to be healed simply because they "claim" it.

Faith teachers are wrong on another point. They emphasize healing results are based on the amount of faith a person possesses. They claim everyone who exercises *enough* faith will be healed. They teach doubt *always* blocks God's divine power from healing.

But Mark 9:24 proves that their teaching is wrong. We know that Jesus mercifully healed even the son of a man who admitted to unbelief. In addition, the faith teachers claim that even negative thinking will block God's power. But this is also wrong since the Bible tells us David prayed in a state of acute depression, and yet his prayer was answered (2 Samuel 15:30-32; 17:1-23).

There is another reason why the "faith" teachers are wrong about a Christian "claiming" his healing. There is not *one* Scripture verse that teaches us to "claim our healing." No Scripture anywhere tells us that Christ's death provides physical healing now merely on the basis of our claiming it.

For example, concerning salvation, the Bible repeatedly promises "whosoever will may come." But concerning claiming one's healing, there is not a single "whosoever will claim" promise in all of Scripture.

If we listen closely to the apostle James, we find he stresses the calling of elders and their "prayer of faith" for healing. He does not mention an individual "claiming" his healing (James 5:1-5).

Those who say we must "claim our healing" should also examine the biblical use of the word "claim." In the New International Version, there are about 45 uses of the word "claim." Again, not one of them refers to healing. But many times the word is used in a negative sense where men claim things that are false, things that they have no right to claim.

For example, the Bible says, "If we claim to be without sin, we deceive ourselves and the truth is not in us" (1 John 1:8 NIV). "If we claim to have fellowship with Him and yet walk in the darkness, we lie and do not live by the truth" (1 John 1:6 NIV). "They claim to know God, but by their actions they deny Him" (Titus 1:16). "You have tested those who claim to be apostles but are not and have found them false" (Revelation 2:2). God tells Job "who has a claim against me that I must pay?" God says that no one has any claims upon him (Job 41:11). Yet God does ask us to call to Him; He promises to consider our requests, but tells us to leave the result with His sovereignty. Still, nowhere does God ask believers to automatically claim their healing from Him.

Contrary to the teaching of the faith healers, the Bible states:

1. If a person is sick, he can call for the elders of the church to come and pray for his recovery. James states, "Is any one of you sick? He should call the elders of the church to pray over him and anoint him with oil in the name of the Lord. And the prayer offered in faith will make the sick person well; the Lord will raise him up . . ." (James 5:14,15 NIV).

James says two things. First, you should call the church elders for your sickness. Second, you do not claim healing by yourself.

2. According to James, if a sick person is not healed, it would seem to be due to the lack of faith on the part of those who prayed for him, not the lack of faith of the sick person.

3. There can be no doubt that God asks His people to individually bring their needs and requests to Him (Philippians 4:6).

4. Even though we are encouraged to make our requests to God, He does not guarantee to fulfill our requests; He may still decline them. In such cases God says that His grace is sufficient and that even in our weakness God's power can be made manifest. Paul states: "Three times I pleaded with the Lord to take it [a thorn in his flesh] away from me. But he said to me, 'my grace is sufficient for you, for My power is made perfect in weakness.' Therefore I will boast all the more gladly about my weaknesses, so that Christ's power may rest on me. That is why, for Christ's sake, I delight in weaknesses, in insults, in hardships, in persecutions, in difficulties. For when I am weak, then I am strong" (2 Corinthians 12:8-10 NIV).

Peter said "Let those who suffer according to the will of God entrust their souls to a faithful Creator in doing what is right" (1 Peter 4:19). Christ's death will one day perfectly heal every believer both spiritually and physically (Romans 8:30). Until that day, we must accept that each of us will, in some way, suffer from the natural consequences of living in a fallen and imperfect, sin-cursed world.

However, this does not imply passivity or resignation. David prayed fervently for God to spare his son, for he said, "Who knows, the Lord may be gracious to me, that the child may live" (2 Samuel 12:22).

All of these verses should be included in our thinking concerning healing.

Question 18

What other views do Christian Positive Thinkers hold?

It is our view that these faith teachers have misread the plain meaning of the words of the Bible in their context. We will now prove that these faith teachers have misread the plain meaning of the Bible.

Gloria Copeland, Kenneth's wife, is a good example of how these faith teachers not only misinterpret but occasionally deliberately delete the words of Scripture that deny their view. For example, Gloria Copeland quotes Daniel 3:17,18, which is the story of Shadrach, Meshach, and Abednego speaking to Nebuchadnezzar before they were to be thrown into the fiery furnace. These servants of God told the king, "[God] will deliver us out of your hand, O king. But even if He does not, let it be known to you, O king, that we are not going to serve your gods. . . ." Here these men tell us they believe it could be God's will *not* to save them, but they will still trust and serve Him just like Job who said, "Though He slay me, I will hope in Him" (Job 13:15). But this goes against the theology of Gloria and Kenneth Copeland and the other faith teachers who say Christians should overcome in every circumstance. Since the words of Daniel 3:18 didn't fit her view, Gloria deleted them. When she quotes Daniel 3:18, the phrase "but even if he does not" is deleted.[114] She actually cites a Scripture in her defense that were it quoted in full would disprove the point she is making.

Consider the following areas that the "faith" teaching has distorted.

God

Faith teaching has distorted both the sovereignty of God and the will of God. God is no longer sovereign if He can be forced to act on the basis of what men do. Thus, in some cases His will can be replaced with man's will. In essence, what God's sovereignty lacks, human sovereignty supplies. Not even God will interfere with the believer's "divine rights."[115]

Jesus and the Atonement

Faith teachers have redefined the mission of Jesus Christ to incorporate their beliefs. For example, John Osteen teaches, "Did Jesus die for your prosperity? Yes."[116] Robert Tilton teaches, "Jesus came to deliver man from failure, and to cause him to be once again a success. . . . Christians who do not believe in divine healing, who do not believe in prosperity—they do not believe in what was atoned for at Calvary."[117] Charles Capps teaches Jesus came and died for us to get Adam's power back to rule and dominate the earth.[118] Gloria Copeland states, *"You have a title deed to prosperity. Jesus bought and paid for your prosperity just like He bought and paid for your healing and your salvation. . . . This prosperity already belongs to you."*[119] Here you can see these four faith teachers are saying that because of Jesus' death on the cross, He bought and paid for your healing or success *now*. Their conclusion is that (even if it takes time to manifest) you can claim success or immediate healing by faith.

This is wrong. Why? First, because it is another misinterpretation of Scripture; namely, Isaiah 53:4,5 and Matthew 8:17 which we have just commented upon.

Secondly, it is wrong because the Bible plainly teaches that the average Christian, the apostles, and Jesus Himself did not teach or hold this view. Physical healing is not the instantaneous gift assumed by the faith teachers. For example, the apostle Paul himself had a physical infirmity or bodily illness he simply had to live with (Galatians 4:13,14; 2 Corinthians 12:7-10). Paul told Timothy to take a little wine "for the sake of your stomach [problems] *and* your frequent ailments" (1 Timothy 5:23, emphasis added). Paul said, "Trophimus I left sick at Miletus" (2 Timothy 4:20). Paul never once told Timothy or anyone else to "claim your healing." He clearly did not believe the death of Christ healed believers' illnesses. Otherwise, how did such great men of faith as Paul and Timothy fail to know and teach that Christ died for our illnesses? Nor was Christ's death a guarantee of success in this life. To the contrary, by worldly standards Paul, the apostles, and the early church were highly unsuccessful (Romans 8:35,36; 1 Corinthians 4:9-17; 15:30; 2 Corinthians 4:7-11). These godly men accepted the fact of their sicknesses and tribulations. Even Jesus also accepted and expected sickness and hardship among believers (Matthew 25:44; Luke 21:17). In fact, Jesus Himself taught that sickness could be to the glory of God. Jesus said of Lazarus, "This sickness is not unto death, but for the glory of God, that the Son of God may be glorified by it" (John 11:4).

Faith

In prosperity thinking, faith is similar to the power of magic. John Osteen states, ". . . faith reaches out into the invisible area. It creates the physical realm out of invisible truths."[120] Here the faith teachers ascribe faith as a force to be exerted upon God forcing Him to act in our behalf. But this is wrong. The Bible nowhere states that God relinquished His will to each one of our wills. He knows that would be chaos.

Man

In Positive Confession, man is considered "a god" or a godlike being.[121] In some ways man is the ruler of God, who is his servant. Like the genie in the bottle, man decides what he wants and then commands or demands God to do his bidding. In some teachings, man comes close to deification. Robert Tilton no longer always thanks God for his food; rather, *he* speaks to the food and pronounces a divine blessing upon it.[122]

As Charles Capps states, "Natural men [can] become supernatural"; "Supernatural men that never existed before . . . [and are] no longer totally subject to their natural ability."[123] For example, the miracles done in the book of Acts were not done solely and directly by God but by believers exercising their supernatural powers and influence on others. In Acts 14:8-10 when Paul told the cripple "stand up," the result is that "spirit words received into his [the cripple's] spirit released spiritual power in his physical body. This creative ability of spirit words formed in his spirit and produced physical results."[124]

Nevertheless, the idea that men are gods is denied in the Bible. Even Paul, a man of great faith, never considered himself a god. For example, in

Acts 14:11-15 God healed a man through Paul. "And when the multitudes saw what Paul had done, they raised their voice, saying in the Lycaonian language, 'The gods have become like men and have come down to us.' " But Paul's response was not, "Yes, we are gods and you, too, can learn how to exercise the miracle power of faith." The Scripture says, "But when the apostles, Barnabas and Paul, heard of it, they tore their robes and rushed out into the crowd, crying out and saying, 'Men, why are you doing these things? We are also men of the same nature as you, and preach the gospel to you in order that you should turn from these vain things to a living God. . . .' "

Angels

The prosperity movement is overly obsessed with the demonic and has distorted biblical teaching on the angels. Many teach that physical illness results from demons. They do this even though Scripture clearly distinguishes physical illness and demon possession (Luke 8:2). Frances Hunter, for example, teaches "a demon takes a look at a woman and says, 'Wow, I think I will lay a little cancer on her . . .' so he jumps into her body . . . and before long, the woman discovers she has cancer of the breast. . . ."[125] Not only does such teaching produce fear of demons in people, it offers a cruel and false hope of a "quick fix" by "exorcism" to those with serious illness. The logical conclusion of reading some of the faith teachers' instruction has been to lead many people into fear and bondage to demons. An example of how far this can be taken is seen by Don Basham's teaching that postnasal drip, fingernail biting, and arthritis of the knees, among many other normal ailments, can be caused by demons.[126]

Conclusion

Many people have been influenced by false teaching in the church. Some of them have been hurt because these teachings have not worked. For example, the "Faith Assembly" of Hobart Freeman has resulted in the deaths of almost 100 people because his people were told that seeking medical help was supposedly a "sin" and a "denial of faith."[127] Instead they were to claim their healing. But sadly in claiming their healing the sick all died one by one. This is just one of the terrible consequences of false teaching. Not surprisingly, many of the other people felt betrayed and felt like giving up on Christianity.

Jesus stated that false teachings will lead to harmful consequences (Matthew 7:17; 24:11,12; Acts 20:30), but He said there is a way out. Those who truly live by His Word, the Bible, can stand the pressures of life because their lives are built on His Word, the solid rock (Matthew 7:24-27). He promises those who know and obey His Word that they will be set free (John 8:31,32). Have you neglected to learn and obey His Word, relying instead on spiritual experiences and unbiblical faith?

If you are hurt, feel betrayed, and feel like giving up on Christianity, what can you do? First, you should not continue to fellowship where false teachings are taught (Romans 16:17). Diligently search until you find a church where the Word of God is honored and taught accurately, a church where the pastor challenges you to study the Scripture for yourself. A good church will have a pastor who loves teaching God's Word and will show it by the number of hours he spends in personal Bible study. Often he will have increased his knowledge of the Word of God by years of study in an evangelical seminary. He will let you know when there are differences of interpretation on a particularly difficult verse and will challenge you to think through these verses in context on your own.

Second, you must learn the Word of God yourself. Paul encouraged Timothy to continue in the things he had "learned and become convinced of" (2 Timothy 3:14). Every Christian needs to take the time and effort to learn the basic doctrines of the Bible so they will know when it is being "wrongly divided" (misinterpreted—2 Timothy 2:15). To start, it would be very helpful for you to have a high-quality study Bible like the NIV Study Bible, the New King James in the Thompson Chain Reference edition, or a study edition of the New American Standard Bible.

You should also visit a Christian bookstore and purchase some good commentaries and resource tools for personal study.[128]

Once you start to learn the Bible, try and help those still caught in false teachings. The Bible encourages us to reprove those following false teachings "severely that they may be sound in the faith" (Titus 1:13).

Finally, we ask some of you to consider whether you have substituted a technique of salvation for salvation itself. Is what you consider "faith" in God really nothing more than a mechanical technique to manipulate God for your own ends? In John 6:26,27 Jesus said that many people followed Him only to satisfy their own hunger. He said that instead of following Him for "food that perishes" they should rather seek the "food that endures to eternal life." Jesus went on to explain that His food that endures to eternal life was not anything material that we can possess; rather it is true knowledge of God himself (John 6:33-35).

Augustine spoke of this true knowledge in his commentary on Psalm 73. There he said that God Himself should be our only treasure and reward. To seek anything but God alone is not to seek for God. Does this depict you? Do you love God for Himself alone or for what you can get out of Him?

If you admit you are guilty of the above, God wants you to repent and ask for His forgiveness. If you have doubts about your relationship with God as to your salvation, you may wish to pray the following prayer:

> Dear Lord Jesus, I am sorry for my sin of ignoring You and putting my own selfish desires first. I now happily receive You as my Lord and Savior, Your gift of forgiveness of my sins, and Your gift of eternal life which You promised to those who would ask You (1 John 2:25; Ephesians 1:7). As a result of Your coming into my life, help me to know Your Word and turn away from false teaching (2 Peter 3:18; Romans 16:17). Thank You for hearing my prayer and making me a Christian (John 1:12).

CULT WATCH

APPENDICES

RECOMMENDED READING

NOTES

Appendix A

The Reorganized Church
of Latter-day Saints

The Reorganized Church of Latter-day Saints (RLDS) has a different history, and some different teachings than the Utah church. It rejects polygamy and the fact that Smith taught and practiced it; it also rejects the early Mormon Adam-God theory and baptism for the dead. But it is still Mormon and still an anti-Christian, unbiblical religion. The Reorganized Church denies the Trinity, accepts continuous revelation, the two Mormon priesthoods, and has a humanistic anthropology.[1] We may note the following:

1. It denies biblical authority.

The Reorganized Church accepts Smith's *Inspired Version* of the Bible which contains numerous errors and additions to the Word of God. It also believes in the Book of Mormon and *Doctrine and Covenants* as revealed scripture.

2. It rejects salvation by grace.

As with Utah Mormons, the Reorganized Church accepts the necessity of baptism, good works, and personal righteousness for salvation.

3. It is exclusive.

The Reorganized Church teaches that it alone is the true church of God and that Christianity is an apostate religion.

4. It denies the Trinity.

Walter Martin observes that the Trinity is "redefined so that there is genuine confusion as to the nature of God, the functions of the members of the Trinity, and the place and application of the Trinity in historic Christian theology."[2]

Although some Christians think that the Reorganized Church is not Mormon and that it is a Christian denomination, no religion that denies biblical authority, the nature of God, and the true means of salvation can possibly be a Christian religion.

Appendix B

"I haven't read any translation that is as diabolical and as damnable as the JW so-called translation. . . . They (the Society) hate Jesus Christ."

Dr. Julius Mantey; "Distortions
of the New Testament"
Tape "T-2" available from
Witness, Inc., Clayton, CA
(See note 120)

Letter dated July 11, 1974
(See note 65, pp. 11-12.)

Watchtower Bible & Tract Society
117 Adams St.
Brooklyn, New York 11201

Dear Sirs:

I have a copy of your letter addressed to CARIS in Santa Ana, California, and I am writing to express my disagreement with statements made in that letter, as well as in quotations you have made from the Dana-Mantey Greek Grammar.

1) Your statement: "their work allows for the rendering found in the *Kingdom Interlinear Translation of the Greek Scriptures* [KIT] at John 1:1." There is no statement in our grammar that was ever meant to imply that "a god" was a permissible translation in John 1:1.

A. We had no "rule" to argue in support of the trinity.

B. Neither did we state that we did have such intention. We were simply delineating the facts inherent in biblical language.

C. Your quotation from p. 148 (3) was in a paragraph under the heading: "*With the Subject in a Copulative Sentence.*" Two examples occur there to illustrate that "the article points out the subject in these examples." But we made no statement in this paragraph about the predicate except that "as it stands the other persons of the trinity may be implied in *theos.*" And isn't that the opposite of what your translation "a god" infers? You quoted me out of context. On pages 139 and 149 (VI) in our grammar we stated: "without the article *theos* signifies divine essence . . . *theos en ho logos* emphasizes Christ's participation in the essence of the divine nature." Our interpretation is in agreement with that in NEB and the TEV: "What God was, the Word was"; and with that of Barclay: "The nature of the Word was the same as the nature of God," which you quoted in your letter to CARIS.

2) Since Colwell's and Harner's articles in *JBL [Journal of Biblical Literature]*, especially that of Harner, it is neither scholarly nor reasonable to translate John 1:1 "The Word was a god." Word order has made obsolete and incorrect such a rendering.

3) Your quotation of Colwell's rule is inadequate because it quotes only a part of his findings. You did not quote this strong assertion: "A predicate nominative which precedes the verb cannot be translated as an indefinite or a 'qualitative' noun solely because of the absence of the article."

4) Prof. Harner, vol. 92:1 (1973) in *JBL,* has gone beyond Colwell's research and has discovered that anarthrous predicate nouns preceding the verb function primarily to

express the nature or character of the subject. He found this true in 53 passages in the Gospel of John and 8 in the Gospel of Mark. Both scholars wrote that when indefiniteness was intended the gospel writers regularly placed the predicate noun after the verb, and both Colwell and Harner have stated that *theos* in John 1:1 is not indefinite and should not be translated "a god." Watchtower writers appear to be the only ones advocating such a translation now. The evidence appears to be 99% against them.

5) Your statement in your letter that the sacred text itself should guide one and "not just someone's rule book." We agree with you. But our study proves that Jehovah's Witnesses do the opposite of that whenever the "sacred text" differs with their heretical beliefs. For example the translation of *kolasis* as *cutting off* when punishment is the only meaning cited in the lexicons for it. The mistranslation of *ego eimi* as "I have been" in John 8:58. The addition of "for all time" in Heb. 9:27 when nothing in the Greek New Testament supports it. The attempt to belittle Christ by mistranslating *arche tes ktiseos* "beginning of the creation" when he is magnified as "the creator of all things" (John 1:2) and as "equal with God" (Phil. 2:6) before he humbled himself and lived in a human body here on earth. Your quotation of "The Father is greater than I am" (John 14:28) to prove that Jesus was not equal to God overlooks the fact stated in Phil. 2:6-8, when Jesus said that he was still in his voluntary state of humiliation. That state ended when he ascended to heaven. Why the attempt to deliberately deceive people by mispunctuation by placing a comma after "today" in Luke 23:43 when in the Greek, Latin, German and all English translations except yours, *even in the Greek in your KIT*, the comma occurs after *lego* (I say)—"Today you will be with me in Paradise." Also 2 Cor. 5:8, "to be out of the body and at home with the Lord." These passages teach that the redeemed go immediately to heaven after death, which does not agree with your teachings that death ends all life until the resurrection. Cf. Ps. 23:6 and Heb. 1:10.

The above are only a few examples of Watchtower mistranslations and perversions of God's Word.

In view of the preceding facts, especially because you have been quoting me out of context, I herewith request you not to quote the *Manual Grammar of the Greek New Testament* again, which you have been doing for 24 years. Also that you not quote it or me in any of your publications from this time on.

Also that you publicly and immediately apologize in the Watchtower magazine, since my words had no relevance to the absence of the article before *theos* in John 1:1. And please write to CARIS and state that you misused and misquoted my "rule."

On the page before the *Preface* in the grammar are these words: "All rights reserved—no part of this book may be reproduced in any form without permission in writing from the publisher."

If you have such permission, please send me a photocopy of it.

If you do not heed these requests you will suffer the consequences.

Regretfully yours,

Julius R. Mantey

(Note: A slight grammatical correction was made in this letter.)

Appendix C

How does one find deliverance
from the occult?

The following material is intended as a brief, general guide to help pastors and concerned Christians assist those who are suffering from occult involvement. Because our research has primarily been from the literature, the authors have had comparatively little personal counseling experience with the occultly oppressed. However, Dr. Kurt Koch has had 40 years of counseling the occultly oppressed and his book *Occult Bondage and Deliverance* is highly recommended. Most of the following material is adapted from pages 85-131. For a complete treatment, the reader should consult the full text and other relevant literature.* We should emphasize that we are primarily dealing with occult oppression; further, we are listing steps that have proven effective, not rules to be slavishly followed.

First and foremost, a correct diagnosis is essential; for example, mental illness must not be mistaken for occult bondage (pp. 133-190). A person must truly be experiencing demonic oppression from real occult activities; otherwise, misdiagnosis can cause serious problems. How does one determine if a person is suffering from occult oppression? Obviously, the counselor must be aware of the causes (e.g., occult activity) and symptoms (e.g., see pp. 283-87) of this malady and also be involved in some type of counseling of the person in question. Accurate information is essential to accurate diagnosis.*

Second, it must be recognized that a genuine battle is in progress. A very real enemy has been encountered, and this enemy is dangerous. But it must also be realized that Christ has obtained victory. Because a real battle has been engaged, Dr. Koch cautions that people are not to rush into the area of occult counseling. Rather, they should seriously look to God for a leading in this area. Spiritual maturity and spiritual insight are vital:

> Without a commission from God, a Christian should not venture too far into the area of the demonic and the occult. There are certain rules that have to be obeyed. . . . People with a sensitive nervous system or maybe with an occult oppression of their own should never attempt to do any work in this field. Recent converts and young women should also refrain from this type of work (pp. 87,88).

Third, we need to recognize God's sovereignty. Christ and Christ alone is the source of deliverance. The usual procedures—psychology, ritual, hypnosis, meditation, etc. are useless and may compound the problem. Further, God does not require our "often complicated counseling procedures." However, deliverance without any counseling at all is rare. Also, full deliverance may take weeks, months, or sometimes years; or by God's sovereignty it may require only a few hours.

Fourth, all paraphernalia of occultism must be destroyed (Acts 19:19). "Magical books and occult objects carry with them a hidden ban. Anyone not prepared to rid himself of this ban will be unable to free himself from the influence of the powers of darkness" (p. 90). "Yet even the little figures made out of precious stones which often originate from heathen temples have to be destroyed if the owner finds he cannot free himself from his occult oppression" (p. 92).

---

* e.g., Kurt Koch, *Christian Counseling and Occultism*; John W. Montgomery, ed., *Demon Possession*; C. Fred Dickason, *Demon Possession and the Christian*.

In addition, all occult contacts and friendship must be broken and not even gifts from occultists should be accepted. In the difficult case of a saved person living with parents who are occultists, it may even be necessary for them to secure other living arrangements. If such persons are attacked by demons and/or their spiritual life declines while they are praying for their parents, Dr. Koch advises "the children of spiritistic families not to pray for their parents at all if they are still engaged in occult practices" (p. 93). "Inexperienced counselors, however, will be unable to appreciate decisions of this nature, for they will have little knowledge of the terrible attacks which can be leveled by the powers of darkness" (p. 94). Perhaps prayer could resume after their Christian life has been sufficiently strengthened or the conditions change. Apparently, because the powers of darkness may attempt to strike back without mercy, such advice needs to be heeded more than one would expect. Battles should be undertaken only when the participant is fully equipped.

Fifth, deliverance from the power of the occult requires complete surrender to Christ on the part of both counselor and counselee. Our first responsibility must be to Christ and our relationship to Him. We cannot help others in so difficult an area until we ourselves are securely grounded as Christians. Every person who really wants to be delivered from the hold of the occult must be prepared to commit his life entirely to Christ. Further, "When a person is delivered from a state of occult subjection, he must withhold nothing in his life from the Lord. These areas which are not surrendered to his Lord will soon be occupied again by the enemy" (p. 126). If Jesus Christ Himself is truly our Lord, then He will protect us from the lordship of others; but if our commitment is halfhearted, we may be asking for unnecessary problems.

Sixth, the occultly oppressed person must acknowledge and confess his participation in occult activity as sin, because such practices are sinful before God and require confession (Deuteronomy 18:9-12; 1 John 1:9). In addition, confession must be voluntary, or it is worthless. The purpose of confession is to bring into the light that which is occult (hidden, secret). Dr. Koch advises that confession be made in the presence of a mature Christian counselor. "Occultly oppressed people should, in fact, make an open confession of every single hidden thing in their lives in order to remove the very last foothold of the enemy" (p. 98). Further, "The confession of a subjected person should not only cover the occult, but also every other department of his life" (p. 99). In other words, nothing should be allowed to build up or develop which may give the devil an opportunity (Ephesians 4:27).

In addition, a prayer renouncing everything occult is important:

> In the normal way the thing that follows confession is absolution—the promise of the forgiveness of sins. In my counseling work among the occultly oppressed, however, I have found that I have had to abandon this sequence since the subjected person usually finds it impossible to grasp the fact that his sins have been forgiven. He is simply unable to believe. A barrier seems to lie in his way. I, therefore, always encourage the victim of occultism to pray a prayer of renunciation first of all (p. 99).

Further:

> In counseling the occultly oppressed, a prayer of renunciation is, however, of great significance. The question is "why?" Every sin connected with sorcery is basically a contract with the powers of darkness. By means of sorcery, the arch enemy of mankind gains the right of ownership over a person's life. The same is true even if it is only the sins of a person's parents or grandparents that are involved. The devil is well acquainted with the second commandment which ends, "for I the Lord your God am a jealous God, visiting the iniquity of the fathers upon the children to the third and the fourth generation of those who hate me" (p. 100).

The powers of darkness may continue to claim their "right" of ownership although often the descendants of occult practitioners remain unaware of the fact, perhaps since they have had no contact with sorcery themselves. Nevertheless, immediately after a person in this situation is converted, Satan makes his claim felt.

> In praying a prayer of renunciation, a person cancels Satan's right both officially and judicially. The counselor and any other Christian brothers present act as witnesses to this annulment of ownership. Although many modern theologians ridicule the whole idea, the devil is in earnest. Hundreds of examples could be quoted to show just how seriously he takes the matter. When the occult oppression is minimal, the person who has made his confession will have little difficulty in repeating a prayer of renunciation after the counselor. The prayer can take the form "In the name of Jesus I renounce all the works of the devil together with the occult practices of my forefathers, and I subscribe myself to the Lord Jesus Christ, my Lord and Savior, both now and forever. In the name of the Father, and of the Son, and of the Holy Spirit. Amen."
> The prayer is not a formula. Every time it is prayed it can take a different form. In severe cases of oppression, on the other hand, a number of complications can arise when it comes to praying a prayer of renunciation (pp. 100-101).

For example, the person may be unable to bring his hands together to pray, or his lips or vocal chords may be unusable. He may fall into a trance when it comes to renouncing the devil. "What can we do in circumstances like this? One can either command the evil powers in the name of Jesus, or else call some other Christian brothers to join in praying for the subjected person" (p. 101). Renunciation may be followed by a remarkable change for the better. Nevertheless, "not everyone experiences such elated feeling after deliverance but the change of ownership is still valid no matter how one feels. . . . Renunciation is particularly important in cases where natives are converted out of a heathen background" (p. 102).

Seventh, it is vital to assure the individual that in Christ his sins have been forgiven, and that he now possesses an eternal salvation that cannot be taken from him. No matter how bad a person's sins may have been, they have been forgiven. Appropriate Scripture passages may be read such as John 5:24; 6:47; 19:30; Romans 5:20; Galatians 1:4; Ephesians 1:7,13,14; Colossians 1:14; 1 Peter 1:3-5,18,19; Hebrews 1:3; Isaiah 53:4-7; 1 Peter 2:24; 1 John 1:7-9; etc.

It is also to be recognized that counseling should involve teamwork. The support of other Christians, church elders, etc., is important. As Koch explains, "Counseling the occultly oppressed is really a matter of teamwork. The individual counselor is far too weak to take upon his own shoulders all the problems he meets" (p. 105). For example, people with occult subjection will often suffer their first attacks after they seek to follow Christ and serve Him. In other words, the battle often does not begin until a person receives Christ. Further, "there is a possibility that if a person puts too much of his own effort into trying to help the demonically oppressed that a transference will take place" (p. 105).

Eighth, prayer is another critical aspect of counseling. People who are delivered from the occult are still vulnerable even after being delivered. It is thus vital that a small group of Christians take upon themselves to continue to pray for them and care for them after their conversion. Sometimes Christians do not recognize how important this is. Many converted occultists have struggled tremendously because they could find no one in the church to help them.

> If necessary, the group need only consist of two Christians. They should meet together at least twice or three times a week for perhaps a

quarter of an hour at a time in order to pray for the oppressed person. The best thing is for the subjected person to be present as well, yet this is not absolutely necessary. Neither is it essential for the oppressed person to have made an open confession before all the members of the group. This need only have been made before the counselor at the very start (p. 106).

When a person is delivered from occult oppression, it is also crucial that he grow as a Christian. He must really lay hold of the four basic spiritual elements comprising Christian discipleship: study in the Word of God, Christian fellowship, continuous prayer, and communion. Further, the new Christian must be grounded in the study of basic Christian doctrine and Christian evidences.

Sometimes those counseling the occultly oppressed will discover that the demons have returned into a person's life, and at this point, it seems the battle is greater than before.

> Very often one finds that the powers of darkness return when a person is liberated in a Christian atmosphere, and then has to return and live in an atmosphere of occultism and sorcery. This is frequently what happens in the case of young people from spiritistic families who are converted when away from home and later have to return and live in the demonically affected house of their parents (p. 119).
>
> People who have been delivered from occult oppression and yet have to return again and live in an occult or spiritistic atmosphere never find real and lasting peace. I usually find that I have to advise young people stemming from such environments, "Stay away from your parents—or from your uncle, aunt, or relation—if they are not prepared to forsake their occult practices and interests." This advice is not always appreciated, however. In fact, on occasions I have been actually rebuked for having given a person advice of this nature. Finally, repeating what we have just been saying, anyone who fails to act on all that the Bible says for our protection will live in continuous danger of falling victim once more to the influence of the exorcised spirits (p. 120).

No matter how difficult or how wearying the counseling of occultly oppressed people may be, the truth remains that the victory is won because of what Christ has accomplished (p. 124). Counselors need to believe God's promises and act in faith even in what seem to be hopeless situations. No situation is finally hopeless, for with God all things are possible. Further, the mere fact that a battle continues to rage is not evidence that the battle will be lost. Many times in biblical history and throughout church history, spiritual battles have been undertaken which have required great endurance, perseverance, patience, and faith. In the area of counseling, those with occult oppression, and in the area of biblical demonology in general, there is much that is not known and, therefore, our reliance on Christ is all the more important. Finally:

> It is also very important to remember when counseling and caring for the occultly oppressed that this kind of counsel will only thrive in the right spiritual atmosphere. One must never look upon a person and his needs as just another "case," or as some new "sensation" or "object of investigation." True deliverance will never be forthcoming in an unscriptural atmosphere—even if the battle for the oppressed person appears to be very dramatic. We must be on our guard against every kind of excess, and above all against exhibitionism. Let us therefore be: Sound in our faith, Sober in our thoughts, Honest and scriptural in our attitude (p. 128).

Appendix D

Who was Nostradamus and
was he a genuine "prophet"?

Nostradamus was a sixteenth-century astrologer, Kabbalist, and medical doctor having something of a celebrity status in twentieth-century America. Whatever Nostradamus was, he was not a genuine prophet. First, it is an undeniable fact that Nostradamus gave numerous false prophecies. Second, his prophecies are so vague and unclear that they have no single "correct" interpretation. This is proven by the fact that all his modern "interpreters" contradict one another. Nostradamus himself confessed that the vague manner in which he wrote his "prophecies" was so that "they could not possibly be understood until they were interpreted after the event and by it."[1] Further, not a single genuine prophecy of Nostradamus has ever been proved. One hundred thirty-one specific prophecies (having names, dates, or places) have been identified in Nostradamus' writings, and all 131 turned out to be false. His deliberately obscure style of writing has caused critics to allege that he was little more than a con man. Even the occult encyclopedia *Man, Myth and Magic* observes the possibility "that Nostradamus composed them [the 'prophecies'] with tongue in cheek, as he was well aware that there is an enduring market for prophecies and particularly for veiled ones."[2] Consider the following characteristic prophecy by Nostradamus:

> Scythe by the Pond, in conjunction with Sagittarius at the high point of its ascendant—disease, famine, death by soldiery—the century/age draws near its renewal (Century I, verse 16).[3]

The possible "interpretations" of this passage are endless. The point is that deliberately enigmatic "prophecies" have no proper interpretation, and therefore no proper fulfillment. People merely read into these prophecies many different "revelations," none of which are correct. All this is why one critic observes,

> The marvelous prophecies of Michel de Nostredame, upon sober examination, turn out to be a tiresome collection of vague, punning, seemingly badly constructed verses written by a man who, in his other work, showed that he was quite capable of writing correct, concise French. The printers served him poorly, committing errors that make his centuries [prophecies composed of four line verses arranged in groups of 100] even more delightful to those who find obscurity profound. . . . From a distance of more than 400 years, I fancy I can hear a bearded Frenchman laughing at the naivety of his 20th century dupes.[4]

Recommended Reading

Mormonism

Jerald and Sandra Tanner, *The Changing World of Mormonism*, Moody, 1986.

D. Michael Quinn, *Early Mormonism and the Magic World View*, Signature Books, 1987.

The reader desiring invaluable resource materials on Mormonism should write for the annotated book list from Utah Lighthouse Ministry, Box 1884, Salt Lake City, UT.

Jehovah's Witnesses

General Critical Treatments

(Starred texts contain photo documentation of rare documents.)

*Duane Magnani, *Point/Counterpoint: A Refutation of the Jehovah's Witnesses' Book Reasoning From the Scriptures, Vol. 1: False Prophets*, Witness, Inc., carries a large number of important critical works on the Witnesses in the area of history, doctrine, and morality. See their publications list.

Danger at Your Door, Witness, Inc., 1987.

Dialogue With Jehovah's Witnesses, Witness, Inc., 1987.

Raymond Franz, *Crisis of Conscience*, Commentary Press, 1983.

Edmond Gruss, *Apostles of Denial: An Examination and Exposé of the History, Doctrines and Claims of the Jehovah's Witnesses*, Baker.

On The New World Translation

Robert H. Countess, *The Jehovah's Witnesses' New Testament: A Critical Analysis of the New World Translation of the Christian Greek Scriptures*, Presbyterian & Reformed, 1987.

Prophecy

Edmond Gruss, *The Jehovah's Witnesses and Prophetic Speculation*, Presbyterian & Reformed, 1972.

Carl Olof Jonsson, *The Gentile Times Reconsidered*, Good News Defenders, 1983.

On the Doctrine of the Trinity

E. Calvin Beisner, *God in Three Persons*, Tyndale House, 1984.

Edward Henry Bickersteth, *The Trinity*, Kregel, 1976.

Robert Glenn Gromacki, *The Virgin Birth: Doctrine of Deity*, Thomas Nelson, 1974. [Reprinted as *The Virgin Birth of Christ*, Baker, 1981.]

The Masonic Lodge

Transcript, "Christianity and the Masonic Lodge: Are They Compatible?" (guests: William Mankin, Dr. Walter Martin), The John Ankerberg Evangelistic Association, 1985.

Committee on Secret Societies of the Ninth General Assembly of the Orthodox Presbyterian Church (meeting at Rochester, NY, June 2-5, 1942), *Christ or the Lodge?* Great Commission Publications, n.d.

Stephen Knight, *The Brotherhood: The Explosive Exposé of the Secret World of the Freemasons*, Grenada Publishing, Ltd./Panther Books, 1983.

Transcript, "The Masonic Lodge: What Goes on Behind Closed Doors?" (guests: Jack Harris, William Mankin, Dr. Walter Martin, Paul Pantzer), The John Ankerberg Evangelistic Association, 1986.

Shildes Johnson, *Is Masonry a Religion?*, Institute for Contemporary Christianity, 1978.

Martin L. Wagner, *Freemasonry: An Interpretation*, nd., np. (distributed by Missionary Service and Supply, Route 2, Columbiana, OH 44408).

J. W. Acker, *Strange Altars: A Scriptural Appraisal of the Lodge*, Concordia, 1959.

Alva J. McClain, *Freemasonry and Christianity*, BMH Books, 1977.

Alphonse Cerza, *Let There Be Light: A Study in Anti Masonry*, The Masonic Service Association, 1983.

"Checking It Out" (Masonic Affiliates), *News & Views*, August 1986, The John Ankerberg Evangelistic Association.

The New Age Movement

Ankerberg, John and Weldon, John, *Can You Trust Your Doctor? The Complete Guide to New Age Medicine and It's Threat to Your Family*, Wolgemuth & Hyatt, 1991.

Groothuis, Douglas R., *Unmasking the New Age*, InterVarsity, 1986.

Hoyt, Karen, and the Spiritual Counterfeits Project, *The New Age Rage*, Fleming H. Revell, 1987.

North, Gary, *Unholy Spirits*, Dominion Press, 1987.

Reisser, Paul and Teri, and Weldon, John, *New Age Medicine*, Global, 1988.

Hunt, Dave, *The Seduction of Christianity*, Harvest House, 1986.

Brooke, Tal, *Riders of the Cosmic Circuit*, Lion, 1986.

Schaeffer, Francis, *True Spirituality*, Tyndale, 1976.

Weldon, John, and Levitt, Zola, *Psychic Healing: An Exposé of an Occult Phenomenon*, Moody Press, 1982.

Wilson, Clifford, and Weldon, John, *Psychic Forces and Occult Shock*, Global, 1986.

Geisler, Norman L., and Watkins, William D., *Perspectives: Understanding and Evaluating Today's World Views*, Here's Life Publishers, 1984.

Raschke, Carl A., *The Interruption of Eternity: Modern Gnosticism and the Origins of the New Religious Consciousness*, Nelson-Hall, 1980.

Stalker, Douglas, and Glymour, Clark, *Examining Holistic Medicine*, Prometheus Books, 1985.

Elliott, Miller, "Channeling: Spiritistic Revelations for the New Age," part one, *Christian Research Journal*, Fall, 1987, pp. 9-15.

Pement, Eric, *The 1988 Directory of Cult Research Organizations*, Cornerstone Press, 1988.

Wilson, Clifford, and Weldon, John, *Close Encounters: A Better Explanation*, Master Books, 1978.

"For Additional Information"

The following organizations can provide additional information on a variety of New Age philosophies, religions, trends, and phenomena:

1. Spiritual Counterfeits Project, P.O. Box 4308, Berkeley, CA 94704. Their order number is 415-540-0300. Their information hotline number is 415-540-5767 (Monday and Wednesday 10 A.M.—2 P.M. Pacific Time).

2. Christian Research Institute, P.O. Box 500, San Juan Capistrano, CA 92693-0500; phone number 714-855-9926.

3. The Skeptical Inquirer (Committee for the Scientific Investigation of the Claims of the Paranormal, 3159 Bailey Avenue, Buffalo, NY 14215-0229.) Although this organization writes from a largely rationalistic perspective, its journal contains a number of helpful critiques and analyses of many New Age phenomena and philosophies.

Spirit Guides

Gasson, Raphael, *The Challenging Counterfeit*, Logos [Bridge], 1970.

Earnest, Victor, *I Talked with Spirits*, Tyndale House, 1971.

North, Gary, *Unholy Spirits: Occultism and New Age Humanism*, Dominion Press, 1986.

Montgomery, John Warwick (ed.), *Demon Possession: A Medical, Historical, Anthropological and Theological Symposium*, Bethany Fellowship, 1976.

Unger, Merrill, *The Haunting of Bishop Pike*, Tyndale House, 1971.

————, *Biblical Demonology: A Study of the Spiritual Forces Behind the Present World Unrest*, Scripture Press, 1971.

————, *Demons in the World Today*, Tyndale House, 1972.

Irvine, Doreen, *Freed from Witchcraft*, Thomas Nelson, 1973.

Gruss, Edmond, *The Ouija Board: Doorway to the Occult*, Moody, 1975.

Keene, M. Lamar, *The Psychic Mafia: The True and Shocking Confessions of a Famous Medium*, St. Martin's Press, 1976.

Koch, Kurt, and Lechler, Alfred, *Occult Bondage and Deliverance*, Kregel, 1970.

Michaelsen, Johanna, *The Beautiful Side of Evil*, Harvest House, 1982.

Weldon, John, and Levitt, Zola, *Psychic Healing: An Exposé of an Occult Phenomenon*, Moody Press, 1982.

Nevius, John L., *Demon Possession*, Kregel, 1970, rpt.

SCP Journal, *Eckankar: A Hard Look at a New Religion*, Spiritual Counterfeits Project, Berkeley, CA, 1979.

SCP Journal, *Spiritism: The Medium and the Message, Spiritual Counterfeits Project*, Berkeley, CA, 1987.

Miller, Elliott, "Channeling: Spiritistic Revelation for the New Age," *Christian Research Journal*, Fall, 1987.

Goodrick-Clarke, Nicholas, *The Occult Roots of Naziism: the Ariosophists of Austria and Germany 1890-1935*, The Aquarian Press [England], 1985.

Angebert, Jean-Michel, *The Occult and the Third Reich*, McGraw-Hill, 1975.

Alexander, Ben, *Out From Darkness*, College Press, 1986.

Astrology

Strohmer, Charles, *What Your Horoscope Doesn't Tell You*, Tyndale, 1988.

Ankerberg, John, Weldon, John, *Astrology: Do the Heavens Rule Our Destiny*, Harvest House, 1989.

Bjornstad, James and Johnson, Shildes, *Stars, Signs and Salvation In The Age of Aquarius*, Bethany, 1971.

Bayly, Joseph, *What About Horoscopes?*, David C. Cook, 1970.

Adam, Ben, *Astrology: The Ancient Conspiracy*, Bethany, 1963.

Culver, R. B. and Ianna, P. A., *The Gemini Syndrome: A Scientific Evaluation of Astrology*, Prometheus Books, 1984. Retitled, *Astrology: True or False: A Scientific Evaluation*, 1988.

Jerome, Lawrence E., *Astrology Disproved*, Prometheus Books, 1977.

Gauquelin, Michael, *The Scientific Basis of Astrology: Myth or Reality*, Stein and Day, 1973.

Gauquelin, Michael, *Dreams and Illusions of Astrology*, Prometheus Books, 1979.

Gallant, Roy, *Astrology: Sense or Nonsense*, Doubleday, 1974.

Dean, Geoffrey, "Does Astrology Need to Be True?" Parts 1 & 2, *The Skeptical Inquirer*, Vol. 9, Numbers 2 & 3.

Bok, Bart J. and Jerome, Lawrence E., *Objections to Astrology*, Prometheus Books, 1975.

Montgomery, John Warwick, *Principalities and Powers*, Bethany, 1973.

Peterson, William J., *Astrology and the Bible*, Victor Books, 1972.

Neher, A., *The Psychology of Transcendence*, Prentice Hall, 1980.

Morey, Robert A., *Horoscopes and the Christian*, Bethany, 1981.

Snyder, John, *Reincarnation or Resurrection?*, Moody, 1984.

Ankerberg, John and Weldon, John, *The Facts on Spirit Guides* and *The Facts on the New Age Movement*, Harvest House, 1988.

The Occult

Gary North, *Unholy Spirits: Occultism and New Age Humanism*, Dominion, 1986.

Merrill Unger, *Biblical Demonology*, Scripture Press, 1971.

Kurt Koch, *Occult Bondage and Deliverance*, Kregel, 1970.

John Warwick Montgomery, ed., *Demon Possession*, Bethany, 1976.

John Ankerberg, John Weldon, *Astrology: Do the Heavens Rule Our Destiny?*, Harvest House, 1989.

Doreen Irvine, *Freed From Witchcraft*, Nelson, 1973.

False Teaching in the Church

On True Christian Faith:

Schaeffer, Francis, *True Spirituality*, Tyndale.

Packer, J. I., *God's Words: Studies of Key Bible Themes*, InterVarsity.

Cambron, Mark, *Bible Doctrines: Beliefs That Matter*, Zondervan.

Milne, Bruce, *Know the Truth*, InterVarsity.

Critiques of Modern Psychology

Schweigerdt, Bruce, "The Gnostic Influence on Psychology: Effects of the Common Heresy," *Journal of Psychology and Theology*, Vol. 10, number 3.

Gross, Martin L., *The Psychological Society: The Impact—and the Failure—of Psychiatry, Psychotherapy, Psychoanalysis, and the Psychological Revolution*, Random House.

Bobgan, Martin and Deidre, *Psycho-Heresy*, Eastgate.

Szasz, Thomas, *The Myth of Psychotherapy*, Doubleday.

Kilpatrick, William, *Psychological Seduction: The Failure of Modern Psychology*, Nelson.

Vitz, Paul, *Psychology As Religion, the Cult of Self-Worship*, Eerdmans.

Wood, Garth, *The Myth of Neurosis: Overcoming the Illness Excuse*, Harper & Row.

Rushdoony, R. J., *Freud*, Presbyterian and Reformed.

Cosgrove, Mark, *Psychology Gone Awry: An Analysis of Psychological World Views*, Zondervan.

Kilpatrick, William Kirk, *The Emperor's New Clothes: The Naked Truths About the New Psychology*, Crossway Books.

Lasch, Christopher, *The Culture of Narcissism*, W. W. Norton and Company.

Browback, Paul, *The Dangers of Self-Love*, Moody Press.

Wallach, Michael, and Lisa Wallach, *Psychology: Sanction for Selfishness*, W. H. Freeman and Company.

Tennov, Dorothy, *Psychotherapy: The Hazardous Cure*, Abelard-Schuman.

Stuart, Richard, *Trick or Treatment: How and When Psychotherapy Fails*, Research Press.

Carl Jung

Wilson, Colin, *Lord of the Underworld: Jung and the Twentieth Century*, Wellingborough, Northamptonshire, England: the Aquarian Press.

Stern, Paul J., *C. J. Jung: The Haunted Prophet*, Dell/Delta.

Fodor, Nandor, *Freud, Jung and Occultism*, University Books.

LaDage, Alta J., *Occult Psychology: A Comparison of Jungian Psychology and the Modern Qabalah*, Llewellyn.

Hoeller, Stephan, *The Gnostic Jung and the Seven Sermons to the Dead*, Quest.

Jung, C. G., *Psychology and the Occult*, Princeton University Press.

————, *Memories, Dreams, Reflections*, Vintage.

The Integration of Psychology and Theology

Collins, Gary, *Can You Trust Psychology?*, InterVarsity.

Carter, John, D., and Bruce Narramore, *The Integration of Psychology and Theology*, Zondervan.

Fleck, J. Roland, and John D. Carter, *Psychology and Christianity: Integrative Readings*, Abingdon.

Kirwan, William T., *Biblical Concepts for Christian Counseling: A Case for Integrating Psychology and Theology*, Baker.

Farnsworth, Kirk E., *Whole-Hearted Integration*, Baker, 1985.

Related to Christian Aberrations

D.R. McConnel, *A Different Gospel, A Historical and Biblical Analysis of the Modern Faith Movement*, Hendrickson, 1988.

Johnson, Arthur, *Faith Misguided: Exposing the Dangers of Mysticism*, Moody.

Parker, Larry, *We Let Our Son Die*, Harvest House.

Eareckson, Joni, *A Step Further*, Zondervan.

Bussell, Harold, *Unholy Devotion*, Zondervan.

Barrs, Jerram, *Shepherds and Sheep*, InterVarsity.

Wells, David F., "Self-Esteem: The New Confusion: A Critical Assessment of Schuller's New Reformation," *TSF Bulletin*, November-December, 1983.

DaSilva, Antonio, "The Theology of Success Movement," *Themelios*, April, 1986.

Sarles, Ken, "A Theological Evaluation of the Prosperity Gospel," *Bibliotheca Sacra*, October-December, 1986.

Machen, Jay Greshem, *What is Faith?*, Eerdmans.

McCullough, Donald, *Back to Reality—Avoiding the Pitfalls of Positive Thinking*, InterVarsity.

DeHaan, Richard, *How to Recogonize a Good Church.*

MacArthur, John, *The Charismatics*, Zondervan.

Bulle, Florence, *God Wants You Rich and Other Enticing Doctrines*, Bethany.

Matzat, Don, *Inner Healing: Deliverance or Deception?*, Harvest House.

Mayhue, Richard, *Divine Healing Today*, Moody Press.

Matta, Judith A., *The Born-Again Jesus of the Word-Faith Teaching*, Spirit of Truth Ministries, Fullerton, California.

Hunt, Dave, and T. A. McMahon, *The Seduction of Christianity* and *America: The Sorcerer's New Apprentice—The Rise of New Age Shamanism*, Harvest House.

Magliato, Joe, *The Wall Street Gospel*, Harvest House.

Farah, Charles, *From the Pinnacle of the Temple*, Logos.

DilLavou, Bruce, "The Problems of Positive Confession," *CAI Newsletter*, Summer, 1983, pp. 6-11 (on Paul Yonggi Cho).

Martin, Walter, cassette, "The Errors of Positive Confession," Christian Research Institute.

Barron, Bruce, *The Health and Wealth Gospel: What's Going on Today in a Movement That Has Shaped the Faith of Millions?*, InterVarsity.

Onken, Brian, "The Atonement of Christ and the 'Faith' Message," *Forward* magazine, Vol. 7, No. 1, Christian Research Institute.

Gudel, Joseph, "The New Reformation? The Faulty Gospel of Robert Schuller," *Forward* magazine, Spring, 1985, Christian Research Institute.

MacArthur, John, "Questions for Robert Schuller," *Moody Monthly*, May, 1983.

McClain, Elissa, "Should the Church Apologize to Unity?," *Christian Research Journal*, Winter-Spring, 1987.

Fee, Gordon, "The Disease of the Health and Wealth Gospels," *SCP Newsletter*, Spring, 1985.

Brandt, Steven, "Is Faith a High Wire Act?," *Eternity*, July-August, 1981.

Packer, James, "Poor Health May Be the Best Remedy," *Christianity Today*, May 21, 1982.

Moore, William, "Nine Half-Truths on Healing," *Eternity*, May, 1983.

Roberts, Patti, *Ashes to Gold*, Word.

"Inner Healing Issue," Spiritual Counterfeits Project, *SCP Journal*, Vol. 4, No. 1.

Notes

Foreword

1. There are an estimated 6-7 million Mormons; 2-3 million Jehovah's Witnesses; 4-6 million Masons; 10-15 million New Agers; 10-20 million occultists and spiritists, 10-20 millions followers of astrology, and 5-10 million believers in Positive Confession.
2. See Walter Martin, Norman Klann, *The Christian Science Myth* (Grand Rapids, MI: Zondervan, 1962), pp. 151-171; Walter Martin, Norman Klann, *Jehovah of the Watchtower*, rev. (Chicago: Moody, 1974), pp. 91-104, cf. Joel S. Williams, *Ethical Issues in Compulsory Medical Treatment: A Study of Jehovah's Witnessess and Blood Transfusion*, Ph.D. dissertation (Waco, TX: Baylor University, 1987).
3. See pp. 319, 328.
4. George H. Gallup, Jr., Frank Newport, "Belief in Paranormal Phenomena Among Adult Americans," *The Skeptical Inquirer*, Winter, 1991, pp. 137-46.
5. Syndicated column for December 23, 1990.
6. *Webster's Third New International Dictionary* (unabridged) supplies the following definitions of the term "cult" or "cultic":

   > (1) religious practice: worship; (2) a system of beliefs and ritual connected with worship of a deity or a spirit, or a group of deities or spirits; (3) the rites, ceremonies and practices of a religion as the *cultus* of Roman Catholicism, involving ceremonial veneration paid to God, Virgin Mary or the saints; (4) a religion regarded as unorthodox or spurious; (5) a system for curing disease based upon dogma or principles set forth to the exclusion of scientific evidence; and (6) excessive devotion to a person, idea or thing.

   The first four definitions, at least, are applicable to the topics in this book. There are also cults that can only be defined in negative terms. Here, at least from a Christian perspective, a cult may be briefly defined as "any religious organization (not a standard world religion) 1) promoting the indoctrination ('to teach to accept the system of thought uncritically') of nonbiblical theology; 2) demanding submission to an unbiblical authoritarian structure; and 3) promoting excessive spiritual and/or psychological regulation or dependence."
   Dr. Gordon Lewis provides another definition, this time of an allegedly biblical group: "A religious group claiming to be based on Christ and the Bible, but whose characteristic teachings contradict the essentials of Christian teachings, whose standard of life contradicts the essentials of Christian ethics and whose standards of leadership contradict the standards of Christian ministerial standards.'"*
   A cult should also be distinguished from what we may term an aberrational Christian group that is more or less doctrinally sound, but contains many of the behavioral aberrations found in cults. A cult has heretical doctrines generally not found in aberrational Christian sects while aberrational Christian sects have truly regenerated individuals generally not found in cults. But even aberrational Christian groups may have elements of serious doctrinal error, such as the Positive Confession movement and the modalistic (unitarian) United Pentecostal Church.
   Nevertheless, an aberrational Christian sect is one whose doctrinal teachings are generally in accord with historic Christianity but whose standards of life or leadership are not. In aberrational Christian sects, certain unbiblical beliefs may be held in order to justify the sect's lifestyle. Such teachings are an aftereffect of aberrational practices, hence these groups may deny 1) the universal priesthood of believers; 2) full forgiveness of sins; 3) independent Bible study; 4) universal accountability (leaders should be accountable to someone); 5) the truth that ministers are servants. Members of such groups may be termed schismatic sheep and 2 Timothy 2:23-26; Titus 1:9; 3:1,2,10,11; and Romans 16:17 applied to the situation.
7. Robert F. Elwood, Jr., *Religious and Spiritual Groups in Modern America* (Englewood Cliffs, NJ: Prentice Hall, 1973), p. 12. Dr. Weldon's research into 70 of the new religions has confirmed the spiritistic influence upon modern religions and cults.
8. E.g., D. R. McConnell, *A Different Gospel: A Historical and Biblical Analysis of the Modern Faith Movement* (Peabody, MA: Hendrickson, 1988), pp. 15-29, passim; John Weldon, "Positive Confession and the Occult," parts 1 and 2, *News and Views*, June and July 1988 (Chattanooga, TN: Ankerberg Theological Research Institute).
9. Ibid.
10. Fenwicke L. Holmes, *Ernest Holmes: His Life and Times* (New York: Dodd, Mead & Co., 1970), back cover.
11. See J. I. Packer, *Knowing God and God's Words* (InterVarsity), Francis Schaeffer, *True Spirituality* (Tyndale).
12. James Dunn, "The Pentecostals" in Tim Dowley, et al., eds., *Eerdmans Handbook to the History of Christianity* (Grand Rapids, MI: Eerdmands, 1977), p. 619; John Weldon, "Monarchianism: Dynamic and Modalistic," ms.
13. See John Ankerberg, John Weldon, *The Case for Jesus the Messiah: Incredible Prophesies that Prove God Exists*; and *Do the Resurrection Accounts Conflict? and What Proof Is There that Jesus Rose from the Dead?* (Chattanooga, TN: Ankerberg Theological Research Institute, 1989 and 1990).
14. See Note 13 and C.S. Lewis, *Mere Christianity* (MacMillian), Henry Morris, *Many Infallible Proofs* (Santee, CA: Master Books, 1988), Norman Geisler and William Nix, *A General Introduction to the Bible*, rev. (Chicago: Moody, 1986), Rene Pache, *The Inspiration and Authority of Scripture* (Chicago: Moody, 1975).
15. Terry C. Muck, "Truth's Intrepid Ambassador," *Christianity Today*, November 19, 1990, p. 34.
16. See Note 13, *Do the Resurrection Accounts Conflict?* pp. 154-181.

---

* At the November 1983 Christian Research Institute Cults Conference, El Toro, CA.

Part One—Mormonism

1. See e.g., Walter Martin, *The Maze of Mormonism* (Santa Ana, CA: Vision House, 1978), pp. 16-21; Einar Anderson, *The Inside Story of Mormonism* (Grand Rapids, MI: Kregel Publications, 1974), pp. ix, 69; *Christianity Today*, Oct. 2, 1981, p. 70; *The Utah Evangel*, Nov., 1981.
2. Harry Ropp, *The Mormon Papers: Are the Mormon Scriptures Reliable?* (Downers Grove, IL: InterVarsity, 1977), pp. 13, 119.
3. Copy of letter from the Protestant Chapel Council, Navy Air Station, Alamedia, CA, to Chief of Chaplains, RADM, Alvin B. Koeneman, Office of the Chief of Navy Operations, Department of the Navy, Washington, D.C., n.d.
4. For a critical evaluation see Gordon H. Fraser, *Joseph and the Golden Plates: A Close Look at the Book of Mormon* (Eugene, OR: Gordon H. Fraser, 1978). The traditional view is that the Book of Mormon story covers North and South America. Some modern Brigham Young University (BYU) scholars accept a more limited geography and believe e.g., that the hill Cumorah was in Southern Mexico.
5. Joseph Fielding Smith, comp., *Teachings of the Prophet Joseph Smith* (Salt Lake City: Deseret Book Company, 1977), p. 350.
6. Joseph Smith, *History of the Church of Jesus Christ of Latter-day Saints*, 6 Vols. (Salt Lake City: Deseret Book Company, 1951), Vol. 5, p. 289, Vol. 6, p. 78. Introduction and notes by B. H. Roberts.
7. Joseph Smith, *History of the Church*, Vol. 6, pp. 408-09.
8. Bruce R. McConkie, *Doctrines of Salvation: Sermons and Writings of Joseph Fielding Smith*, Vol. 1 (Salt Lake City: Bookcraft, 1976), pp. 189-90.
9. Brigham Young, *Journal of Discourses*, Vol. 7, p. 289. This is a photo lithographic reprint of the original 1860 edition published in London by the Latter-day Saints' Book Depot, 30 Florence Street, Cross Street, Islington.
10. Joseph F. Smith, *Gospel Doctrine: Selections from the Sermons and Writings of Joseph F. Smith* (Salt Lake City: Deseret Book Company, 1975), p. 479; cf. p. 471.
11. See e.g., Jerald Tanner and Sandra Tanner, *The Changing World of Mormonism* (Chicago, IL: Moody Press, 1981), Chapters 4, 14, 17, 18, and pp. 587-89.
12. *Christianity Today*, Oct. 2, 1981, p. 70, citing Mormon official Robert Blackman; Walter Martin refers to 26,000 full-time missionaries in Martin, *The Maze of Mormonism*, p. 16.
13. Martin, *The Maze of Mormonism*, p. 21. *The Utah Evangel*, Mar. 1982, p. 13.
14. Ibid., pp. 16-21; cf. *Mormon Corporate Empire*.
15. Tanner and Tanner, *The Changing World of Mormonism*, pp. 148-70.
16. Joseph Smith, *The Pearl of Great Price* (Salt Lake City, UT: The Church of Jesus Christ of Latter-day Saints, 1967), "Writings of Joseph Smith," 2, p. 46.
17. Ibid., pp. 47-48.
18. Joseph Smith, *History of the Church of Jesus Christ of Latter-day Saints*, Vol. 1 (Salt Lake City, UT: Deseret Book Company, 1976), p. 8.
19. That the Christian denominations of Joseph Smith's time taught biblical doctrine is established by a study of the respective theological teaching of that period.
20. For example, demons routinely impersonate good angels, the spirits of the dead, and even Jesus Christ Himself. See Raphael Gasson, *The Challenging Counterfeit* (Plainfield, NJ: Logos, 1971) and "Spirit Guides" (Part 5) herein.
21. Joseph Smith, *History of the Church*, Vol. 1, p. 9.
22. For a critique, see Gordon H. Fraser, *What Does the Book of Mormon Teach? An examination of the Historical and Scientific Statements of The Book of Mormon* (Chicago, IL: Moody Press, 1964).
23. Walter Martin, *The Kingdom of the Cults* (Minneapolis, MN: Bethany, 1970), p. 154.
24. Joseph Smith, *History of the Church*, Vol. 1, pp. 39-48, 80.
25. See *The Doctrine and Covenants of the Church of Jesus Christ of Latter-day Saints* (Salt Lake City, UT: The Church of Jesus Christ of Latter-day Saints, 1968), pp. vi-viii for a chronological listing.
26. See Gasson, *The Challanging Counterfeit*; Victor Ernest, *I Talked With Spirits* (Wheaton, IL: Tyndale, 1971).
27. Orson Pratt, *The Seer*, Vol. 2, No. 4, Apr. 1854, in *The Seer*, (compilation, n.p., n.d.), p. 255.
28. *Doctrine and Covenants* 1:30.
29. Pratt, *The Seer*, p. 255.
30. Bruce McConkie, *Doctrinal New Testament Commentary*, Vol. 2 (Salt Lake City, UT: Bookcraft, 1976), p. 113; cf. pp. 366, 458-59, 506-07.
31. Bruce McConkie, *Mormon Doctrine*, 2nd ed. (Salt Lake City, UT: Bookcraft, 1977), p. 626.
32. Deseret Sunday School Union, *The Master's Church, Course A* (Salt Lake City, UT: Deseret Sunday School, Union, 1969), p. 6.
33. Ropp, *The Mormon Papers*, p. 119.
34. Ibid., p. 13.
35. Copy of letter from the Protestant Chapel Council, Naval Air Station, Alameda, CA, to Chief of Chaplains, RADM Alvin B. Koeneman, Office of the Chief of Naval Operations, Department of the Navy, Washington, DC, n.d.
36. Anthony Hoekema, *The Four Major Cults* (Grand Rapids, MI: Eerdmans, 1970), p. 30.
37. Gordon Fraser, *Is Mormonism Christian?* (Chicago, IL: Moody Press, 1977), p. 10.
38. Martin, *The Maze of Mormonism*, p. 45.
39. Tanner and Tanner, *The Changing World of Mormonism*, p. 559.
40. The bibliography in Tanner and Tanner, *The Changing World of Mormonism*, is representative.
41. Tanner and Tanner, *The Changing World of Mormonism*, pp. 192-203.
42. *Journal of Discourses*, Vol. 6 (Salt Lake City, UT: 1967, reprint of original, 1855 ed., Liverpool, England: F.D. Richards, publisher), p. 198.
43. *Elders Journal*, Joseph Smith, ed., Vol. 1, No. 4, pp. 59-60; from Jerald Tanner and Sandra Tanner, *Mormonism—Shadow or Reality?* (Salt Lake City, UT: Utah Lighthouse Ministry, 1972), p. 3.
44. Joseph Fielding Smith, *Teachings of the Prophet Joseph Smith*, p. 322.
45. Tanner and Tanner, *The Changing World of Mormonism*, pp. 398-416.
46. Joseph Smith, *History of the Church*, Vol. 1, p. lxxxvi.
47. Ibid.
48. *Journal of Discourses*, Vol. 8, p. 199.
49. Ibid., Vol. 8, p. 171.
50. Ibid., Vol. 6, p. 167.

51. Ibid., Vol. 6, p. 163; Vol. 13, p. 225.
52. *Pamphlets by Orson Pratt*, p. 38; cited in Jerald Tanner and Sandra Tanner, *The Case Against Mormonism*, Vol. 1 (Salt Lake City, UT: Utah Lighthouse Ministry, 1967), p. 6.
53. Pratt, *The Seer*, May 1854, Vol. 2, No. 5, pp. 259-60.
54. Ibid., Vol. 2, No. 3, pp. 237, 239-40.
55. Joseph Fielding Smith, *Doctrines of Salvation*, Vol. 3, comp. Bruce McConkie (Salt Lake City, UT: Bookcraft, 1976), pp. 267, 287.
56. McConkie, *Mormon Doctrine*, p. 137-38.
57. Ibid., p. 132.
58. Ibid., passim.
59. McConkie, *Doctrinal New Testament Commentary*, Vol. 2, p. 274.
60. Ibid., Vol. 2, p. 280.
61. Ibid., Vol. 3, p. 85.
62. Ibid., Vol. 3, pp. 547, 550-51.
63. See e.g., Martin, Walter R., *Kingdom of the Cults* (Minneapolis, MN: Bethany House, 1987).
64. Statement by Richard L. Evans, a member of the Council of Twelve, as cited in Leo Rosten, *Religions of America* (New York: Simon and Schuster, 1975), p. 189.
65. J. F. Smith, comp., *Teachings of the Prophet*, p. 370.
66. McConkie, *Mormon Doctrine*, p. 317.
67. Ibid., pp. 576-77.
68. J. F. Smith, *Teachings of the Prophet*, p. 347; Duane S. Crowther, *Life Everlasting* (Salt Lake City, UT: Bookcraft, 1988), pp. 360-61.
69. McConkie, *Doctrinal New Testament Commentary*, Vol. 2, p. 78.
70. Joseph Smith, *History of the Church*, Vol. 6, p. 305.
71. J. F. Smith, *Teachings of the Prophet*, pp. 345-46.
72. Ibid., p. 371.
73. Ibid., p. 181.
74. McConkie, *Mormon Doctrine*, p. 250.
75. McConkie, *Doctrinal New Testament Commentary*, Vol. 2, p. 160.
76. *Journal of Discourses*, Vol. 13, p. 308.
77. Pratt, *The Seer*, Nov., 1853, Vol. 1, No. 11, p. 172.
78. Crowther, *Life Everlasting*, p. 340.
79. *Journal of Discourses*, Vol. 3, p. 93.
80. Milton R. Hunter, *The Gospel Through the Ages* (Salt Lake City, UT: Deseret Books, 1958), pp. 104, 114-15, cited in Tanner and Tanner, *The Changing World of Mormonism*, p. 177.
81. *Salt Lake Tribune*, Oct. 6, 1974 p. 1; from Tanner and Tanner, *The Changing World of Mormonism*, p. 188.
82. *What the Mormons Think of . . . Christ*, pamphlet (The Church of Jesus Christ of Latter-day Saints n.d., n.p.), pp. 25-26.
83. Rev. Frank S. Morley, *What We Can Learn from the Church of Jesus Christ of Latter-day Saints: by a Protestant Minister* (Salt Lake City, UT: Deseret News Press, n.d.), p. 3.
84. James Talmage, *A Study of the Articles of Faith* (Salt Lake City, UT: The Church of Jesus Christ of Latter-day Saints, 1974), p. 471.
85. J. H. Evans, *An American Prophet* (1933), p. 241, cited in Hoekema, *The Four Major Cults*, p. 54.
86. McConkie, *Doctrinal New Testament Commentary*, Vol. 3, p. 238.
87. McConkie, *Mormon Doctrine*, p. 129.
88. Ibid., p. 257.
89. Milton Hunter, *The Gospel Through the Ages* (1958), p. 21, from Tanner and Tanner, *The Changing World of Mormonism*, p. 519.
90. McConkie, *Mormon Doctrine*, p. 169; cf. J. F. Smith, *Doctrines of Salvation*, Vol. 1, p. 75.
91. J. F. Smith, *Doctrines of Salvation*, Vol. 1, p. 18.
92. Carlfred B. Broderick, in *Dialogue: A Journal of Mormon Thought*, Autumn, 1967, pp. 100-01, from Tanner and Tanner, *The Changing World of Mormonism*, p. 180.
93. J. F. Smith, *Doctrines of Salvation*, Vol. 1, p. 18.
94. McConkie, *Mormon Doctrine*, p. 547.
95. Brigham Young in *Deseret News*, Oct. 10, 1866, from Tanner and Tanner, *The Changing World of Mormonism*, p. 180.
96. Pratt, *The Seer*, Nov. 1853, Vol. 1, No. 11, p. 172.
97. James Talmage, *Jesus the Christ* (Salt Lake City, UT: Deseret Book Company, 1976), p. 31.
98. McConkie, *Mormon Doctrine*, p. 116.
99. McConkie, *Mormon Doctrine*, pp. 176-77, 234, 670; McConkie, *Doctrinal New Testament Commentary*, Vol. 3, pp. 284-85.
100. Talmage, *Articles of Faith*, p. 107.
101. J. F. Smith, *Doctrines of Salvation*, Vol. 2, p. 139.
102. McConkie, *Doctrinal New Testament Commentary*, Vol. 2, p. 229.
103. e.g., *The Book of Mormon*: 2 Nephi 25:23; Alma 7:16; Mosiah 5:7,8; 13:27,28; 2 Nephi 9:23,24; *Doctrine and Covenants*, 7:37; 132:12.
104. *Journal of Discourses*, Vol. 3, p. 269.
105. Talmage, *Jesus the Christ*, p. 5.
106. Joseph Fielding Smith, *The Way to Perfection* (Salt Lake City, UT: Deseret Book Company, 1975), p. 189.
107. McConkie, *Doctrinal New Testament Commentary*, Vol. 2, p. 294; cf. p. 279.
108. McConkie, *Mormon Doctrine*, p. 61.
109. *The Book of Mormon*: Helaman 14:15,16; 2 Nephi 2:26.
110. Crowther, *Life Everlasting*, p. 233; *What the Mormons Think of . . . Christ*, p. 28.
111. e.g., *The Master's Church, Course A*, p. 96; McConkie, *Doctrinal New Testament Commentary*, Vol. 2, pp. 242-43; Talmage, *Articles of Faith*, pp. 87-89.
112. *What the Mormons Think of . . . Christ*, pp. 27-28.
113. *Journal of Discourses*, Vol. 4, p. 220.
114. Tanner and Tanner, *The Changing World of Mormonism*, pp. 490-504; cf. John Ahmanson, *Secret History: An Eye Witness Account of the Rise of Mormonism* (Chicago, IL: Moody Press, 1984); Stephen Naifeh and Gregory White

Smith, *The Mormon Murders: A True Story of Greed, Forgery, Deceit, and Death* (New York, NY: Weidenfeld and Nicholson, 1988).

115. *Journal of Discourses*, Vol. 21, p. 81.
116. cf., Tanner and Tanner, *The Changing World of Mormonism*; Martin, *The Maze of Mormonism*, etc.
117. *Journal of Discourses*, Vol. 14, p. 216.
118. *The Master's Church, Course A*, p. 225.
119. McConkie, *Doctrinal New Testament Commentary*, Vol. 2, p. 274.
120. Joseph Smith, *History of the Church*, Vol. 1, p. xci.
121. cf. F. F. Bruce, *The New Testament Documents: Are They Reliable?* (Downers Grove, IL: InterVarsity Press, 1969); Norman L. Geisler, William E. Nix, *A General Introduction to the Bible*, rev. ed. (Chicago, IL: Moody, 1986).
122. *Dialogue: A Journal of Mormon Thought*, Autumn 1966, p. 29; David L. McKay, *Gospel Ideals*, p. 85; John A. Widtsow, *Joseph Smith, Seeker After Truth*, p. 19; Paul Cheesman, "An Analysis of the Accounts Relating Joseph Smith's Early Visions," BYU graduate thesis, May 1975, p. 75, cited in Tanner and Tanner, *The Changing World of Mormonism*, p. 151; Jerald Tanner and Sandra Tanner, *Joseph Smith's Strange Account of the First Vision* (Salt Lake City, UT: Utah Lighthouse Ministry, n.d.), p. 1; Tanner and Tanner, *Mormonism: Shadow or Reality?* p. 143; Martin, *The Maze of Mormonism*, pp. 26-30, cf. Tanner and Tanner, *The Changing World of Mormonism*, Chapter 6.
123. Tanner and Tanner, *The Changing World of Mormonism*, p. 148.
124. Ibid., pp. 10, 149-55.
125. Wesley P. Walters, *New Light on Mormon, Origins from the Palmyra (New York) Revival* (n.p., 1967), cf. Tanner and Tanner, *The Changing World of Mormonism*, pp. 166-71 and Marvin W. Cowan, *Mormon Claims Answered* (Salt Lake City, UT: Marvin W. Cowan), pp. 1-10.
126. Tanner and Tanner, *The Changing World of Mormonism*, pp. 155-56.
127. Ibid., p. 156.
128. Ibid., pp. 148-71.
129. Hugh Nibley, *An Approach to The Book of Mormon* (1957), p. 13, cited in Tanner and Tanner, *The Case Against Mormonism*, Vol. 2, p. 63.
130. Joseph Fielding Smith, *Answers to Gospel Questions*, Vol. 2 (Salt Lake City, UT: Deseret Book Company, 1976), p. 199.
131. e.g., Jerald Tanner and Sandra Tanner, *Joseph Smith and Money Digging* (Salt Lake City, UT: Utah Lighthouse Ministry, 1970).
132. *The Saints Herald*, May 19, 1888, p. 310, from Tanner and Tanner, *The Changing World of Mormonism*, p. 81.
133. Fawn Brodie, *No Man Knows My History: The Life of Joseph Smith* (New York, NY: Alfred A. Knopf, rev. 1976), p. 69.
134. Ibid., pp. 69-70, citing *Millennial Harbinger*, Vol. 2, Feb. 18, 1931, p. 85.
135. B.H. Roberts, *Studies of The Book of Mormon*, available from Utah Lighthouse Ministry, Box 1884, Salt Lake City, UT 84110.
136. See e.g., Hal Hougey, *A Parallel—The Basis of The Book of Mormon: B. H. Roberts "Parallel" of The Book of Mormon to View of the Hebrews* (Concord, CA: Pacific Publishing Company, 1963), p. 4; Ropp, *The Mormon Papers*, p. 36; cf. Ethan Smith, *View of the Hebrews*, available from Utah Lighthouse Ministry, Box 1884, Salt Lake City, UT 84110.
137. Hoekema, *The Four Major Cults*, p. 85.
138. Tanner and Tanner, *The Case Against Mormonism*, Vol. 2, pp. 87-102.
139. Fraser, *Is Mormonism Christian?*, p. 143; cf. p. 145.
140. This letter and many others like it are reproduced in Jerry and Marian Bodine, *Whom Can You Trust?* (Santa Ana, CA: Christ for the Cults, 1979), p. 16.
141. Ibid., p. 3, citing letter of Frank Roberts, Jr., Director, to Mr. Marvin Cowan, Jan. 24, 1963.
142. Ibid., p. 13, citing letter of Mr. Hermansen to Mr. Gregory R. Shannon, May 29, 1978.
143. See Sir William Ramsay, *The Bearing of Recent Discovery on the Trustworthiness of the New Testament* (Grand Rapids, MI: Baker Book House, 1979, reprint); Tanner and Tanner, *The Changing World of Mormonism*, pp. 140-41; cf. Jerald Tanner and Sandra Tanner, *Archeology and The Book of Mormon*, available from Utah Lighthouse Ministry, Box 1884, Salt Lake City, UT 84110.
144. Martin, *The Maze of Mormonism*, pp. 68-69; cf. Fraser, *Joseph and the Golden Plates*.
145. See "The Testimony of the Three Witnesses" in the front of *The Book of Mormon*.
146. See Ropp, *The Mormon Papers*, Chapter 4, Appendix C; Tanner and Tanner, *The Changing World of Mormonism*, pp. 38-63; *Joseph Smith Begins His Work*, Vol. 2 (photo reprint of the 1833 *Book of Commandments* and the 1835 *Doctrine and Covenants*), available from Utah Lighthouse Ministry, Box 1884, Salt Lake City, UT 84110.
147. e.g., J. F. Smith, *Doctrines of Salvation*, Vol. 1, p. 170; and Tanner and Tanner, *The Changing World of Mormonism*, p. 39.
148. Available from Utah Lighthouse Ministry, Box 1884, Salt Lake City, UT 84110.
149. Ibid.
150. Tanner and Tanner, *The Changing World of Mormonism*, pp. 329-63.
151. See the following titles available from Utah Lighthouse Ministry, Box 1884, Salt Lake City, UT 84110: Wesley Walters, *Joseph Smith Among the Egyptians*; H. Michael Marquardt, *The Book of Abraham Papyrus Found*; *Joseph Smith's Egyptian Alphabet and Grammar*; and F. S. Spaulding, *Why Egyptologists Reject The Book of Abraham*.
152. See e.g., Tanner and Tanner, *The Changing World of Mormonism*, pp. 29-66; see also Jerald and Sandra Tanner, *Falsification of Joseph Smith's History*; D. Michael Quinn, "On Being a Mormon Historian," available from Utah Lighthouse Ministry, Box 1884, Salt Lake City, UT 84110; Tanner and Tanner, *Mormon Spies, Hughes and the CIA* (Salt Lake City, UT: Utah Lighthouse Ministry).
153. See the materials from Tanner and Tanner, Utah Lighthouse Ministry, Box 1884, Salt Lake City, UT 84110.
154. Martin, *Kingdom of the Cults*, p. 181.
155. Tanner and Tanner, *The Changing World of Mormonism*.
156. *The Evening and Morning Star*, July 1833, p. 1.
157. McConkie, *Doctrinal New Testament Commentary*, Vol. 1, p. 252.
158. Talmage, *Articles of Faith*, pp. 7-8.
159. *Journal of Discourses*, Vol. 10, p. 344.
160. *Journal of Discourses*, Vol. 13, p. 362.
161. Clause J. Hansen, *Dialogue: A Journal of Mormon Thought*, Autumn 1966, p. 74.
162. J. F. Smith, *The Way to Perfection* (1935 ed.), p. 270.
163. Ropp, *The Mormon Papers*, p. 64; cf. "Rebellion in South Carolina," *Evening and Morning Star*, Feb. 1833.
164. Tanner and Tanner, *The Changing World of Mormonism*, pp. 428-30.

165. Ibid., pp. 417-30.
166. *Mormonia: A Quarterly Bibliography of Works on Mormonism*, Fall 1972, p. 89.
167. *Salt Lake Tribune*, Oct. 7, 1972, pp. 22-23 cited in Tanner and Tanner, *Mormonism Like Watergate? An Answer to Hugh Nibley*, 1974, p. 4.
168. Foreword in Tanner and Tanner, *The Changing World of Mormonism*, p. 11.
169. Talmage, *Articles of Faith*, p. 296.
170. Ibid., p. 311.
171. Ibid.
172. e.g., *Journal of Discourses*, Vol. 2, p. 338; Vol. 3, pp. 155-57.
173. *Doctrine and Covenants* 93:1; 67:10-14; McConkie, *Mormon Doctrine*, p. 644; *Journal of Discourses*, Vol. 1, pp. 13-15; Vol. 2, pp. 44-46; see Question 23.
174. McConkie, *Mormon Doctrine*, p. 650, citing *Doctrine and Covenants* 102:2,9,23; 107:39; 128:11.
175. McConkie, *Mormon Doctrine*, p. 645.
176. e.g., *Journal of Discourses*, Vol. 16, p. 46; *The Book of Mormon*, Moroni 10:4,5.
177. Martin, *The Maze of Mormonism*, p. 220; cf. J. F. Smith, *The Way to Perfection*, pp. 318-19; McConkie, *Doctrinal New Testament Commentary*, pp. 225-26; McConkie, *Mormon Doctrine*, pp. 35-36, 762.
178. Available from Utah Lighthouse Ministry, Box 1884, Salt Lake City, UT 84110.
179. Martin, *The Maze of Mormonism*, p. 211.
180. Tanner and Tanner, *The Changing World of Mormonism*, p. 10; Einar Anderson, *Inside Story of Mormonism* (Grand Rapids, MI: Kregel, 1974), p. 22.
181. Kurt Koch, *Christian Counseling and Occultism* (Grand Rapids, MI: Kregel 1972), pp. 184-87.
182. *Deseret News*, May 29, 1852; cf. Tanner and Tanner, *The Changing World of Mormonism*, p. 159.
183. e.g., Tanner and Tanner, *The Changing World of Mormonism*, pp. 77-85.
184. Ibid., pp. 67-69.
185. Ibid., pp. 88-91; cf. Jack Adamson and Reed Durham, Jr., *No Help For the Widow's Son: Mormonism and Masonry* (Nauvoo, IL: Martin Publishing Company, 1980), pp. 32-33.
186. Tanner and Tanner, *The Changing World of Mormonism*, pp. 67-80.
187. Ibid., pp. 80-84; cf. Tanner and Tanner, *Joseph Smith and Money Digging*, p. 7.
188. Tanner and Tanner, *Joseph Smith and Money Digging*, pp. 11-13.
189. Martin, *The Maze of Mormonism*, p. 218; see Question 23.
190. J. F. Smith, *Teachings of the Prophet*, p. 326, 243, 338, 363.
191. *Journal of Discourses*, Vol. 6, p. 349; cf. J. F. Smith, *Teachings of the Prophet Joseph Smith*, pp. 222-23, 180, 191-93, 363.
192. Joseph Smith, *Improvement Era*, Vol. 39, Apr. 1936, p. 200; *Times and Seasons*, Vol. 2, p. 546, cited in Joseph Heinerman, *Spirit World Manifestations; Accounts of Divine Aid in Genealogical and Temple and Other Assistance to Latter-day Saints* (Salt Lake City, UT: Joseph Lyon and Associates, 1986).
193. Heinerman, *Spirit World Manifestations*, p. 29.
194. McConkie, *Doctrinal New Testament Commentary*, Vol. 3, pp. 140-41; LeGrand Richards, *A Marvelous Work and a Wonder* (Salt Lake City, UT: Deseret Book Company, 1977).
195. e.g., J. F. Smith, *Answers to Gospel Questions*, Vol. 1, p. 47; Joseph Smith, *History of the Church*, Vol. 2, p. 380; Vol. 4, p. 231.
196. Parley P. Pratt, "Spiritual Communication," *Journal of Discourses*, Vol. 2, pp. 44-45.
197. Charles Penrose, *Mormon Doctrine* (1888), pp. 40-41, cited in Martin, *The Maze of Mormonism*, p. 225.
198. J. F. Smith, *Gospel Doctrine*, pp. 436-37.
199. e.g., *Journal of Discourses*, Vol. 3, p. 369; Vol. 7, p. 240; Crowther, *Life Everlasting*, p. 60; *Deseret Weekly News*, Vol. 53, p. 112.
200. *Journal of Discourses*, Vol. 7, p. 240.
201. John A. Widtsoe, *Discourses of Brigham Young* (Salt Lake City, UT: Deseret Book Company, 1976), pp. 378-80, citing *Journal of Discourses*, Vol. 7, p. 332; Vol. 6, p. 349.
202. John Ankerberg and John Weldon, *The Facts on Spirit Guides* (Eugene, OR: Harvest House, 1988), and *The Facts on the Occult* (Eugene, OR: Harvest House, 1991); Merrill Unger, *Biblical Demonology* (Wheaton, IL: Scripture Press, 1971); Gasson, *The Challenging Counterfeit.*.
203. Joseph Heinerman, *Eternal Testimonies: Inspired Testimonies of Latter-day Saints* (Salt Lake City, UT: Magazine Printing and Publishing, 1982).
204. Heinerman, *Spirit World Manifestations*, pp. 7, 277, 280.
205. Crowther, *Life Everlasting*, p. 151.
206. Floyd McElveen, *Will the Saints Go Marching In?* (Glendale, CA: Regal, 1977), p. 168.
207. McConkie, *Mormon Doctrine*, p. 39.
208. J. F. Smith, *Teachings of the Prophet*, p. 364.
209. J. F. Smith, *Doctrines of Salvation*, Vol. 1., p. 324.
210. *Journal of Discourses*, Vol. 10., p. 250.
211. See note 152.
212. See note 153.

Part Two—Jehovah's Witnesses

(Note: Most Jehovah's Witnesses' materials are published anonymously by the Watchtower Bible and Tract Society [WBTS], Brooklyn, NY. Few are listed with a specific author. See note 73.)

1. Edmond Gruss, *Apostles of Denial: An Examination and Exposé of the History, Doctrines and Claims of the Jehovah's Witnesses* (Grand Rapids, MI: Baker, 1972), pp. 14-16.
2. C. J. Woodworth and George H. Fisher, comp. and ed., *The Finished Mystery*, Vol. 7 of *Studies in the Scriptures*, 1918 ed. (Brooklyn, NY: International Bible Students Assoc., 1917), p. 387; cited in Gruss, *Apostles of Denial*, p. 21.
3. *The Watchtower*, Sept. 15, 1910, p. 298, from Chicago Bible Students, *Reprints of the Original Watchtower and Herald of Christ's Presence*, 12 volumes plus index (Chicago, IL: Chicago Bible Students, n.d.)
4. *The Watchtower*, Aug. 15, 1981, pp. 28-29.
5. See Gruss, *Apostles of Denial*, Chapter 5.
6. Ibid., p. 76.

7. Raymond Franz, *Crisis of Conscience* (Atlanta, GA: Commentary, 1983), pp. 345, 347, 354, 290-291, 303, 25-26, 51, 137-39, 147-48, 164-223, 9-10, 16, 41, 47, 238-39, 344, 52-65, 195, 29-52, 97, 245, 257.
8. *Life Everlasting in the Freedom of the Sons of God* (WBTS, 1966), p. 181.
9. Edmond Gruss, *We Left Jehovah's Witnesses—A Non-Prophet Organization* (Nutley, NJ: Presbyterian & Reformed, 1974), p. 78.
10. *The Watchtower*, Mar. 1, 1979, p. 16.
11. *The Watchtower*, July 15, 1960, p. 439, cited in Michael Van Buskirk, *The Scholastic Dishonesty of the Watchtower* (Santa Ana, CA: CARIS, 1976), p. 26.
12. H. Montague, "Watchtower Congregations: Communion or Conflict?" (Costa Mesa, CA: CARIS), p. 7. See Duane Magnani, *The Watchtower Files: Dialogue with a Jehovah's Witness* (Minneapolis, MN: Bethany Fellowship, 1985), p. 17, for documentation from court records of a statement by Nathan H. Knorr that *The Watchtower* is the word of God "without any qualification whatsoever."
13. Gruss, *We Left Jehovah's Witnesses*, p. 41.
14. *You Can Live Forever in Paradise on Earth* (WBTS, 1982), p. 212.
15. *Blood, Medicine and the Law of God* (WBTS, 1961), p. 55. Cited in Duane Magnani and Arthur Barrett, *Dialogue with Jehovah's Witnesses*, two volumes (Witness, Inc., P.O. Box 597, Clayton, CA, 1983), Vol. 2, p. 371.
16. William and Joan Cetnar, *Questions for Jehovah's Witnesses* (William J. Cetnar: R.D. #3, Kunkletown, PA, 1983), p. 26; Magani, *Dialogue With a Jehovah's Witness*, Vol. 2, pp. 368-74. For a refutation of this view, see Jerry Bergman, *Jehovah's Witnesses and Blood Transfusions* (St. Louis, MO: Personal Freedom Outreach, n.d.); Martin, *Jehovah of the Watchtower*, rev. ed. (Chicago: Moody Press, 1974), pp. 91-105.
17. *Man's Salvation Out of World Distress at Hand!* (WBTS, 1975), p. 335.
18. *The Watchtower*, Sept. 1, 1979, p. 21.
19. J. F. Rutherford, *Preparation* (WBTS, 1933), pp. 19-20.
20. J. F. Rutherford, *Religion* (WBTS, 1940), p. 104. Cited in Gruss, *Apostles of Denial*, p. 63.
21. *The Watchtower*, Sept. 1, 1979, p. 8.
22. *The Watchtower*, Oct. 1, 1952, pp. 596-604. Cited in Martin, *Jehovah of the Watchtower*, p. 109.
23. C. T. Russell, *Studies in the Scriptures*, Volume 7: *The Finished Mystery*, p. 410. Cited in W. M. Nelson and R. K. Smith, "Jehovah's Witnesses, Part 2, Their Mission," in David Hesselgrave, ed., *Dynamic Religious Movements: Case Studies of Rapidly Growing Religious Movements Around the World* (Grand Rapids, MI: Baker, 1978), p. 181.
24. *Aid to Bible Understanding* (WBTS, 1971), p. 665; Duane Magnani, *The Heavenly Weatherman* (Clayton, CA: Witness, Inc., 1987), pp. 1-8, 42-50, 246-51, etc.
25. *Then Is Finished the Mystery of God* (WBTS, 1969), p. 10.
26. J. F. Rutherford, *Uncovered* (WBTS, 1937), pp. 48-49. Cited in Charles S. Braden, *These Also Believe: A Study of Modern American Cults and Minority Religious Movements* (NY: Macmillan, 1970), p. 371. *Let God Be True* (WBTS, 1976), p. 82, states, "Satan is the originator of the 'Trinity' doctrine."
27. *Let God Be True* (WBTS, 1946), p. 83; *Things in Which It Is Impossible for God to Lie* (WBTS, 1965), p. 259; *The Watchtower*, July, 1982, pp. 2-3.
28. The verses listed with each of these five points should be read in a good, modern translation like the New International Version or the New American Standard Bible, since some were mistranslated in the King James Version and in the New World Translation. See Questions 13 and 14.
29. For an indepth study of the historical development of the doctrine of the Trinity from apostolic times through the final form of the Nicene Creed adopted at the Council of Constantinople in A.D. 381, including a line-by-line comparison of the Creed with New Testament teaching, see E. Calvin Beisner, *God in Three Persons* (Wheaton, IL: Tyndale House, 1984).
30. *Is This Life All There Is?* (WBTS, 1974), p. 99.
31. C. T. Russell, *Studies in the Scriptures*, Vol. 5: *The Atonement Between God and Man* (East Rutherford, NJ: Dawn Bible Students Assoc., reprint of 1899 ed., n.d.,) p. 60.
32. *Aid to Bible Understanding*, p. 1152.
33. *The Watchtower*, Aug. 22, 1976, pp. 25-26; *Aid to Bible Understanding*, p. 918.
34. *Let God Be True*, p. 65.
35. *The Watchtower*, Aug. 15, 1976, p. 495; cf. *The Watchtower*, May 15, 1932, p. 155; Nov. 1, 1919, p. 332-33.
36. Russell, *The Atonement Between God and Man*, p. 454; cf. note 36.
37. *The Truth Shall Make You Free* (WBTS, 1943), p. 264; Hoekema, *The Four Major Cults* (Grand Rapids, MI: Eerdmans, 1970), p. 272; James Bjornstad, *Counterfeits at Your Door* (Glendale, CA: Regal, 1979), pp. 67-68, 92-94; Nelson and Smith in Hesselgrave, *Dynamic Religious Movements*, pp. 178-79; *Things in Which It Is Impossible*, p. 219; *Let Your Name Be Sanctified* (WBTS, 1961), p. 272; *Man's Salvation Out of World Distress at Hand!* (WBTS, 1975), pp. 42-43; *The Watchtower*, Jan. 15, 1980, p. 31; *Make Sure of All Things, Hold Fast to What Is Fine* (WBTS, 1965), p. 255.
38. *Reasoning From the Scriptures* (WBTS, 1985), pp. 95-98. However, in *Studies in the Scriptures*, Volume 4: *The Battle of Armageddon*, p. 621, Russell wrote, "Our Lord, the appointed King, is now present, since October 1874, A.D., according to the testimony of the prophets, to those who have ears to hear it...."
39. See *Aid to Bible Understanding*, p. 437, and the discussion in Hoekema, *The Four Major Cults*, pp. 279-85.
40. *Reasoning From the Scriptures*, pp. 76-77.
41. *You May Survive Armageddon into God's New World* (WBTS, 1955), p. 356.
42. The Witnesses may in places define God's grace properly, but they do not live as if it were true. See Gruss, *We Left Jehovah's Witnesses*, pp. 131-32; Magnani, *The Watchtower Files: Dialogue with a Jehovah's Witness* (Minneapolis, MN: Bethany Fellowship, 1985), Chapter 13.
43. *Making Your Family Life Happy* (WBTS, 1978), pp. 182-183.
44. *The Watchtower*, May 1, 1979, p. 20; cf. *The Watchtower*, May 1, 1980, p. 13; also Aug. 1, 1981, p. 20.
45. *Life Everlasting in the Freedom of the Sons of God* (WBTS, 1966), p. 400.
46. *Aid to Bible Understanding*, p. 437; *You May Survive Armageddon*, pp. 356-57; Gruss, *We Left Jehovah's Witnesses*, pp. 131-32.
47. Discussions with members, former members, and *Reasoning From the Scriptures*, p. 277. See note 50.
48. *All Scripture Is Inspired by God and Beneficial* (WBTS, 1963), pp. 326, 327-30.
49. *The New World Translation of the Holy Scriptures* (WBTS, 1961), p. 5.
50. *The Kingdom Interlinear Translation of the Greek Scriptures* (WBTS, 1969), p. 5; *Reasoning From the Scriptures*, p. 277, states: "We have not used any scholar's name for reference or recommendations because . . . the translation must be appraised on its own merits."
51. Cited in Gruss, *Apostles of Denial*, pp. 32-33, 219; Gruss has seen the original court transcripts himself. This is a rather startling admission, for the control of men by spirits sounds more like demonism than divine inspiration.

One mediumistic translator of the Bible, who claimed that his translation originated in the spirit world, handled several passages similarly to how the Society handles them. The 1937 New Testament translation by occult medium Johannes Greber translates John 1:1, Hebrews 1:8, and other passages the way the NWT does. Indeed, the Society quotes Greber's translation to support its own. See note 115. If indeed translators were "controlled by angels of various ranks," it was by unholy angels—demons. Only they would have so twisted the translation. See note 120. For documentation as to parallels between the NWT and this mediumistic translation, see William and Joan Cetnar, *Questions for Jehovah's Witnesses*, pp. 48-55.

52. Julius Mantey, *Depth Exploration in the New Testament* (NY: Vantage Press, 1980), pp. 136-37.
53. Bruce M. Metzger, "The Jehovah's Witnesses and Jesus Christ: A Biblical and Theological Appraisal," rpt. of *Theology Today* article, Apr. 1953 (Princeton, NJ: Theological Book Agency), p. 74.
54. Robert Countess, *The Jehovah's Witnesses' New Testament: A Critical Analysis of the New World Translation of the Christian Greek Scriptures* (Phillipsburg, NJ: Presbyterian & Reformed, 1987), pp. 91, 93.
55. H. H. Rowley, "How Not to Translate the Bible," *The Expository Times*, Nov. 1953, pp. 41-42; cf. Jan. 1956, cited by Gruss, *Apostles of Denial*, pp. 212-13.
56. *The Watchtower*, Mar. 15, 1972, p. 189.
57. *The Watchtower*, Sept. 1, 1979, p. 30.
58. A. T. Robertson, *A Grammar of the Greek New Testament in the Light of Historical Research* (Nashville, TN: Broadman Press, 1934), p. 786.
59. C. Kuehne, "The Greek Article and the Doctrine of Christ's Deity," *Journal of Theology*, Church of the Lutheran Confession, Vol. 13, Nos. 3-4, Vol. 14, Nos. 1-4, Sept. 1973-Dec. 1974. Cited in the CARIS *Newsletter* (P.O. Box 1783, Santa Ana, CA), May 1978, Vol. 2, No. 2. (Condensed version by Michael Van Buskirk endorsed as accurate by Kuehne; "Letters," CARIS *Newsletter*, Vol. 2, No. 3.)
60. Metzger, "The Jehovah's Witnesses and Jesus Christ," p. 79.
61. H. E. Dana and Julius R. Mantey, *A Manual Grammar of the Greek New Testament* (Toronto: Macmillan, 1957), p. 147.
62. A. T. Robertson, *Word Pictures in the New Testament*, 6 volumes (Nashville, TN: Broadman, 1933), Vol. 6, p. 147.
63. *Make Sure of All Things*, p. 364.
64. See, for example, Alston Hurd Chase and Henry Phillips, Jr., *A New Introduction to Greek*, third ed. (Cambridge, MA: Harvard University Press, 1972), p. 41.
65. The Society has given four *different* grammatical constructions for *ego eimi*. See Michael Van Buskirk, *The Scholastic Dishonesty of the Watchtower* (Santa Ana, CA: CARIS, 1976), p. 20.
66. *The Kingdom Interlinear Translation of the Greek Scriptures*, p. 467.
67. James Hope Moulton and William Milligan, *The Vocabulary of the Greek Testament* (Grand Rapids, MI: Eerdmans, 1976), p. 352, citing from B. P. Grenfell and A. S. Hunt, eds., *The Oxyrhynchus Papyri*, Vol. 5 (London: 1898-1927), p. 840.
68. Mantey, *Depth Exploration*, p. 142.
69. Ibid., p. 143.
70. *Aid to Bible Understanding*, p. 1344.
71. *The Watchtower*, July 1, 1943, p. 203; Mar. 15, 1971, p. 189; Apr. 1, 1972, p. 197; Jan. 15, 1959, pp. 40-41; *The Nations Shall Know That I Am Jehovah—How?* (WBTS, 1971), pp. 58, 70-71.
72. *Aid to Bible Understanding*, p. 1348.
73. Reprints of early editions of *The Watchtower* are available in *Reprints of the Original Watchtower and Herald of Christ's Presence*, 1879-1916, Vols. 1-12, from Chicago Bible Students, Box 6016, Chicago, IL 60680.
74. N. H. Barbour and C. T. Russell, *Three Worlds and the Harvest of This World* (Rochester: Barbour and Russell, 1877), p. 17; cited in Gruss, *The Jehovah's Witnesses and Prophetic Speculation* (Nutley, NJ: Presbyterian & Reformed, 1972), p. 82.
75. *Zion's Watchtower and Herald of Christ's Presence*, January, 1886, p. 1 (*Reprints*, Vol. 2, p. 817. See note 73).
76. C. T. Russell, *The Time Is at Hand* (Allegheny, PA: WBTS, 1889), p. 101; cited in Gruss, *Jehovah's Witnesses and Prophetic Speculation*, p. 83.
77. C. T. Russell, *The New Creation* (WBTS, 1904), p. 579; cited in Gruss, *Jehovah's Witnesses and Prophetic Speculation*, p. 84.
78. *The Watchtower*, May 1, 1914, p. 134 (*Reprints*, p. 5450).
79. Ibid., pp. 23-26.
80. J. F. Rutherford, *Millions Now Living Will Never Die* (WBTS, 1920), pp. 97, 105, 140; Gruss, *Jehovah's Witnesses and Prophetic Speculation*, p. 87.
81. J. F. Rutherford, *Light*, Vol. 2 (WBTS, 1930), p. 327; cited in Gruss, *Jehovah's Witnesses and Prophetic Speculation*, p. 89.
82. J. F. Rutherford, *Vindication*, Vol. 1 (WBTS, 1931), p. 147.
83. J. F. Rutherford, *Preparation*, p. 11.
84. Ibid., pp. 16-18.
85. J. F. Rutherford, *Salvation* (WBTS, 1939), p. 310; cited in Gruss, *Jehovah's Witnesses and Prophetic Speculation*, p. 89.
86. Copies on file. Thanks to Professor Edmond C. Gruss for supplying them.
87. *Let God Be True* (WBTS, 1946), p. 194.
88. *This Means Everlasting Life* (WBTS, 1950), p. 311; cited in Gruss, *Jehovah's Witnesses and Prophetic Speculation*, p. 93.
89. *You May Survive Armageddon*, p. 11; cf. p. 362. This statement is from a speech given in 1953.
90. Ibid., p. 331.
91. *From Paradise Lost to Paradise Regained* (WBTS, 1958), p. 205.
92. See the discussion with photo documentation in Magnani, *Dialogue with a Jehovah's Witness*, Vol 2, pp. 53-55 and Gruss, *The Jehovah's Witnesses and Prophetic Speculation*, pp. 13-15; *Then Is Finished the Mystery of God* (WBTS, 1969), pp. 364-71.
93. *True Peace and Security—From What Source?* (WBTS, 1973), p. 83.
94. *God's Kingdom of a Thousand Years Has Approached* (WBTS, 1973), p. 44.
95. *Man's Salvation Out of World Distress at Hand*, p. 312.
96. Ibid., p. 349.
97. Ibid., pp. 283-284.
98. Ibid., p. 309.
99. Ibid., p. 287. Under oath, legal counsel for the Society, Hayden C. Covington, also admitted the prophecy was false, and that it nevertheless had to be accepted by Witnesses to preserve "unity at all costs." See transcript in Gruss, *The Jehovah's Witnesses and Prophetic Speculation*, pp. 99-101.
100. *1975 Yearbook of Jehovah's Witnesses* (WBTS, 1974), p. 76.
101. Ibid., pp. 145-46.

102. *1980 Yearbook of Jehovah's Witnesses* (WBTS, 1979), pp. 30-31.
103. *1975 Yearbook of Jehovah's Witnesses*, p. 245.
104. Additional documentation of false prophecies and the Watchtower Society's suppression of vital information can be found in Gruss, *The Jehovah's Witnesses and Prophetic Speculation*, and in former 25-year member Carl Olof Jonsson's *The Gentile Times Reconsidered* (La Jolla, CA: Good News Defenders, 1983), citing original documentation.
105. Gruss, *Apostles of Denial*, pp. 232-34, citing original documentation.
106. William and Joan Cetnar, *Questions for Jehovah's Witnesses*, p. 30. All but the first illustration are taken from Gruss, *We Left Jehovah's Witnesses*, pp. 156-59, citing original documentation.
107. Gruss, *Apostles of Denial*, p. 104; cf. pp. 56-66, 76.
108. William J. Schnell, *Jehovah's Witnesses Errors Exposed* (Grand Rapids, MI: Baker, 1975), p. 13.
109. cf. the Russell-White debate of 1908; J. F. Rutherford, *Reconciliation* (WBTS, 1928), pp. 175-76; *The New World* (WBTS, 1942), pp. 360-61; *Let God Be True* (WBTS, 1946), pp. 79; 1952, p. 98.
110. Their official history has also been altered. See Gruss, *Apostles of Denial*, pp. 19-37.
111. *1975 Yearbook of Jehovah's Witnesses*, p. 245.
112. J. F. Rutherford, *Prophecy* (WBTS, 1929), pp. 67-68; *Awake!* Mar. 22, 1963.
113. See note 115, under Roy Goodrich.
114. For primary documentation consult Martin, *Jehovah of the Watchtower*, pp. 19-23; Gruss, *Apostles of Denial*, pp. 27, 45, 294-95; Gruss, *Jehovah's Witnesses and Prophetic Speculation*, Chapter 6; Hoekema, *The Four Major Cults*, p. 243; Van Baalen, *The Chaos of the Cults*, p. 259; Gruss, *We Left Jehovah's Witnesses*, pp. 7, 65-66, 70, 74-75, 80-81, 83, 111, 118-19, 129; Montague, "Watchtower Congregations: Communion or Conflict?"; Hesselgrave, *Dynamic Religious Movements*, p. 183. For problems on the high incidence of mental illness among Jehovah's Witnesses, see Dr. Jerry Bergman, *The Mental Health of Jehovah's Witnesses* (Clayton, CA: Witness, Inc., 1987).
115. William and Joan Cetnar, *Questions for Jehovah's Witnesses*, p. 53 (cf. pp. 48-55). The Johannes Greber translation is cited in, e.g., *Make Sure of All Things*, p. 489. Greber was a spirit medium who claimed his translation originated in the spirit world. It translates John 1:1, Hebrews 1:8 and other passages the way the NWT does. See note 51. Roy Goodrich, head of the Jehovah's Witness splinter sect Back to the Bible Way, discusses the Society's involvement with psychometry and radionics in his "Demonism and the Watchtower." These are spiritistic forms of medical diagnosis. See John Weldon and Zola Levitt, *Psychic Healing* (Chicago: Moody Press, 1982), pp. 53-65. The last known address of Back to the Bible Way was 517 N.E. Second St., Ft. Lauderdale, FL 33301.
116. Rutherford, *Riches* (WBTS, 1936), p. 316, and *Vindication*, Vol. 3 (WBTS, 1932), p. 250.
117. William and Joan Cetnar, *Questions for Jehovah's Witnesses*, p. 55.
118. Rutherford, *Preparation*, pp. 35-38, 67.
119. *The Watchtower*, Apr. 1, 1972, p. 200; cf. Sept. 1, 1932, p. 263.
120. Much of this information was supplied by Duane Magnani of Witness, Inc., P.O. Box 597, Clayton, CA 94517. For further information and documentation as to the Society's claim to direction and guidance from the spirit world see Witness, Inc.'s tape "Angels of the New Light" and the text *The Heavenly Weatherman* (p. 3). A free catalogue of materials may be requested.
121. Raymond Franz, *Crisis of Conscience*, p. 31.
122. *Is This Life All There Is?*, p. 99.

Part Three—The Masonic Lodge

1. In *The Secret Teachings of the Masonic Lodge: A Christian Appraisal* (Moody Press, 1990), we cover many important additional facts and issues in Masonry that space does not permit us to address here. We cover not only the Blue Lodge, but also the York and Scottish Rites. Together, these combine 40 additional degrees of Masonry (10 in the York Rite and 30 in the Scottish Rite) that a Mason may complete. However, most Masons complete only the Blue Lodge, and this is why we have concentrated upon it here.

   For those needing information on the following subjects, we suggest they consult our book. The issues we discuss include: the worldwide influence and global goals of Masonry, how Masonry is influencing the church, a specific analysis of the theology of Masonry on the topics of God, Jesus Christ, salvation, life after death, and its views on the Bible. In addition, we show how Masonry is related to the ancient mystery religions; what characteristics it has in common with cultism; how Masonry encourages occult involvement; and many other important issues, such as Masonic oaths.
2. For details consult Ankerberg and Weldon, *The Secret Teachings of the Masonic Lodge*; and, for example, Martin L. Wagner, *Freemasonry: An Interpretation*, n.d., n.p. (distributed by Missionary Service and Supply, Route 2, Columbiana, OH 44408); *Los Angeles Times* Wire Services, "Anglican Synod Condemns Freemasonry," *Los Angeles Times*, July 14, 1987.
3. Henry C. Clausen, *Clausen's Commentaries on Morals and Dogma* (The Supreme Council, 33rd Degree, Ancient and Accepted Scottish Rite of Freemasonry, Southern Jurisdiction of the USA, 1976), p. 148.
4. Stephen Knight, *The Brotherhood: The Explosive Exposé of the Secret World of the Freemasons* (London: Grenada Publishing, Ltd./Panther Books, 1983), p. 234.
5. Editorial by Francis G. Paul, The Sovereign Grand Commander, "The Test Never Changes," *The Northern Light: A Window for Freemasonry*, May 1988.
6. Henry Wilson Coil, *Freemasonry Through Six Centuries*, Vol. 1 (Richmond, VA: Macoy Publishing and Masonic Supply, 1967), pp. 131, 152; "Christianity and the Masonic Lodge: Are They Compatible?" transcript from the John Ankerberg Evangelistic Association (Chattanooga, TN, 1985), p. 3. Guests were William Mankin and Dr. Walter Martin; Shildes Johnson, *Is Masonry a Religion?* (Oakland, NJ: Institute for Contemporary Christianity, 1978), p. 12.
7. Albert Mackey, *Mackey's Revised Encyclopedia of Freemasonry*, rev. and enlarged by Robert I. Clegg, Vol. 1 (Richmond, VA: Macoy Publishing and Masonic Supply, 1966), p. 269.
8. Ibid.
9. Ibid.
10. Henry Wilson Coil, *A Comprehensive View of Freemasonry* (Richmond, VA: Macoy Publishing and Masonic Supply Co., 1973), p. 234.
11. Mackey, *Mackey's Revised Encyclopedia*, Vol. 1, p. 378.
12. "Christianity and the Masonic Lodge," pp. 3, 5.

13. "The Masonic Lodge: What Goes On Behind Closed Doors?" transcript from the John Ankerberg Evangelistic Association (Chattanooga, TN, 1986), p. 29. Guests were Jack Harris, William Mankin, Dr. Walter Martin, and Paul Pantzer.
14. See H. V. B. Voorhis, *Facts for Freemasons: A Storehouse of Masonic Knowledge in Question and Answer Form*, rev. ed. (Richmond, VA: Macoy Publishing and Masonic Supply, 1979), p. 172; Alphonse Cerza, *Transactions of the Missouri Lodge of Research*, Vol. 34 (1978-1979) of *A Masonic Reader's Guide*, Thomas C. Warden, ed., (1980), pp. 8, 148; Silas H. Shepherd et al., *Little Masonic Library*, Vol. 1 (Richmond, VA: Macoy Publishing and Masonic Supply, 1977), p. 130.
15. H. L. Haywood, *The Newly-Made Mason: What He and Every Mason Should Know About Masonry* (Richmond, VA: Macoy Publishing and Masonic Supply, 1973); cf. Henry Pirtle, *Kentucky Monitor: Complete Monitorial Ceremonies of the Blue Lodge* (Louisville, KY: Standard Printing Co., 1921).
16. "Christianity and the Masonic Lodge: Are They Compatible?" transcript from the John Ankerberg Evangelistic Association (Chattanooga, TN, 1985), p. 2. Guests were William Mankin and Dr. Walter Martin; cf. Alphonse Cerza, *Let There Be Light: A Study in Anti-Masonry* (Silver Spring, MD: The Masonic Service Association, 1983), p. 41.
17. "Christianity and the Masonic Lodge," p. 2.
18. Cerza, *Let There Be Light*, p. 41.
19. *Webster's New World Dictionary*, Second Collegiate Edition (New York: Simon & Schuster, 1984).
20. Henry Wilson Coil, *Coil's Masonic Encyclopedia* (New York: Macoy Publishing and Masonic Supply, 1961), p. 512.
21. Mackey, *Mackey's Revised Encyclopedia*, Vol. 2, p. 847.
22. "Christianity and the Masonic Lodge," p. 2.
23. *Monitor of the Lodge: Monitorial Instructions in the Three Degrees of Symbolic Masonry* (Grand Lodge of Texas, A. F. and A. M., Grand Lodge of Texas, 1982), p. 83.
24. Malcom C. Duncan, *Masonic Ritual and Monitor* (New York: David Mckay Co., n.d.), p. 129, emphasis added.
25. Ibid., p. 50, emphasis added; cf. *Monitor of the Lodge*, p. 88.
26. Coil, *Coil's Masonic Encyclopedia*, p. 512, emphasis added.
27. "Christianity and the Masonic Lodge," p. 2; Cerza, *Let There Be Light*, p. 41.
28. *Webster's New World Dictionary*.
29. Coil, *Coil's Masonic Encyclopedia*, p. 512, emphasis added.
30. Ibid.
31. Ibid.
32. Coil, *Coil's Masonic Encyclopedia*, p. 516; Duncan, *Masonic Ritual and Monitor*, p. 226.
33. *Oxford American Dictionary* (New York: Avon, 1982).
34. *Webster's New Twentieth Century Dictionary*, 2nd ed. unabridged (Collins-World, 1978).
35. Joseph Fort Newton, *The Religion of Masonry: An Interpretation* (Richmond, VA: Macoy Publishing and Masonic Supply Co., Inc., 1969), pp. 58-59.
36. *Webster's New Twentieth Century Dictionary*.
37. Allen E. Roberts, *The Craft and Its Symbols: Opening the Door to Masonic Symbolism* (Richmond, VA: Macoy Publishing and Masonic Supply, 1974), pp. 57, 64.
38. George Simmons and Robert Macoy, *Standard Masonic Monitor of the Degrees of Entered Apprentice, Fellow Craft and Master Mason* (Richmond, VA: Macoy Publishing and Masonic Supply, 1984), p. 17.
39. Carl H. Claudy, *Foreign Countries: A Gateway to the Interpretation and Development of Certain Symbols of Freemasonry* (Richmond, VA: Macoy Publishing and Masonic Supply, 1971), p. 23, emphasis added.
40. Albert Pike, *Morals and Dogma of the Ancient and Accepted Scottish Rite of Freemasonry* (Charleston, SC: The Supreme Council of the 33rd Degree for the Southern Jurisdiction of the United States, 1906), p. 526, emphasis added.
41. Coil, *Coil's Masonic Encyclopedia*, p. 513.
42. *Webster's New World Dictionary*.
43. Coil, *Coil's Masonic Encyclopedia*, p. 512.
44. Ibid.
45. Mackey, *Mackey's Revised Encyclopedia*, Vol. 2, p. 847, emphasis added.
46. Ibid., p. 847-48.
47 Coil, *Coil's Masonic Encyclopedia*, p. 513.
48. "Christianity and the Masonic Lodge: Are They Compatible?" p. 5.
49. Allen E. Roberts, *The Craft and Its Symbols: Opening the Door to Masonic Symbolism* (Richmond, VA: Macoy Publishing and Masonic Supply, 1974), pp. 62, 80.
50. Ibid., p. xi; cf. 11.
51. Albert G. Mackey, *The Symbolism of Freemasonry: Illustrating and Explaining Its Science and Philosophy, Its Legends, Myths, and Symbols* (Chicago, IL: Charles T. Powner Co., 1975), p. 5, emphasis added.
52. Ibid., pp. 148, 158.
53. Roberts, *The Craft and Its Symbols*, p. 21.
54. Mackey, *The Symbolism of Freemasonry*, pp. 148, 158.
55. Malcom C. Duncan, *Masonic Ritual and Monitor* (New York: David Mckay Co., n.d.), p. 29; cf. "The Masonic Lodge: What Goes On Behind Closed Doors?" transcript from the John Ankerberg Evangelistic Association (Chattanooga, TN, 1986), p. 4. Guests were Jack Harris, William Mankin, Dr. Walter Martin, and Paul Pantzer.
56. Albert Mackey, *The Manual of the Lodge* (New York: Clark Maynard, 1870), p. 20; cf. "The Masonic Lodge: What Goes On," p. 5.
57. Henry Wilson Coil, *Coil's Masonic Encyclopedia* (New York: Macoy Publishing and Masonic Supply, 1961), p. 375.
58. Roberts, *The Craft and Its Symbols*, p. 84.
59. Ibid., p. 21.
60. Ibid., p. 84.
61. Duncan, *Masonic Ritual and Monitor*, p. 30, emphasis added; cf. Carl H. Claudy, *Foreign Countries: A Gateway to the Interpretation and Development of Certain Symbols of Freemasonry* (Richmond, VA: Macoy Publishing and Masonic Supply, 1971), p. 23; and George Simmons and Robert Macoy, *Standard Masonic Monitor of the Degrees of Entered Apprentice, Fellow Craft and Master Mason* (Richmond, VA: Macoy Publishing and Masonic Supply, 1984), p. 17.
62. Claudy, *Foreign Countries*, p. 24.
63. Foster Bailey, *The Spirit of Masonry* (Hampstead, London: Lucius Press, Ltd., 1972), p. 110.
64. Ibid.
65. Coil, *Coil's Masonic Encyclopedia*, pp. 516-17.
66. Martin L. Wagner, *Freemasonry: An Interpretation* (dist. by Missionary Service and Supply, Route 2, Columbiana, OH 44408), p. 284; *Baptists and Freemasonry*, The Baptist Union of Scotland (endorsed by the Baptist Union of Great Britain and Ireland), (Baptist Church House, 1987), pp. 4-5.

67. Wagner, *Freemasonry: An Interpretation*, pp. 281-351.
68. Ibid., pp. 137-355.
69. Ibid., pp. 288-302.
70. Ibid., p. 321.
71. Ibid., p. 300.
72. Albert Pike, *Morals and Dogma*, p. 223.
73. Ibid., pp. 295-96.
74. Wagner, *Freemasonry: An Interpretation*, pp. 288-302.
75. Ibid. See note 1.
76. e.g., Duncan, *Masonic Ritual and Monitor*, p. 226.
77. Coil, *Coil's Masonic Encyclopedia*, p. 516.
78. Duncan, *Masonic Ritual and Monitor*, p. 226.
79. Wagner, *Freemasonry: An Interpretation*, pp. 338-39.
80. Edmond Ronayne, *The Master's Carpet; or Masonry and Baal-Worship—Identical* (dist. by Missionary Service and Supply, Route 2, Columbia, OH 44408); A. E. Cundall, "Baal," in Merrill C. Tenney, ed., Vol. 1 *The Zondervan Pictorial Encyclopedia of the Bible* (Grand Rapids, MI: Zondervan, 1975); "Baal" in *Encyclopedia Britannica—Micropedia*, Vol. 1 (Chicago, IL: University of Chicago, 1978); "Baal" in *The New Schaff-Herzog Encyclopedia of Religious Knowledge*, Vol. 1 (Grand Rapids, MI: Baker, 1977), pp. 390-93; Lewis Bayles Payton, "Baal, Beel, Bel" in James Hastings, ed., *Encyclopedia of Religion and Ethics*, Vol. 2 (New York: Charles Schribner's Sons, n.d.); George A. Barton, "Baalzebub and Beelzaboul" in Hastings, *Encyclopedia of Religion and Ethics*, subsequent article; W. L. Liefeld, "Mystery Religions" in Merrill C. Tenney, *The Zondervan Pictorial Encyclopedia of the Bible*, Vol. 4 (Grand Rapids, MI: Zondervan, 1977); John Gray, "Baal—The Dying and Rising God" in Richard Cavendish, ed., *Man, Myth and Magic: An Illustrated Encyclopedia of the Supernatural*, Vol. 2 (New York: Marshall Cavendish Corp., 1970).
81. E. Ronayne, *Chapter Masonry* (Chicago: Ezra A. Cook, 1984), p. 126.
82. Shepherd et al., *Little Masonic Library*, Vol. 5, p. 51; Coil, *Coil's Masonic Encyclopedia*, pp. 516-17; Wagner, *Freemasonry: An Interpretation*, pp. 321-51.
83. J. W. Acker, *Strange Altars: A Scriptural Appraisal of the Lodge* (St. Louis, MO: Concordia, 1959), p. 37, emphasis added.
84. Carl H. Claudy, *Introduction to Freemasonry*, Vol. 2 (Washington, D.C.: The Temple Publishers, 1984), p. 110.
85. Pike, *Morals and Dogma*, p. 525.
86. Henry C. Clausen, *Clausen's Commentaries on Morals and Dogma* (The Supreme Council, 33rd Degree, Ancient and Accepted Scottish Rite of Freemasonry, Southern Jurisdiction of the USA, 1976), p. 159.
87. Acker, *Strange Altars*, p. 34; e.g., Jim Shaw and Tom McKenney, *The Deadly Deception: Freemasonry Exposed by One of Its Top Leaders* (Lafayette, LA: Huntington House, 1988), pp. 126-27.
88. Shaw and McKenney, *The Deadly Deception*, p. 127; cf. Clausen, *Practice and Procedure*, pp. 75-77.
89. Clausen, *Clausen's Commentaries on Morals and Dogma*, p. 157.
90. Pike, *Morals and Dogma*, p. 525.
91. Ronayne, *The Master's Carpet*, p. 87.
92. Albert Pike, *Liturgy of the Ancient and Accepted Scottish Rite of Freemasonry for the Southern Jurisdiction of the United States*, Part 2 (Washington, D.C.: The Supreme Council, 33rd Degree of the Ancient and Accepted Scottish Rite of Freemasonry of the Southern Jurisdiction of the USA, 1982), p. 202, emphasis added.
93. Shepherd et al., *Little Masonic Library*, Vol. 5, pp. 51-52.
94. Ibid., pp. 47-52; *Liturgy of the Ancient*, pp. 137, 202.
95. Mackey, *Mackey's Revised Encyclopedia*, Vol. 1, p. 133; Shepherd et al., *Little Masonic Library*, Vol. 1, p. 132.
96. Coil, *Coil's Masonic Encyclopedia*, p. 520, emphasis added.
97. Mackey, *Mackey's Revised Encyclopedia*, Vol. 1, p. 133.
98. Holy Bible, Temple Illustrated ed. (Nashville, TN: A. J. Holman Co., 1968), pp. 3-4.
99. Shepherd et al., *Little Masonic Library*, Vol. 1, p. 132.
100. Roberts, *The Craft and Its Symbols*, p. 76.
101. Simmons and Macoy, *Standard Masonic Monitor*, p. 111; cf. Duncan, *Masonic Ritual and Monitor*, p. 129.
102. Roberts, *The Craft and Its Symbols*, p. 31.
103. Simmons and Macoy, *Standard Masonic Monitor*, p. 29, emphasis added.
104. Holy Bible, Temple Illustrated ed., p. 4.
105. Mackey, *The Symbolism of Freemasonry*, p. 135.
106. Roberts, *The Craft and Its Symbols*, p. 62; Duncan, *Masonic Ritual and Monitor*, pp. 130-31.
107. "The Masonic Lodge: What Goes On?" p. 35.
108. Pike, *Morals and Dogma*, p. 30.
109. Simmons and Macoy, *Standard Masonic Monitor*, p. 125.
110. Cerza, *Let There Be Light*, p. 53.
111. Coil, *Coil's Masonic Encyclopedia*, p. 512.
112. See C. S. Lewis, *Mere Christianity* (MacMillan); Henry M. Morris, *Many Infallible Proofs* (Master Books); and Os Guinness, *In Two Minds* (InterVarsity).
113. e.g., *Leaves from Georgia Masonry* (Educational and Historical Commission of the Grand Lodge of Georgia, 1947), pp. 74-75.

Part Four—The New Age Movement

1. Shirley MacLaine, *Out on a Limb* (New York: Bantam, 1983), p. 268.
2. Robert Lindsay, "Spiritual Concepts Drawing a Different Breed of Adherent," *New York Times*, Sept. 29, 1986, p. 1; Robert Burroughs, "Americans Get Religion in the New Age," *Christianity Today*, May 16, 1986, pp. 1, 17; Douglas Groothuis, *Unmasking the New Age* (Downers Grove, IL: InterVarsity Press, 1986).
3. From Nina Easton, "Shirley MacLaine's Mysticism for the Masses," *The Los Angeles Times Magazine*, Sep. 6, 1987, p. 33.
4. Ibid.
5. Ibid., p. 8.
6. Brooks Alexander, "Theology From the Twilight Zone," *Christianity Today*, Sep. 18, 1987, p. 22.
7. e.g., *The Los Angeles Times*, Oct. 3, 1986, Part IX, p. 1.

8. *The Los Angeles Times*, Aug. 6, 1986, Part II, p. 1.
9. Kenneth Feder, "Spooks, Spirits, and College Students," *The Humanist*, May-June, 1985.
10. e.g., on scientific mysticism see Dean C. Halverson, "Science: Quantum Physics and Quantum Leaps," in Karen Hoyt and the Spiritual Counterfeits Project, *The New Age Rage* (Old Tappan, NJ: Revell, 1987), pp. 74-90; on the military see Martin Ebon, *Psychic Warfare* (New York: McGraw-Hill, 1983); Ronald McRae, *Mind Wars: The True Story of Secret Government Research into Military Potential of Psychic Weapons* (New York: St. Martin's Press, 1984). See also the *Spiritual Counterfeits Project Journal*, Vol. 7, No. 1 (P.O. Box 4308, Berkeley, CA 94704) and Marie Sengler and Brian Van Der Horst, "The Inner Directed," *New Realities*, Vol. 3, No. 6 (1980).
11. Easton, "Shirley MacLaine's Mysticism," p. 10.
12. Ibid; cf. Elliot Miller, "Channeling: Spiritistic Revelations for the New Age," *Christian Research Journal*, Fall 1987, p. 14.
13. Easton, "Shirley MacLaine's Mysticism," p. 7.
14. Among his books are *Up From Eden, The Atman Project, No Boundary, Transformations of Consciousness* (ed.) and *The Spectrum of Consciousness*.
15. The best illustration of this is *The Journal of Transpersonal Psychology*, which began in 1969 and is considered the leading journal in the field. The past president of the Association for Transpersonal Psychology, publisher of the Journal, is Dr. Frances Vaughan. She observes, "The transpersonal perspective sees the Eastern spiritual disciplines and Western scientific approaches to psychology as complementary." Frances Vaughan, "The Transpersonal Perspective: A Personal Overview," *The Journal of Transpersonal Psychology*, Vol. 14, No. 1, p. 37.
16. Walter Truett Anderson, *The Upstart Spring: Esalen and the American Awakening* (Menlo Park, CA: Addison-Wesley, 1983), p. 104.
17. Taken from the televised miniseries "Out on a Limb," 1987.
18. N. Kasturi, *Sathyam-Shivam-Sundaram: The Life of Bhagavan Sri Sathya Sai Baba Part 3* (Brindavan Whitefield, Bangalore, India: Sri Sathya Sai Foundation, 1973), p. 112.
19. Bhagwan Shree Rajneesh, "I am the Messiah Here and Now," *Sannyas* Magazine, No. 5 (Sep.-Oct.), 1978) p. 34; Rajneesh, *The Book of the Secrets*, Vol. 1 (San Francisco: Harper & Row, 1974), p. 22.
20. Rajneesh in Swami Anand Yarti, *The Sound of Running Water: A Photobiography of Bhagwan Shree Rajneesh and His Work, 1974-1978* (Poona, India: Poona Rajneesh Foundation, 1980), p. 382.
21. Vivekananda in Swami Nikhilananda (compiler), *Vivekananda The Yogas and Other Works* (New York: Ramabrishna-Vivekananda Center, 1953), rev., p. 530.
22. Ibid.
23. Rajneesh, *The Book of the Secrets*, Vol. 1, p. 399. Rajneesh is explaining spiritual wisdom to Arjuna, the warrior in the *Bhagavad Gita*.
24. e.g., "Seth's" views on reconstructing psychology along New Age lines in Jane Roberts' *The Nature of Human Personality* (1974); *Adventures in Consciousness: An Introduction to Aspect Psychology* (1975); and *Psychic Politics: An Aspect Psychology Book* (1976).
25. Stanislav Grof, ed., *Ancient Wisdom and Modern Science* (New York: State University of New York Press, 1984), esp. pp. v-xxxi; 3-31.
26. For example, consider a statement on the back cover of *The Eye of Shiva: Eastern Mysticism and Science* (New York: William Morrow, 1981), "Amaury de Riencourt maintains that the 'higher state of consciousness' of the meditating yogi, the 'enlightenment' of Eastern mysticism, is not a dream state but a true description of reality. He believes that this consciousness, symbolized by the Eye of Shiva, can provide the appropriate model for further research in physics. Furthermore, he argues that this 'hidden level of existence' can unite Eastern and Western traditions and end forever the dualisms of Western thought."
27. John Ferguson, *An Illustrated Encyclopedia of Mysticism and the Mystery Religions* (New York: Seabury Press, 1977), p. 148; Brad Steiger, *Revelation: The Divine Fire* (1973); Walter Pahnke, "Implications of L.S.D. and Experimental Mysticism," in Charles Tart, ed., *Altered States of Consciousness* (New York: Wiley and Sons, 1969), pp. 399-428; Robert Crookall, *The Interpretation of Cosmic and Mystical Experience* (Cambridge: James Clark & Co., 1969); W. T. Stace, *Mysticism and Philosophy* (New York: MacMillan, 1960); R. M. Bucke, *Cosmic Consciousness* (New York: E. P. Dutton, 1901); Lawrence LeShan, *Toward a General Theory of the Paranormal* (New York: Parapsychology Foundation, 1969).
28. The first major text on "channeling" discussing these and other entities from a New Age perspective is Jon Klimo, *Channeling: Investigations on Receiving Information from Paranormal Sources* (Los Angeles: Jeremy P. Tarcher, 1987).
29. Lynn Smith, "The New Chic Metaphysical Fad of Channeling," *Los Angeles Times*, Dec. 5, 1986, Part V; cf. Katherine Lowry, "Channelers: Mouthpieces of the Spirits," *Omni* Magazine, Oct. 1987.
30. Kilmo, P., e.g., Laeh Garfield, *Companions in Spirit: A Guide to Working with Your Spirit Helpers* (Berkeley, CA: Celestial Arts, 1984); Robin Westen, *Channelers: A New Age Directory* (New York: Putnam, 1988); Roman and Packer, *Opening to Channel: How to Connect with Your Guide* (Tiburon, CA: H.J. Kramer, 1987); Cathryn Ridle, *Channeling: How to Reach Out to Your Spirit Guides* (New York: Bantam, 1988).
31. See also *Metapsychology: The Journal of Discarnate Intelligence*.
32. Lowry, "Channelers: Mouthpieces," p. 22.
33. Alexander, "Theology From the Twilight Zone," p. 22.
34. This was a national poll conducted by the University of Chicago's National Opinion Research Council; see the report in Andrew Greeley, "Mysticism Goes Mainstream," *American Health*, Jan.-Feb. 1987.
35. Lowry, "Channelers: Mouthpieces."
36. Carol Ostrom, "Pastor Resigns, Sticks with Disputed Belief" in *The Seattle Times*, July 28, 1986, Part B.
37. For a critique of *God Calling* see Edmond Gruss, "A Critical Look at a Christian Best Seller," *Personal Freedom Outreach Newsletter*, Vol. 6, No. 3 (P.O. Box 26062, St. Louis, MO 63136).
38. See *Time Magazine*, Nov. 13, 1972, and *New Realities*, Richard Bach Interview, Nov.-Dec., 1984, p. 56. Bach was also indebted to "Seth."
39. See p. 9 in the critique of channeling in the *Spiritual Counterfeits Project Journal*, Vol. 7, No. 1 (P.O. Box 4308, Berkeley, CA, 1987).
40. See "Agartha: Journey to the Stars," and Mentor, "Man as God: Learning to Channel," in *Holistic Life Magazine*, Summer 1985, p. 22.
41. Collectively the NAM is a combination of related pantheistic beliefs: 1) monism, the belief that all true reality is divine, with the corollary that the phenomenal universe is outwardly an illusion (*maya*) but inwardly divine in its true essence; 2) panentheism, the belief that the universe is God's "body" and so God is more than the physical universe; 3) pantheism, the belief that the physical universe is God.

42. See Walter Martin, *Kingdom of the Cults* (Minneapolis: Bethany, 1987) and Walter Martin, ed., *The New Cults* (Santa Ana: Vision House, 1984).
43. e.g., David Fetcho, "David Fetcho's Story: Last Meditation/Lotus Adept," *Spiritual Counterfeits Project Special Collection Journal*, Winter 1984, p. 33.
44. Rajneesh, *I Am the Gate* (San Francisco: Perennial Library, 1978), p. 16.
45. Napoleon Hill, *Grow Rich with Peace of Mind* (New York: Ballantine, 1982), pp. 158, 160.
46. e.g., his *Positive Imaging* (New York: Ballantine, 1983).
47. Robert Schuller, *Peace of Mind Through Possibility Thinking* (New York: Jove/Berkeley, 1985), pp. 130-38.
48. K. Bottomly, J. French, "Christians Meditate, Too," *Yoga Journal*, May-June, 1984, pp. 26-28, 48.
49. See E. S. Gallegos "Animal Imagery, the Chakra System and Psychotherapy," *The Journal of Transpersonal Psychology*, Vol. 15, No. 2.
50. See David Benner, ed., *Baker Encyclopedia of Psychology* (1985), under these listings. See also under "transpersonal psychology," "psychosynthesis," "bioenergetics," and "hypnosis."
51. For an analysis of these and other topics see Reisser, Reisser and Weldon, *New Age Medicine* (Downers Grove, IL: InterVarsity, 1988) and Ankerberg and Weldon, *Can You Trust Your Doctor?* (Wolgemuth & Hyatt, 1991).
52. Ibid., Chapter 9.
53. See Clifford Wilson and John Weldon, *Psychic Forces* (Chattanooga, TN: Global), Section III.
54. Robert Muller in *New Genesis: Shaping a Global Spirituality* (New York: Doubleday, 1984), discusses several of these. See Peter Russell, *The Global Brain: Speculations on the Evolutionary Leap to Planetary Consciousness* (Los Angeles: J. P. Tarcher, 1983), and Daisaku Ikeda, *The Toynbee-Ikeda Dialogue* (1976), p. 243.
55. Muller, *New Genesis*, pp. 47-49, 89-90, 120-27.
56. This is the view of New Age cultural commentator Theodore Rozak, in *The Unfinished Animal* (New York: Harper & Row, 1977), pp. 17-18; see Charles Tart, ed., *Transpersonal Psychologies* (New York: Harper & Row, 1977); Seymour Boorstein, ed., *Transpersonal Psychotherapy* (Palo Alto, CA: Science and Behavior Books, Inc., 1980); Alta J. LaDage, *Occult Psychology: A Comparison of Jungian Psychology and the Modern Quabalah* (St. Paul, MN: Llewellyn, 1978); John Levy "Transpersonal Psychology and Jungian Psychology" and Shawn Steggles et al., "Gestalt Therapy and Eastern Philosophies: A Partially Annotated Bibliography," *Journal of Humanistic Psychology*, Spring 1983; Carl Rogers, *A Way of Being* (Boston: Houghton Mifflin Co., 1980), pp. 82-92, 100-02, 129-32, 253-56, 312-15, 343-52; Richard D. Mann, *The Light of Consciousness: Explorations in Transpersonal Psychology* (Albany: State University of New York Press, 1984); Roger Walsh, et al., *Beyond Ego: Transpersonal Dimensions in Psychology* (Los Angeles: J. P. Tarcher, 1980).
57. e.g., Margot Adler, *Drawing Down the Moon: Witches, Druids, Goddess-Worshippers, and other Pagans in America Today* (New York: Viking Press, 1979), pp. 21-29, 58, 64, 95-113, 150-54, 385; Maury Terry, *The Ultimate Evil: An Investigation of America's Most Dangerous Satanic Cult* (Garden City, NY: Dolphin, 1987), pp. xi-xiii; 499-512; Carl A. Raschke, "Satanism and the Devolution of the New Religions," *Spiritual Counterfeits Project Newsletter*, Vol. 11, No. 3, pp. 22-29.
58. Yarti, *The Sound of Running Water*, p. 364.
59. Terry, *The Ultimate Evil*, pp. xi-xiii; 499-512.
60. As stated on the Oprah Winfrey Show, Feb. 17, 1988.
61. Mircea Eliade, *Occultism, Witchcraft and Cultural Fashions* (Chicago: University of Chicago Press, 1976), p. 71; Tal Brooke, *Riders of the Cosmic Circuit* (Batavia, IL: Lion, 1986), pp. 199-208.
62. Mary Lutyens, *Krishnamurti: The Years of Awakening* (New York: Avon, 1976), p. 203.
63. Pat Rodegast, *Emmanuel's Book* (Weston, CT: Friends Press, 1986), pp. 132, 198-99, 200, 201, 227, 232, 205, 161.
64. Ibid., pp. 228, 208, xx, 145, 223, 151, 88.
65. Ibid., pp. 39, 29, 33, 30, 42, 44, 243, 169-72.
66. Ibid., pp. 138, xix, 142-143, 153, 222, 239-241, 72, 74, 76-77, 78.
67. Johanna Michaelsen, *The Beautiful Side of Evil* (Eugene, OR: Harvest House, 1982), p. 148.
68. Doreen Irvine, *Freed From Witchcraft* (Nashville, TN: Thomas Nelson, 1973), pp. 123-26.
69. Raphael Gasson, *The Challenging Counterfeit* (Plainfield, NJ: Logos, 1970), p. 36.
70. Ibid., p. 83.
71. Many spiritual teachers or leaders admit their occultic training, e.g., Paul Twitchell in *The Flute of God* (San Diego: Illuminated Way Press, 1975), p. 118, and Brad Steiger, *In My Soul I Am Free* (San Diego: Illuminated Way Press, n.d.), pp. 82-83; Werner Erhard, founder of est in W. W. Bartley, *Werner Erhard, the Transformation of a Man: The Founding of est* (New York: Clarkson N. Porter, 1978), pp. 14, 37, 75-76, 81-82, 118-19, 145, 148, 158. Autobiographies of such leaders often reveal such involvement, e.g., for Jose Silva, founder of Silva Mind Control, *I Have a Hunch: The Autobiography of Jose Silva* (Laredo, TX: Institute of Psychorientology, 1983), Chapters 10, 17, 21, 23, 29; for Earlyne Chaney, cofounder of Astara, *Remembering: The Autobiography of a Mystic* (Los Angeles: Astara, 1974), Chapters 9-16; Paramahansa Yogananda, founder of the Self-Realization Fellowship, *Autobiography of a Yogi* (Los Angeles: Self-Realization Fellowship, 1973), Chapters 14, 43.
72. See Malachi Martin, *Hostage to the Devil* (New York: Bantam, 1980) for examples.
73. See Kurt Koch, *Occult Bondage and Deliverance* (Grand Rapids, MI: Kregel, 1970); John Warwick Montgomery, ed., *Demon Possession* (Minneapolis, MN: Bethany, 1976).
74. See Martin Ebon, ed., *The Satan Trap: Dangers of the Occult* (Garden City, NY: Doubleday, 1976); and Emma Bragdon, *A Sourcebook for Helping People in Spiritual Emergency*, 1987, part of her Ph.D. dissertation of the same title on record at the Institute for Transpersonal Psychology in Menlo Park, CA.
75. See Koch, *Occult Bondage and Deliverance*, and for the counseling professional his *Christian Counseling and Occultism* (Grand Rapids, MI: Kregel, 1972).
76. John Stott, *Becoming a Christian* (Downers Grove, IL: InterVarsity, 1950), pp. 25-26.

Part Five—Spirit Guides

1. Alan Gauld, *The Founders of Psychical Research* (New York: Schocken Books, 1968), p. 24.
2. William James, "Report on Mrs. Piper's Hodgson Control," *Proceedings of the English Society for Psychical Research*, Vol. 23, pp. 1-121, from Klimo, *Channeling: Investigations*, p. 238. By "demons" James refers to evil spirits in general and not necessarily in a biblical sense.
3. Klimo, *Channeling: Investigations*, pp. 1, 24,27; Brooks Alexander, "Theology from the Twilight Zone," *Christianity Today*, Sep. 18, 1987, p. 22.

4. Nina Easton, "Shirley MacLaine's Mysticism for the Masses," *The Los Angeles Times Magazine*, Sep. 6, 1987, p. 33; Klimo, *Channeling: Investigations*, pp. 44, 48-49; Katherine Lowry, "Channelers: Mouthpieces of the Spirits," *Omni Magazine*, Oct. 1987, p. 22.
5. Slater Brown, *The Heyday of Spiritualism* (New York: Pocket Books, 1972), pp. 159-60.
6. Nandor Fodor cites the *North American Review*, Apr. 1855, as accurate in giving the figure of nearly two million spiritists in 1855. Nandor Fodor, *An Encyclopedia of Psychic Science* (Secaucus, NJ: Citadel, 1974), p. 362; Alfred Douglas, *Extra-Sensory Powers: A Century of Psychical Research* (Woodstock, New York: Overlook Press, 1977), p. 54. On the authority of the editor of the *Home Journal* he cites 40,000 spiritualists in New York in 1853; Gauld, *The Founders of Psychical Research*, p. 15.
7. This is evident from any number of historical studies. See Paul Kurtz, "Introduction: More Than a Century of Psychical Research," in Paul Kurtz, ed., *A Skeptic's Handbook of Parapsychology* (Buffalo, NY: Prometheus, 1985), pp. xii-xiv; John Beloff, "Historical Overview" in Benjamin B. Wolman, ed., *Handbook of Parapsychology* (New York: Van Nostrand Reinhold, 1977), pp. 4-7; J. B. Rhine, "A Century of Parapsychology" in Martin Ebon, ed., *The Signet Handbook of Parapsychology* (New York: Signet, 1978), p. 11.
8. See e.g., E. J. Dingwall, "The Need for Responsibility in Parapsychology: My Sixty Years in Psychical Research" in Paul Kurtz, *A Skeptic's Handbook of Parapsychology*, pp. 161, 174.
9. Lynn Smith, "The New Chic Metaphysical Fad of Channeling," *Los Angeles Times*, Dec. 5, 1986, Part 5.
10. Easton, "Shirley MacLaine's Mysticism," pp. 8-10, 32-34; Klimo, *Channeling: Investigations*, p. 49; John Ankerberg and John Weldon, *The Facts On The New Age Movement* (Chattanooga, TN: The John Ankerberg Evangelistic Association, 1988), pp. 6-7, 13-15.
11. Brooks Alexander, "Theology from the Twilight Zone," p. 22; Klimo, *Channeling: Investigations*, p. 42.
12. Klimo, *Channeling: Investigations*, pp. 4-6, 62-68; Easton, "Shirley MacLaine's Mysticism," p. 10. Various magazines devoted exclusively to channeling include *Spirit Speaks, Metapsychology: The Journal of Discarnate Intelligence,* and *The Channel Sourceletter* (Ottawa).
13. e.g., Mark Vaz, "Psychic!—The Many Faces of Kevin Ryerson" (interview), *Yoga Journal*, July/Aug. 1986, pp. 26-29, 92; Klimo, *Channeling: Investigations*, pp. 3, 20, 39, 64-69, 131-32, 167, 237-53, 205-320; Stephan Schwartz, *The Secret Vaults of Time: Psychic Archaeology and the Quest for Man's Beginning* (New York: Grosset & Dunlap, 1978); Gerald G. Jampolsky, *Goodbye to Guilt: Releasing Fear Through Forgiveness* (New York: Bantam, 1985), (based on *A Course in Miracles*); Jane Roberts, *Adventures in Consciousness: An Introduction to Aspect Psychology* (1975); John Weldon and Zola Levitt, *Psychic Healing* (Chicago: Moody Press, 1982), pp. 7-22, 42-46.
14. A. Harwood, *Rx: Spiritist as Needed* (New York: John Wiley & Sons, 1977), cited in Albert Villoldo and Stanley Krippner, *Healing States: A Journey Into the World of Spiritual Healing and Shamanism* (New York: Fireside/Simon & Schuster, 1987), p. 198.
15. Klimo, *Channeling: Investigations*, pp. 61-64, 67; George W. Meek, ed., *Healers and the Healing Process* (Wheaton, IL: Theosophical Publishing/Quest Book, 1977), pp. 13-70.
16. Walter Martin, *The Kingdom of the Cults* (Minneapolis, MN: Bethany, 1985), rev., p. 227. Martin estimates over 4 million spiritists in South America.
17. Vaz, "Psychic!—The Many Faces," p. 27.
18. Klimo, *Channeling: Investigations*, p. 45.
19. Ibid., pp. 43-44.
20. Ibid., pp. 48-49.
21. According to Merv Griffin, "The Merv Griffin Show," July 25, 1986.
22. Klimo, *Channeling: Investigations*, p. 49.
23. Erika Bourguignon, ed., *Religion, Altered States of Consciousness and Social Change* (Columbia: Ohio State University Press, 1973), pp. 16-17; Table 2.
24. Orthodox Christianity and Judaism are almost alone in the universal condemnation of seeking to contact the spirit world. The practice is accepted, variously, among Hindus, Buddhists, Sufis, Sikhs, Muslims, Kabbalists, Taoists, Animists, etc. See the extensive discussion in James Hastings, ed., *Encyclopedia of Religion and Ethics* (New York: Charles Scribner's Sons, n.d.), Vol. 4, pp. 565-636.
25. This is proven beyond reasonable doubt by both the history of the occult and the modern data from parapsychology. See e.g., Douglas, *Extra-Sensory Powers*, pp. 87-360; Gauld, *The Founders of Psychical Research*, pp. 153-364; Naomi Hintze and Gaither Pratt, *The Psychic Realm, What Can You Believe?* (New York: Random House, 1975), pp. 135-223; Norma Bowles and Fran Hynds, *Psi-search* (San Francisco: Harper & Row, 1978), pp. 51-91.
26. John Warwick Montgomery, ed., *Demon Possession: A Medical, Historical, Anthropological and Theological Symposium* (Minneapolis, MN: Bethany Fellowship, 1976); Malachi Martin, *Hostage to the Devil: The Possession and Exorcism of Five Living Americans* (New York: Bantam, 1977); William M. Alexander, *Demonic Possession in the New Testament: Its Historical, Medical and Theological Aspects* (Grand Rapids, MI: Baker, 1980); John L. Nevius, *Demon Possession* (Grand Rapids, MI: Kregel, 1970).
27. Satprem, *Sri Aurobindo or the Adventure of Consciousness* (New York: Harper & Row, 1974), p. 199, cf., 197, 201.
28. Robert Monroe, *Journeys Out of the Body* (Garden City, NY: Anchor Books, 1973), pp. 138-39.
29. Samuel M. Warren, *A Compendium of the Theological Writings of Emanuel Swedenborg* (New York: Swedenborg Foundation, 1977), p. 618. See Slater Brown, *The Heyday of Spiritualism*, p. 63.
30. Emanuel Swedenborg, *The True Christian Religion* (New York: E. P. Dutton, 1936), pp. 667-69; Emanuel Swedenborg, *Heaven and Its Wonders and Hell* (New York: Swedenborg Foundation, 1940), pp. 265-68; Rev. John Whitehead, *Posthumous Theological Works of Emanuel Swedenborg*, Vol. 1 (New York: Swedenborg Foundation, 1969), p. 452; Samuel M. Warren, *A Compendium of the Theological Writings of Emanuel Swedenborg* (New York: Swedenborg Foundation, 1977), pp. 376-77.
31. e.g., Nevius, *Demon Possession*, p. 322; Chapters. 2, 8-10, 14-18.
32. Note the descriptions in Jane Roberts, *Seth Speaks* (Englewood Cliffs, NJ: Prentice Hall, 1972), pp. 1-2 and back cover photographs; Klimo, *Channeling: Investigations*, p. 185.
33. e.g., guru Sri Chinmoy has produced thousands of paintings by automatic painting. In less than two hours on June 26, 1975 Sri Chinmoy painted 500 paintings. *Sri Chinmoy* (Jamaica, NY: Aum Publications, n.d.), pp. 15-18; Rosemary Brown, *Unfinished Symphonies* (New York: William Morrow & Company, 1971). Medium Rosemary Brown has composed hundreds of musical pieces in styles very similar to the famous dead composers she claims work through her.
34. Klimo, *Channeling: Investigations*, pp. 185-86; Raphael Gasson, *The Challenging Counterfeit* (Plainfield, NJ: Logos, 1970), pp. 83, 87.
35. Klimo, *Channeling: Investigations*. Chapter 6 discusses many of these forms.

36. Clifford Wilson and John Weldon, *Psychic Forces and Occult Shock* (Greenville, NC: Global Publishers, 1987), pp. 282-83.
37. Klimo, *Channeling: Investigations*, pp. 46-47, 50, 61, 64; Edward Rosenfeld, *The Book of Highs: 250 Ways to Alter Consciousness Without Drugs* (New York: Quadrangle/The New York Times Book Company, 1973).
38. Edmond C. Gruss, *The Ouija Board: Doorway to the Occult* (Chicago: Moody Press, 1975); Stoker Hunt, *Ouija: The Most Dangerous Game* (New York: Perennial/Harper & Row, 1985).
39. Gasson, *The Challenging Counterfeit*, Chapter 1; Victor Ernest, *I Talked with Spirits* (Wheaton, IL: Tyndale House, 1971), Chapter 1.
40. Klimo, *Channeling: Investigations*, p. 3.
41. Ibid., p. 1; Ankerberg and Weldon, *The Facts on The New Age Movement*, pp. 15-16.
42. Ibid., pp. 5, 18, 168-84; Elliott Miller, "Channeling—Spiritistic Revelations for the New Age" (Part One), *Christian Research Journal*, Fall 1987, p. 14.
43. Pat Rodegast and Judith Stanton, *Emmanuel's Book: A Manual for Living Comfortably in the Cosmos* (New York: Some Friends of Emmanuel, 1985), p. xxi.
44. e.g., Klimo, *Channeling: Investigations*, pp. 14, 20, 39, 131-32, 205-320; see Wilson and Weldon, *Psychic Forces*, Part 3.
45. C. S. Lewis, *The Screwtape Letters* (New York: MacMillan, 1943, 1969), pp. 32-33.
46. e.g., Klimo, *Channeling: Investigations*, pp. 39, 131-32, 184, 237-53.
47. Ibid., pp. 183-84.
48. Another analysis will be found in Miller, "Channeling—Spiritistic Revelations," Part 2.
49. Martin Ebon observes, "The mesmeric, or hypnotic, trance bears a close resemblance to the mediumistic trance." Martin Ebon, "History of Parapsychology" in Martin Ebon, ed., *The Signet Handbook of Parapsychology* (New York: Signet, 1978), p. 24. Edgar Cayce became a medium through hypnosis. See Thomas Sugrue, *There is a River* (New York: Holt, Rinehart and Winston, 1942); Alan Spraggett, *Ross Peterson: The New Edgar Cayce* (Garden City, NY: Doubleday, 1977), pp. 14-15; see also Simeon Edmunds, *Hypnotism and ESP* (Los Angeles: Wilshire Books, 1969), pp. 61-155; Simeon Edmunds, *Hypnosis: Key to Psychic Powers* (New York: Samuel Weiser, 1968), pp. 9-63; Eric J. Dingwall, ed., *Abnormal Hypnotic Phenomena: A Survey of 19th Century Cases*, Vol. 4 (New York: Barnes and Noble, 1967).
50. Edmunds, *Hypnosis: Key to Psychic Powers*; Frank Podmore, *Mediums of the 19th Century*, Vols. 1 and 2 (New Hyde Park, NY: University Books, 1963), Vols. 1 and 2; Leslie Shepard, *Encyclopedia of Occultism and Parapsychology* (Detroit, MI: Gale Research Company, 1979), article under "Hypnosis"; Hiroshi Motoyama, *Hypnosis and Religious Superconsciousness* (Tokyo, Japan: The Institute of Religious Psychology, 1971).
51. In fact spirit incorporation resembles a state of deep hypnosis. See Albert Villoldo and Stanley Krippner, *Healing States: A Journey Into the World of Spiritual Healing and Shamanism* (New York: Simon and Schuster, 1987), pp. 197-98; cf., Klimo, *Channeling: Investigations*, pp. 38, 219-27.
52. The Troops for Truddi Chase (Introduction and Epilogue by Robert A. Phillips, Jr.); *When Rabbit Howls* (New York: E. P. Dutton, 1987), pp. xvii, xxiii, 387-93, 411-15. See note 54.
53. Villoldo and Krippner, *Healing States*, pp. 20-21, 38, 197; Klimo, *Channeling: Investigations*, pp. 237-47.
54. e.g., Robert A. Phillips in the Introduction and Epilogue to *The Troops for Truddi Chase* by Robert A. Phillips, Jr., p. x, observes: "Dr. [Frank] Putnam has discovered [in observing over 200 cases] that there are significant differences in brain wave patterns, voice tone and inflection, eye responses to stimuli and other responses to both physical and psychological stimuli among the personalities even though they are found in the same body. My own clinical observation has noted differences in handwriting, syntax, voice, accent, facial appearance, and body stance . . . . The growing body of data indicates that the personalities (or "persons" as some multiples prefer to call them) are quite different and in fact are unique individuals."
55. Kenneth Ring, *Heading Toward Omega: In Search of the Meaning of the Near-Death Experience* (New York: Quill/William Morrow, 1985), esp. Chapters. 3-9. John Weldon and Zola Levitt, *Is There Life After Death?* (Eugene, OR: Harvest House, 1977); *Anabiosis: The Journal of Near-Death Studies*, volumes to the present.
56. Ben G. Hester, *Dowsing: An Exposé of Hidden Occult Forces* (Arlington, CA: Ben G. Hester, 4883 Headrick Avenue, Arlington, CA 92505, 1984), rev. 1984, $7.95.
57. Clifford Wilson and John Weldon, *Close Encounters: A Better Explanation* (San Diego: Master Books, 1978).
58. Clifford Wilson and John Weldon, *Psychic Forces and Occult Shock* (Chattanooga, TN: Global Publishers, 1987), pp. 331-454.
59. e.g., Klimo, *Channeling: Investigations*, pp. 6-8; John Ferguson, *An Illustrated Encyclopedia of Mysticism and the Mystery Religions* (New York: Seabury, 1977), p. 148.
60. John Weldon and Zola Levitt, *Psychic Healing* (Chicago: Moody Press, 1982); Paul Reisser, Teri Reisser and John Weldon, *New Age Medicine* (Downers Grove, IL: InterVarsity, 1988).
61. Klimo, *Channeling: Investigations*, pp. 242-47.
62. Hans Bender, "Mediumistic Psychoses" in *Telepathy, Clairvoyance, and Psychokinesis* (Munich: Piper Publishers, 1983).
63. Kurt Koch and Alfred Lechler, *Occult Bondage and Deliverance* (Grand Rapids, MI: Kregel, 1970), p. 31; Part 2; Kurt Koch, *Demonology, Past and Present* (Grand Rapids, MI: Kregel, 1973), pp. 41-42.
64. Wilson Van Dusen, *The Presence of Other Worlds* (San Francisco: Harper & Row, 1974), pp. 117-18, 135-37. In this book he correlates the experiences of the powerful medium Emanuel Swedenborg with his own mental patients.
65. Harry Thomsen, *The New Religions of Japan* (Rutland, VT: Charles E. Tuttle, 1971), pp. 15-18. In *Soka Gakkai: Japan's Militant Buddhists* (John Knox, 1968), p. 28, Noah S. Brannen observes that one-third of the popular religions of Japan began from special revelation by a god or spirit being.
66. Thomsen, *New Religions of Japan*, p. 200.
67. Robert S. Ellwood, Jr., *Religious and Spiritual Groups in Modern America* (Englewood Cliffs, NJ: Prentice Hall, 1973), p. 12 where he states, "The cult phenomena could almost be called a modern resurgence of shamanism." Mr. Weldon's eight years of research into 65 modern religious cults and sects revealed spiritistic origins or associations in every one.
68. Klimo, *Channeling: Investigations*, p. 8; his arguments here concerning Christianity (pp. 85-90) involve a false interpretation of the Bible.
69. These religions accept spiritistic revelations.
70. John Weldon, *The Encyclopedia of Contemporary American Religions, Sects and Cults*, unpublished.
71. Ibid.
72. e.g., ". . . Kal [the devil] is the Jehovah of the Jewish faith and the Father of the Christian teachings . . ."; "Therefore we really see [Jesus] as a son of Kal . . ." Paul Twitchell, *The Precepts of Eckankar* (Eckankar, ASOST,

n.d.), No. 11, p. 6, and his *Letters to a Chela* (Eckankar, ASOST, 1972) first series, No. 3, p. 1. See the analysis in SCP Journal, *Eckankar: A Hard Look at a New Religion* (Berkeley, CA: Spiritual Counterfeits Project), Vol. 3, No. 1, 1979, pp. 26-28. The Radhasoami Sect from which Eckankar was derived has certain teachings in common with the Cathars of the later Middle Ages who also taught the biblical God was the devil. See Williston Walker et al., *A History of the Christian Church*, 4th ed., 1985, p. 302.

73. David Lane, "Eckankar in Turmoil, Part 1," *Understanding Cults and Spiritual Movements— Research Series*, Vol. 2, No. 1 (Del Mar, CA: Del Mar Press), pp. 1-6, 17-19.

74. SCP Journal, *Eckankar: A Hard Look*, pp. 7-22.

75. Ibid., pp. 1-55; Lane, "Eckankar in Turmoil, Part 1," pp. 1-6, 17-15.

76. SCP Journal, *Eckankar: A Hard Look*, pp. 14-21, 45-47.

77. Ibid., pp. 42-44.

78. Ibid., pp. 24-27.

79. Ibid., pp. 6-22.

80. Ibid., pp. 34-37.

81. Ibid., and Lane, "Eckankar in Turmoil, Part 1," Vol. 2, No. 1.

82. SCP Journal, *Eckankar: A Hard Look*, p. 39.

83. Klimo, *Channeling: Investigations*, p. 297.

84. Ibid.

85. Ibid., p. 296.

86. Colin Wilson, *Mysteries: An Investigation Into the Occult, the Paranormal and the Supernatural* (New York: G. P. Putnam's Sons, 1978), pp. 460, 484.

87. James Hastings, ed., *Encyclopedia of Religion and Ethics*, Vol. 4, pp. 565-636.

88. e.g., lifelong occultist David Conway, "A Word About Demons," in his *Magic: An Occult Primer* (New York: Bantam, 1973), pp. 196-99. He discusses how evil the demons are and the damage they can do, noting their chief aim is to destroy men, especially occultists.

89. John Warwick Montgomery, *Demon Possession*, (Bethany, 1976); T. K. Oesterreich, *Possession: Demonical and Other* (Citadel, 1974); Malachi Martin, *Hostage to the Devil* (Bantam, 1977); no author, *Demon Experiences in Many Lands— A Compilation* (Chicago: Moody Press, 1960).

90. Doreen Irvine, *Freed from Witchcraft* (Thomas Nelson, 1978), p. 138.

91. M. Scott Peck, *People of the Lie: The Hope for Healing Human Evil* (New York: Simon & Schuster, 1983), p. 190.

92. See William Lane Craig, *The Son Rises* (Chicago: Moody Press, 1987) for a stalwart historical defense of the resurrection.

93. C. S. Lewis, *The Screwtape Letters* (New York: MacMillan, 1971), p vii.

94. John Warwick Montgomery, *Principalities and Powers* (Minneapolis, MN: Bethany, 1973), p. 146.

95. John Warwick Montgomery, ed., *Demon Possession*, p. 232.

96. Edmond Gruss, *The Ouija Board: Doorway to the Occult* (Chicago: Moody Press, 1975), pp. 83-94.

97. On human sacrifice see Nigel Davies, *Human Sacrifice in History and Today* (New York: William Morrow, 1981), pp. 13-28, 84-87, 92-98, 275-89; *The Chattanooga Times*, Mar. 25, 1988, where a 7-year-old girl is murdered by a Hindu priest in a ritual offering to a goddess; and Maury Terry, *The Ultimate Evil: An Investigation of America's Most Dangerous Satanic Cult* (Garden City, NY: Doubleday/Dolphin, 1987), introduction, Chapter 25.

98. On the Atlanta slayings, Sondra A. O'Neal (Emory University in Atlanta), *King City: Fathers of Anguish, of Blood: The True Story Behind the Atlanta Murders* (unpublished).

99. Robert Somerlott, *Here, Mr. Splitfoot* (New York: Viking, 1971), p. 12; Gruss, *The Ouija Board*, recommends Dr. Charles C. Cumberland's *Mexican Revolution: Genesis Under Madero* which identifies Francisco I. Madero, the originator of the Mexican revolution, as a leader of spiritism in Mexico. According to a report in the *Wall Street Journal*, June 12, 1987, a similar situation may currently exist in Panama.

100. *Los Angeles Times*, Oct. 4, 1977.

101. Nandor Fodor, *An Encyclopedia of Psychic Science*, p. 266; Bhagwan Shree Rajneesh, "Suicide or Sannyas," *Sannyas*, No. 2, 1978, pp. 27-31; Gruss, *The Ouija Board*; J. D. Pearce-Higgins, "Dangers of the Occult (Garden City, NY: Doubleday, 1976), pp. 232-36; Doreen Irvine, *Freed From Witchcraft* (Nashville: Thomas Nelson), p. 121; J. D. Pearce-Higgins, "Dangers of Automatism," *Spiritual Frontiers*, Autumn 1970, p. 216; Morton Kelsey, *The Christian and the Supernatural* (Minneapolis: Augsburg, 1976), p. 41.

102. Elliott O'Donnell, *The Menace of Spiritualism* (New York: Frederick A. Stokes, 1920), p. xii.

103. *Human Behavior*, Sep. 1977, pp. 26-27.

104. J. N. D. Anderson in *The World's Religions* (Grand Rapids, MI: Eerdman's, 1968), p. 55; J. M. Rodwell, trans., *The Koran* (New York: Dutton, 1977), preface, pp. 5, 13-14; William Miller, *A Christian Response to Islam* (NJ: Presbyterian and Reformed, 1977), pp. 19-20; and Sura 32:22, 44:29, in Rodwell text.

105. Thomas Sugrue, *There is a River*, p. 210.

106. Holistic Life Magazine, Summer 1985, p. 30: For another example, see Laeh Garfield, *Companions in Spirit: A Guide to Working with your Spirit Helpers* (Berkeley, CA: Celestial Arts, 1984), pp. 92-93.

107. Andrija Puharich, *Uri* (New York: Bantam, 1975), pp. 173, 188-89.

108. as told by his friend Colin Wilson, *Mysteries*, p. 451.

109. Gasson, *The Challenging Counterfeit*, p. 130.

110. Kurt Koch cites a figure of 9 out of 10 cases of occult involvement harming people, supported by "many thousands of examples" (Koch and Lechler, *Occult Bondage and Deliverance*, p. 30).

111. Nandor Fodor, *An Encyclopedia of Psychic Science*, pp. 233-38; Gasson, *The Challenging Counterfeit*, p. 87.

112. Dr. Nandor Fodor, *An Encyclopedia of Psychic Science*, p. 234, observes: "After prolonged exercise of mediumship intemperance often sets in. The reason is a craving for stimulants following the exhaustion and depletion felt after the seance. Many mediums have been known who succumbed to the craving and died of delirium tremens "; the editors of Psychic Magazine, *Psychics: Indepth Interviews*, pp. 16-17; cf., Ford's autobiography *Unknown but Known: My Adventure into the Meditative Dimension* (New York: Harper & Row, 1968).

113. Merrill Unger, *The Haunting of Bishop Pike* (Wheaton, IL: Tyndale House, 1971).

114. Keene, M. Lamar, *The Psychic Mafia: The True and Shocking Confessions of a Famous Medium*, (New York: St. Martins Press, 1976), p. 142.

115. Fodor, *An Encyclopedia of Psychic Science*, mentions cases of mediums who were weighed during ectoplasmic manifestations and lost from 10-118 pounds; the weight of the medium's body apparently decreases proportionately to the spirit's use of the medium's body to produce the materialized "phantom," which, in one case weighed from 52-77 pounds. See Arthur Conan Doyle, *The History of Spiritualism* (New York: Arno, 1975), Vol. 1, p. 278.

116. Joseph Millard, *Edgar Cayce* (Fawcett Gold Metal, 1967), pp. 98, 104-116, 156, 198-201.
117. Keene, *The Psychic Mafia*, pp. 133, 140; Fodor, *An Encyclopedia of Psychic Science*, p. 234.
118. Keene, *The Psychic Mafia*, p. 141, observes "cheating, lying, stealing, conning—these are sanctified in the ethics of mediumship as I knew it."
119. Keene, *The Psychic Mafia*, pp. 135, 142; Fodor, *An Encyclopedia of Psychic Science*, p. 234; Carl A. Wickland, *30 Years Among the Dead* (Van Nuys, CA: Newcastle, rpt., 1974), p. 154.
120. Wickland, *Thirty Years Among the Dead*, pp. 17, 95, 116, 185; Martin Ebon (ed.), *The Satan Trap: Dangers of the Occult* (Garden City, NY: Doubleday, 1976).
121. Keene, *The Psychic Mafia*, pp. 147-48.
122. Sri Chinmoy, *Astrology, the Supernatural and the Beyond* (Jamaica, NY: Angi Press, 1973), p. 62.
123. Kurt Koch, *Occult Bondage and Deliverance*, p. 31; Kurt Koch, *Occult ABC* (Germany: Literature Mission Aglasterhausen, Inc.), p. 238.
124. Fodor, *An Encyclopedia of Psychic Science*, p. 235; Hereword Carrington, *Your Psychic Powers and How to Develop Them* (Van Nuys, CA: Newcastle, 1975), p. 62.
125. Fodor, *An Encyclopedia of Psychic Science*, p. 235.
126. Malachi Martin, *Hostage to the Devil*, p. 419; cf., 385-488.
127. Ibid., p. 418.
128. Ibid., p. 485.
129. Gasson, *The Challenging Counterfeit*, Ernest, *I Talked with Spirits*.

Part Six—Astrology

1. *The Los Angeles Times*, Sep. 3, 1975, p. 1.
2. Donald Regan, *For the Record: From Wall Street to Washington* (New York: Harcourt Brace Jovanovich, 1988), p. 3.
3. June Wakefield, *Cosmic Astrology: The Religion of the Stars* (Lakemont, GA: CSA Press, 1968), p. 22.
4. Charles E.O. Carter, *The Principles of Astrology* (Wheaton, IL: Theosophical Publishing House, 1977), p. 13.
5. Theodore Laurence, *The Foundation Book of Astrology* (Secaucus, NJ: University Books, 1973), p. 13.
6. Jeff Mayo, *Astrology* (London: Hodder, and Stoughton, 1978), p. 15.
7. Owen S. Rachleff, *Sky Diamonds: The New Astrology* (New York: Popular Library, 1976), p. 15.
8. For example, "Ascendant," "Aspect," "House," "Sextile," "Cusp," "Sesquiquadrate," "Imum Coeli," "Ecliptic," "Opposition," "Quadruplicity," "Quincunx," "Trine," "Zodiac," "Descending Node," etc.
9. Neither is there agreement on the value of the aspects, which also leads to widely different interpretations.
10. John Anthony West and Jan Gerhard Toonder, *The Case for Astrology* (Baltimore, MD: Penguin Books, 1973), p. 1.
11. Lawrence E. Jerome, *Astrology Disproved* (Buffalo, NY: Prometheus Books, 1977), p. 1.
12. Bernard Gittelson, *Intangible Evidence* (New York: Simon and Schuster, 1987), p. 338.
13. The Gallup poll for Oct. 19, 1975. See R. B. Culver and P. A. Ianna, *The Gemini Syndrome: A Scientific Evaluation of Astrology* (St. Buffalo, NY: Prometheus Books, 1984), p. 2.
14. Derek Parker and Julia Parker, *The Compleat Astrology* (New York: Bantam, 1978), p. 178.
15. "News and Comment," *The Skeptical Inquirer*, Vol. 9, No. 2, pp. 113-14. The May 1988 Gallup Poll indicated overall belief in astrology was down, but this poll did not include the aftereffects of the White House revelations.
16. Geoffrey Dean, "Does Astrology Need to Be True? Part One: A Look at the Real Thing," *The Skeptical Inquirer*, Vol. 11, No. 2, p. 167.
17. Parker and Parker, *The Compleat Astrology*, p. 60.
18. e.g., see Eden Gray, *A Complete Guide to the Tarot* (New York: Bantam, 1980), pp. 204-27; also Javane & Bunker's *Numerology and the Divine Triangle* (Para Research, 1980), which integrates numerology, Tarot, and astrology as does John Sandbach's *Degree Analysis: Dwadashamsas and Deeper Meanings* (Seek It, 1983). Dane Rudhyar, Liz Greene, and Stephen Arroyo are three leading astrologers currently integrating psychology with astrology. See Joanne Sanders, "Connecting Therapy to the Heavens," *The Common Boundary*, Jan./Feb. 1987, pp. 11-14; also Alice Howell, *Jungian Symbolism in Astrology* (Wheaton, IL: Quest, 1987). West and Toonder, *The Case for Astrology*, pp. 221-27; Roy A. Gallant, *Astrology: Sense or Nonsense* (Garden City, NY: Doubleday, 1974), pp. 14-19. Gittelson, *Intangible Evidence*, pp. 350-353; on medical astrology, see Harry F. Darling, M.D., *Essentials of Medical Astrology* (Tempe, AZ: AFA, 1981); Omar V. Garrison, *Medical Astrology: How the Stars Influence Your Health* (New York: Warner, 1973); cf., Barb Bok and Lawrence E. Jerome, *Objections to Astrology* (Buffalo, NY: Prometheus Books, 1975), p. 46; C. Norman Shealy, *Occult Medicine Can Save Your Life* (New York: Bantam, 1977), p. 117; Gallant, *Astrology: Sense or Nonsense*, pp. 115-116. On Hinduism and Theosophy, see James Braha, *Ancient Hindu Astrology for the Modern Western Astrologer* (N. Miami, FL: Hermetician Press, 1986); Edward K. Wilson, Jr., *The Astrology of Theosophy* (Tempe, AZ: AFA, 1982).
19. Dean, "Does Astrology Need to Be True?", p. 167.
20. Joyce Wadler, "The President's Astrologers," *People Weekly*, May 23, 1988, p. 111; Gittelson, *Intangible Evidence*, pp. 352-53.
21. e.g., Mae Wilson-Ludlam taught the first accredited high school astrology course in 1972. The July 1988 AFA Convention handbook and book tables indicated several astrologers taught astrology at high school or college campuses e.g., Louise Bronley at Emory University.
22. Culver and Ianna, *The Gemini Syndrome*, p. 2.
23. From M. Kurt Goedelman, "Seeking Guidance From the Stars of Heaven," *Personal Freedom Outreach*, July/Sept. 1988, p. 5. This is probably exaggerated, although it is widely agreed that a significant number of major corporations do use astrology.
24. *The Los Angeles Times*, July 5, 1985, p. 1.
25. Henry Weingarten, *A Modern Introduction to Astrology* (New York: ASI Publishers, 1974), p. 28.
26. e.g., The American Federation of Astrologers in Tempe, Arizona offer tapes on this from past conventions. The July 1988 convention in Las Vegas also offered courses on the subject.
27. *The Los Angeles Times*, July 5, 1985, p. 1.
28. Geoffrey Dean, "Does Astrology Need To be True, Part 2—The Answer is No," *The Skeptical Inquirer*, Vol. 11, No. 3, p. 262.
29. E. Howe, "Astrology," in Richard Cavendish, ed., *Man, Myth and Magic: An Illustrated Encyclopedia of the Supernatural*, Vol. 1 (New York: Marshal Cavendish Corporation), p. 149.

30. e.g., Culver and Ianna, *The Gemini Syndrome*, pp. ix-218. See Question 23 and our *Astrology: Do the Heavens Rule Our Destiny?* (Harvest House, 1989).
31. John Weldon, *Hazards of Psychic Involvement*, unpublished, 1986, pp. 1-389. See the writings on the occult by Dr. Kurt Koch e.g., *Between Christ and Satan* (Grand Rapids, MI: Kregel, 1962) and Dr. Merrill Unger (e.g., *Demons in the World Today* (Wheaton, IL: Tyndale, 1972). Also see Edmond Gruss, *The Ouija Board: Doorway to the Occult* (Chicago: Moody, 1975), pp. 59-112; Merrill Unger, *The Haunting of Bishop Pike* (Wheaton, IL: Tyndale, 1971); Personal testimonies include Doreen Irvine, *Freed From Witchcraft* (Nashville: Thomas Nelson, 1973); Johanna Michaelsen, *The Beautiful Side of Evil* (Eugene, OR: Harvest House, 1982); Raphael Gasson, *The Challenging Counterfeit* (Plainfield, NJ: Logos, 1970); and Malachi Martin, *Hostage to the Devil: The Possession and Exorcism of Five Living Americans* (NY: Bantam, 1977).
32. See Merrill Unger, *Biblical Demonology* (Wheaton, IL: Scripture Press, 1971); C. Fred Dickason, *Angels: Elect and Evil* (Chicago, IL: Moody Press, 1975); and Merrill Unger, *Demons in the World Today*.
33. Significantly, in eight of ten courses taken at random during the July 4-8, 1988 American Federation of Astrology convention in Las Vegas, NV, the astrology instructors admitted to having spirit-guides. The definition cited is from Merrill Unger, *Biblical Demonology*, p. 119.
34. Apart from the literature that could be cited, this was admitted by most of the dozens of astrologers we talked with at the July 1988 American Federation of Astrologers convention in Las Vegas, Nevada.
35. *The Los Angeles Times*, Jan. 15, 1975.
36. Ibid.
37. Carter, *The Principles of Astrology*, p. 14.
38. in Gittelson, *Intangible Evidence*, p. 350.
39. Clifford Wilson and John Weldon, *Psychic Forces* (Chattanooga, TN: Global, 1987), pp. 331-345.
40. In addition, at the May 1988 AFA convention 20-year astrologer Rev. Irene Diamond told us the spirits personally led her into astrology and that all her books on astrology were produced by spirit dictation and/or automatic writing. The current AFA president, Doris Chase Doane, told us that the spirits' efforts through the occult Church of Light (founded by C. C. Zain) is "very important to the work of astrology."
41. Alice Bailey, *Esoteric Astrology*, Vol. 3 of *A Treatise on the Seven Rays* (London: Lucius Trust, 1982).
42. Margaret H. Gammon, *Astrology and the Edgar Cayce Readings* (Virginia Beach: A.R.E. Press, 1987) p. viii.
43. Ibid., p. 15; reading no. 3744-3.
44. West and Toonder, *The Case for Astrology*, pp. 107-08.
45. Daniel Logan, *The Reluctant Prophet* (1980), pp. 63-65, 169-70.
46. Marcus Allen, *Astrology for the New Age: An Intuitive Approach* (Sebastopol, CA: CRCS Publications, 1979), pp. 2, 6. A brief perusal of over 500 books authored by astrologers at the July 1988 convention revealed that many astrologers, if not most, were into other forms of the occult. This was also true for most of the astrologers we talked with.
47. "Sepharial," *A Manual of Occultism* (New York: Samuel Weiser, 1978), p. 3.
48. Sybil Leek, *My Life in Astrology* (Englewood Cliffs, NJ: Prentice Hall, 1972), p. 11.
49. Ibid., p. 12.
50. Ibid., pp. 19, 31, 48.
51. Doreen Valiente, *An ABC of Witchcraft Past and Present* (New York: St. Martin's Press, 1973), p. 21.
52. Ibid., p. 23.
53. Dean Rudhyar, *The Practice of Astrology* (New York: Penguin Books, 1975), p. 21.
54. Weingarten, *A Modern Introduction to Astrology*, p. 77.
55. Richard Cavendish, *The Black Arts* (New York: G.P. Putnam's Sons, 1967), pp. 219, 222, 225.
56. Keith Thomas, *Religion and the Decline of Magic* (New York: Charles Scribner's Sons, 1971), Chapter 21.
57. Ibid., p. 634.
58. Bok and Jerome, *Objections to Astrology*, p. 225.
59. Ibid., p. 76.
60. John Warwick Montgomery, *Principalities and Powers* (Minneapolis, MN: Bethany, 1976), p. 96.
61. Edward J. Moody, "Magical Therapy: An Anthropological Investigation of Contemporary Satanism," in Irving I. Zaretsky and Mark P. Leone, *Religious Movements in Contemporary America* (Princeton, NJ: Princeton University Press, 1974), pp. 362-63.
62. In 17 years of reading New Age, Eastern, psychic, and occult literature this was acknowledged in every text read.
63. Gittelson, *Intangible Evidence*, pp. 348, 353.
64. Charles Strohmer, *What Your Horoscope Doesn't Tell You* (Wheaton, IL: Tyndale House, 1988), pp. 45-55.
65. Robert Leichtman, M.D., "Clairvoyant Diagnosis," in the *Journal of Holistic Health* (San Diego: Association for Holistic Health/Mandala Society, 1977), p. 40.
66. Parker and Parker, *The Compleat Astrology*, p. 129.
67. Jeanne Avery, *The Rising Sun: Your Astrological Mask* (Garden City, NY: Doubleday, 1982), p. 396.
68. Syndey Omarr, *My World of Astrology* (Hollywood, CA: Wilshire Book Company, 1965), p. 21.
69. Ralph Metzner, *Maps of Consciousness* (New York: Collier, 1976), p. 126.
70. Parker and Parker, *The Compleat Astrology*, pp. 88-96, 145.
71. Colin Wilson, *The Occult: A History* (New York: Vintage Books, 1973), p. 250.
72. Howe, in Cavendish (ed.) *Man, Myth, Magic*, pp. 153-54.
73. Michael Shallis, "The Problem of Astrological Research," *Correlation*, Vol. 1, no. 2, pp. 41-46 from Kelly and Krutzen, "Humanistic Astrology: A Critique," *The Skeptical Inquirer*, Vol. 8, No. 1, p. 73.
74. Gittelson, *Intangible Evidence*, p. 354.
75. Ibid., pp. 353-54.
76. Ibid., pp. 29, 306-08, 282-83.
77. Metzner, *Maps of Consciousness*, p. 111.
78. Allen, *Astrology for the New Age*, p. 6.
79. Rudhyar, *The Practice of Astrology*, pp. 130, 136.
80. Leek, *My Life in Astrology*, pp. 19, 202.
81. Gittelson, *Intangible Evidence*, pp. 348-49.
82. Isabel M. Hickey, *Astrology: A Cosmic Science* (Watertown, MA: privately published, 1974), pp. 275-76.
83. Robert A. Morey, *Horoscopes and the Christian* (Minneapolis, MN: Bethany, 1981), p. 54.
84. Ronald Davison, *Synastry: Understanding Human Relations Through Astrology* (New York: ASI Publishers, 1978), p. 94.

85. Allen, *Astrology for the New Age*, p. 117.
86. Rudhyar, *The Practice of Astrology*, p. 8.
87. Davison, *Astrology*, (New York: ARC Books, 1970), p. 12.
88. Mayo, *Astrology*, p. 7.
89. Joseph F. Goodavage, *Astrology: The Space Age Science* (New York: Signet, 1967), p. xi.
90. For illustrations see James Sire, *Scripture Twisting* (Downers Grove, IL: InterVarsity, 1982).
91. James Bjornstad and Shildes Johnson, *Stars Signs and Salvation in the Age of Aquarius* (Minneapolis, MN: Bethany, 1971), pp. 36-90.
92. Gallant, *Astrology: Sense or Nonsense*, p. 111.
93. For a very brief review see Bjornstad and Johnson, *Star Signs and Salvation*, pp. 88-89.
94. In the thirteenth to sixteenth centuries astrology was variously practiced in the church, in part due to the influence of Thomas Aquinas.
95. Morey, *Horoscopes and the Christian*, pp. 48-49.
96. Jeane Dixon, *Yesterday, Today and Forever: How Astrology Can Help You Find Your Place in God's Plan* (New York: Bantam, 1977), p. 6.
97. Ibid., pp. 7-9.
98. Ibid., p. 12.
99. Ibid., p. 502.
100. John Warwick Montgomery, *Principalities and Powers* (Minneapolis, MN: Bethany, 1976), p. 110.
101. Letter on file dated June 2, 1986.
102. Clifford Wilson and John Weldon, *Psychic Forces* (Chattanooga, TN: Global, 1987), see section on Christian parapsychology.
103. Promotional brochure for AFA Golden Anniversary Convention included with product price list, Winter 1987-1988. But a week-long visit to their July 1988 convention revealed that many of the astrologers had spirit guides and practiced other forms of the occult. The President and First Vice President of the AFA are both spiritists.
104. The Gauquelin research; Mark Urban-Lurain, *Astrology as Science: A Statistical Approach* (Tempe, AZ: American Federation of Astrologers, 1984), see pp. 1, 10-11, 32-33; Jeannette Glenn, *How To Prove Astrology* (Tempe, AZ: American Federation of Astrologers, 1981), see p. 13.
105. Dean, "Does Astrology Need To be True, Part 1," p. 167; Urban-Luraine, *Astrology as Science*, p. 1.
106. Dean, "Does Astrology Need To be True, Part 1," p. 175, citing I. W. Kelly, R. Culver and P. J. Loptson, 1986, "Arguments of the Astrologers: A Critical Examination" in Bisivas et al., eds., *Cosmic Perspectives* (India's Science Circle, India).
107. Kelly and Saklofske, "Alternative Explanations in Science: The Extroversion-Introversion Astrological Effect," in *The Skeptical Inquirer*, Vol. 5, No. 4, p. 35. This contains a summary of the events.
108. Culver and Ianna, *The Gemini Syndrome*, p. 216. The controversy may be traced in *The Skeptical Inquirer*, Vol. 4, No. 2, pp. 19-64; Vol. 5, No. 4, pp. 62-65; Vol. 6, No. 2, p. 67; and Vol. 7, No. 3, pp. 77-82.
109. Michael Gauquelin, "Zodiac and Personality: An Empirical Study," *The Skeptical Inquirer*, Vol. 6, No. 3, p. 57.
110. Ibid., pp. 57-64.
111. Michael Gauquelin, *The Scientific Basis of Astrology: Myth or Reality* (New York: Stein and Day, 1973), p. 145.
112. Dean et al., "The Guardian Astrology Study: A Critique and Reanalysis," *The Skeptical Inquirer*, Vol. 9, No. 4, pp. 327-37.
113. Mechler et al., "Response to the National Enquirer Astrology Study," *The Skeptical Inquirer*, Vol. 5, No. 2, pp. 34-41.
114. Cited in Dean, "Does Astrology Need To be True, Part 1," p. 178.
115. Ibid., p. 173.
116. e.g., Gittelson, *Intangible Evidence*, p. 355.
117. Ralph Bastedo, "An Empirical Test of Popular Astrology," *The Skeptical Inquirer*, Vol. 3, No. 1, p. 34.
118. Kurtz and Fraknoi, "Tests of Astrology Do Not Support Its Claims," *The Skeptical Inquirer*, Vol. 9, No. 3, p. 211.
119. John McGervey, "A Statistical Test of Sun-sign Astrology," *The Zetetic*, Vol. 1, No. 2, p. 53.
120. Dean, "Does Astrology Need To be True, Part 2," p. 267.
121. Douglas Lackey, "Controlled Test of Perceived Horoscope Accuracy," *The Skeptical Inquirer*, Vol. 6, No. 1, p. 30; Dean, "Does Astrology Need To be True, Part 1," pp. 179-80.
122. Dean, "Does Astrology Need To be True, Part 2," p. 263.
123. Ibid.
124. Ibid, p. 267.
125. These are summarized in Kelly et al., "The Moon Was Full and Nothing Happened," *The Skeptical Inquirer*, Vol. 10, No. 2, p. 139.
126. Culver and Ianna, *The Gemini Syndrome*, pp. 169-79.
127. Kurtz and Fraknoi, "Tests of Astrology," pp. 210-11.
128. Dean, "Does Astrology Need To be True, Part 2," p. 265.
129. Letters to the editor, "The Humanist," Nov./Dec., 1978, p. 24.
130. West and Toonder, *The Case for Astrology*, p. 155.
131. Weingarten, *The Study of Astrology*, pp. 129-30.
132. Carter, *The Principles of Astrology*, p. v.
133. S. Best, "Astrological Counseling and Psychotherapy: Critique and Recommendations," *Astrological Journal*, Vol. 25, No. 3, pp. 182-89 from Dean, "Does Astrology Need To be True, Part Part 2," p. 268.
134. Stephen Arroyo, *Astrology, Psychology and the Four Elements: An Energy Approach to Astrology and Its Use in the Counseling Arts* (Davis, CA: CRCS Publications, 1978), pp. 24-25.
135. Dean, "Does Astrology Need To be True," Parts 2 and 3.
136. Gittelson, *Intangible Evidence*, pp. 282-83.
137. Strohmer, *What Your Horoscope Doesn't Tell You*, p. 51.
138. John Manolesco, *Scientific Astrology* (New York: Pinnacle Books, 1973), p. 125; cf. Garrison, *Medical Astrology*, pp. 147, 11-15, 137-46.
139. Manolesco, *Scientific Astrology*, p. 125.
140. Kurt Koch, *Satan's Devices* (Grand Rapids, MI: Kregel, 1978), p. 20.
141. Kurt Koch, *Between Christ and Satan* (Grand Rapids, MI: Kregel, 1962), pp. 11-12.
142. Bastedo, "An Empirical Test of Popular Astrology," p. 31; Frances Sakoian and Lewis Acker, *The Astrologers Handbook* (New York: Harper and Row, 1973), pp. 94-95.

143. Bok and Jerome, *Objections to Astrology*, p. 50.
144. Rosenblum, Bernard, *The Astrologer's Guide to Counseling*, Reno, NV: CRCS Publications 1983), pp. 120-21.
145. Book review in *The Zetetic Scholar*, 1979, Nos. 3 & 4, pp. 83-85, cf. his *From Humanistic to Transpersonal Astrology* (Palo Alto, CA: The Seed Center, 1975), p. 12 and Manolesco, *Scientific Astrology*, p. 27.
146. Strohmer, *What Your Horoscope Doesn't Tell You*, p. 55.
147. Alan Onken, *Astrology, Evolution and Revolution: A Path to Higher Consciousness Through Astrology*. New York: Bantam, 1976), p. 85.
148. Manolesco, *Scientific Astrology*, p. 33.
149. Mayo, *Astrology*, p. 4.
150. Jess Stern, *A Time For Astrology* (New York: Signet, 1972), pp. 210-15.
151. Allen, *Astrology for the New Age*, p. 56.
152. Kurt Koch, *The Devil's Alphabet* (Grand Rapids, MI: Kregel, 1969), pp. 17-18.
153. Strohmer, *What Your Horoscope Doesn't Tell You*, p. 47.
154. Kurt Koch, *Satan's Devices*, pp. 20-21.
155. For growth in the Christian life, Francis Schaeffer's *True Spirituality* and J. I. Packer's *God's Words* are very helpful.

Part Seven—The Occult

1. Nandor Fodor, *Encyclopedia of Psychic Science* (Secaucus, NJ: Citadel, 1974), p. 235.
2. See e.g., Joseph Millard, *Edgar Cayce: Mystery Man of Miracles* (Greenwich, CT: Fawcett, 1967), who correctly describes Cayce as a "puppet controlled by forces beyond human comprehension" (p. 73); cf. Gary North, *Unholy Spirits: Occultism and New Age Humanism* (Fort Worth, TX: Dominion Press, 1986), pp. 198-200.
3. Raphael Gasson, *The Challenging Counterfeit* (Plainfield, NJ: Logos, 1966), pp. 35-36.
4. Doreen Irvine, *Freed from Witchcraft* (Nashville, TN: Thomas Nelson, 1973), p. 130.
5. Ibid., pp. 103-07, 110-12, 130-31.
6. Ibid., p. 168.
7. Mircea Eliade, *Occultism, Witchcraft and Cultural Fashions* (Chicago, IL: The University Chicago Press, 1976), p. 69.
8. Colin Wilson, *The Occult: A History* (New York: Vintage Books/Random House, 1973), p. 456.
9. Nat Freedland, *The Occult Explosion* (Berkeley, CA: Berkeley Medallion, 1972), p. 3.
10. C. A. Burland, *Beyond Science* (New York: Grossett and Dunlap, 1972), p. 9.
11. Merrill F. Unger, *Demons in the World Today* (Wheaton, IL: Tyndale House, 1972), p. 18.
12. Arthur Lyons, *The Second Coming: Satanism in America* (New York: Dodd, Mead, 1970), pp. 3, 5; cf. his *Satan Wants You: The Cult of Devil Worship in America* (New York: Mysterious Press, 1988), and Ted Schwarz, Duane Empey, *Satanism: Is Your Family Safe?* (Grand Rapids, MI: Zondervan, 1988).
13. Maury Terry, *The Ultimate Evil: An Investigation into America's Most Dangerous Satanic Cult* (Garden City, NY: Dolphin/Doubleday, 1987), p. 511.
14. Numerous polls have been conducted over the last two decades; contact the Gallup, Roper, and the University of Chicago's National Opinion Research Council organizations, respectively.
15. This was a national poll conducted by the University of Chicago's National Opinion Research Council; see the report in Andrew Greeley, "Mysticism Goes Mainstream," *American Health*, Jan.-Feb. 1987.
16. Katherine Lowry, "Channelers: Mouthpieces of the Spirits," *Omni*, Oct. 1987, p. 22.
17. Jon Klimo, *Channeling: Investigations on Receiving Information from Paranormal Sources* (Los Angeles, CA: Jeremy P. Tarcher, 1987), p. 1.
18. Cited in *Christianity Today*, Nov. 17, 1989, p. 50.
19. See John Ankerberg, John Weldon *Can You Trust Your Doctor? The Complete Guide to New Age Medicine and Its Threat to Your Family* (Nashville, TN: Wolgemuth and Hyatt, 1991).
20. Consider, for example, transpersonal and Jungian psychology; New Age Medicine, transpersonal and Montessori education, spiritistic influence in Hollywood, New Age business seminars; parapsychology and the misapplication of quantum physics as an alleged "scientific" justification for New Age occultism; Christian parapsychology and panentheistic Process Theology.
21. John Keel, *UFO's: Operation Trojan Horse* (New York: G. P. Putnam's Sons, 1970), pp. 215, 299.
22. Whitley Strieber, *Communion: A True Story* (New York: Beech Tree Books/William Morrow, 1987), pp. 14-15.
23. Brooks Alexander, "Theology from the Twilight Zone," *Christianity Today*, Sept. 18, 1987, p. 24; cf. John Ankerberg, John Weldon, *The Facts on Spirit Guides* (Eugene, OR: Harvest House, 1989).
24. *The Oxford American Dictionary* (New York: Avon, 1982), p. 617.
25. Philip B. Gove, ed., *Webster's Third New International Dictionary*, unabridged (Springfield, MA: Merriam-Webster, 1981), p. 1560.
26. June G. Bletzer, *The Donning International Encyclopedic Psychic Dictionary* (Norfolk, VA: The Donning Company, 1987), p. 439.
27. "Occult," in *Encyclopedia Britannica*, Micropaedia, Volume 7, p. 469.
28. Ron Enroth, "The Occult," in Walter A. Ellwell, ed., *Evangelical Dictionary of Theology* (Grand Rapids, MI: Baker, 1984), p. 787.
29. John Ankerberg, John Weldon, *Astrology: Do The Heavens Rule Our Destiny?* (Eugene, OR: Harvest House, 1989), slightly rev. from pp. 161-62.
30. William D. Halsey, ed. director, *MacMillan Dictionary for Students* (New York: McMillan, 1984), p. 57.
31. "Monism," in Paul Edwards, ed., *The Encyclopedia of Philosophy*, Vol. 5 (New York, MacMillan Publishing Company and The Free Press, 1972), p. 363.
32. David Conway, *Magic: An Occult Primer* (New York: Bantam, 1973), p. 35.
33. Gary North, *Unholy Spirits*, pp. 59-61.
34. Conway, *Magic: An Occult Primer*, pp. 29-30.
35. Charles Manson, letter to the editor, *Radix*, Nov.-Dec. 1976, p. 2.
36. Michael Harner, *The Way of the Shaman* (New York: Bantam, 1986), p. 54.
37. Mircea Eliade, *Shamanism: Archaic Techniques of Ecstasy* (Princeton, NJ: Bollingen/Princeton University Press, 1974); see the comments by Dr. Robert S. Ellwood, Jr. in *Religious and Spiritual Groups in Modern America* (Englewood Cliffs, NJ: Prentice-Hall, 1973), "The [recent] cult phenomena could almost be called a modern resurgence of Shamanism," p. 10; also Tal Brooke, *Riders of the Cosmic Circuit: Rajneesh, Sai Baba, Muktananda . . . God's of the New Age* (Batavia, IL: Lion, 1986); cf. Mircea Eliade, *From Primitives to Zen: A Thematic Source Book of the History of Religions* (New York: Harper and Row, 1977).

38. Sayed Idries Shah, *Oriental Magic*, (New York: E. P. Dutton, 1973), p. 123.
39. Louis Jacolliot, *Occult Science in India and Among the Ancients* (New Hyde Park, NY: University Books, 1971), p. 201.
40. Ibid., p. 204.
41. Jess Stearn, *Adventures into the Psychic* (New York, Signet, 1982), p. 163.
42. Doreen Irvine, *Freed from Witchcraft*, p. 96.
43. Ibid., p. 123.
44. Ibid., p. 7.
45. David Conway, *Magic: An Occult Primer*, p. 19.
46. Charles Panati, *Supersenses* (Garden City, NY: Anchor/Doubleday, 1976), p. 102.
47. George W. Meek, "The Healers in Brazil, England, U.S.A., and U.S.S.R.," in George W. Meek, ed., *Healers and the Healing Process: A Report on Ten Years of Research by Fourteen World Famous Investigators* (Wheaton, IL: Theosophical/Quest, 1977), p. 32.
48. Jeanne Pontius Rindge, "Perspective—A Overview of Paranormal Healing," in Meek, ed., *Healers and the Healing Process*, p. 17.
49. Hans Naegeli-Osjord, "Psychiatric and Psychological Considerations," in Meek, ed., *Healers and the Healing Process*, p. 80.
50. Danny Korem, "Waging War Against Deception," *Christianity Today*, Apr. 18, 1986, p. 32.
51. Robert A. Morey, *Reincarnation And Christianity* (Minneapolis, MN: Bethany, 1980), p. 25.
52. J. I. Packer, *God's Words: Studies of Key Bible Themes* (Downers Grove, IL: InterVarsity, 1981), pp. 83-84.
53. Denis De Rougemont, *The Devil's Share: An Essay on the Diabolic in Modern Society* (New York: Meridian Books, 1956), pp. 20-21.
54. Satprem, trans. from the French by Tehmi, *Sri Aurbindo, or The Adventure of Consciousness* (New York: Harper and Row, 1968), p. 199.
55. Guy L. Playfair, *The Unknown Power* (New York: Pocket Books, 1975), p. 240; cf. pp. 253-54; Clifford Wilson, John Weldon, *Psychic Forces and Occult Shock* (Chattanooga, TN: Global, 1987), Chapter 30.
56. Kurt Koch, *Christian Counselling And Occultism: The Counselling of the Psychically Disturbed and Those Oppressed Through Involvement in Occultism* (Grand Rapids, MI: Kregel, 1978), p. 181; cf., Kurt Koch, *Satan's Devices* (Grand Rapids, MI: Kregel, 1980), p. 162.
57. Robert A. Monroe, *Journeys Out of the Body* (Garden City, NY: Anchor/Doubleday, 1973), pp. 138-39.
58. Samuel M. Warren, *A Compendium of the Theological Writings of Emanual Swedenborg* (New York: Swedenborg Foundation, 1977), p. 618.
59. Victor Ernest, *I Talked with Spirits* (Wheaton, IL: Tyndale, 1971); Raphael Gasson, *The Challenging Counterfeit* (Plainfield, NJ: Logos, 1970); Ben Alexander, *Out From Darkness: The True Story of a Medium Who Escapes the Occult* (Joplin, MO: College Press, 1986); Johanna Michaelsen, *The Beautiful Side of Evil* (Eugene, OR: Harvest House, 1982); cf. Merrill Unger, *The Haunting of Bishop Pike* (Wheaton, IL: Tyndale, 1971).
60. Tal Brooke, *Riders of the Cosmic Circuit*, p. 172.
61. Louisa Rhine, *PSI—What Is It—An Introduction to Parapsychology* (New York: Harper and Row, 1975), p. 2.
62. David Hammond, "Psychic Evolution and You," *Psychic*, Apr. 1976, p. 21.
63. Howard M. Zimmerman, "Introduction," in Benjamin B. Wolman, ed., *Handbook of Parapsychology* (New York: Van Nostrand Reinehold Co., 1977), p. xvii, etc.
64. Martin Ebon, ed., *The Satan Trap: Dangers of the Occult* (Garden City, NY: Doubleday & Co., 1976).
65. See Question 17.
66. See e.g., Clifford Wilson and John Weldon, *Psychic Forces and Occult Shock* (Chattanooga, TN: Global, 1987), Chapters 22-25.
67. Benjamin B. Wolman, *Handbook of Parapsychology*, pp. 5, 27-29; Gardner Murphy, *The Challenge of Psychical Research* (New York: Harper-Colophon Books, 1970), p. 185.
68. Wilson and Weldon, *Psychic Forces and Occult Shock*, pp. 343-49; see the discussion in Alfred Douglas, *Extra-Sensory Powers: A Century of Psychical Research* (Woodstock, NY: Overlook Press, 1977), especially Chapter 4, "Early Investigations"; also Alan Gauld, *The Founders of Psychical Research* (New York: Shocken Books, 1968).
69. D. Scott Rogo, *Parapsychology: A Century of Inquiry* (New York: Dell, 1975), p. 44.
70. Nandor Fodor, *Encyclopedia of Psychic Science*, p. 316.
71. E. Garth Moore, *Try the Spirits: Christianity and Psychical Research* (New York: Oxford University Press, 1977); Charles E. Cluff, *Parapsychology and the Christian Faith* (Valley Forge, PA: Judson Press, 1976); H. Richard Neff, *Psychic Phenomena and Religion: ESP, Prayer, Healing, Survival* (Philadelphia, PA: The Westminster Press, 1974); Morton T. Kelsey, *The Christian and the Supernatural* (Minneapolis, MN: Augsburg, 1976); John J. Heaney, *The Sacred and the Psychic: Parapsychology and Christian Theology* (New York: Paulist Press, 1984).
72. William V. Rauscher, "Faith and Science," in Martin Ebon, ed., *The Signet Handbook of Parapsychology* (New York: New American Library, 1978), pp. 163, 168.
73. H. Richard Neff, *Psychic Phenomena and Religion*, p. 167.
74. James C. Crosson, "Parapsychology and the Christian Faith," *Parapsychology Review*, Sept.-Oct. 1977, Vol. 8, No. 5, p. 15.
75. United Presbyterian Church, Advisory Council on Discipleship and Worship, *Report On Occult And Psychic Activities*, 1976, p. 7; Mrs. Margueritte Harmon Bro, a medium and cofounder of The Spiritual Frontiers Fellowship, was one of the seven persons serving on the task force; cf. Wilson and Weldon, *Psychic Forces and Occult Shock*, pp. 424-25 and chapters 26-29.
76. For examples see Wilson and Weldon, *Psychic Forces & Occult Shock*, pp. 425-28.
77. Kurt Koch, *Satan's Devices* (Grand Rapids, MI: Kregel, 1988), p. 159.
78. e.g., Morton Kelsey, *The Christian and the Supernatural*, pp. 92-95.
79. e.g., Jane Roberts, *Seth: Dreams and Projection of Consciousness* (Walpole, NH: Stillpoint, 1986), pp. 193, 350.
80. Personal correspondence from Brooks Alexander, Jan. 25, 1985.
81. e.g., Malachi Martin, *Hostage to the Devil: The Possession and Exorcism of Five Living Americans* (New York: Bantam, 1977), pp. 521-30.
82. Ankerberg and Weldon, *The Facts on Spirit Guides*, pp. 38-41.
83. Henry Griss, William Dick, *The New Soviet Psychic Discoveries: A Firsthand Report on the Latest Breakthroughs in Russian Parapsychology* (Englewood Cliffs, NJ: Prentice-Hall, 1978), pp. 28-31.
84. Aleister Crowley, *Magic in Theory and Practice* (New York: Castel, n.d.), pp. 127, 152-53, from North, *Unholy Spirits*, p. 286; Leslie A. Shepherd, *Encyclopedia of Occultism and Parapsychology*, Vol. 1 (Detroit, MI: Gale Research Company, 1979), p. 203; cf. J. Symonds, K. Grant, *The Confessions of Aleister Crowley* (New York: Bantam, 1971), pp. 575-76.

85. Kurt Koch, *Satan's Devices*, p. 238.
86. Kurt Koch, *Between Christ and Satan* (Grand Rapids, MI: Kregel, 1976), p. 102.
87. For Arigo: John G. Fuller, *Arigo: Surgeon of the Rusty Knife* (New York: Pocket Books, 1975), p. 237; For Gurdjieff. J. G. Bennett, *Gurdjieff: Making a New World* (New York: Harper & Row, 1973), p. 160; For Gurney: D. Scott Rogo, *Parapsychology: A Century of Inquiry*, p. 66; For Branham: William Branham, *Footprints on the Sands of Time: The Autobiography of William Marion Branham* (Jeffersonville, IN: Spoken Word, 1976), p. 705; For Rudrananda: Da Free John (his disciple), *The Enlightenment of the Whole Body* (Middletown, CA: Dawn Horse Press, 1978), p. 14.
88. For Garrett's parents: Norma Bowles, Fran Hynds, *Psi-Search* (New York: Harper & Row, 1978), p. 89; For Krishnamurti and Nityananda: Mary Lutyens, *Krishnamurti: The Years of Awakening* (New York: Avon, 1976), p. 347.
89. For Wedgewood: Lutyens, *Krishnamurti: The Years of Awakening*, p. 308; John Weldon, *The Hazards of Psychic Involvement*, ms., 1988.
90. Kurt Koch, *Satan's Devices*, p. 188.
91. Kurt Koch, *Christian Counselling and Occultism*, p. 184.
92. Ibid., pp. 187-88.
93. Merrill Unger, *Demons in the World Today*, p. 95.
94. Ibid., p. 50.
95. John Warwick Montgomery, *Principalities and Powers: The World of the Occult* (Minneapolis, MN: Bethany, 1973), p. 149.
96. e.g., Bhagwan Shree Rajneesh, "Suicide or Sannyas," *Sannyas*, Mar. Apr 1978, No. 2, pp. 26-33; cf. Rajneesh, "Who Is the Master?" *Sannyas*, July-Aug. 1980, No. 4, p. 33.
97. Kelsey, *The Christian and the Supernatural*, p. 41.
98. Sri Chinmoy, *Astrology, The Supernatural and the Beyond* (Jamaica, NY: Agni Press, 1973), pp. 94-95.
99. Wickland, *Thirty Years Among the Dead*, p. 29.
100. Ibid., p. 8.
101. Ibid., p. 132.
102. Ibid., p. 17.
103. Ibid., p. 116.
104. Kurt Koch, *Occult Bondage and Deliverance* (Grand Rapids, MI: Kregel, 1970), p. 31.
105. Kurt Koch, *Demonology Past and Present* (Grand Rapids, MI: Kregel, 1973), pp. 41-42.
106. Anita Muhl, *Automatic Writing: An Approach to the Unconscious* (New York: Helix Press, 1963), pp. 51.
107. As reported in John Dart, "Peril in Occult Demonic Encounters Cited," *Los Angeles Times*, Dec. 30, 1977.
108. C. Fred Dickason, *Demon Possession and the Christian: A New Perspective* (Chicago, IL: Moody Press, 1987), p. 37.
109. Irvine, *Freed from Witchcraft*, p. 138.
110. Ankerberg, Weldon, *The Facts on Spirit Guides*, passim.
111. M. Scott Peck, *People of the Lie: The Hope for Healing Human Evil* (New York: Simon and Schuster, 1983), p. 190.
112. Montgomery, *Principalities and Powers*, p. 146.
113. Erika Bouguignon, ed., *Religion, Altered States of Consciousness and Social Change* (Columbus, OH: Ohio State University Press, 1973), pp. 16-17, Table 2.
114. Martin Ebon, *The Devil's Bride: Exorcism Past and Present* (New York: Harper and Row, 1974), p. 11.
115. Ibid., p. 12.
116. John S. Mbiti, *African Religions and Philosophy* (New York: Anchor/Doubleday, 1970), p. 106.
117. e.g., Martin, *Hostage to the Devil*, passim; John Warwick Montgomery, ed., *Demon Possession* (Minneapolis, MN: Bethany, 1976); John L. Nevius, *Demon Possession* (Grand Rapids: MI, Kregel, 1970); T. K. Oesterreich, *Possession: Demonical and Other Among Primitive Races in Antiquity, The Middle Ages and Modern Times* (Secaucus, NJ: Citadel, 1974); articles on mediumism and related subjects in Shephard, ed., *Encyclopedia of Occultism and Parapsychology*; I. M. Lewis, *Ecstatic Religion: An Anthropological Study of Spirit Possession and Shamanism* (Baltimore, MD: Penguin Books, 1975).
118. Conway, *Magic: An Occult Primer*, pp. 130-32.
119. Unger, *Demons in the World Today*, p. 28; cf. p. 72.
120. Ibid., p. 99, citing Brad Steiger, *Sex and Satanism* (New York: Ace, 1969).
121. Irvine, *Freed from Witchcraft*, pp. 90-91, 96.
122. e.g., Conway, *Magic: An Occult Primer*, pp. 127-33.
123. Bhagwan Shree Rajneesh, *The Book of the Secrets: Discourses on "Vigyana Bhairava Tantra,"* Vol. 1 (New York: Harper Colophon, 1977), pp. 22, 36-37.
124. Ibid., p. 399; cf. Rajneesh, *The Mustard Seed* (New York: Harper and Row, 1975), p. 69.
125. F. Max Muller, trans., *The Upanisads*, Part 1 (New York: Dover, 1962); citing *Kaushitaki Upanishad* 3: 1,2.
126. A. C. Bhaktivedanta Swami Prabhupada, *Bhagavad-gita As It Is: Complete Edition* (New York: Collier, 1973).
127. Maharishi Mahesh Yogi, *On the Bhagavad-Gita: A New Translation and Commentary* (Baltimore, MD: Penguin, 1974), p. 76.
128. Charles Manson, letter to the editor, *Radix*, Nov.-Dec. 1976, p. 2.
129. Vincent Bugliosi, *Helter Skelter* (New York: Bantam, 1975), p. 624; "Charles Manson: Portrait in Terror," Feb. 16, 1976, Channel 7, KABC-TV, Los Angeles, 11:30 p.m.; description by Bugliosi.
130. Mircea Eliade, *Yoga, Immortality and Freedom* (Princeton, NJ: Princeton University Press/Bollingen, 1973), p. 263.
131. Ibid., p. 205; cf. pp. 205-07.
132. Eliade, *Occultism, Witchcraft, and Cultural Fashions*, p. 71.
133. For example, in 1989 the accused witch Sarah Aldrete and a homosexual occultist named Constanzo were alleged by police authorities to be involved in at least 15 known human sacrifices and possibly scores of other murders in Matamoros, Mexico near the Texas border with Mexico. They combined "nontraditional" Satanism with a folk religion, Palo Mayombe.
134. Cited by Margaret Gaddis, "Teachers of Delusion," in Ebon, ed., *The Satan Trap: Dangers of the Occult*, p. 57.
135. For Ramirez, *Los Angeles Times*, Oct. 24, 1985; for Berkowitz, Maury Terry, *The Ultimate Evil*; cf. *The Fortean Times*, Summer 1980, p. 34.
136. Dr. Sondra O'Neale, *King City: Fathers of Anguish, Children of Blood: The True Story Behind the Atlanta Murders* (unpublished; copy on file). At the time of her writing, Dr. O'Neale was a professor at Emory University in Atlanta.
137. Cited in *Christianity Today*, Dec. 15, 1978, p. 38.
138. Kurt Koch, *Between Christ and Satan*; Joan Halifax-Grof, "Hex Death," *Parapsychology Review*, Oct. 1974; n.a., *Demon Experiences in Many Lands: A Compilation* (Chicago, IL: Moody Press, 1978), p. 22; Mike Warnke, *The Satan Seller* (Plainfield, NJ: Logos, 1972), p. 66; Eliade, *Shamanism: Archaic Techniques of Ecstasy*, p. 106.

139. "The Devil Worshippers," transcript from "20/20," May 16, 1985.
140. Terry, *The Ultimate Evil*, pp. xi-xiii, 1-16, 347, 507-12.
141. Ibid, p. 347.
142. Ibid, picture inserts after p. 346.
143. Richard Cavendish, *The Black Arts* (New York: G.P. Putnam & Sons, 1967), pp. 247, 249. Cf. Nigel Davies, *Human Sacrifice in History and Today* (New York: William Morrow, 1981); Alastair Scolri, *Murder For Magic: Witchcraft in Africa* (London: Cassell & Co., 1965); R. C. Zaehner, *Our Savage God: The Perverse Use of Eastern Thought* (New York: Sheed & Ward, 1974); Larry Kahaner, *Cults That Kill: Probing the Underworld of Occult Crime* (New York: Warner, 1988); M. Paul Dove, *Indian Underworld* (New York: E.P. Dutton & Co., 1940).
144. Ma Satya Bharti, *Death Comes Dancing* (London: Rutledge, Kegan Paul, 1981), p. 52.
145. Carl A. Raschke, "Satanism and the Devolution of the 'New Religions,'" *SCP Journal*, Fall 1985; Patricia Weaver, "Ritual Abuse, Pornography, and the Occult," *SCP Newsletter*, Vol. 14, No. 4; Gary North, "Magic, Envy, and Foreign Aid" in *Unholy Spirits*, pp. 273-88.
146. Brochure, North American Conferences, San Demas, CA; cf. Cultural Hermeneutics Project, "Summit on Satanism," Glorieta Baptist Conference Center, Glorieta, NM, Oct. 31–Nov. 4, 1990; *Minnesota Police Chief*, Sept. 1989, pp. 33-45, provides an illustration of how police departments are now recognizing the relationship between certain occult practices and criminal activity.

Part Eight—False Teaching in the Church

1. The illustration is taken from Erwin Lutzer, "Toward a Philosophy of Counseling," *Moody Monthly*, Feb. 1983, pp. 81-83.
2. See footnote 4.
3. e.g., David Brenner, ed., *Baker Encyclopedia of Psychology* (Grand Rapids, MI: Baker Books, 1985), p. v. This volume for Christian psychologists has over 1000 entries, many of them secular techniques of psychotherapy.
4. e.g., H. Newton Maloney states, "We do not get from scripture those basic therapeutic ingredients which establish relationships. We get them from client-centered therapy, the writings of Carl Rogers...," transcript, "Is Christianity Compatible with Psychotherapy?" 1983, p. 21, from The John Ankerberg Show; Stephen Allison and H. Newton Maloney, "Filipino Psychic Surgery: Myth, Magic or Miracle," *Journal of Religion and Health*, Spring 1981, pp. 48-61.
5. Brenner, *Baker Encyclopedia of Psychology*, p. V; Gary Collins, *Can You Trust Psychology?* (Downers Grove, IL: InterVarsity Press, 1988), pp. 51, 169; John Carter and Bruce Narramore, *The Integration of Psychology and Theology* (Grand Rapids, MI: Zondervan, 1979), p. 48.
6. This premise is variously reflected in the integrationist literature. See Recommended Reading.
7. These are the claims of much secular and materialistic, rationalistic psychology, but not all. Many texts have noted the general antagonism of secular psychology to Christian faith. For an illustration see Albert Ellis, "Is Religiosity Pathological," *Free Inquiry*, Spring, 1988, p. 27. See also "Critiques" under Recommended Reading.
8. Jung believed "all talk of God (is) mythological," and that Protestant theologians only engaged in mythologizing. G. Adler, ed., *C. G. Jung Letters*, Trans. by R. F. Hall (London: Routledge, 1976), Vol. 2, p. 262, from Thomas Szasz, *The Myth of Psychotherapy* (Garden City, NY: Doubleday, 1978), p. 173; C. G. Jung, *Psychology and Religion, West and East* (Princeton University Press, 1975), pp. 193-200.
9. Colin Wilson *Lord of the Underworld: Jung in the 20th Century* (Wellingborough, North Hamptonshire: Aquarian Press, 1984), p. 9. Occult authority Wilson shares this view.
10. C. G. Jung, *The Undiscovered Self* (New York: Mentor, 1958), p. 58; C. G. Jung, *Memories, Dreams, Reflections* (New York: Vintage, 1965), pp. 195-205, 373; Nandor Fodor, *Freud, Jung and Occultism* (New Hyde Park, New York: University Books, 1971), p. 67.
11. Jung, *Memories, Dreams, Reflections*, pp. 182-89; Wilson, *Lord of the Underworld*, pp. 27-32.
12. Ibid.
13. Jung, *Memories, Dreams, Reflections*, pp. 186-91.
14. Gene Lall, "C. G. Jung and Astrology," in Joanne Sanders, "Connecting Therapy to the Heavens," *The Common Boundary*, Vol. 5, no. 1; Jung, *Memories, Dreams, Reflections*, pp. 274-84; Martin Ebon, "Jung's First Medium," *Psychic*, May-June 1976, pp. 42-47.
15. e.g., Wilson, *Lord of the Underworld*, especially chapter 4, p. 134; Jung, *Memories, Dreams, Reflections*, pp. 4, 183, 189-92.
16. Jung, *Memories, Dreams, Reflections*, pp. 170-222.
17. e.g., Morton Kelsey, *The Christian and the Supernatural* (Augsburg, 1976), pp. 79-80 and *Christo-Psychology* (New York: Crossroad, 1982), pp. 131-138; Alta J. LaDage, *Occult Psychology: A Comparison of Jungian Psychology and the Modern Qabalah* (St. Paul, MN: Llewellyn, 1978). This is also true particularly in the field of transpersonal psychology.
18. Jung, *Memories, Dreams, Reflections*, pp. 181-86.
19. e.g., see "Analytical Psychology," in Brenner, *Baker Encyclopedia of Psychology*, pp. 55-58.
20. See Question 4; for a critique see Don Matzat, *Inner Healing: Deliverance or Deception?* (Eugene, OR: Harvest House, 1987); for an illustration of Jungian and occultic ideas and practices in Christian dreamwork see L. M. Savary; P. Berne and S. K. Williams, *Dreams and Spiritual Growth: A Christian Approach to Dream Work* (New York: Pallis Press, 1984). In Jane Roberts, *Seth Dreams and Projection of Consciousness* (Stillpoint, 1986), dreams become the method to contact spirits.
21. Jung, *Memories, Dreams, Reflections*, pp. 4, 192.
22. e.g., Ibid., pp. x-xi, 55-59; Paul J. Stern, *C. G. Jung: The Haunted Prophet* (New York: Delta, 1977), pp. 251-56.
23. Matzat, *Inner Healing*, pp. 47-137.
24. Ibid.
25. Ibid., pp. 99-120.
26. Dave Hazard in *Charisma* magazine, Sept. 1986, p. 49. From Matzat, *Inner Healing*, p. 117.
27. e.g., LaDage, *Occult Psychology*, pp. 103, 120, 122, 156; Jung, *Memories, Dreams, Reflections*, pp. 183-92.
28. e.g., Shakti Gawain, *Living in the Light* (Mill Valley, CA: Whatever, 1986), pp. 14-25; in her book, *Creative Visualization* (San Rafael, CA: New World Library, 1978), she identifies spirit-guides with the "inner counselor" contacted by imagination (pp. 89-93, 101-02).

29. Mary Watkins, *Invisible Guests: The Development of Imaginale Dialogues* (Hillsdale, NJ: The Analytic Press, 1986), pp. 91-100; chapters 11 and 12.
30. Ibid., p. 99.
31. Ibid., p. 92.
32. Jung, *Memories, Dreams, Reflections*, p. 184.
33. e.g., Laeh Garfield, *Companions in Spirit: A Guide to Working with Your Spirit Helpers* (Berkeley, CA: Celestial Arts, 1984); Mike Samuels and Hal Bennett, *Spirit Guides: Access to Inner Worlds* (New York: Random House, 1974).
34. The many allegedly Christian societies endorsing parapsychology and Christian spiritism, such as the Spiritual Frontiers Fellowship, only compound this problem.
35. Norman Vincent Peale, *Positive Imaging: The Powerful Way to Change Your Life* (New York: Ballantine, 1983), pp. 16-17.
36. Helen Keller, *My Religion* (New York: The Swedenborg Foundation, 1974), pp. 7-37.
37. Kenneth Copeland, "Take Time to Pray," *Believers Voice of Victory*, Feb. 1987, p. 9.
38. Kenneth Copeland, "What Happened from the Cross to the Throne" (cassette tape, Fort Worth, TX: Kenneth Copeland Ministries, n.d.). See the analyses in Brian Onken, "The Atonement of Christ and the 'Faith' Message," *Forward* magazine, Vol. 7, No. 1, 1984, pp. 1, 10-15.
39. Kenneth Hagin, *The Name of Jesus* (Tulsa, OK: Faith Library Publications, 1981), p. 31; also, Kenneth Hagin, *The New Birth* (Tulsa, OK; Faith Library, 1978), p. 10; also, Kenneth Hagin, "Made Alive," *The Word of Faith*, Apr. 1982, p. 3; cf. Onken, "The Atonement."
40. Charles Capps, *The Tongue—A Creative Force* (Tulsa, OK: Harrison House, 1976), pp. 63-100; John Osteen, *The Sixth Sense . . . Faith* (Houston, TX: John Austin Publications, 1980), pp. 1-29. See *News and Views*, June and July 1988, the John Ankerberg Evangelistic Association, for details.
41. Charles Capps, *Dynamics of Faith and Confession* (Dallas, TX: Word of Faith, 1983), p. 97; cf. pp. 78-82, 96-97.
42. Morton Kelsey, *The Christian and the Supernatural* (Minneapolis, MN: Augsburg, 1976), pp. 92-95.
43. Agnes Sanford, *The Healing Gifts of the Spirit* (New York: Trumpet, 1977), pp. 170-71; Agnes Sanford, *The Healing Power of the Bible* (New York: Lippincott, 1969), pp. 205-21.
44. E. W. Kenyon, *The Hidden Man: An Unveiling of the Subconscious Mind* (Linwood, WA: Kenyon's Gospel Publishing Society, 1970), pp. 119, 126.
45. Napoleon Hill, *Grow Rich! with Peace of Mind* (New York: Fawcett Crest, 1982) pp. 158-59.
46. Jerry Savelle, *Living in Divine Prosperity* (Tulsa, OK: Harrison House, 1982), p. 55.
47. See J. I. Packer, *God's Words: Studies of Key Bible Themes* (Downers Grove, IL: InterVarsity Press, 1981).
48. Robert Schuller, *You Can Become the Person You Want to Be* (Old Tappan, NJ: Revell, 1976), p. 12.
49. Ibid., pp. 39-48.
50. Ibid., pp. 12, 65.
51. Ibid., pp. 66, 73, 109.
52. Robert Schuller, *Peace of Mind Through Possibility Thinking* (New York: Jove, 1985), pp. 129-31.
53. Ibid., pp. 131-32.
54. John Weldon, Zola Levitt, *The Transcendental Explosion* (Eugene, OR: Harvest House, 1975). See especially Maharishi Mahesh Yogi, *Transcendental Meditation* (New York: Signet, 1968) and his *On the Bahagavad Gita: A New Translation and Commentary*, of chapters 1-6 (New York: Penguin, 1969).
55. Schuller, *Peace of Mind*, p. 131.
56. Weldon, *The Transcendental Explosion*, Appendix 1; R. D. Scott, *Transcendental Misconceptions* (San Diego, CA: Beta Books), pp. 89-99.
57. Schuller, *Peace of Mind*, p. 132.
58. e.g., Daniel Goleman, *The Varieties of the Meditative Experience* (New York: Dutton, 1977).
59. Robert Schuller, *Self Esteem: The New Reformation* (Waco, TX: Word, 1982), pp. 26-27, 63-65, 135.
60. *Christianity Today*, Oct. 5, 1984, p. 13. For critiques of Schuller see Recommended Reading and John McArthur, "Questions for Robert Schuller," *Moody Monthly*, May 1983, p. 10.
61. Oral Roberts, *A Daily Guide to Miracles and Successful Living Through Seed Faith* (Tulsa, OK: Pinoak Publications, 1976), pp. 17-28, 35, 48-52.
62. Ibid., p. 53.
63. Ibid., p. 52.
64. Ibid., p. 50.
65. *Christianity Today*, Mar. 15, 1985, p. 44.
66. Patti Roberts, *Ashes to Gold* (Waco, TX: Word, 1983), pp. 119-20.
67. Ibid., pp. 120-23.
68. Roberts, *A Daily Guide to Miracles*, p. 63.
69. Ibid., pp. 66-68.
70. Ibid., p. 68.
71. Ibid.
72. For illustrations see James Sire, *Scripture Twisting* (Downers Grove, IL: InterVarsity Press, 1985).
73. Roberts, *A Daily Guide to Miracles*, p. 68.
74. Ibid., p. 65.
75. Colon Brown, ed., *The New International Dictionary of New Testament Theology*, Vol. 1 (Grand Rapids, MI: Zondervan, 1975), p. 215.
76. Capps, *Dynamics of Faith and Confession*, p. 47.
77. e.g., Charles Capps, *Why Tragedy Happens to Christians* (Tulsa, OK: Harrison House, 1980), pp. 12-15. See Questions 17,18; Robert Tilton, *To Catch a Thief* (Dallas, TX: Word of Faith), p. 38.
78. e.g., Robert Tilton, *God's Laws of Success* (Dallas, TX: Word of Faith, 1985), pp. 2-4.
79. e.g., Charles Capps, *The Tongue: A Creative Force* (Tulsa, OK: Harrison House, 1976), pp. 35-75; Kenyon, *The Hidden Man*, p. 119.
80. Capps, *Dynamics of Faith and Confession*, p. 83.
81. e.g., Gloria Copeland, *God's Will Is Prosperity* (Ft. Worth, TX: Kenneth Copeland Ministries, 1978), pp. 84-91; Charles Capps, *Success Motivation Through the Word* (Tulsa, OK: Harrison House, 1982), pp. 143-49; Kenneth Hagin, *I Believe in Visions* (Tulsa, OK: Kenneth Hagin Ministries, 1984), pp. 93-96, 129-33.
82. Capps, *The Tongue: A Creative Force*, p. 108.
83. e.g., Kenneth Copeland, *The Laws of Prosperity* (Ft. Worth, TX: Kenneth Copeland Ministries, 1974), pp. 70, 100; Capps, *Releasing the Ability of God*, pp. 100-04; Capps, Capps, *Changing the Seen*, pp. 47-48; Capps, *The Tongue: A*

Creative Force, p. 40; c.f. Bruce Barron, *The Health and Wealth Gospel* (Downers Grove, IL: InterVarsity, 1987), pp. 108-118.
84. Ibid., p. 106.
85. Kenneth Copeland, *The Force of Faith* (Fort Worth, TX: Kenneth Copeland Publications, n.d.), p. 17.
86. Tilton, *To Catch A Thief*, p. 1.
87. Kenneth Hagin, *New Thresholds of Faith* (Tulsa, OK: Kenneth Hagin Ministries, 1985), p. 55.
88. Kenneth Hagin, *The Name of Jesus* (Tulsa, OK: Kenneth Hagin Ministries), p. 9, from Barron, *The Health and Wealth Gospel*, p. 119.
89. Catalogue of materials distributed in 1985 by Jerry Savelle Ministries, p. 20, from Barron, *The Health and Wealth Gospel*, p. 120.
90. Savelle, *Living in Divine Prosperity* pp. 8-9.
91. Kenyon, *The Hidden Man*, p. 50.
92. Kenneth Hagin, *Redeemed from Poverty, Sickness and Death* (Tulsa, OK: Kenneth Hagin Ministries, 1983), p. 3.
93. Hagin, *New Thresholds of Faith*, p. 55.
94. Ibid., p. 84.
95. Kenneth Copeland, *Walking in the Realm of the Miraculous* (Fort Worth, TX: Kenneth Copeland Ministries, n.d.), p. 15.
96. Kenneth Copeland, *The Force of Faith* (Fort Worth, TX: Kenneth Copeland Publications, n.d.), p. 10.
97. Capps, *The Tongue: A Creative Force*, p. 54.
98. Ibid., p. 81.
99. Ibid., p. 85.
100. Tilton, *To Catch a Thief*, pp. 88-89.
101. Paul Yonggi Cho, *The Fourth Dimension* (Plainfield, NJ: Logos, 1979), pp. 18-39.
102. Ibid., pp. 38-53.
103. Ibid., p. 31.
104. Ibid., pp. 40-41.
105. Ibid., p. 51.
106. Ibid., pp. 59, 51-60.
107. Ibid., p. 58.
108. Stephen Strang, "Cho's Problem with Prosperity: An Exclusive Interview with Paul Yonggi Cho," *Charisma* magazine, Mar. 1988, pp. 69-71.
109. Paul Yonggi Cho, *Salvation, Health and Prosperity: Our Three-Fold Blessings in Christ* (Almonte Springs, FL: Creation House, 1987), p. 12.
110. Ibid., p. 139.
111. e.g., Larry Parker, *We Let Our Son Die* (Eugene, OR: Harvest House, 1980); Walter Martin, *The Christian Science Myth* (Grand Rapids, MI: Zondervan, 1962), Chapter 8, pp. 151-72; Walter Martin, *Jehovah of the Watchtower* (Chicago, IL: Moody Press, 1974), chapter 5, pp. 91-105.
112. Barron, *The Health and Wealth Gospel*, pp. 123-46.
113. Kenneth Copeland, *The Laws of Prosperity*, (Fort Worth, TX: Kenneth Copeland Ministries, 1974), p. 70.
114. Gloria Copeland, *God's Will is Prosperity*, Fort Worth, TX: Kenneth Copeland Ministries, 1978), p. 110.
115. See the excellent analysis in Ken Sarles, "A Theological Evaluation of the Prosperity Gospel," *Bibliotheca Sacra*, Oct.-Dec. 1986, pp. 340-42.
116. Osteen, *The Sixth Sense*, p. 23.
117. Tilton, *God's Laws of Success*, pp. 3-4.
118. Capps, *The Tongue: A Creative Force*, p. 12.
119. Copeland, *God's Will Is Prosperity*, p. 40.
120. Osteen, *The Sixth Sense*, p. 21.
121. Copeland, *The Laws of Prosperity*, p. 15; Copeland, *Walking in the Realm of the Miraculous*, p. 79.
122. Tilton, *God's Laws of Success*, p. 176.
123. Capps, *The Tongue: A Creative Force*, p. 98.
124. Ibid., p. 97.
125. Sarles, "A Theological Evaluation," pp. 344-345.
126. Basham, *Can a Christian Have a Demon?*; See *News and Views*, July 1988 (The John Ankerberg Evangelistic Association).
127. See the details in Barron, *The Heath and Wealth Gospel*, pp. 19-30.
128. e.g., Frank Gaebelein, *The Expositor's Bible Commentary* (12 vols.); W. Elwell, ed., *Evangelical Dictionary of Theology*; Walvoord and Zuck, *The Bible Knowledge Commentary* (2 vols.); M. Tenney, ed., *The Zondervan Pictorial Encyclopedia of the Bible*.

Appendix A—Mormonism

1. Gordon Fraser, *Sects of the Latter-day Saints*, Part 1: The Reorganized Church; Part 2: Polygamous Sects (Hubbard, OR: Gordon H. Fraser, 1978), pp. 22-60.
2. Martin, *The Maze of Mormonism*, p. 311.

Appendix D—The Occult

1. James Randi, "Nostradamus: The Prophet For All Seasons," *The Skeptical Enquirer*, Fall 1982, p. 31.
2. "Nostradamus," in Cavendish, ed., *Man, Myth and Magic*, Vol. 15 (Freeport, NY: Marshall Cavendish, 1983), p. 2017.
3. Randi, "Nostradamus, The Prophet," p. 32.
4. Ibid., p. 36.

Index of Persons

Muller, Robert 136, 154
Muktananda, Swami 136
Packer, J. I. 150
Peale, Norman Vincent 149
Pursel, Jach 135, 141
Rajneesh, Bhagwan Shree 136-137, 140, 149, 155
"Ramtha" 141
Reddy, Helen 135
Rodegast, Pat 157
Russell, A. J. 141
"Saint Germain" 141
Schaeffer, Francis 150
Schuchman, Helen 142
Schuller, Robert 149
"Seth" 136, 141
Shealey, Norman 136
Stalin, Joseph 157
Stone, Clement 149
Tart, Charles 136
Terry, Maury 152
Torres, Penney 135
Turner, Tina 135
Vivekananda, Swami 137
Weldon, John 152, 161
Wierwille, Victor Paul 148
Wilbur, Ken 135
Winfrey, Oprah 135
York, Michael 135
Young, Meredith Lady 142

Spirit Guides

Alexander, Ben 198
Ankerberg, John 191
Aurobindo, Sri 171
Bailey, Alice 187
Ballard, Guy 187
Bender, Hans 186
Berg, David 187
"Carl" 197-198
Chaney, Earlyne 187
Chimnoy, Sri 187, 197
Cayce, Edgar 195-196
Dass, Ram 187
Eddy, Mary Baker 187
"Emmanuel" 177
Ernest, Victor 198
Evans, Linda 168
Ford, Authur 197
Gasson, Raphael 198
Geller, Uri 195
Gless, Sharon 168
Gibran, Kahlil 183
Gross, Darwin 189
Gruss, Edmond 193
Huxley, Aldous 197
Irvine, Doreen 191
"Jesus" 181-182
"John" 170
Johnson, Julian 188
Jones, Jim 173
Keene, M. Lamar 171, 196
Knight, J. Z. 170, 195
Klemp, Harold 188
Klimo, John 189
Koch, Kurt 197, 199
Krishnamurti, Jiddhu 187
Kubler-Ross, Elizabeth 195
MacLaine, Shirley 168, 170
"Lazaris" 168, 170
Lewis, C. S. 178, 191
"Lily" 182
Millard, Joseph 196
Mohammad 195
Monroe, Robert 171
Montgomery, John Warwick 192
Montgomery, Ruth 169
Moon, Sun Myung 187

"Moroni" 187
Peck, M. Scott 191
Pike, Bishop 196
Prophet, Elizabeth Claire 187
Puharich, Andrija 195
Pursel, Jach 168, 170
Rajneesh, Bhagwan Shree 187
"Ramtha" 170, 180-181
Roberts, Jane 169, 174, 196
Ryerson, Kevin 170
Rodgast, Pat 177
"Salem" 195
Satprem 171
Schucman, Helen 169, 181
"Seth" 169, 182
Singh, Kirpal 188
Singh, Sawan 188
Slade, William 197
Slater, Bill 195
Smith, Joseph 187
Swedenborg, Emanuel 171, 172
Twitchell, Paul 187-188
VanDusen, Wilson 186
Vaughn, Bernard 194
Wilson, Colin 190
Weldon, John 191, 193
Yogananda, Paramahansa 187
York, Michael 168

Astrology

Addey, John 236
Allen, Marcus 219, 222
Andrew, Prince 211
Armistead, Julian 218
Bacall, Lauren 211
Bailey, Alice 214
Barrett, Rona 214
Best, S. 237
Blavatsky, Helena P. 214-215
Brahe, Tycho 227
Birmingham, Carolyn 236
Carter, Charles E. O. 214, 237
Cavendish, Richard 216
Cayce, Edgar 214
Collins, Joan 211
Davidson, W. M. 237
Davison, Ronald 221
Dean, Geoffrey 211, 213
Diana, Princess 211
Dickinson, Angie 211
Diller, Phyllis 211
Dixon, Jean 226-227
Eysenck, H. J. 231-232
Fonda, Jane & Peter 211
Francis, Arlene 211
Gittelson, Bernard 217, 238
Goodavage, Joseph 223
Gosselin, Jane 218
Gauquelin, Michael 230, 232-233
Hawn, Goldie 211
Hussey, Olivia 211
Jaynes, Charles 218
Jerome, Lawrence 216
Kepler, Johann 227
Koch, Kurt 239
Kurtz, Paul 236
Leek, Sybil 215, 221
Leightman, Robert 218
Manolesco, John 240
Mayo, Jeff 223, 241
McGervy, John 235
Metzner, Ralph 219
Michaan, Colette 214
Moody, Edward J. 216
Montgomery, John Warwick 217
Morey, Robert 221, 226
Newton-John, Olivia 221

Subject Index

Note: Parenthetical numbers refer to footnote numbers on the page given.

378

About the Authors

John Ankerberg is host of the nationally televised, award-winning "The John Ankerberg Show" carried on more than 39,000 outlets every week in all 50 states, reaching a potential audience of almost 80 million homes. The show offers an opportunity for discussion and debate on widely varying topics, bringing together Christian and non-Christian religious leaders and leading secular authorities. Ankerberg has lectured on 80 college and university campuses and addressed large audiences in mass meetings in Asia, Africa and North and South America. He has the B.A. degree from the University of Illinois, the M.A. degree in Church History and the History of Christian Thought and the M.Div. degree both from Trinity Seminary and has a doctorate degree from Bethel Theological Seminary.

Dr. Ankerberg has personally researched and hosted over a dozen separate debates concerning the topics in this volume alone. Other televised debates have included such subjects as the creation-evolution issue, abortion, Armstrongism, the Baha'i Faith, Edgar Cayce, Silva Mind Control, Roman Catholicism, Secular Humanism, Seventh Day Adventism, the Unification Church, Unity School of Christianity, the Church of Christ, the United Pentecostal Church, the historic evidence for the Resurrection of Christ, thanatology, Messianic prophecy, homosexuality, New Age Medicine, Christianity and psychotherapy, rock music, the Playboy Philosophy, religion and government, and other topics.

John Weldon is an honors graduate in sociology from California State University, San Diego and has a master's degree in Christian Apologetics from the Simon Greenleaf School of Law in Anaheim, California (summa cum laude); the M.Div. and D.Min. degrees from Luther Rice Seminary in Atlanta, Georgia (the latter with an emphasis in cultic studies); and a third master's degree issued jointly with William Carey International University, Pasedena, California and Pacific College of Graduate Studies, Melbourne, Australia. His thesis for Pacific College involved a study of psychic healing. He also has the Ph.D. in comparative religion, with an emphasis on Eastern religion from the latter institution. Dr. Weldon has studied alternate religious movements and phenomena in depth for 20 years. He has written books on topics as diverse as UFOs, near-death experiences, Transcendental Meditation, Psychic Healing, New Age Medicine, and fantasy role playing games. In addition to being author or co-author of 25 books, many related to topics in this volume, he is working on a ten-volume critique of the New Age Movement and finishing an 8000-page theological and critical analysis of 70 of the new religions.

Other Books by John Ankerberg and John Weldon

Behind the Mask of Mormonism
The Coming Darkness
Encyclopedia of New Age Beliefs

THE FACTS ON SERIES
The Facts on Abortion
The Facts on Angels
The Facts on Astrology
The Facts on Creation vs. Evolution
The Facts on the Faith Movement
The Facts on False Teaching in the Church
The Facts on Halloween
The Facts on Hinduism
The Facts on Holistic Health and the New Medicine
The Facts on Homosexuality
The Facts on Islam
The Facts on the Jehovah's Witnesses
The Facts on Jesus the Messiah
The Facts on the King James Only Debate
The Facts on Life After Death
The Facts on the Masonic Lodge
The Facts on the Mind Sciences
The Facts on the Mormon Church
The Facts on Near-Death Experiences
The Facts on the New Age Movement
The Facts on the Occult
The Facts on Psychic Readings
The Facts on Rock Music
The Facts on Roman Catholicism
The Facts on Self-Esteem, Psychology and the Recovery Movement
The Facts on Spirit Guides
The Facts on UFOs and Other Supernatural Phenomena

Knowing the Truth About Jesus the Messiah
Knowing the Truth About Salvation
Knowing the Truth About the Resurrection
Knowing the Truth About the Trinity
Protestants and Catholics: Do They Now Agree?
Protestants and Catholics: Do They Now Agree? (Video)

Other Good
Harvest House Reading

THE GOD MAKERS
by *Ed Decker* and *Dave Hunt*

This unique expose on Mormonism is factual, carefully researched, and fully documented. *The God Makers* provides staggering new insights that go beyond the explosive film of the same title. An excellent tool in reaching Mormons.

THE INTERNATIONAL INDUCTIVE STUDY BIBLE
(NASB & NIV)

The first of its kind in Bible publishing history, *The International Inductive Study Bible* teaches you how to unearth the treasures of God's Word for yourself. Includes study helps, four-color maps and charts, and a concordance.

DEATH OF A GURU
by *Rabi Maharaj* with *Dave Hunt*

Descended from a long line of Brahmin priests and trained as a yogi, Rabindranath Maharaj becomes a great Hindu leader. His autobiography, written by bestselling author Dave Hunt, traces his difficult search for meaning, his increasing disillusionment, and his struggle to choose between Hinduism and Christ.

CHRISTIANITY IN CRISIS
by *Hank Hanegraff*

A growing number of church leaders are spreading distorted doctrines that undermine the very core of biblical Christianity. Hank Hanegraff carefully documents the surprising blasphemies and widespread teaching of the Faith movement.

WHAT YOU NEED TO KNOW ABOUT MORMONISM
by *Ed Decker*

A docudrama adaptation of a video/film by the same title, shows the dramatic encounter that results when two Mormons and a Christian have an opportunity to discuss their beliefs. *The Mormon Dilemma* models typical conversations between Christians and Mormons and shows Christians how to respond with love and truth.